group dynamics AND TEAM BUILDING

group dynamics AND TEAM BUILDING

R K SAHU

EXCEL BOOKS

ISBN: 978-81-7446-823-9

First Edition: New Delhi, 2010

EXCEL BOOKS
A-45, Naraina, Phase I,
New Delhi-110 028

Published by Anurag Jain for Excel Books, A-45, Naraina, Phase I, New Delhi-110 028 and printed by him at Excel Printers, C-205, Naraina, Phase I, New Delhi-110 028

Brief Contents

Detailed Contents

Preface

Once Henry Ford, the architect of Automobile Industry, said, "Coming together is beginning, keeping together is progress and working together is success". This is the essence of working in teams. He further echoed the same thought, when he said, "You can take my factories, burn up my buildings, but give me my people and I will build the business right back again". What does this mean? It simply means, that teams can do wonders.

If an organisation has a pool of highly qualified people, a lot of resources and avenues to deliver or market to capture, but lacks team spirit then sooner or later the organisation is destined for doom. On the contrary, if an organisation has a group of ordinary people with heart-to-heart bonding amongst them, transparency, role clarity, excellent interpersonal communication and relations, having shared values with unity of direction, moving towards a common goal, they will certainly tide over all crises as a team and eventually cherish the pleasure of achievement of their common goal.

Human resource has great potential, which can be harnessed and unleashed by strengthening and nurturing the quality of team bonding. Team spirit is fundamental for any group effort, like organising a picnic or a religious function, or accomplishing any project involving two or more people or achieving business objectives of an organisation or organising a political rally or running successfully a government, right from setting its programmes and goals to executing its plans and achieving the end results.

The success of the organisation depends on the teamwork but there is dearth of resource books and publications on the subject of Team Building. This book is an endeavor to fill in this deficiency. I have made efforts to incorporate all the related topics required for team building, like the overall understanding of group dynamics, stages involved in team building process, characteristics of high performing teams, etc. I have also included and discussed elaborately on the dynamics of conflicts within and between teams and different ways of resolving conflicts. This book will be a great resource for the CEOs, functional heads and all managers, who are in the role of team leaders. This will also serve as a textbook for the management institutes, management teachers and students alike as well as management trainers and consultants on team building.

Dr R K SAHU

About the Author

Dr RK Sahu is the founder Director of Human Resource Development Centre, New Delhi. Dr Sahu has held a senior managerial position with HMT and as HR Chief of Usha Beltron. He has trained over 15,000 management professionals on Leadership, Team Building and other management areas during the last 14 years.

Dr Sahu has undertaken training and management consultancy assignments for over 360 companies including 24 factories of Hindustan Unilever, Nepal Lever, Tata Motors, Indian Oil, NHPC, Pepsi, Whirlpool, Coca Cola, Cadbury, Godrej, Electrolux, Becton Dickinson, Eureka Forbes, Parle Products, Polyplex, ICI, Ranbaxy, Jyoti CNC, PPAP, Hero Honda, KRIBHCO, Eicher Motors, HINDALCO, BALCO, NALCO, Hindustan Zinc, Hindustan Latex, Oil India, GRASIM, Lafarge, Rico Auto, SMC, MICO, Gujarat Gas, Delphi, Moser Baer, Mitsubishi, Thomson Press, Torrent Pharma, and UB Group to name a few. Besides training, he has provided consultancy services to his clients for implementation of 5S, Kaizen, Zero Defect, Competency Mapping, Balanced Scorecard, Performance Management System, Psychometric Testing and other HR systems.

Dr Sahu has designed training modules for over 50 subjects like TQM, Productivity, Leadership, Quality, Wastage Control and Cost Reduction, and various managerial, attitudinal and motivational subjects like time management, creative problem-solving and decision making, training for trainers, competency mapping, emotional intelligence, balanced scorecard, man management skills, psychometric testing, etc.

His research papers have been published in various papers and journals like the *Times of India*, *Economic Times*, *Personnel Today*, *India Journal for Training and Development*, etc. He has authored some best selling books like *Training for Development*, *Performance Management System*, *Competency Mapping* and *Strategic Leadership* published by Excel Books.

CHAPTER

1

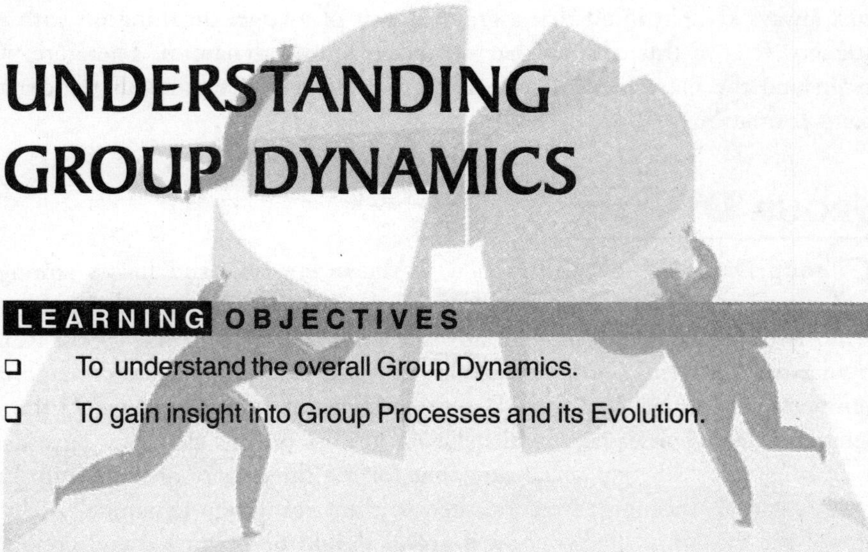

UNDERSTANDING GROUP DYNAMICS

LEARNING OBJECTIVES

- To understand the overall Group Dynamics.
- To gain insight into Group Processes and its Evolution.

INTRODUCTION

Our main aim apparently, is to understand why individuals form groups. Let us ask you some questions: How old were you when you first joined a group? How many different groups do you belong to? How would you identify a group leader? Does your behaviour change when you are with different groups? Have you ever led a group? In what sense were you the leader? What were the results?

If you start answering these questions on your own, you will find that understanding group behaviour and the properties of groups are essential to being both a good manager and an effective member of groups. A manager spends half of his time in some formal or informal meetings, where a group of people gets together to solve problems or make plans. So the manager himself acts as a member of a group with other managers or colleagues.

There are also many examples where the manager decides to take a decision on his own or to rely on groups by holding meetings or making committees. In management, small groups with which he interacts are very important for a manager. It may consist of his peers or colleagues, other managers, specialists or others who really help the manager to take an effective decision. You might have also come across instances of well-knit and cohesive groups, which really make a superior performance under a good leader. For all these purposes, you must try to gain understanding of how to manage a group and how to become a more effective group member. In order to develop the above two objectives, you must always keep in mind that a group is part of a larger organization with which it interacts. It is in this context that we talk of group dynamics. Therefore, we must understand the meaning of Group Dynamics before we talk about the dynamics of group formation.

Group Dynamics

Group Dynamics is concerned with the interaction and forces among group members in a social situation. It is important to understand the dynamics of members of formal or informal groups in the organization. In the 1930s, Kurt Lewin popularized the term, Group Dynamics to mean interaction of forces among group members in a social situation. The three styles of leaderships are Authoritarian, Democratic and Laissez-faire, which Lewin (1939) and his associates have developed by creating three different social situations for the three styles of leadership. In course of time, various meanings were attached to the term 'group dynamics' (Kelly 1974). One of the meanings suggests **how a group should be organized and conducted.** In democratic leadership, member participation and overall cooperation are emphasized. Another meaning of Group Dynamics is that it is a set of techniques. In various group exercises, it tries to make the leader as well as the member effective. An attempt is made to make the above members play their roles in a management situation of a group discussions, team building, finding out various solutions to problems by brainstorming and understanding ourselves in relation to others while we transact or interact with others. Such exercises are also provided in situations where only members are present and no leader exists to direct or control the group. All these exercises are techniques to develop both the individual as well as the organisation in which he or she works. The last meaning of the term, Group Dynamics, is closest to Lewin's use of the term suggesting internal nature of the groups as to how they are formed, what their structures and processes are, how they function and affect individual members, other groups and the organization. In this unit, our main attention will be focused on the third meaning of the term. You will appreciate therefore, the plan here to start with defining a group and then consider the dynamics of group formation.

What is a Group?

A group is any number of people who:

- have a common purpose or objective

- interact with each other to accomplish their objective
- are aware of one another
- perceive themselves to be part of the group.

This is the way Huse and Bowditch (1977) defined a group. You were asked at the beginning as to how many different groups you belonged to. You may see, from the above definition that throughout our lives, we belong to many different groups. Families are groups, a cricket team is a group, a club is a group, drama and music organizations are all groups. You can thus apply the concept of group to various examples of religion, politics, consumers, sports, etc. as the case may be. In management, we primarily talk of groups at work. In most organizations, getting the work done requires group efforts. Thus, a manager must know how to manage an individual by knowing the individual dynamics, such as his values, personality, perceptions and attitudes as discussed earlier. Also a manager must know how to manage a group by understanding Group Dynamics.

At this point, the number of people as contained in the definition of the group, should not be taken too literally, At some point, the number of people may become too large to fit the rest of the definition. For example, all the people of India cannot interact with each other. Also, each group has a common objective, but the member who belongs to it may have other personal objectives. For example, a life insurance agent may like to become a member of a parent-teacher association of a school to help promote the development process of its students. But belonging to that association will also help him to increase his or her contact to ensure more and more people, so he gets more commission for as many members as he can sell the insurance to.

What is most important in the content of the definition of a group is to be aware of each other in a group. This awareness is seldom there, when we look at an aggregation of people. They are mere collections, different from what we call a group, where members see themselves as belonging to a group in order to interact and achieve the common objectives of the group. Moreover, such kind of interaction may be over a long or short period of time. In waiting for a bus, passengers make a queue. All of them have a common purpose, that is, to enter the bus after buying tickets. We cannot call them a group, although they have a common purpose. Suddenly a person breaks the queue to go ahead. All the others get together to prevent that person from gatecrashing and getting his ticket ahead of those standing in the queue before him. That moment, a group is formed. Perhaps, after controlling that person from getting a ticket out of turn, the others keep continuing to talk to each other but the common purpose of keeping the queue-breaker has vanished. The group disappears and the numbers of people become an aggregation or a collection.

THE DYNAMICS OF GROUP FORMATION

From the above example, it becomes imperative that you should understand why people form into groups. Some people believe that it is because of propinquity or affiliating with one another that individuals form into groups. In a room people sitting nearer to each other make a group more easily than people sitting at opposite ends of a room. This kind of affiliation of people with each other is due to spatial or geographical nearness. But it does not help us to understand some of the complexities of group formation, which are more than mere affiliations due to physical or geographical nearness. It will do you good to know some major theories of group formation in brief.

Theories of Group Formation

1. Homans (1950) explained the basis of group formation in terms of activities, interactions and sentiments of people. These three elements are directly related to each other. In the above example of controlling a queue-breaker in the line, the **required activities** are the **assigned** tasks at which people work. All others **knew** their turn and how to exercise it especially, with a sudden change of then created by the queue breaker. The **required interaction** takes place when any one person's activity **follows** or is **influenced** by the activity of another. In this example, the person whose turn was dislocated by the queue-breaker influences all others activities. As soon as he pushes out the person (the queue-breaker) or tells him not to do it, all others follow him. Hence required interaction may be verbal (telling him not to break the queue) or non-verbal (pushing him out of the queue). One can see the activities and the interactions. But as **sentiments** are the feelings or attitudes of a person towards others, his likes or dislikes, approval or disapproval, can only be inferred from the behaviour. After the activity of throwing out the queue-breaker changes, the interactions also change. In the above example, people talk to each other in a very informal way after they succeeded in throwing out the queue-breaker. These informal interactions, known as emergent interactions, change the activities into informal or emergent activities, such as people reorganiing their queue and ensuring that no other intruder comes in out of turn etc. All these activities emerge because of the sentiments or feelings of the people.

   You will notice that the more activities people share, the more numerous will be their interactions and the stronger will be their mutual sentiments. Therefore, in turn, with more interactions among persons, the more will be their shared activities and sentiments. Again in turn the more sentiments the person has for one another, the more will be their shared activities and interactions. Homan's theory, therefore, explains the formation of groups on the basis of people's interaction with each other. People are not only physically together, but they also solve problems, attain goals, facilitate coordination, reduce tension and achieve a balance. In an organization, the participants interact with each other in this manner and tend to form into powerful groups.

2. Newcomb (1961) states a theory known as balance theory of group formation, which explains group formation on the basis of attractions of persons towards each other as they have similar attitudes towards common objects or goals. For example, person A and B will interact and form a relationship because of their common attitudes and values towards C.

   A Balance Theory of group formation:

   - Common attitudes and values
   - Politics
   - Religion
   - Literature
   - Work
   - Aesthetics
   - Authority
   - Marriage

   If A and B form a relationship or a group, they will strive to maintain a symmetrical balance between the attraction and the common values. Whenever this relationship between A and B becomes unbalanced, both of them try to restore the balance. If the balance cannot be restored, then their relationship is dissolved. Both affiliation and interaction play a significant role in the balance theory.

3. Thaibaut and Kelly (1959) talk of another theory of group formation, stating the outcome of interaction as the basis of group formation. The outcome of a relationship should be rewarding in order to have attraction or affiliation among the persons or members of a group. Persons derive personal and social satisfaction from having interactions with each other. If they incur anxiety or frustration or embarrassment or fatigue in such interactions, then that interaction becomes a cost for them rather than a reward. Thaibaut and Kelly's theory of group formation is known as exchange theory of reward and cost outcomes. You will appreciate that there are affiliation, interaction and common attitudes—all playing roles in the exchange theory.

What do Groups offer to Individuals?

For individuals, there are some very practical reasons to join a group or forming a group. If you are hungry, you can satisfy your need for food by eating. This need for food involves others too. You need money to buy food, but in order to have money you must work for it or have someone give it to you. Very few people can live alone or in isolation, like Robinson Crusoe. Most of us can satisfy our needs only with or through other people. Let us see what some of the needs are that groups help us to satisfy.

❖ Safety and Security Needs

Do you remember the very first question asking you as to how old you were when you first joined a group? The answer is, perhaps you joined in a group in your preschool years in a nursery classroom. You learnt to protect yourself by being in a group. A newborn baby has to be protected from a hostile world and therefore he or she belongs to a group by depending on it for its security and comfort. In the nursery class, a teacher asks the small kids who broke the toy and seldom gets an answer. All the kids keep quiet. Although young, they protect their members by not disclosing anybody's name or pointing to anyone in a group. A teenager at the adolescent stage derives social support from his group when he or she strives for individual independence in taking decisions and actions. You may like to appreciate how group is a source of support to an individual in an organisation. Workers become members of a union and thus feel more secure to be with the group.

Even in emergency activities of putting off fire, the fire fighters depend on each other for protection; similarly, coal miners depend heavily on each other for protection. These are cases where individuals doing hazardous jobs like the above derive physiological and psychological support from the groups. They need to be physically together, even if they know that this may increase their collective danger. This helps them to be more confident and able to perform well, less fearful and more responsible to carry out their duties.

❖ Relatedness or Belongingness Needs

You might have noticed many persons in your working life, who are very isolated or who prefer to be absent from work most of the times or an organisation having high turnover of employees or frequent change of employees. Studies show such phenomena occur where people are unable to belong to groups. This is because of the fact that all of us are social beings and belonging to or relating to groups satisfies a number of social needs. We get emotional support from a group, which is particularly helpful at times of stress. In normal situations, as is seen in Hawthorne studies, affiliation to a group has a major influence on human behaviour in organizations. When we are isolated from human communication and companionship, we simply lose touch with reality.

❖ Esteem and Growth Needs

When you do a piece of work, you get a praise from others. This gives a sense of recognition, which fulfils your esteem, need (being recognised) and also brings a sense of fulfillment of your need for growth towards further achievement of good work and career prospects.

We should now make ourselves familiar with many kinds of groups and many different ways to classify them. We should concentrate on both formal and informal groups existing in organizations. We shall talk of other groups, but in brief.

TYPES OF GROUPS

❖ Formal Groups

These groups are established by the organisation to accomplish specific tasks. According to Cartwright and Zander (1974) these groups include **command groups,** which consists of managers and their direct subordinates; and committees and task forces which are created to carry out specific organizational assignments or activities. For example, In an educational institution there are three broad formal groups of teachers, students and administration. In the command group, the top administrator or principal or head of the institution has heads of departments of different disciplines as his direct subordinates. Various commitments to look at academic activities of teaching and research are made to carry out the specific activities such as selecting students, making of a curriculum, developing teaching and evaluation methods, moderating performance, etc. in each department for a specific disciplines, having their command groups, committees and task force as well as administrative staff of various levels and categories (such as academic, accounts, audit, sports, etc).

In all cases, command groups and committees continue to exist where as task forces are usually established to solve a particular problem. They are disbanded after the work is done. The idea of task is more applicable to manufacturing or service organizations rather than research institutions. In the later kind of organizations, task forces consists of managers, technical experts from research, development, marketing, production and purchasing departments, to make sure that each new product passes through smoothly from the idea stage through the production stage and into market.

❖ Informal Groups

These groups are formed within the structure of the organisation but by the members themselves rather than by the organisation. Sometimes they do not have the approval of the management. Basically, informal groups are formed to satisfy social needs on the job. Sometimes, they are formed to perform a task better, sometimes they are formed to hold production at a certain level. In a rigid system of organisation, these informal groups meet fairly regularly to cut short the rigid bureaucratic practices of the management.

❖ Primary Groups

Cooley (1911) defined and analyzed primary groups as those characterized by intimate, face-to-face association and cooperation. They are primary in several senses, but chiefly in that they are fundamental in forming the social nature and ideals of the individuals.

Example of primary group is family and the peer group. Many people use the term small group interchangeably with primary group. But the small group only meets the criterion of small size for face-to-face interaction and communication to occur. In addition to being small, a primary group must have a feeling of comradeship, loyalty and a common sense of values among all its members. Thus, all primary groups are small groups, but not all small groups are primary.

The logic of primary goods is extended to work groups in Hawthorne's studies. These work groups have primary group qualities, which tremendously influence individual behaviour irrespective of contact or environmental conditions.

❖ Membership Groups

These are the ones to which the individual actually belongs. Examples: clubs, cooperative societies, worker's unions etc.

❖ Reference Groups

These are the ones with which an individual identifies or to which he would like to belong. Examples: Socially or professionally prestigious groups with which the individual would like to belong.

❖ In-groups

The in-groups represent a clustering of individuals holding prevailing values in a society or at least having a dominant place in social functioning. Examples: Members of a team, family members.

❖ Out-groups

The out-groups are the conglomerates looked upon as subordinate or marginal in the future. Examples: Street performers for an office worker, a hawker for a surgeon. Whenever there is a win-lose situation in a competitive task, members of win or lose group show tremendous in-group feelings within themselves. Their group, in relation to the other group, is also called an out-group.

Group Role

Shakespeare said, "All the world is a stage, and all the men and women merely players." By this term, we mean a set of expected behaviour patterns attributed to someone occupying a given position in a social unit. The understanding of role behaviour would be dramatically simplified if each of us chose one role and "played it out" regularly and consistently. We are required to play a number of diverse roles, both on and off our jobs. As we shall see, one of the tasks is understanding behaviour is grasping the role that a person is currently playing.

For example, on his job, Mr. 'X' is a plant manager with an electrical company, a large electrical equipment manufacturer. He has a number of roles to fulfill on that job; for instance that of an electrical company's employee, a member of the middle management, an electrical engineer and the primary company spokesman in the community. Off the job, he finds himself playing still more roles: husband, father, Rotarian, tennis player, a member of the Thunderbird country club and president of homeowner's association. Many of these roles are compatible, while some create conflicts. For example, how does his religious involvement influence his managerial decisions regarding lay offs, expense account padding, or providing accurate information to government agencies. Thus, we are all required to play a number of roles and our behaviour varies with the role we are playing.

Role Identify and Perception

There are certain attitudes and actual behaviours consistent with the role and they create the role identity. People have the ability to shift roles rapidly when they recognise that situation and its demand clearly requires major changes. For example, when union stewards were promoted to foreman's position, it was found that their attitudes changed from pro-union to pro-management within a few months of their promotion. When it had to be later rescinded because of economic difficulties in the firm, it was found that the demoted foreman had once again adopted their pro-union attitudes.

When the situation is more vague and the role one has to play is less clear, people often revert to old identities. In spite of the fact that some of the former losers were now winners by society's standards, they found it very difficult to deal with the winners' role, when placed in an environment in which they had always been losers. With the role requirements ill-defined, identities became clouded, and individuals reverted back to old patterns of behaviour.

One's own view of how one is supposed to act in a given situation is a role perception, based on an interpretation of how we believe we are supposed to behave, we engage in certain types of behaviour. Where do we get these perceptions? One author suggests that we all learn roles from such media as movies, books and television and from friends. If this is true, we might propose that many persons may have formed their role identities perceiving their favourite character. Of course, the primary reason apprenticeship programmes exist in many trades and professions are to allow individuals to watch an 'expert' so they can to act as they are supposed to.

Role Expectations and Conflict

Role expectations are defined as how others believe you should act in a given situation. How you behave is determined, to a large part, by the role defined in the context in which you are acting. The role of a parliament member is viewed as having propriety and dignity, whereas a football coach is seen as aggressive, dynamic and inspiring to his players. When role expectations are concentrated into generalized categories, we have role stereotypes. During the last few decades we have seen a major change in the general population's role stereotypes of females. In 1950, a woman's role was to stay home, take care of the house, bring up children, and generally care for her husband. Today, most of us no longer hold this stereotypes. Girls can aspire to be doctors, lawyers, managers and astronauts, as well the more traditional activities of nurse, school teachers, secretary or house wife. In other words, many of us have changed our role expectations of women and, similarly many women carry new role perceptions.

In the workplace, it can be helpful to look at the role expectations through the perspective of the psychological contract, an unwritten agreement, existing between employee and the employer. It sets our mutual expectations—what management expects from workers and vice-versa. In effect, this contract defines the behavioural expectations that go with every role. Management is expected to treat employees justly, provide acceptable working conditions, clearly communicate what is a fair day's work and give feedback on how well the employee is doing. In turn, employees are expected to respond by demonstrating a good attitude, follow directions, and show loyalty to the organisation.

When an individual is confronted by divergent roles' expectations, the result is role conflict. It exists when an individual finds that compliance with one entails conflict with another. At the extreme, it would include situations where two or more role expectations are mutually contradictory.

The issues of ethics in business demonstrate a well-publicized area of role conflict among corporate executives. A recent study found that 57 percent of Harvard *Business Review* readers had experienced the dilemma of having to choose between what was profitable for their firms and what was ethical.

Spatial Influences on Role

Research evidence indicates that the way individuals position themselves within a group, that is, the spatial arrangement that they voluntarily develop, is far from random.

Spatial factors can also determine who within a group will be chosen or accepted for a leadership role. When one wants to take on the role of adversary or to emphasize superior-subordinate relationships, it is natural to place a barrier between himself and others to identify a we-they distinction.

This may more readily be illustrated by comparing a traditional classroom situation, where the instructor stands in front of the class before a podium, with the students in clearly established neat rows and columns, and a less structured situation with the chairs geographically dispersed about in a circle and the instructor taking one of the seats in the circle. The latter positioning can be expected to increase group interaction, reduce the feeling of superior-subordinate interaction, and place the instructor or more equal footings with the students.

Implications of Formal and Informal Groups for Management

Formal Groups: Committees

As defined earlier, formal groups are established by the organisation to accomplish specific tasks. These groups include command groups, committees and task forces. In this section, we should further clarify committee organisation as an important type of formally designated group and its implication for management.

Committees are special kinds of groups which serve the following purposes in an organisation:

(a) Exchanging views and information

(b) Recommending action

(c) Generating ideas

(d) Making decisions

The size of the committees is usually kept small. It is to encourage good quality of decisions. Communication among members is, thus, limited to few. With increase in the size of committee, many members feel less willing or threatened to participate actively.

The chairperson of the committees provides directions to the committee to fulfill the objectives of the committee. He or she should be a person of open mind and a careful listener. He or she should allow members to voice their opinions and should not place his or her opinion above those of others. He or she should involve everyone in the activities of the committee and in the ideas of the members. He or she should help the committee focus on the task at hand and on the progress made.

The members of the committee should cooperate with each other to achieve the purpose of the committee. To a great extent, the image of a committee depends on the cooperation of members with each other. They should have stronger motivation to accomplish the task. They should have effective communication with each other. There should be more ideas generated in the group, along with increased satisfaction and performance of the members. It is the chairperson who should try to ensure communication, satisfaction and productivity among the members of the committee.

With today's organizations becoming increasingly large and complex, the committee form of organisation will, undoubtedly become more important and more widely used in future. The modern manager must learn how his committees or teams or commissions boards or groups or task forces should be effectively formed and should function, no matter whether he is in a government or educational or religious or business organisation. In other words, this kind of a group management will become more popular as well as important in times to come.

Meetings of members in a committee may be time-consuming and costly in so far as individual's time is concerned. Committees are also criticized for not making the members responsible for bad decisions or mistakes. Many individuals use the committee as a shield to avoid personal responsibility for bad decisions or mistakes. In fact, all committee members as well as chairperson should be made responsible for all decisions. It is in the interest of the committee to differentiate between very conscientious members who voted against a wrong decision as well as those who took a particular decision and can defend it to the end. Many decisions taken by committee may or may not be liked by members of the organisation who are likely to be affected by it.

In spite of all the above shortcomings that are likely to be there, the future manager must learn to arrive at an improved decision through the combined and integrated judgment of the committee members. He or she can reduce conflict in the group, facilitate coordination of various groups in the organisation and increase commitment and motivation of members of the organisation through participation.

Committees, which are, thus, the formally designated groups of the organisation, are assuming more importance in day-to-day functioning at any organizational level. Today, they are acknowledged as significant features of group dynamics in organizational behaviour.

Informal Groups

Informal groups plays a significant role in the dynamics of organizational behaviour. A formal group has officially prescribed goals and relationships, which an informal groups does not have. But we cannot think of these two groups as separate entities, as they coexist and they are inseparable. An illustration will make it clear. When an engineer designs the plans and technology for a new factory and when an architect designs the office for layout, they are also designing the social relations that will prevail in the organization. The formal organization of the management determines where men will work and what opportunities they will have to contact each other during the day. Also the rates of pay, work conditions and other aspects of the jobs as decided by the management are important too. This is because of the fact that every person is told formally where and how he or she is to worl , with whom to come into contact. Obviously, one develops friendships with the ‚eople one most often comes across. In fact, those employees who have the greatest opportunities to make contacts on the job make the largest numbers of friends. In course of time, they may be in the best position to become leaders of the group.

Remember for yourself, who was the first person you had contact with when you joined your present work organization? How frequently did you meet them? In course of time, have you noticed that you have became a member of your work group having made contacts with quite a number of people—trying to share your problems with them and their problems with you? This is how a work group is formed. As time passes, your affiliation with certain groups becomes more meaningful and strong.

Based on contacts and common interests such friendships and groups made by employees arise out of the life of the organization. Once these groups are formed, they develop a life of their own. The process is dynamic and self-generating and makes the work groups an organization in itself.

Characteristics of Effective Work Groups

In managing the organization, you have to understand how groups can be made into effective work groups. The factors that influence the work groups effectiveness are norms, cohesion and leadership. Let us see how each one of them contributes to making the group effective to achieve the objectives of the organization.

Group Norms

When the group functions for a period of time, to attain certain objectives it develops norms or standards of behaviour. A norm is a rule. This tells the individual of how to behave in a particular group. An individual may be a member of a welfare group, a chess club, his family and his work group. You will see the different kinds of the behaviour the same individual in the different groups.

You may also notice that sometimes the norm is formal and is accepted by the group that way. For example, all workers of a particular group wear safety glasses while operating on a particular machine. On the other hand, a norm can be informal arising out of the interactions and feelings of the people. All the members of the task groups decide to keep their output high by regulating their pace of work. For example, a number of typists decide to attain a target of fifty pages of neat typing every day. So they do it.

It is also possible that another group may like to keep its output low, again because of some emergent activities, interactions and feelings of the group. So it is important to know what behaviour is significant for the group, which helps to develop the norms. In other words, having high or low output is equally influenced by what the group prescribed for its members as well as what other activities, interactions and feelings develop among the members in case of doing work.

We also find another characteristics of norms: some norms are applicable to some people, only and not to all. For example, a manager of a group behaves differently, from others members of the groups. His or her behaviour is what others expect of him or her in a given position. When a new member joins the group, he or she expected to follow the norms more closely than the senior members.

Some norms have central importance and are accepted by every one of the group while others have less importance. A worker who remains absent and does not do any work will not last long in an organization. A relevant group norm is one, which is neither central nor absolutely essential to follow but is worthwhile and desirable.

Some of us conform to all the norms of the groups, some of us select only pivotal norms for acceptance, still others reject all the values and norms of the group. It is usually seen that complete conformity to norms as in first case and complete rejection of the norms, as in the last one, have undesirable consequences. A completely confirming individual losses his or her ability to influence the group. An individual who rejects the all group norms is likely to be expelled from the group. It is, therefore, advisable that the individual exercises his or her choice of acceptance of the norm quite discreetly.

It is equally important to understand that with increase in size of the group, norms are less likely to be accepted. It is also true that more intelligent persons are less likely to confirm to norms. You may notice that as the group increases in size, there are chances that subgroups may prove difficult to maintain with uniform conformity all the time.

The last characteristics of the norm are those that allow possible deviations. An individual who deviates too far gets punished. When the union is on strike, its members attending to work are punished by being boycotted by the group.

Ask yourself the following questions in the positions of a manager:

- What have you understood about the norms when you are formal leader of a group and when you are the member of the other group?
- Have you understood what the norms of the other groups are?
- Do you know which are the central norms?
- Do people conform to norms completely?
- Do people wait for their leader to speak first in a meeting?
- Do people come in time for meetings?
- Is disagreement allowed?
- Do people have a common style of clothing?

As a manager, you must also try to understand why people opt to lower their output and if need be, you should try to develop trust among your members in order to be able to influence and change or modify the norms of your group. Your effectiveness as a manager will increase with a high level of trust between you and your group members.

Group Cohesiveness

This means the degree to which group members are motivated to remain within the group and consequently behave in a similar ways. A cohesive group also helps the members in their satisfaction of needs and attainment of goals.

What are the factors that affect the group cohesiveness?

Size of the group: With very few people in a group, you may fall short of skilled hands to do a good job. With a large number of people you may find it difficult to communicate and identify the best talent. At the same time, the individual member may not be happy with his or her interactions with the group. In the first case, there is a breakdown of the task and in the second case, reaching out to people is difficult.

Proximity or geography of the group: Nearness or working closely together helps in group cohesiveness. It helps face-to-face contact. A small isolated work group is cohesive and will work better to attain its goals.

Outside pressure: This binds together all the members against a common enemy and thus makes it members forget their differences. You might have been observed how groups become cohesive under outside pressures where there is (i) competition with other groups or (ii) reaction against the supervisor who closely supervises the work or (iii) union-management conflict or (iv) lack of trust between the manager and his group or (v) even mistrust between two groups.

Accomplishing group goals: As the group becomes more cohesive, the members become more motivated to accomplish its goal and behave in similar ways. Accomplishing group goals increase the cohesion of the group. Falling to accomplish the group goals reduces the group cohesiveness.

It is necessary to remember that it is not always desirable to have group cohesiveness, which may result in going against the objectives of the work group. For example, workers being highly cohesive may decide to work against the management. So you must find out what the harmful effects are likely to be of a cohesive group. Examples of rejection of new ideas by cohesive group members are not uncommon. At times, these members feel that they know the best. The kind of feeling is known as 'group think' where members show tremendous desire for unanimity. A great deal of solidarity and loyalty to the group overrides the motivation of the members to consider different courses of action logically and in a realistic manner. In government administration, many significant decisions are made on the basis of group think principles, which have been quite unfortunate for a large number of people.

As a manager you must make a cohesive group to accomplish organizational goals. You have to give information, get the resources of your members to accomplish the task and hold frequent open meetings.

Group Leadership

Leadership is the ability to influence the behaviour of others. Any effective work group wanting to accomplish its task gaining some sort of social satisfaction and having some sense of contribution and growth should like to look up to a leader to help reach these goals.

Informal leaders often emerge from the activities, interactions, sentiments of the ongoing group. They may help the group to accomplish its task or fulfill its social goals. You will always notice that formal task instructions comes from the supervisor, but informal help comes from the informal leader.

Informal leader may be lower in official status than the formal leader, but he helps the group satisfy both personal and organizational goals. If this job is done by the formal leader, then there will be no informal leader emerging out of the group.

If the informal leader helps in attaining the organizational goals, then he becomes task-oriented like a formal leader. There may be chances that social leader will emerge to maintain a balance between organizational and personal needs.

In order to be effective as a manager you must recognize the existence of informal leaders and work with them to develop group norms of high productivity, build more cohesion and enable the members to have their social needs satisfied.

MANAGING GROUP PRODUCTIVITY

In your role as manager, you will do well to remember some useful ways to make your work group effective.

❖ Content

While having a meeting with your group members try to understand the subject matter of the task to be performed by the committee. This will help you to see the problems clearly. And solve it to:

- Decide about the size of the committee (having about five to fifteen members) and include experts in the committee to solve your problem.
- Distribute the agenda before the meeting is held to all the members.
- Specify the timings of the meetings.
- Encourage persons to present their ideas and do not encourage them to pick up the first feasible solution to a problem. Allow them to think of various alternative solutions.
- Periodically summarize the discussion and restate the current position of the committee as to whether the committee has to finally decide on a solution or only recommend a solution to a high authority/advise the higher authority.

❖ Process

This involves how the content is handled or discussed by the members. Benne and Sheats (1948) describe three effective ways to approach the group processes.

One of the ways the content is handled, is by group task activities. You may intimate and orient the groups to its goals, coordinate, give and seek information about the problem.

Another way may be through the group building activities like encouraging members to cooperate with each other. This is the group building activity which helps a manager to establish better group relationships.

Still another way the group members satisfy their needs is through self-serving activities. Members satisfy their needs at the cost of others. You might have noticed that more behave in a dominating manner, more try to get attention, more behave aggressively and more withdraw while working in the group. Persons engaged in the group activities are only serving their own purpose or interest rather than helping the group to achieve its goals.

You must try to understand the differences between the content and process to make the group more effective. Too much of task activity and too little of group building activity is not a good way to make an effective work group.

Self-serving activities are signs of non-constructive satisfaction of valid personal needs and are disruptive. They reduce the ability of the group to its objectives.

Many times, we overlook the fact that people can be both emotional and rational in understanding the content and process of work. Emotions are realities that have to be take care of. A good manager must not neglect the group building activity as it may make group and committee meetings ineffective. He or she should draw on the influence of the informal group by integrating its objectives with those of formal group as well as try to keep the formal activities from unnecessarily disrupting the informal organization.

GROUPS IN MOTION

So far we have been looking at some of the key elements or variables that make up a group, its properties or dimensions, from an analytical point of view, rather as if we are dissecting a dead fish. But groups are alive; they do not stand still in time and space. The analytical approach needs to be complemented by a holistic view of the moving, living, dynamic whole. Until you have seen a shoal of fish gliding together, suddenly turning silver-sided around an invisible centre of gravity, you have not understood groups.

Not only is the group moving as a unit, but the various elements within it are constantly interacting. A change in procedure will affect the atmosphere, which will affect the participation pattern, which will affect cohesion, which will affect morale and so on.

Various attempts have been made to discern phases or patterns within the constant flux of group life. Many theorists in the Group Dynamics movement, for example, made analogies describing the process of group formation as a spiral, a series of cycles, or a series of stages, which succeed each other as growth occurs.

Groups would work on a problem, and then as if by agreement withdraw from it, only to return to the same ground some time later, but upon a higher plane. Knowledge of this spiralling effect was useful, not least because it helped me as a teacher to time my interventions. For instance, it was worth waiting for the 'upward thermals' before making comments. Remarks made when the group was not in a' work phase or cycle, but 'resting' or withdrawing, were not as likely to be effective.

Consistent and identifiable stages of development in all groups probably do not exist. Group growth is a gradual process in which themes and subtleness may intertwine but in which the dramatic quality is the wholeness. The closest analogy to my mind is a musical symphony, with tunes, phrases, moods interwoven into a moving pattern.

Any breakdown into phases by a process of analysis therefore, runs the double risk of oversimplifying and also destroying that' very holistic quality which constitutes the group. Analysis leads to abstraction, which in turn, leads us away from the concrete, unique, whole group with whom you may be working the design office or its equivalent.

There are probably no clear and finite *stages* of development. But that does not mean there are no consistent sequential changes. Not every teenager goes through a stage of moodiness, but there are changes in that period of life which tend to be accompanied by moodiness. Not every mother feels postnatal depression, but there is a strong tendency for that to happen.

This is the nearest we can get to regularity. It does appear that in some groups change takes a cyclic or spiral form, with movement backwards and forwards. In other groups change seems to happen in sudden leaps and bounds, interspersed with plateau periods where no change occurs. In other groups, there are regressive movements as well as dramatic arid unpredictable spurts. Again, you may be able to think of analogies in the development of individuals you know well — or indeed in your own life history. You should bear these factors in mind when considering the group development model in Box 1.1.

BOX 1.1 Group Development

	Group Structure	Task Activity
Forming	Considerable anxiety, testing to discover the nature of the situation what help can be expected from leader or convener and what behaviour will or will not be appropriate.	What is the task? Members seek the answers to that basic question together with knowledge of the rules and the methods to be employed.
Storming	Conflict emerges between sub-groups; the authority and/or competence of the leader is challenged. Opinions polarize.	The value and feasibility of the task is questioned. People react Emotionally against Its demand.

Contd....

	Individuals react against efforts of the leader or group to control them.	
Norming	The group begins to harmonise; its experiences group cohesion or unity for the first time. Norms emerge as those in conflict are reconciled and resistance is overcome. Mutual support develops.	Co-operation on the task begins; plans are made and work standards laid down. communication of views and feelings develop.
Performing	The group structures Itself or accepts a structure which fits most appropriately its common task. Roles are seen in terms functional to the task and flexibility between them develops.	Constructive work on the task surges ahead; progress is experienced as more of the group's energy is applied to being effective in the area of their common task.

These phrases are fairly recognisable to any normally perceptive person with experience in work groups. Where there is an unresolved problem of who is in charge, for example, a power struggle may develop among members who desire to have things move their way or who may enjoy controlling others or power for its own sake. Such people in such unresolved control situations will tend to engage in various persuasive methods of controlling others, such as advice giving, argument or confrontation. Strategies for manipulating others may be resorted to, possibly in subgroups outside the total group. People may appeal in vain to the appointed or elected leader to check this competition for power. Others may argue against all forms of control, as if enjoying the apparent freedom in lack of any organisation.

The resolution of this phase, and the eventual emergence of the group into the stage of performance, is not the end of the story. The group, which is already a team in ore, may go on to become the refined metal of a high performance team.

The group may equally lapse into decline, the *dorming* phase. Here, group structure becomes governed by routine and systems — everything has to go through 'proper channels' and the group spirit becomes ossified into a comfortable and cosy togetherness. Task activity falls off in quantity and quality, but the group does not really mind. It is so satisfied by past achievements that it is content to leave the unconquered peaks to the young thrusting groups coming into being all around them.

Not all groups behave in this way. Some complete their job and disperse. Some complete a job and say 'that was enjoyable, can we find something else to do.'

What Needs are Present in the Life of Every Group?

The needs of the group can be summarised as follows:

BOX 1.2 Needs of the Group

Task	The need to accomplish something — build a house, sing an anthem, determine a budget, plan a conference, solve a problem, climb a mountain. The need of the group is to try to accomplish this task. So long as this task remains undone, there will be a tension in the group and an urge to complete the task. The task is *what* the group is talking about or working on. The task is usually seen in terms of *things* rather than people.
Group	The need to develop and maintain working relationships among the members so that the group task can be accomplished. This is called the maintenance need of the group. Maintenance refers primarily to *people* and their relationships with each other. It concerns *how* people relate to each other *as* they work at the group task. Unless members listen to each other, for example, and try to build upon each other's suggestions it will be very difficult, and often impossible, for the group to accomplish its task. Yet maintenance is frequently neglected in groups. How long would a fleet of jet airliners be able to operate if they were not serviced, refuelled and otherwise maintained?
Individual	The needs of individuals come with them into groups. People work in groups not only because of interest in the task to be accomplished but also because membership of groups fulfils their various needs. Why do people work in the first place? They work because they are hungry, they are thirsty and they need somewhere to sleep. Even today, when we use money as a means of exchange, most of our salary goes in satisfying those basic needs. But a satisfied need ceases to motivate. Once you have enough food and drink, once you have a house, other needs rise up in the human heart. You become interested in a pension, job security and safety of work. If those security needs are satisfied by good company policy and through the welfare state, people do not then turn round and say 'Thank you, we are now fully satisfied'. Instead, they discover other areas of need bubbling up within them: the quality of relationships in working life; respect from others and self respect; and then the need for 'self-actualization', a fulfillment of one's potential by growth. The needs for physical satisfaction and security are stronger and more deep-rooted. If they are threatened then we jump back and defend them. The needs for self-esteem, the respect of others and self-fulfilment are weaker, but they are more distinctively human. If such needs can be met *along with* and not *at the expense of the* group task and maintenance needs, then the group will tend to be more effective.

As you will see from Figure 1.1, the circles overlap. If you achieve the common task the effects will flow into the group circle and help to create a sense of unity. And they will also influence the individual circle. In fact, you can work round the diagram. If you have a good group, for example, you are more likely to achieve the task. If the individuals concerned are fully involved and motivated, then they are going to give much more to the task and much more to the group. By contrast, if you imagine a black circle totally eclipsing the task circle that would symbolise a total failure of the task area. You would then have taken quite a chunk out of the group area, and a similar one out of the individual circle too. If you could put that black circle over the group maintenance area, then again it would show that lack of group cohesiveness will affect the other two circles.

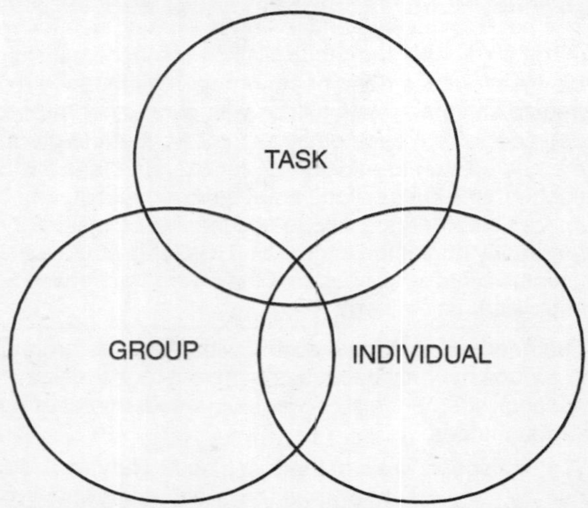

FIGURE 1.1 **Three Areas of Need**

Needs and Leadership Functions

In order that the task and maintenance needs be met, certain *functions* have to be performed. A function is what you do as opposed to a quality or trait.

In this chapter listed the 'roles' or functions introduced by Benne and Sheats in the late 1940s. Observers in Group Dynamics training laboratories found these rather long; moreover we found it difficult to use two separate forms at once. Therefore, various efforts were made to produce a composite list.

One such working categorisation, suggested by Gibb and Gibb influenced my subsequent efforts. They indicated five broad categories of leadership functions:

Initiating: Keeping the group action moving, or getting it going (for example, suggesting action step, pointing out goal, proposing procedure, clarifying)

Regulating: Influencing the direction and tempo of the group's work (for example, summarising, pointing out time limits, restating goal)

Informing: Bringing information or opinion to the group

Supporting: Creating an emotional climate that holds group together, makes it easy for members to contribute to work on the task (for example, harmonising, relieving tension, voicing group feeling, encouraging)

Evaluating: Helping the group to evaluate its decisions, goals or procedures (for example, testing for consensus, noting group process)

A group needs all five of these types of function if it is to accomplish its task and maintain its cohesiveness. Early in a group's work initiating functions are much needed. Later, as solutions are proposed, informing and regulating functions may assume much more importance. Supporting functions are needed all the way along. The evaluating function becomes especially relevant as the group nears the end of its work. Group work will be effective, then, to the degree that needed group functions are supplied at the time they are needed.

❖ Some Implications

Sooner or later all three kinds of needs present in every group must be met to some extent in order to achieve effectiveness and satisfaction. When needed functions are missing, group progress is slow and uneven.

This does not imply that at every moment exactly one third of the group's attention and energy should be devoted to each of these three kinds of needs. Over a period of time, there may be great fluctuations in the amount of group attention and energy directed to anyone of these needs. The amount of energy to be allocated depends upon the ability of the members to diagnose which of the three needs is most pressing at every moment, and their ability to meet this perceived need.

The performing of one function may help to meet two or even three needs simultaneously. Most people usually have preferences for providing one or another function most often, such as the inveterate summariser. Hence the tendency to use the word 'role' in the context of group life. But most people can at least potentially make more than one functional contribution.

Group Processes

Process issues, you may recall, revolve around the underlying ways in which a group works. Again, to repeat an earlier point, it is not the same as group maintenance. In this and the following chapter, we shall draw out some more lessons about group processes which are relevant to teamwork today.

In order to clothe, the rather nebulous concept of process we have chosen three examples: responses to authority, response to frustration and decision-making procedures. These are obviously not directly connected with each other. Taken together, however, they can take us some steps further in understanding more fully what goes on in groups.

In each section you should bear in mind the Group Dynamics provenance for these ideas. But we have selected these particular instances of group process because we have experienced them many times in working groups and we have found the work of psychologists here illuminating rather than obfuscating.

All groups need to use some procedures — ways of working — to get things done. In formal business meetings we are accustomed to a set of rules or procedures. Informal groups usually use less rigid procedures. The choice of procedures has a direct effect on such other aspects of group life as atmosphere, participation and cohesion. Choosing procedures that are appropriate to the situation and the work to be done may require a degree of flexibility and inventiveness by a group.

CHECKLIST

- How does the group determine its practices or agenda?
- How does it make decisions — by vote, silent assent, consensus?
- How does it discover and make use of the resources of its members?
- How does the work of various members, subgroups and activities get coordinated?
- How does it evaluate its work?

Decision Making

Group processes revolve around the core of decision making. How are decisions made? Or do they just happen? That is a central issue for groups.

Take the case of a group of doctors working together in a primary healthcare team in Bristol. There are four doctors together with district nurses and health visitors making up this team. The senior partner is a woman aged 51, and the other doctors — all men — are aged 29, 32 and 35. At one meeting, the younger doctors proposed that if disagreements arose about matters concerning the group practice, decisions should be taken by vote. The senior partner put her foot down and insisted that decisions should be by consensus. Do you think she was right to do so?

Decisions occur — or do not, as the case may be — by a variety of methods.

Here you will see group processes at work in the following ways:

Apathy: Nobody is sufficiently interested or concerned to get the group to operate, that is, deciding not to decide by tacit agreement.

Plops: A decision suggested by an individual to which there is no response. Plopping often occurs in a new group confronted by many problems; in a group where a number of the members have fairly equal status; when a member is overly aggressive; when a member has difficulty in articulating.

Self-authorised: A decision made by an individual who assumes authority to do decisions so. When such a decision is proposed, the group as a whole often finds it easier to accept than reject, even though some individuals may not be in agreement. The decision is thus by default.

Pairing: A decision made by two members of the group joining forces. Such 'hand-clasping' sometimes emerges so suddenly that it catches the other members of the group off guard and at the same time presents them with another problem (how to deal with the two people at once).

Topic-jumping: A decision to cut short by the inappropriate intrusion of another topic. Topic-jumping confuses the issue confronting the group and thus changes the nature of the decision.

Minority group: A decision agreed upon in advance by several members of the group. Cliques are present in almost every group, and their prearranged decision may be very good. But the effect of collusion can be to destroy group cohesiveness and a sense of trust.

Majority group: A decision made by some form of voting. The traditional procedure of taking a vote often seems to be the only way in which to reach a decision under the given circumstances. Nonetheless the minority may remain against the decision despite the vote and therefore, not likely to act on it.

Does anyone disagree: A decision made by pressure not to disagree. When confronted by such a question, several persons who really disagree strongly or who have not had opportunity to express their opinion on the issue, might show real reluctance to voice opposition with no apparent support.

Note that Figure. 1.2 on decision making in groups includes *true consensus* and *false consensus.* In the latter, everyone *appears* to agree but when the decision is acted upon each member seems to have different ideas about the decision or to have reserved the right not to implement it. Some members may have only pretended to agree in the first place, hoping the matter would be forgotten or that the decision could subsequently be fudged.

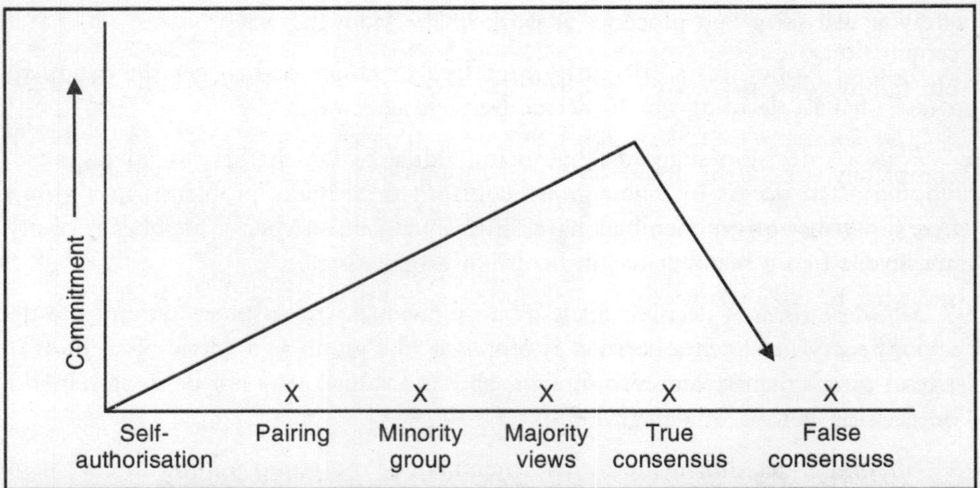

FIGURE 1.2 **Ways of Reaching a Decision**

True consensus is not always possible even if it is normally desirable, because it can be very time consuming. It occurs when communication has been sufficiently open for all to feel they have had a fair chance to influence decision and the 'feeling of the meeting' emerges without voting. The following definition is worth bearing in mind:

When alternatives have been debated thoroughly by the group and everyone is prepared to accept that in the circumstances one particular solution is the best way forward, even though it might not be *every* person's preferred solution.

The most important test is that everyone is prepared to *act* as though it was their preferred solution.

Responses to Authority

Not all the processes at work below the surface — or on it — in group life are concerned with making decisions or constitute procedures for tackling common goals. Under the umbrella of group processes, we can look at two recurring patterns in group life: the different responses to the leader's authority and the tendency of groups to withdraw or 'take flight' when faced with difficulty.

The T-group began with the trainer asking the group to 'become a group' and then sitting back, apparently leaving them to their own devices.

This overt behaviour, apparently a complete abdication from the leadership role, sparked off several reactions in groups, which in time became fairly predictable. Although conditioned and sharpened by the T-group environment, they are latent in all of us and you will have experienced some of them in daily life at work in certain situations. The first pair, for example, would be recognised by most of us in our family roles as children and parents:

Dependency: Members look to others to tell them what to do. They are completely dependent upon the 'authority figure' and are lost without him.

Counterdependency: Members resist authority, especially from the leader. They are hostile to any attempt to curtail their freedom. 'What right have you got to tell me what to do?'

The *dependency* and *counter dependency* phases we go through as children in regard to our parents and teachers can get fixed. There are adults who carry around with them these latent attitudes towards those in authority.

The dependent person clearly needs to be nurtured coaxed, counselled and coached into taking a less dependent stance in regard to authority. It is not easy, because the pattern of dependency can be stamped on a person's nature by parents and teachers.

In dealing with counterdependence, it is important to realise first that these hostile, frustrated feelings are not being directed at you personally. They are often the by-product left in the human soul of overdominant parents or autocratic teachers. In weaning someone from counterdependency you should not parade your authority; your legitimate authority should stem from your knowledge and personality.

In emerging from these two states (and counterdependency can be the flipside of dependency) we have to go through the stage of *independence.* The independent person is neither dependent nor counterdependent to a leader. The adjective carries good overtones of autonomy and freedom.

Independence can also mean: 'I am going to have nothing to do with you'. In this case the person severs himself from the offending source of authority, if need be by force or flight. This may be necessary if that authority has tried to keep you in leading-strings or is authoritarian in its behaviour. Otherwise independence is a natural phase of growing up.

Yet it is not the end of the story. For independence in the second sense contravenes the elementary principle of reciprocity: that we are made for, and made in, a fundamental process of giving and receiving. The natural end of our striving, then, is the state of *interdependence,* the social commerce of free and equal individuals who accept that their skills, natures and needs are complementary.

Fight and Flight

When faced with a difficulty, especially one that is threatening, humans can either stand their ground and fight or they can take flight. This behaviour can be categorised as follows:

Fighting and dominating: Disagreeing; asserting personal dominance; attacking whatever is believed to be responsible for the cause of stress. It is common, for example, to blame others – individuals, groups, institutions, ideas.

Flight and withdrawal: Staying out of discussion; daydreaming; sulking; running away physically or psychologically.

Pairing: In pairing, individuals seek reassurance from other individuals about their feelings of anxiety or discomfort.

But sometimes, the whole group may take a fighting stance. Doubtless, you can think of groups who have become belligerent. What is not so obvious, however, is when a group is *taking flight* in a psychological way from a dangerous area.

You may notice symptoms include a higher degree of rather artificial playacting or 'larking about'. Nervous humour and jokes are often symptoms of tension, for laughter is a safety valve. This is why groups often laugh at jokes or remarks that are not really funny.

An intriguing method of group flight occurs when the discussion shifts from the particular to the *general* and stays there. It can be a form of flight, for example, to discuss the problem of leadership today' rather than tackle the central issue in the group, which is: 'You, Jack, are not giving us any Leadership'.

It is of course not always true that groups who are talking in general or theoretical terms are evading some problem within their own life. Sometimes, their very reason for being there is explore such areas in an intellectual fashion. But you should able to judge when it is flight into the general or abstract. As a form of veering away mentally from a problem or difficulty they should be tackling, it can afflict all groups in all places.

Defence Mechanism

The flight into abstract or general discourse is an example of a largely unconscious group response (although a cunning member may manipulate the discussion in that direction if he wants no decision to be taken). But individuals also develop conscious responses to anxiety making situations. Some of them get 'institutionalised' in their psychological make-up. These can sometimes help to explain why a person may be acting or reacting in a certain way.

One important recourse of the group is the so-called defence mechanism. The identification of them was one of the more useful outcomes of Sigmund Freud's work. Defence mechanisms, he believed, are employed by individuals to reduce or overcome anxiety. They provide some insights into human behaviour in groups.

BOX 1.3 Some Depth Mind Strategies

Displacement	For example, where a subordinate is annoyed at his boss and punishes his own subordinates or some other person.
Repression	A process by which unacceptable desires or impulses are excluded from consciousness and left to operate in the unconscious, for example, where an individual blocks out or represses an unpleasant experience.
Regression	Reversion to an earlier mental or behavioural level, for example, when an adult behaves in a childish fashion.
Over-reaction	For example, becoming excessively bureaucratic or rule-abiding.
Projection	The act of externalising or objectifying what is primarily subjective; for example, projecting one's own thoughts or desires onto others.
Fixation	An obsessive or unhealthy preoccupation or attachment; for example, a persistent concentration on a supposed threat or enemy.
Sublimation	Directing the energy of (an impulse) from its primitive aim to one that is ethically or culturally higher; for example, a naturally aggressive person who becomes an attacking hockey centre forward.

It is unwise to play the role of amateur psychologist if you are a leader or manager, for a little learning is a dangerous thing. But Freud's categories can sometimes throw light on the thought processes or behaviour of individuals in relationships. It may be, too, that groups that have been together for a time will also develop their own defence mechanisms. It also may displace, repress, overreact, project and form fixations. In other words, these can be group as well as individual phenomena. As always, the price of freedom is eternal vigilance.

CHAPTER

2

BUILDING TEAMS

LEARNING OBJECTIVES

- To familiarise with the interrelation between Groups, Teams and Team Development Process.
- To understand the key to Team Leadership and Essence of Teams.

GROUPS ARE FUNDAMENTAL UNITS OF ORGANISATION

From the beginning of time, people have formed groups. Groups provide the basis for family living, protection, waging war, government, recreation and work. Group behaviour has ranged from total chaos to dramatic success, but it is increasingly evident that groups enjoy their greatest success when they become more productive units called teams.

Managers in many organisations seem content with group performance. This is often because they have not thought beyond what is being accomplished to what might be achieved under slightly different circumstances. Other leaders using the same number of people, doing similar tasks with the same technology, somehow manage to improve productivity dramatically by establishing a climate where people are willing to give their best and work together in teams.

A comparison of teams and groups is shown on the next page. Check (√) the characteristics representative of the unit of which you are currently a part.

TABLE 2.1 Groups versus Teams

Groups	Teams
❑ Members think they are grouped together for administrative purposes only. Individuals work independently; sometimes at cross purposes with others.	❑ Members recognise their inter dependence and understand both personal and team goals are best accomplished with mutual support. Time is not wasted struggling over "turf" or attempting personal gain at the expense of others.
❑ Members tend to focus on themselves because they are not sufficiently involved in planning the unit's objectives. They approach their job simply as a hired hand.	❑ Members feel a sense of ownership for their jobs and unit because they are commited to goals they helped establish.
❑ Members are told what to do rather than being asked what the best approach would be. Suggestions are not encouraged.	❑ Members contribute to the organisation's success by applying their unique talent and knowledge to team objectives.
❑ Members distrust the motives of colleagues because they do not understand the role of other members, expressions of opinion or disagreement are considered divisive or non-supportive.	❑ Members work in a climate of trust and are encouraged to openly express ideas, opinions, disagreements and feelings. Questions are welcomed.
❑ Members are so cautious about what they say that real understanding is not possible. Game playing may occur and communications traps set to catch the unwary.	❑ Members practice open and honest communication. They make an effort to understand each other's point of view.
❑ Members may receive good training but are limited in applying it to the job by the supervisor or other group members.	❑ Members are encouraged to develop skills and apply what they learn on the job. They receive the support of the team.
❑ Members may find themselves in conflict situations which they do not know how to resolve. Their supervisor may put off intervention until serious damage is done.	❑ Members recognise conflict is a normal aspect of human interaction but they view certain situation as an opportunity for new ideas and creativity. They work to resolve conflict quickly and constructively.
❑ Members may or may not participate in decisions affecting the team. Confirmity often appears more important than positive results.	❑ Members participate in decisions affecting the team but understand their leader must make a final ruling whenever the team cannot decide, or an emergency exists. Positive results, not conformity, are the goal.

Team leaders exhibit different styles than those who are content managing a group. These styles are shaped by each person's life experience and the values they have adopted over the years.

Give today's rapid rate of organisational change, and the changing needs of people, it is important for those "in charge" to re-evaluate and modify their styles on a regular basis. This is the only way they can make the adaptations necessary to continue to be effective.

See below how team-centered leadership differs from group centered management — then make a commitment to creating and supporting a team effort.

Plan to make any needed changes in your style and evaluate the results carefully. Keep making adjustments until you achieve the results desired. Stay on the alert for the additional ways to improve your leadership.

TABLE 2.2 **Differences between Team Centered Managers and Group Centered Managers**

Identify the qualities which best describe you at this time with a tick (√).

Group Centered	Team Centered
❑ Overriding concern to meet current goals inhibits thought about what might be accomplished through reorganizing to enhance member contributions.	❑ Current goals are taken in stride. Can be a visionary about what the people can achieve as a team. Can share vision and act accordingly.
❑ Reactive to upper management, peers and employees. Find it easier to go along with the crowd.	❑ Proactive in most relationships. Exhibits personal style. Can stimulate excitement and action. Inspires teamwork and mutual support.
❑ Willing to involve people in planning and problem solving to some extent, but within limits.	❑ Can get people involved and commited. Makes it easy for teamwork. Allows people to perform.
❑ Resents or distrusts employees who know their jobs better than the managers.	❑ Looks for people who want to excel and can work constructively with others. Feels role is to encourage and facilitate this behaviour.
❑ Sees group problem-solving as a waste of time, or an abdication of managerial responsibility.	❑ Considers problem-solving the responsibility of team members.
❑ Controls information and communicates only what group members need or want to know.	❑ Communicates fully and openly. Welcomes questions. Allows the teams to do its own filtering.
❑ Ignores conflict between staff members or with other groups.	❑ Mediates conflicts before it becomes destructive.
❑ Sometimes slow to recognise individual or group achievements.	❑ Makes an effort to see that both individual and team accomplishments are recognised at the right time in and appropriate manner.
❑ Sometimes modifies group agreements to suit personal convenience.	❑ Keeps commitments and expect the same in return.

TEAM DEVELOPMENT

An Effective Team:

- Has a clear understanding of its goals: overall and immediate.
- Is flexible in selecting its procedure as it works toward its goals.
- Has achieved a high degree of communication and understanding among its members. Communication of personal feelings and attitudes as well as ideas occurs in direct and open fashion because it is considered important to the work of the team.
- Is able to initiate and carry out an effective decision-making, carefully considering minority viewpoints and securing the commitment of all members to important decisions.
- Achieves an appropriate balance between team productivity and the satisfaction of individual needs.
- Provides for sharing of leadership responsibilities.
- Has a high degree of cohesiveness (attractiveness to its members).
- Makes intelligent use of the differing abilities if its members.
- Can be objective about reviewing its own processes. Can face problems and adjust to needed modification.
- Maintains a balance between emotional and rational behaviour, channeling emotionally into productive team effort.

Achieving a Cooperative Team Structure

- Members must interact, give and receive help from one another, and share ideas, information, and resources to help accomplish the team's goals.
- The team goal of getting the task done at the highest level possible must be accepted by everyone, and members need to develop commitment to the Team goal.
- Because the possibility exists of different team members doing different sub-tasks, teams may divide the labour in various ways to accomplish their goals.
- Rewards, if any, must be based upon the quality and quantity of team performance, not individual performance.

Basic Stages of Team Development

There are several basic stages that new teams go through as they move to becoming effective as a team. These stages parallel the Situational Leadership Model different styles of leadership tend to work best at different points in the overall development of the team.

❖ Stage 1 – FORMING

Forming (Getting Acquainted): This first stage is characterized by a sense of uncertainty and awkwardness and perhaps anxiety. Participants may be unsure of what to do and how to do it. The "rules of the road"—team norms and standards have yet to be defined and participants are eagerly looking to find out what is okay and not okay. This phase often shows as tentativeness or even some anxiety on the part of the participants. Leaders need to *set the tone* for team behaviour, activities, and interactions (see Establishing Team Norms below). Most people are polite as they try to put their "best foot forward." The result is a superficial level of harmony and cooperation. This serves the purpose of getting the team started and off the ground in terms of motivation and commitment. Members may tend to verbalize how close they feel to each other, and may develop quite a team spirit due to successful task accomplishment. Leadership at this point should be a combination of High Task/Low Relationship (Telling) in terms of teaching skills and establishing norms moving to High Task/High Relationship (Selling) to get everyone involved and interacting in the team.

- Feeling moderately eager with high expectations.
- Initial period requires lot of adjustments, it is a painful process of misunderstanding.
- Feeling of anxiety: where do I fit? What is expected of me.
- Testing the situations and central figures.
- Depending on authority and hierarchy.
- Needing to find a place and establish oneself.

Development Action

- Get to know and assess one another.
- Examine the function and purpose of the team.
- Look at the skills, knowledge, cohesiveness and balance already present.
- Identify the blocks, frustration and culture.

Possible Pitfalls

- Mistake of jumping to conclusions too quickly and imposing "instant" changes.
- Rigidity in making adjustments.
- Negative responses not tackled.

❖ Stage 2 – STORMING

Storming (Struggling Forward): This next stage is characterized by individual assertive behaviour, which may result in some team instability. Participants have begun to feel comfortable enough with their new environment to take some risks in revealing more of their personalities. Each person wants to feel a sense of individual importance and influence on the team — "finding a niche." This becomes more evident as increasing responsibility is shifted to the team as they move into moderate levels of maturity. The leadership style which may be most effective are High Task/High Relationship (Selling). Leaders should not be surprised if some conflicts develop in the team at this stage. This is part of the natural process of the team becoming self-sustaining.

- Feelings begin to come out into the open.
- Feeling frustrated, anger around goals, tasks and action plans.
- Feeling incompetent and confused.
- Reacting negatively toward leaders and other members.
- Competing for power and/or attention.
- Experiencing a discrepancy between hopes and reality.
- Team copes poorly when real pressure emerges.

Development Action

- Debate risky issues.
- Consider wider options.
- Encourage openness and feedback.
- Handle conflict positively.

Possible Pitfalls

- It takes time to build trust.
- This stage cannot be rushed.
- Some teams are unable to move out of this stage without external help.

❖ Stage 3 – NORMING

Norming (Becoming Personal): This stage is characterized by a growth of affection and establishment of personal relationships. Participants will begin to take responsibility for resolving conflicts and strengthening friendships. The leadership style, which may be most effective, is Low Task/High Relationship (Participating) since the team is competent regarding tasks but needs assistance and support in terms of relationships.

- Ground rules are established.
- Working procedures are agreed.
- Decreasing dissatisfaction.
- Resolving discrepancies between expectations and reality.
- Developing harmony, trust, support and respect.
- Developing self-esteem and confidence.
- Being more open and giving more feedback.
- Sharing responsibility and control.
- Using team language.
- High level of concern for a methodical approach to the task.

Development Action

- Maintain openness.
- Regular team reviews.
- Encourage challenges to established way of doing things.
- Celebrate success.
- Focus on individual as well as team development.

Possible Pitfalls

- Established methods become an end in themselves.
- Creativity is stifled.
- Team forgets to look outwards.

❖ Stage 4 – PERFORMING

Performing (Working Together): This stage is characterized by harmony among Team members. Participants look outwards to see how other people in the Team are doing to make sure all are supported. Decision-making and problem solving will be shared within the Team. At this stage, the Team is mature enough to attend to its own needs both in terms of task and relationship matters. The leadership style, which would be most effective, would be Low Task/Low Relationship (Delegating).

- Shared values

- High flexibility
- Commitment to team goals
- Feeling excited about participating in team activities
- Feeling posting about task successes
- Problem solving approach
- Conflicting views are handled positively and constructively. Issues are resolved by consensus, not majority rule.
- Feeling team strength
- Sharing leadership
- Performance at high levels
- High level of maturity, emotional, problems are effectively handled without threatening its stability.

❖ Stage 5 – TRANSFERENCE

Transference: This is essential in making sure that the trip is not remembered as "just a fun couple days in the woods." It is important that participants be able to transfer the things which they have learnt about themselves and being in a team back to their regular lives. This is accomplished through the debriefing process in transferring the experience.

❖ Stage 6 – NURTURING

Nurturing: Just like development of any plant, the team has also a process. As plants need continuous nourishment and nurturing to bear fruits, teams also need continuous motivation and rewards as well as right environment to bear fruits, i.e. achieve results. The plants will die out, if not provided nourishment in the form of manures and water as well as in absence of oxygen. Similarly, the teams will become inefficient if it lacks right rewards like manures and water, and right environment like oxygen for the plants. We have detailed description of rewards, motivation and work climate/environment is given in subsequent chapters

Establishing Team Norms

Establishing norms is an important part of the first stage of team development, letting people learn "the rules of the road." Many of the team norms that we use in OA are actually underlying goals for the experience (like Team cooperation, minimal impact, etc.).

Team norms can be established in three ways:

- *Stating:* Telling/explaining to people how to behave, e.g., this is how to wear a pack.
- *Modelling:* Demonstrating behaviour for others to adopt, e.g., leaders picking up trash along the trail.
- *Importing:* Bringing in behaviour customary in other social situations, e.g., people will going off into the woods for privacy to go to the bathroom.

These methods often must be combined in order to work effectively. For example, if you want to reinforce minimal impact camping practices you will need to state it as a goal, explain how to accomplish it, and model the behaviour. If the leader simply tells people to pick up trash along the trail, but then walks right by trash without picking it up, the participants become confused as to the norm and may assume that the instruction was merely lip service. Remember, at the beginning of a trip, participants may not know what to expect and may not have previous experience in the outdoors. Direct demonstration is the best way to get things across in this early stage. Before the trip goes out, think about what sort of team norms you want to convey to the team before leaving campus as well as what things you will need to cover during the trip. Below are some examples of things to present to the team.

❖ Norms to Present Pre-trip

- Team cooperation (everyone needs to do their share)
- Minimal impact camping (idea, not specific techniques)
- Safety
- Substance-free trip

❖ Norms to Present During the Trip

- Challenge by choice
- Good communication and listening between team members
- Debriefing
- Respect for others

Team Decision-making

During the course of a trip, there are a number of decisions that will need to be made by the whole team. These might include things like where to camp, which route to take, whether to rest for the afternoon or do a side hikes, etc. Team decision-making can be a powerful learning and growth tool for the team. It can also be a place for conflict to develop. The first thing to determine is whether it is a decision that can and should be made by the team, or with input from the team, or is it a decision to be made solely by the leaders. The leaders will make obviously some issue, such as those that involve safety. To present such a decision to the team suggests that they have authority to make the decision, and if the leaders disagree, they must countermand the Team's decision. Also, some decision-making can lead to splintering the team. Both of these can lead to bad feelings among the team members and damage the positive team spirit and interaction leaders have worked to facilitate. Avoid this problem by thinking ahead and determining what decisions are appropriate for the team to make. It may be better for the leaders to make the decision from their status as authorities, that to give the decision to the team and have the process lead to negative outcomes. Leaders will also need to decide if they should be involved in the decision process, or "sit it out." Sometime the presence and perceived authority of the leaders can slant the decision making process. However, in certain situations, this can work to your advantage as a leader. Making good team decisions involves a process, which the leaders may have to state or model as a norm for the team to follow.

❖ Decision Strategies

Authority Decides: In this case, the decision is made by the leaders by virtue of their role of being responsible for the trip or by some person determined to have the greatest knowledge about the topic. This process can be very effective when the individual(s) have significantly more knowledge than the other members of the team. It is also very efficient in terms of time. In some cases, getting feedback from the team may be essential for the leaders to have all the facts in order to make a good decision. For example, if the leaders have to decide about changing the route, they need to know the physical and mental state of all the participants. The most common scenario for this decision making process is a safety or emergency situation. Here, the leaders need to take charge of the team. Keep in mind that some individuals, even though they may be the most knowledgeable, may not be good at making decisions. Making effective decisions is a skill that all leaders should develop. If things seem to be breaking down and a decision is not being made, you may have to move to another method.

Majority Vote: In this case, members of the team are polled and the option that receives support from the greatest number in the team is chosen. This strategy works well if everyone agrees to be bound by it, and if everyone feels they have a chance to express their viewpoints and needs. However, it can lead to splitting of the team. Once again leaders should evaluate if this method will be a positive or negative experience for the team.

Consensus: This is the most effective method of making a team decision in terms of members feeling included. Consensual decision-making means reaching a decision that all members of the team are willing to support at some level. In order to reach this point, everyone in the team must be given ample time to express their view and time to express their disagreement with other's views. Through a process of negotiation, the team moves to an idea that everyone can place some level of support in. This process can take a great deal of time and "perfect consensus" is almost never reached. Make sure that you have the time before embarked on this as you approach. It is counterproductive to start with the consensus process and then have to give it up to make the decision some other way because you don't have enough time.

In all of these strategies it is important for leaders to model good listening and communication skills. Leaders may need to act as facilitators for effective communication through such things as asking people not to interrupt others, quieting dominant members of the team, and asking quieter members to speak up.

❖ Team Decision Making Process

- Set goal(s) and prioritize them
- Brainstorm options for achieving goals
- Evaluate the different options and examine how the options meet the goal(s)
- Determine the decision-making strategy to be used (see above)

Decide on an option using one of the following criteria:

- Best serves highest priority goals
- Best serves all goals
- Serves goals without creating any negative outcomes
- Creates the least negative outcomes

What is Team Building Process?

Team building process is transforming a group into team by setting goals, clarifying roles and responsibilities, allocating resources, imparting skills, monitoring progress, reviewing and rewarding for achievements.

The entire process of team building can be shown through the following team building process flowchart:

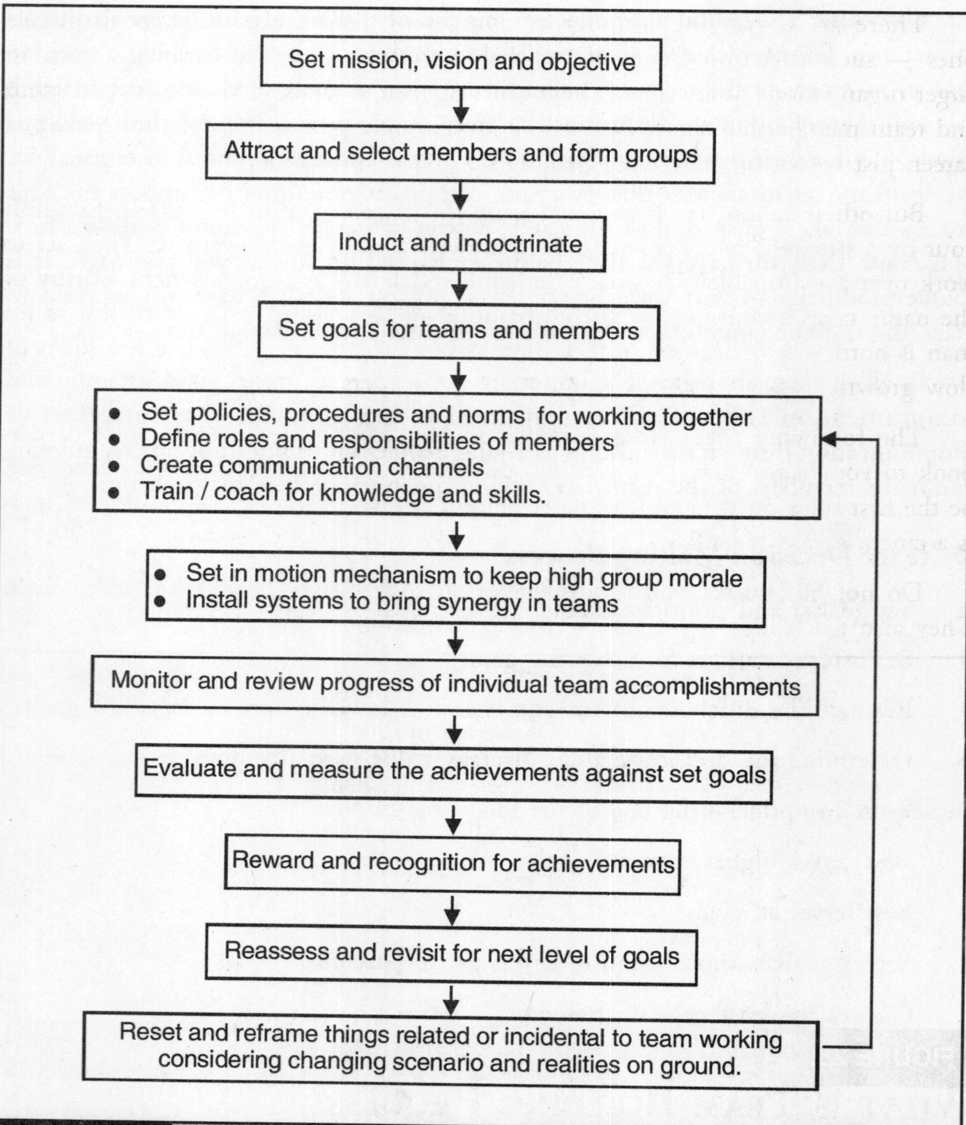

FIGURE 2.1 **Team Building Process Flow Chart**

A Checklist for Team Leaders

We have emphasised the role of the leader in team building. In this chapter, we want to instil the desire, to become more effective in that role. For the more skilled you become as a leader, the more rewarding you will find it to be. Enjoyment increases and the burden lightens.

There are a growing number of courses on leadership skills, both public ones — such as Action Centered Leadership (ACL) — and 'in-company' ones, in larger organisations at any rate. These can help you to develop your own leadership and team membership skills, especially if you attend them at the right time in your career, just before or shortly after taking up a leadership role.

But others cannot teach you leadership — you must learn it yourself. Establish your own strengths and weaknesses as a leader with ruthless objectivity. Then set to work over a reasonable time span. Remember that any self-development worthy of the name takes a considerable stretch of time, so start young if you can. Just as no man is born wise or learned so too, none is born a leader. Confidence is a plant of slow growth.

The following checklist is designed to help you apply the principles of this book to your team now. Doing things differently, making improvements there can be the first steps on your much longer road of self-development as a leader. An inch is a cinch, a yard is hard.

Do not be afraid of making mistakes on that journey. Failures teach success. They also teach humility.

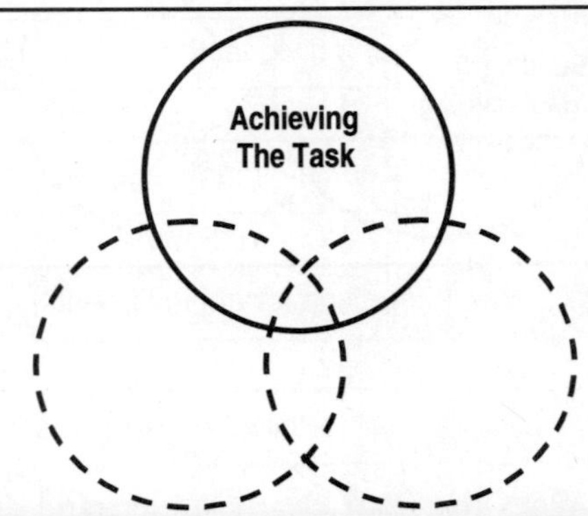

FIGURE 2.2 Step–1

❖ Task

Purpose:	Am I clear what the task is?
Responsibilities:	Am I clear what mine are?
Objectives:	Have I agreed these with my superior, the person accountable for the group?
Programme:	Have I worked one out to reach objectives?
Working conditions:	Are these right for the job?

Resources:	Are these adequate (authority, money, materials)?
Targets:	Has each member clearly defined and agreed them?
Authority:	Is the line of authority clear (accountability chart)?
Training:	Are there any gaps in the specialists skills or abilities of individuals in the group required for the task?
Priorities:	Have I planned the time?
Progress:	Do I check this regularly and evaluate?
Supervision:	In case of my absence who covers for me?
Example:	Do I set standards by my behaviour?

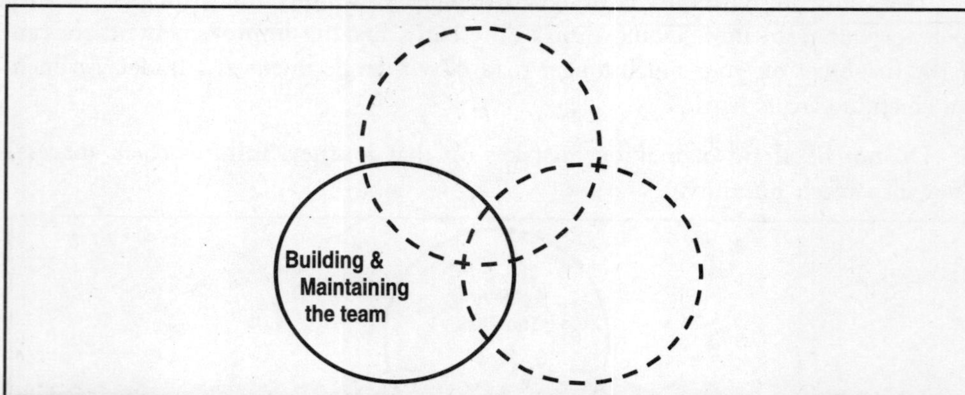

FIGURE 2.3 Step–2

❖ Team Members

Objectives:	Does the term clearly understand and accept them?
Standards:	Do they know what standards of performance are expected?
Safety Standards:	Do they know consequences of infringement?
Size of team:	Is the size correct?
Team members:	Are the right people working together? Is there a need for subgroups to be constituted?
Team spirit:	Do I look for opportunities for building teamwork into jobs? Do methods of pay and bonus help to develop team spirit?
Discipline:	Are the rules seen to be reasonable? Am I fair and impartial in enforcing them?

Grievances: Are grievances dealt with promptly? Do I take action on matters likely to disrupt the group?

Consultation: Is this genuine? Do I encourage and welcome ideas and suggestions?

Briefing: Is this regular? Does it covers current plans, progress and future developments?

Represent: Am I prepared to represent the feelings of the group when required?

Support: Do I visit people at their work when the team is apart? Do I then represent to the individual the whole team in my manner and encouragement?

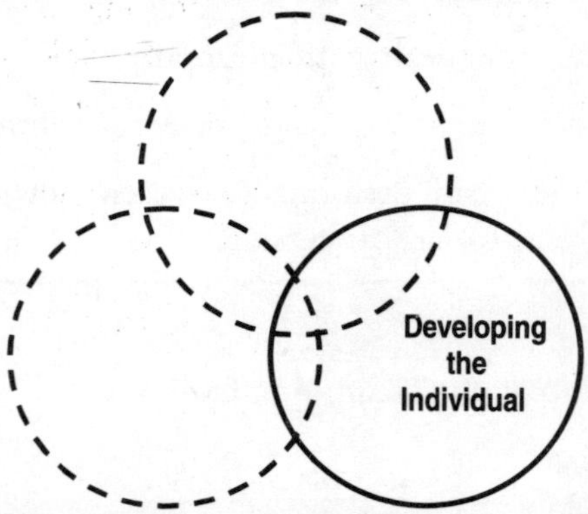

FIGURE 2.4 Step–3

❖ Individual

Targets: Have they been agreed and quantified?

Induction: Does s/he really know the other team members and the organisation?

Achievement: Does s/he know how his/her work contributes to the overall result?

Responsibilities: Has s/he got a clear and accurate job description? Can I delegate more to him/her?

Authority: Does s/he have sufficient authority for his/her task?

Training: Has adequate provision been made for training or retraining both technical and as team member?

Recognition:	Do I emphasise people's successes? In failure, is criticism constructive?
Growth:	Does s/he see the chance of development? Does s/he see some pattern of career?
Performance:	Is this regularly reviewed?
Reward:	Are work, capacity and pay in balance?
The task:	Is s/he in the right job? Has s/he the necessary resources?
The person:	Do I know this person well? What makes him/her different from others?
Time/attention:	Do I spend enough with individuals listening, developing, counselling?
Grievances:	Are these dealt with promptly?
Security:	Does s/he know about pensions, redundancy and so on?
Appraisal:	Is the overall performance of each individual regularly reviewed in face-to-face discussion?

CHECKLIST

Have you selected the Right Team Member?

TASK	**YES**	**NO**
Has s/he an alert intelligence?	☐	☐
Where applicable, has s/he a high level of vocational skills?	☐	☐
Do his or her knowledge/skills complement those of other team members rather than duplicate them?	☐	☐
Is s/he motivated to seek excellence in results and methods of working together?	☐	☐
Does his or her track record really bear out the scores given above?	☐	☐
TEAM		
Will s/he work closely with others in decision making and problem solving without 'rubbing people up the wrong way'?	☐	☐
Does s/he listen?	☐	☐
Is s/he flexible enough to adopt different roles within the group?	☐	☐

Contd...

Can s/he influence others- assertive rather than aggressive?	☐	☐
Will s/he contribute to group morale rather than draw cheques upon it?	☐	☐
INDIVIDUAL		
Has s/he a sense of humour and a degree of tolerance for others?	☐	☐
Has s/he a certain amount of will to achieve ambition, tinged with understanding that s/he cannot do it all alone?	☐	☐
Will s/he develop a feeling of responsibility for the success of the team as a whole, not simply his or her own part in it?	☐	☐
Has s/he integrity?	☐	☐
Does s/he have a realistic perception of his/her strengths and weaknesses?	☐	☐

The Keys to Leadership

To be a leader means to have determination', wrote Lech Walesa. 'It means to be resolute inside and outside, with ourselves and with others'.

The first responsibility of leadership is to define the objective. Achieving the aim is the ultimate test of leadership. Until you know clearly what it is you want to achieve you can't begin to direct other people towards it. When the objective or task is not easy to define the effective leader takes the time to think it out. Without a clear goal there is no such thing as concerned team work. Besides, who will follow a leader who does not know where he is going? 'If a blind man leads a blind man they will both fall into a ditch.'

Once the group's task is settled and the team have accepted, it is the individual's turn. He also needs a clear personal objective/or target. Naturally it must contribute to the overall aim, but the individual must see that it suits his strengths and skills, if possible it should be worked out with the individual concerned, so that he feels it his personal goal. Good targets should be:

- measurable
- time-bound
- realistic
- challenging
- agreed

Make sure each individual knows and feels that his part of the task is making a significant contribution to the group's overall task.

These elements – task, team and individual constitute the core responsibility of the leader. They spring from the three overlapping areas of work group life depicted there as three circles, as in Figure. 2.5 below.

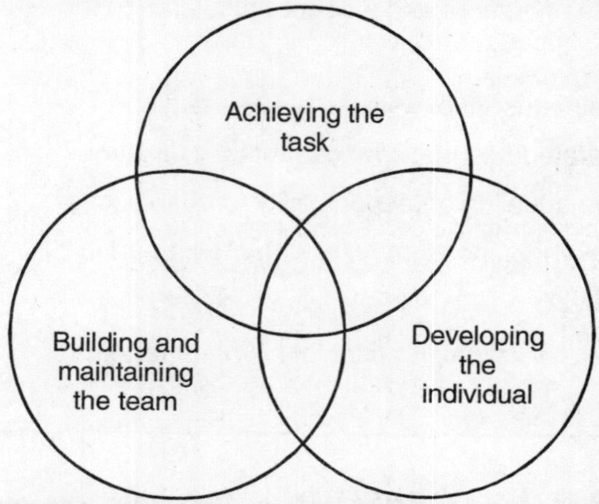

FIGURE 2.5 The Leader's Core Responsibility

To fulfil the three circles of responsibility certain, key functions have to be performed. They are the responsibility of the leader, but that does not mean the leader will do them all himself. They can be shared or delegated in all sorts of ways.

The following Box is by no means definitive – the sheer variety of situations prohibit that — but these general functions are commonly required:

BOX 2.1 Task of Leadership

Planning: Seeking all available information; defining group task, purpose or goal; making a workable plan (in right decision-making framework).

Initiating: Briefing group on aims and plan; explaining *why* aim or plan is necessary; allocating tasks to group members; setting group standards.

Controlling: Maintaining group standards; influencing tempo; ensuring all actions are taken towards objectives; keeping discussion relevant; prodding group to action/decision.

Supporting: Expressing acceptance of persons and their contributions; encouraging group/ individuals; disciplining group/individuals;

Contd...

	creating team spirit; relieving tension with humour; reconciling disagreements or getting others to explore them.
Informing:	Clarifying task and plan; giving new information to the group, that is, keeping them 'in the picture'; receiving information from the group; summarising suggestions and ideas clearly.
Evaluating:	Checking feasibility of an idea; testing the consequences of a proposed solution; evaluating group performance; helping the group to evaluate its own performance against standards.

It must be stressed again that not all these functions will be performed by every leader all the time. In groups of more than three or four there are too many actions required to meet the requirements of task, team and individual for anyone person to do them. But the leader is *accountable* for the three circles. Taken together these functions constitute his role. Although team members may characteristically perform one or other of them — or contribute to several — the leader makes sure that they do so. He may have to do each of them himself as occasion requires. His range of functions will always be wider than any other single member.

Remember that you can be appointed a manager, but you are not a leader until your appointment is ratified in the hearts and minds of those who work for you.

To deal effectively with people you must take time to understand them as persons. They need to be understood both in terms of what they share in common and what differentiates them. How does this particular person differ from all others? You do not have the *right* to know someone but you have the duty to try to do so. That does not mean being matey or familiar. It just means a willingness to spend time talking and listening. Effective leaders get about and meet people.

Give people your respect and trust, some real responsibilities together with a degree of independence and they will reward you with their best.

The 17 Indisputable Laws of Teamwork

To achieve great things, you need a team. Building a winning team requires understanding of these principles. Whatever your goal or project, you need to add value and invest in your team so the end product benefits from more ideas, energy, resources, and perspectives.

❖ The Law of Significance

People try to achieve great things by themselves mainly because of the size of their ego, their level of insecurity, or simple naiveté and temperament. One is too small a number to achieve greatness.

❖ The Law of the Big Picture

The goal is more important than the role. Members must be willing to subordinate their roles and personal agendas to support the team vision. By seeing the big picture, effectively communicating the vision to the team, providing the needed resources, and hiring the right players, leaders can create a more unified team.

❖ The Law of the Niche

All players have a place where they add the most value. Essentially, when the right team member is in the right place, everyone benefits. To be able to put people in their proper places and fully utilize their talents and maximize potential, you need to know your players and the team situation. Evaluate each person's skills, discipline, strengths, emotions, and potential.

❖ The Law of Mount Everest

As the challenge escalates, the need for teamwork elevates. Focus on the team and the dream should take care of itself. The type of challenge determines the type of team you require. A new challenge requires a creative team. An ever-changing challenge requires a fast, flexible team. An Everest-sized challenge requires an experienced team. See who needs direction, support, coaching, or more responsibility. Add members, change leaders to suit the challenge of the moment, and remove ineffective members.

❖ The Law of the Chain

The strength of the team is impacted by its weakest link. When a weak link remains on the team the stronger members identify the weak one, end up having to help him, come to resent him, become less effective, and ultimately question their leader's ability.

❖ The Law of the Catalyst

Winning teams have players who make things happen. These are the catalysts, or the get-it-done-and-then-some people who are naturally intuitive, communicative, passionate, talented, creative people who take the initiative, are responsible, generous, and influential.

❖ The Law of the Compass

A team that embraces a vision becomes focused, energized, and confident. It knows where it's headed and why it's going there. A team should examine its Moral, Intuitive, Historical, Directional, Strategic, and Visionary Compasses. Does the business practice with integrity? Do members stay? Does the team make positive use of anything contributed by previous teams in the organization? Does the strategy serve the vision? Is there a long-range vision to keep the team from being frustrated by short-range failures?

❖ The Law of the Bad Apple

Rotten attitudes ruin a team. The first place to start is with yourself. Do you think the team wouldn't be able to get along without you? Do you secretly believe that recent team successes are attributable to your personal efforts, not the work of the whole team? Do you keep score when it comes to the praise and perks handed out to other team members? Do you have a hard time admitting you made a mistake? If you answered yes to any of these questions, you need to keep your attitude in check.

❖ The Law of Countability

Teammates must be able to count on each other when it counts. Is your integrity unquestionable? Do you perform your work with excellence? Are you dedicated to the team's success? Can people depend on you? Do your actions bring the team together or rip it apart?

❖ The Law of the Price Tag

The team fails to reach its potential when it fails to pay the price. Sacrifice, time commitment, personal development, and unselfishness are part of the price we pay for team success.

❖ The Law of the Scoreboard

The team can make adjustments when it knows where it stands. The scoreboard is essential to evaluating performance at any given time, and is vital to decision-making.

❖ The Law of the Bench

Great teams have great depth. Any team that wants to excel must have good substitutes as well as starters. The key to making the most of the law of the bench is to continually improve the team.

❖ The Law of Identity

Shared values define the team. The type of values you choose for the team will attract the type of members you need. Values give the team a unique identity to its members, potential recruits, clients, and the public. Values must be constantly stated and restated, practiced, and institutionalized.

❖ The Law of Communication

Interaction fuels action. Effective teams have teammates who are constantly talking, and listening to each other. From leader to teammates, teammates to leader, and among teammates, there should be consistency, clarity and courtesy. People should be able to disagree openly, but with respect. Between the team and the public, responsiveness and openness is key.

❖ The Law of the Edge

The difference between two equally talented teams is leadership. A good leader can bring a team to success, provided values, work ethic and vision are in place. The Myth of the Head Table is the belief that on a team, one person is always in charge in every situation. Understand that in particular situations, maybe another person would be best suited for leading the team. The Myth of the Round Table is the belief that everyone is equal, which is not true. The person with greater skill, experience, and productivity in a given area is more important to the team in that area. Compensate where it is due.

❖ The Law of High Morale

When you're winning, nothing hurts. When a team has high morale, it can deal with whatever circumstances are thrown at it.

❖ The Law of Dividends

Investing in the team compounds over time. Make the decision to build a team, and decide who among the team are worth developing. Gather the best team possible, pay the price to develop the team, do things together, delegate responsibility and authority, and give credit for success.

TEAM ROLES

Individual Roles in Teams

❖ "Nobody's perfect but a team can be!"

We've all met people whose characteristics may drive us mad, the person who jumps from idea to idea, the steady plodder, the knocker of ideas, the one who wants action without thinking first, the loyal company worker — they can be very annoying and unproductive when working on their own. However, give them a role in a team and they could help to knock the opposition's socks off.

No one individual can combine all the qualities of a good manager but a team of individuals certainly can — and often does. And it can be in 10 places at once. This is why it is strong teams that are the instrument of sustained and enduring success in management. A team can build up a store of shared and collectively-owned experience, information and judgement that can be passed on as its membership changes.

Belbin's Team Types

Dr. Meredith Belbin, of the Industrial Training Research Unit at Cambridge has developed an understanding of how teams work, and how to make them work better. Belbin's perception is that all members of a management team have a dual role. The first role, the functional one, is obvious: a manager belongs to the team because he is an accountant or production engineer or regional service manager or group marketing executive, or whatever. The second role, the team role, is much less obvious.

Through extensive research at Henley Management College Belbin isolated and identified eight key roles as the ones available to team members. Over the years of his research, first at Henley and subsequently within the real business world extending from Britain to Australia, Dr. Belbin and his colleagues learned to recognise individuals who made a crucial difference to teams and to whose team types he gave descriptive names.

The reason for these names is not always obvious, and the names themselves are sometimes a little misleading. When using them it is the descriptions, not their labels, which are important.

Here are the eight Belbin team types:

❖ Creators

- Plant
- Resource Investigator

Plant

Think of the plant as the one who scatters the seeds, which the others nourish until they bear fruit. The plant was named when it was found that one of the best ways to improve the performance of an ineffective and uninspired team was to 'plant' one of this role in it.

The plant is the team's source of original ideas, suggestions and proposals: the ideas person. The plant tends to be the most imaginative as well as the most intelligent member of the team, and the most likely to start searching for a completely new approach to a problem if the team starts getting bogged down, or to bring a new insight to a line of action already agreed.

- *Positive qualities:* genius, imagination, intellect, knowledge
- *Negative qualities:* up in the clouds, inclined to disregard practical details or protocol.

Resource Investigator

The Resource Investigator (RI) is probably the most immediately likeable member of the team – Relaxed, sociable and gregarious, and easy to interest and enthuse. RI's responses tend to be positive and enthusiastic, though they can dismiss things as quickly as they take them up. The most popular; the salesperson; the diplomat; the 'Fix-It'; extroverted; enthusiastic; curious. The RI's ability to stimulate ideas and encourage innovation can lead people to mistake them for an ideas person, but the RI does not have the radical originality that distinguishes the Plant. They are, however, quick to see the relevance of new ideas.

- *Positive qualities:* a capacity for contacting people and exploring anything new; an ability to respond to challenge
- *Negative qualities:* liable to lose interest once the fascination has passed.

❖ Leaders

- Coordinator
- Shaper

Coordinator

is one of those slightly misleading titles — they are best suited to lead the team even though that may not be their 'formal' role. The Coordinator is the one who presides over the team and coordinates its efforts to meet external goals and targets. They are the social leader; calm; self-confident and controlled.

- *Positive qualities:* a capacity for treating and welcoming all potential contributors on their merits and without prejudice; a strong sense of objectives
- *Negative qualities:* no more than ordinary in terms of intellect or creative ability

Shaper

The Shaper is full of nervous energy: outgoing and emotional, impulsive and impatient, sometimes edgy and easily frustrated. Quick to challenge, and quick to respond to a challenge the Shaper is the task leader of the team. The principal function of the Shaper is to give a shape to the application of the team's efforts, always looking for a pattern in discussions, and trying to unite ideas, objectives and practical considerations into a single feasible project, which the Shaper seeks to push forward urgently to decision and action.

- *Positive qualities:* drive and a readiness to challenge inertia, ineffectiveness, complacency or self-deception
- *Negative qualities:* proneness to provocation, irritation and impatience most prone to paranoia, quick to sense a fight and the first to feel that there is a conspiracy afoot and he is the object or the victim of it.

❖ Implementer

- Team Builder
- Team Implementer

Team Builder

The Team Builder is the most sensitive part of the team; the most aware of individuals' needs and worries, and the one who perceives most clearly the emotional undercurrents within the group. If you want to know the mood of the team ask the Team Builder — supportive; uncompetitive; mediator; socially-oriented; rather mild; sensitive.

- *Positive qualities:* an ability to respond to people and to situations and to promote team spirit.
- *Negative qualities:* indecisiveness at moments of crisis.

Team Implementer

The Implementer is the practical organiser; the one who turns decisions and strategies into defined and manageable tasks that people can actually get on with. If anyone does not know what on earth has been decided and what they are supposed to be doing they will go to the Team Implementer first to find out. A practical organiser; conservative; dutiful; predictable. Research has shown that a high proportion of Team Implementers end up in leading roles in industry — they do the tasks others find too uninteresting but are necessary for progress and survival!

- *Positive qualities:* organising ability, practical common sense, hard-working, self-disciplined.
- *Negative qualities:* lack of flexibility, unresponsive to unproved ideas.

❖ Completers

- Monitor Evaluator
- Completer Finisher

Monitor Evaluator

In a balanced team it is only the Plant and the Monitor-Evaluator who need a high IQ, but by contrast with the Plant, the Monitor-Evaluator is a bit of a cold fish. By temperament serious and not very exciting. The ME's contribution lies in measured and dispassionate analysis rather than creative ideas. Analytically rather than creatively intelligent; sober; unemotional; prudent.

- ***Positive qualities:*** judgement, discretion, hard-heartedness.
- ***Negative qualities:*** lacks inspiration or the ability to motivate others.

Completer Finisher

The Completer Finisher worries about what might go wrong and is never at ease until he/she have personally checked every detail and made sure that everything has been done and nothing has been overlooked. Completer Finishers are not common in business and when you find one, treasure them! Checks details; worries about deadlines; chivvies; painstaking; orderly; conscientious; anxious.

- ***Positive qualities:*** a capacity for follow through, perfectionism.
- ***Negative qualities:*** a tendency to worry about small things, a reluctance to "let go".

Significance of Belbin Team Roles

❖ In General

Where there is an uneven spread of roles in a group, then there may be problems in addressing the task allocated. Therefore it is important for team members to appreciate their own driving team role, know their second and third-best roles and see if these can complement the other group members' roles. In this way an effective team can be constructed.

There is a tendency in top teams for too many 'Shapers' and 'Plants' with few if any 'Completer-Finishers'. This means that everyone likes to talk, wants their own ideas to be accepted by all and relies on others to take the follow-through actions. Another role that often is lacking in top teams is that of 'Monitor-Evaluator' — this person is often seen as trying to prevent things from happening by introducing balance and reality into the discussions.

❖ Specific Teams

Knowing the predominant Belbin roles of your team can often offer an explanation for the dysfunction of the team. This can be adjusted by the leader asking some of the team members to move to their second or third strongest roles. Where there is a role that is not fulfilled at all in the team then either the leader assigns someone to that role or all the team members must take responsibility for ensuring that this role is carried out.

ESSENCE OF TEAMS

Shared Dreams — Shared Directions

We don't have to like each other... but we do need to work together to get the job done." As we think about leadership teams and the impact they have on organizational performance and success, it is important to consider why alignment at the top is needed and how people can work together to provide collective leadership.

The *Webster's Dictionary* explains the word align as "to array on the side of or against a party or cause." It also talks about" to be in or come into precise adjust or correct relevant position. "As I read these descriptions, several images come to mind of what this means in the corporate context." To array on the side of a cause" by implication means that being aligned is about being united by an overarching vision for the organization. A shared dream of sustainable growth — whatever be the industry, product or service. It is this common purpose and shared vision that enables people to develop a set of shared values, beliefs and goals that they strive to live up to and accomplish. This alignment needs to be visible at the very top. This burning ambition for the organization needs to be demonstrated by all members of the top team if they are to be able to drive it down deep through the organization for performance and success. Yet, this talk about vision, dreams and common purpose seems "touchy-feely" and almost elusive. To understand how real it is, let us spend a few minutes talking about the role of top leadership.

There are four key roles of the top leadership team. First, they must be role models for the behaviours and values important for the organization and the aspirations of the company and provide a pathway to accomplish these. They must also establish systems and processes to enable the work to support the accomplishment of these goals. They must remove obstacles to effective implementation of systems and processes. Finally, they must inspire and communicate, communicate, and communicate!

While individual members of the top team may be responsible for specific functions, divisions and performance cells, the collective responsibility of the team is to ensure organizational effectiveness and success. Healthy debate and discussion must be encouraged, but a decision once taken is the collective decision of the team and must be communicated through the organization as such.

For this to be visible to the rest of the organization, members of the top team need to demonstrate their cohesion through their behaviour. How they communicate their support for each other in their functional teams and in wider forums is vitally important. For instance, if we want to build an organization that works with speed and responsiveness to customers' needs, then, the top team must demonstrate their ability to be efficient. This means that they need to trust each other, make quick decisions and follow through with passion and commitment once those decisions are reached. If we want to build an organization where performance, results and positive accountability are the norm then, members of the top team must hold each accountable for their behaviours, the commitments they make and the way they lead their own teams for agreed performance.

This demonstration of the shared values and beliefs is the most important ingredient for building alignment. Without this, it is fair to say that an organization's efforts to establish a culture or transform traditional ways of working will rarely succeed.

The next role of the top leadership team is to create the foundation for effective systems and processes to support the goals. It is only by creating clarity of thought, purpose and action for the organization that the leadership gets the desired results through people. It is through this process that we can make success a habit for the organization. When the organization is clear about the vision and the goals, individuals are able to align their work, and their teams around what is important. They find ways to work through across teams to deliver the goals. Using the demonstrated behaviours of the top leadership team, they are able to work through obstacles and difficulties.

Even as we empower teams down the line to work through their goals, it is imperative for the leadership team to continuously assess organizational effectiveness. By this I mean that members of the leadership team, individually and collectively remain responsible for understanding the reasons why goals are accomplished or not and are, therefore, continuously in touch with reality. It is their responsibility then to quickly modify or eliminate systems and processes, which hamper progress, reinforce the systems that work and demonstrate flexibility to enable performance.

Thus, the process of creating organization clarity, and inducing flexibility and 'nimbleness' is a continuous and reiterative one — this helps the process of learning and institutionalizing patterns for successful behaviour across the organization.

Finally, all of this is possible only through consistent and continuous communication. The process of communication, directly and frequently, repetitively, reinforces what is important for the organization and inspires everybody through the organization to understand and act in desired ways.

Relentless and consistent communication is essential. When instituted with a continuous feedback mechanism, it leads to an effective understanding of informal processes within the organization.

What factors should we consider as we put a top team together, and the underlying pieces that hold these individuals together? It is imperative that we ensure a good match between personal and organizational values. It is, therefore, critical that all the supporting HR processes within the organization find ways of assessing the values match of individuals at the top. There are many implications of having a group of people with very disparate ways of thinking about goals, results, achievement and growth. It is apparent from an analysis of highly successful organizations that values are the unifying piece which determine the manner in which organizations meet their goals and build a sustainable capability.

While building a diverse work force and leadership team makes eminent good business sense, it is important that we understand the organization, the business and the manner in which they serve customers. Having too diverse a background and talent base often means that the decision-making process is slowed down, the ability to reach a consensus is difficult, the pace and manner of implementation of agreed policies varied. All of this is expensive for the organization, and creates a set of dysfunctional dynamics that detract from the primary aim of serving customers.

In too many organizations, we see that a place on the top leadership team is earned by the length of service in the organization or by a proven track record in a functional area. It is vitally important that people on the top team have a passion for excellence demonstrated by performance and experience in at least two or three different functions. Both depth and breadth of experience are important, and as we select people to move into the top leadership slots, we should keep this in mind. What this brings to the table is maturity of thought and action, ability to appreciate views of other functions and perspectives, and above all, ability to think laterally and generate creative thought. Individuals need to have the ambition to move on and get further in their careers; they must continue to demonstrate passion for learning and improvement.

It is important to build in diversity of age and experience to ensure that various schools of thought are adequately represented and that the team constructively challenges direction, process and systems. It is important to consider how an organization is able to encourage calculated risk taking to ensure optimum results. An all-older people often lead to relatively traditional ways of working. Too young a team may lead to a very radical approach. This balance of age and experience at the top is also important to ensure that the various work groups within the organization are represented effectively.

These factors become really important in getting top team alignment. What then are the elements that hold people together? The first and foremost is trust. Too diverse a team impacts the ability to generate trust and a shared vision for the present and the future. The second is team working. If members of the group believe in the value of working with each other to maximize skills and capabilities the message down the line is loud and clear. The third piece is commitment — to the cause, to results, to excellence and to coaching each other to deliver on the promise. The fourth is constructive conflict management and the fifth is creating an environment of open, honest feedback. Organizations that are able to nurture these elements will probably be able to develop an environment of success for everyone who works there.

In difficult and turbulent times, the issue of top team alignment is critical and one that causes organizations the most pain. Whether it is a start up organization, or one in the throes of transformation, the group at the top needs to perform as a team. Individually and collectively, they have an onerous responsibility of steering people and the organization towards sustainable growth and success. It calls for unlearning and relearning new skills and capabilities. It requires a genuine understanding of the people factors that affect performance. It requires an almost selfless focus on including other people and making them a part of your own success. It is not easy, but it has to be done.

Where human beings are involved, success is never ensured. However, we can through thoughtful actions and continuous improvements at least manage the risks associated with leadership and organization—building. In the words of Patrick Lencioni, author of the book "*Four Obsessions of An Extraordinary Executive*" executives must keep two things in mind if they are to make their organizations successful...first there is nothing more important than making their organization healthy, and second there is no substitute for discipline..." It is important for us to be relentless in the pursuit of alignment, for without this the organization flounders in a sea of conflict and despair — without hope and a chance to succeed.

Nurture Your People

1. Use effective assessment tools to understand each individual. There are many effective tools available like the Myers Briggs, Success Insights or Concept 4.2 which provide useful insights into an individual's natural and adapted styles and areas where development is needed.

2. Establish a process for individuals to share profiling information with others on the team to foster genuine understanding amongst them. It is very important that people are able to understand styles of operating, how decisions are made

and how skills are utilized as these have a direct bearing on a team's ability to deliver results.

3. Institute and zealously implement an effective meeting handling process. Establish ground rules for how team decisions will be made, what is acceptable and unacceptable behaviour and the consequences for breaking the rules. This enables the team members to effectively and constructively manage conflicts, help each other to be effective and stay committed to the goals of the organization.
4. Have a regular; structured process for regular off site meetings facilitated preferably by experienced outsiders to discuss issues and to address unresolved issues. Use this process also to reiterate the core values and shared beliefs which drive the organization.
5. Establish an effective process of 360 degree feedback to help the individuals to make timely changes and to learn from each other.
6. Be ruthless about making changes in the team if there are individuals who do not abide by the guiding values and principles, however strong a performance they might deliver. This is the toughest to do, yet vi.ally important if organizations want to build a sustainable organization.
7. Have a well-established performance management system, which is rigorously implemented for the top leadership team. Often, we forget that the leadership team members also need feedback and development.
8. Facilitate a process whereby people know each other at a personal level. Regular informal meetings help to release tension and pressures and create an environment where differences can be resolved amicably.

Making it All Possible

- ***Establish:*** a clear value base.
- ***Induct:*** individuals with a passion for continuous improvement.
- ***Balance:*** diverse talent and backgrounds with company's core competence.
- ***Harmonize:*** age and experience.

❖ Conclusion

In difficult and turbulent times, the issue of top team alignment is critical and one that causes the most pain. Whether it is a start-up organization, or one in the throes of transformation, the group at the top has an onerous responsibility of steering people and the company towards sustainable growth and success.

ESTABLISHING PROFESSIONAL TEAMS

Teams can become the means for change, a means for individual growth and a means for organizational learning. Senge has commented "Individuals learn all the time and yet there is no organizational learning. But if teams learn, they become a microcosm for learning throughout the organization. Insights gained are put into action. Skills developed can be propagated to other individuals and to other teams. The team's accomplishment can set the tone and establish a standard of learning together for the larger organization." (Senge, 1992, p.236)

Since the general move towards using a team approach, there have been certain underlying reasons why organizations have wanted to establish and promote teams. Firstly, there is a belief that productivity will increase when staff is involved in local problem-solving and decision-making. Secondly, teams involve employees in both local and strategic planning, and change implementation. Finally, there is an increased recognition of the value of personal and professional learning, with the team being viewed as a place to share knowledge, learn new skills and take risks. Hence, the modern learning organization implements learning teams to facilitate an increase in productivity, assist in the process of change and develop collaboration.

Developing the Effective Team

A good starting point is to define what a team means. Katzenbach and Smith define a team as: a small number of people with complimentary skills who are committed to a common purpose, performance goals and approach for which they hold themselves mutually accountable. (Katzenbach & Smith, 1998)

This definition outlines the key elements that distinguish a team from a collection of people who just so happen to work together. Teams are different from groups and committees. In a group, there is minimal involvement required, and no personal development is necessary. In a committee, a greater involvement is required, but still no commitment to long-term personal development. Meanwhile, high involvement is necessary in a team, and continuous commitment to personal and professional development is essential.

Once you have an understanding of what a team is, the next step is to have a clear understanding of the fundamental features of an effective team. An effective team must have a shared vision — a commonality of purpose; a genuine reason to exist; ownership of goals and outcomes; the ability to think insightfully; defined time line; interdependence; agreed, defined membership; mutual responsibility and accountability; skills in problem-solving, decision-making, interpersonal, and technical; an environment where they can build on their collective knowledge, skills and understanding; persistence in inquiry.

Building an Effective Leadership Team

The concept of a team approach will not become established without an effective leadership team guiding the overall process. Often, leaders are keen to create a new culture but are unable to find peer support. When the support is not forthcoming, the leadership often retreats to the traditional leader-subordinate role. No one person possesses all the talents necessary to run an effective organization over the long term. Leadership should not be seen as a solo act. Most team members simply do not see themselves as a group. They are not conscious of how they think together and consequently cannot recognize and avoid the barriers to group learning. Leadership teams often work on the wrong things. They find themselves driven by urgency, not by the importance of issues. They spend too much time on managerial issues and not enough on leadership. They plan and budget, deal with staffing, and solve problems. However, they rarely create views of the future, articulate strategy, chart ways to align and mobilize people, or build a framework that will keep them on the path to the future. In this way, they become good at putting out fires, but seldom light any. People with complementary skills who learn to function as a leadership team are more likely to build long-term success.

There are eight steps to achieve this:

Have a clear definition of what the leader does: Most leaders have three aspects to their daily performance — managing, leading, and contributing. In many cases, the components making up each of these tasks is not clearly defined. The leader needs to ask, "If we operated as a leadership team, how would we be different?" Teams must learn to think about their thinking. That is the beginning of the journey toward group self-knowledge. As the group increasingly becomes aware of its learning styles and impediments to learning, the more it is able to learn.

Evaluate performance: What gets measured gets done. This is not about evaluating the strengths and weaknesses of leaders. Rather, what should be asked is how we evaluate the combined leadership effort. If we measure leaders as a group for their combined contributions, they might spend more time leading, and less time managing.

See leadership as a function: One person cannot make the organization successful. Effective leaders understand what it takes to operate successfully, are able to assess their own capabilities, and work cooperatively with others. When the successful leader shares the leadership responsibilities, they give up the idea of the one person having all the answers.

Leadership is a skill to be developed: Leaders need some basic capacity, but the skills of the effective leader are developed with practice. Strengths are sharpened through risk-taking, discussions, dialogues, questioning, collaboration and collegiality.

Take time to view the big picture: The natural tendency is to focus primarily on the immediate, short-term, reactive issues. Effective leaders are able to let go of the less important short-term tasks to work on the future. This shift in work practice requires courage in oneself and faith in fellow leaders. Take the time to reflect, dialogue, and teach others the art of leadership.

Demonstrate your respect for your employees: This respect translates into maximizing human potential. Teams provide an excellent vehicle for getting the best out of people. Teams create a safe and supportive environment where employees are encouraged to try new behaviours, take risks and thus gain confidence. Employees have the opportunity to learn from others. They get to view different styles, methods and approaches. Staff is able to enjoy more successes than by working independently; in this way self-esteem is enhanced. Staff gains a breadth of skills due to the cross-functional nature of teams, which results in enhancing one's ability and value to the company. Leadership teams often work on the wrong things. They find themselves driven by urgency, not by the importance of issues. They spend too much time on managerial issues and not enough on leadership. They rarely create views of the future, articulate strategy, chart ways to align and mobilize people, or build a framework that will keep them on the path to the future... they become good at putting out fires, but seldom light any.

Shared goals are necessary for successful teams: The shared development and implementation of ideas mean there will be shared ownership.

Understand that there are different teams for different needs: The effective leader knows what teams are most effective for different needs. Specific tasks require specific tools.

Moving to the Thinking Team

Once having established the effective team, work can commence on developing the thinking team. Inquiry and learning within the team depends on the ability of the team members to question and explore and the ability of the team to manage this process. The ability to do these things consistently over time is more likely to occur if the team has some tools to assist their thinking. Without the thinking tools, the team can easily fall into "attack and defence" modes that will work against the very nature of inquiry (de Bono, 1990; Senge, 1992, p.237). In many meetings, where thinking tools are not being used, the usual rules of the game are that the initiator defends the idea, with or without help from others, while some of the rest of the participants find reasons why the idea will not work. The final decision usually results in damaged egos and is made according to the power of the individual rather than on the merits of the idea itself. When thinking tools are introduced, the participants are able to move out of the confrontationist mode to the constructive mode and genuinely explore the issues involved (Argyris, 1992). Thinking tools, such as de Bono's CoRT, Argyris' Model1/Model 11, and Hyerle's visual maps, provide a framework for goal- setting, problem-solving and decision-making. The tools make it possible for teams to utilize a range of perspectives, ideas and expertise. Hargreaves tells of the importance of working together. Working together is not just a way of building relationships and collective resolve; it is also a source of learning. It helps people to see problems as things to be solved, not as occasions for blame; to appreciate that conflict is a necessary part of change; to value the different and even dissident voices of more marginal members of the organization; to sort out policy demands, and always to be looking for ways to improve. "(Hargreaves,1997,p.113).

CHAPTER 3

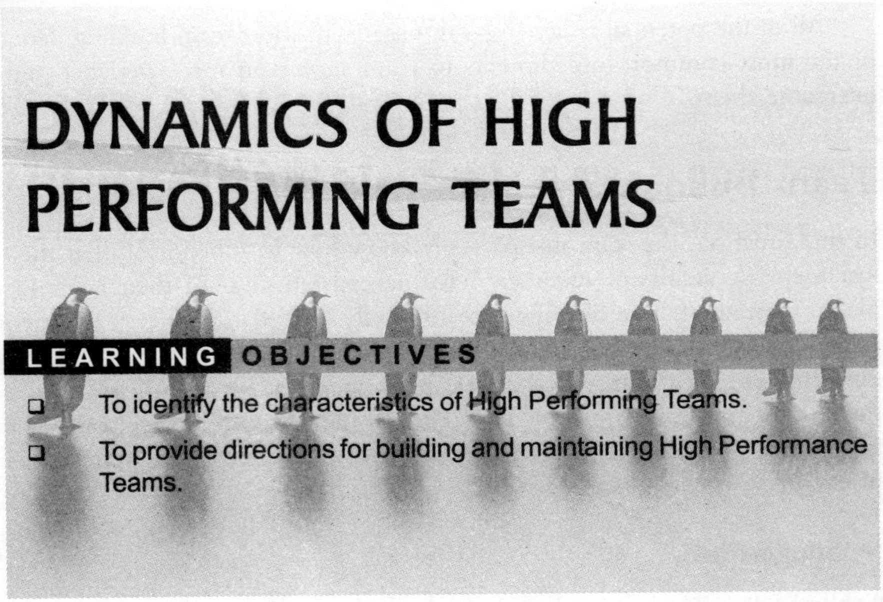

DYNAMICS OF HIGH PERFORMING TEAMS

LEARNING OBJECTIVES

- To identify the characteristics of High Performing Teams.
- To provide directions for building and maintaining High Performance Teams.

TEAM BUILDING: LEADERSHIP STRATEGIES TO ADDRESS TODAY'S MOST COMMON TEAM BUILDING PROBLEMS

Despite the best team building efforts, many organizations are still operating on low power when it comes to producing desired results. They've invested time and dollars in events that supposedly help team members bond and function coherently, yet results are short-term at best.

So what's the problem? Every situation is unique, but here are a few possibilities:

- Some or all members don't want to function as a team. They've become accustomed to operating independently and don't see the value of operating as a whole.
- Team-building isn't linked to business results. Instead, the team experienced artificial feel good exercises. Although the team has learnt about each other's behavioral styles, motivational profiles, individual strengths, etc., they have failed to connect their efforts to desired business outcomes.

- There's no follow-up beyond a onetime event. A successful team building process should be approached strategically, not as a onetime event hoping for the best. It should result in actionable ideas to help the team and organization achieve their goals. Continued learning, action and reinforcement are critical.

All of the potential issues that can negatively affect team building here are some of the most common impediments to team success in my experience and ways to overcome them.

Team Building Impediment 1: Fuzzy Focus

In this situation, the team doesn't really know how to function. Either the team has lost focus on results or members have never been clear of their goals in the first place. Instead, they've become too internally fixated on other team members — judging what they're doing, making assumptions, speculating, back-stabbing, finger-pointing, etc. Without a clear focus, team members frequently react to events in their immediate environment. They become distracted by other team members or simply respond to whatever issue lands in their lap. There's no strategic team focus or energy to move forward.

❖ Suggestion

As the leader, you must step in and clarify big picture goals and expectations. In order to do complete this task effectively, you must communicate the goals in a number ways that appeal to a variety of team members. Some may need a visual representation (e.g., a roadmap); others may need to know the 'why' behind the goals to buy in. Check for clarity. Ask the team to articulate their understanding of the overall goals in their own words. Then clarify or correct as needed.

Team Building Impediment 2: Lack of Leadership

Leadership is critical to help the team succeed. Without it, team members will resort to their own methods. Some will run as far and fast as they can to prove themselves, pushing boundaries and taking on too much risk. Others will sit idle for as long as they can, performing as little as possible, yet complaining about how much work needs to get done. Some leaders are too busy concentrating on their own political or career agenda. Other leaders just don't understand their role or possess good leadership skills.

❖ Suggestion

Conduct regular strategic focus sessions. Strong leaders will help the team focus on the goal (the what) and key strategies (the how). Hold consistent informal one-on-

one development meetings with direct reports to gain feedback, uncover trouble spots and leverage opportunities. If you need to build leadership skills yourself, make that a priority. If you value your career, find a coach or mentor to help you. Remember, in order to develop others – you must first develop yourself.

Team Building Impediment 3: Stuck in Sameness

The team is stuck in practices that may have been established years ago. They've gotten lazy or stopped trying new approaches. New team members may be frustrated by the apparent lack of openness to new ideas or ways of operating. Experienced team members defend the way things have always been done.

❖ Suggestion

Identify one aspect of the team that you would be excited to see change come about. Talk with your team to make sure everyone agrees it would be worth it to affect change in that area. Determine what the best possible outcome could be if the team made the change, adopted a new procedure, tried a new approach or do whatever it is you're suggesting. Then call for ideas from the team on how to make it happen. Generating excitement about new possibilities makes it easier for the team to get unstuck.

The most effective teams can maintain best practices while adapting to new environments or organizational changes. They are not content with sameness or status quo. Their best practices include constantly seeking new and better ways to perform their job. They are not content with going through the motions or frivolous exercises that may help increase awareness, but stop there.

❖ Final Thoughts

It doesn't matter if Bob is blue, green or yellow if he can't connect his self-awareness to results. The same applies at the team level. Team members may find it interesting to learn more about team members, but be sure to help translate learning into results.

Great team leaders spend time clarifying goals, cultivating their own leadership skills and identifying new ways to achieve great results. Not to be confused with micromanaging, an effective leader will check in from time to time to make sure the organization's goals and strategies remain clear. At the same time, they help build capability of individual team members versus taking on the work of the team themselves.

Simply opening productive and constructive communication to a greater degree will help leaders increase their effectiveness and their teams function most effectively.

Leaders often feel unnecessary pressure to tell everyone on the team what to do. Focus on influencing versus doing.

Team building is a means to an end, not an end in itself. What do you want your team to achieve?

How to Build a Teamwork Culture

Do the Hard Stuff for Teams

Fostering teamwork is creating a work culture that values collaboration. In a teamwork environment, people understand and believe that thinking, planning, decisions and actions are better when done cooperatively. People recognize, and even assimilate, the belief that "none of us is as good as all of us."

It's hard to find work places that exemplify teamwork. In America, our institutions such as schools, our family structures, and our pastimes emphasize winning, being the best, and coming out on top. Workers are rarely raised in environments that emphasize true teamwork and collaboration.

Organizations are working on valuing diverse people, ideas, backgrounds, and experiences. We have miles to go before valuing teams and teamwork will be the norm.

You can, however, create a teamwork culture by doing just a few things right.

Admittedly, they're the hard things, but with commitment and appreciation for the value, you can create an overall sense of teamwork in your organization.

Create a Culture of Teamwork

To make teamwork happen, these powerful actions must occur.

- **Executive leaders communicate the clear expectation that teamwork and collaboration are expected.** No one completely owns a work area or process all by himself. People who own work processes and positions are open and receptive to ideas and input from others on the team.
- **Executives model teamwork in their interaction with each other and the rest of the organization.** They maintain teamwork even when things are going wrong and the temptation is to slip back into former team unfriendly behaviour.
- **The organization members talk about and identify the value of a teamwork culture.** If values are formally written and shared, teamwork is one of the key five or six.

- **Teamwork is rewarded and recognized.** The lone ranger, even if she is an excellent producer, is valued less than the person who achieves results with others in teamwork. Compensation, bonuses, and rewards depend on collaborative practices as much as individual contribution and achievement.
- **Important stories and folklore that people discuss within the company emphasize teamwork.** (Remember the year the capsule team reduced scrap by 20 percent?) People who "do well" and are promoted within the company are team players.
- **The performance management system places emphasis and value on teamwork.** Often 360 degree feedback is integrated within the system.

Tips for Team Building

Do you immediately picture your group off at a resort playing games or hanging from ropes when you think of team building? Traditionally, many organizations approached team building this way. Then, they wondered why that wonderful sense of teamwork, experienced at the retreat or seminar, failed to impact long term beliefs and actions back at work.

I'm not averse to retreats, planning sessions, seminars and team building activities, in fact I lead them, but they have to be part of a larger teamwork effort. You will not build teamwork by 'retreating' as a group for a couple of days each year. Think of team building as something you do every single day.

- **Form teams to solve real work issues** and to improve real work processes. Provide training in systematic methods so the team expends its energy on the project, not on figuring out how to work together as a team to approach it.
- **Hold department meetings to review projects and progress**, to obtain broad input, and to coordinate shared work processes. If team members are not getting along, examine the work processes they mutually own. The problem is not usually the personalities of the team members. It's the fact that the team members often haven't agreed on how they will deliver a product or a service or the steps required to get something done.
- **Build fun and shared occasions into the organization's agenda.** Hold pot luck lunches; take the team to a sporting event. Sponsor dinners at a local restaurant. Go hiking or to an amusement park. Hold a monthly company meeting. Sponsor sports teams and encourage cheering team fans.
- **Use icebreakers and teamwork exercises at meetings.** I worked with an organization that held a weekly staff meeting. Participants took turns bringing a "fun" ice breaker to the meeting. These activities were limited to ten minutes,

but they helped participants laugh together and get to know each other — a small investment in a big time sense of team.

- **Celebrate team successes publicly.** Buy everyone the same T-shirt or hat. Put team member names in a drawing for company merchandise and gift certificates. You are limited in teamwork only by your imagination.

Take care of the hard issues above and do the types of teamwork activities listed here. You'll be amazed at the progress you will make in creating a teamwork culture, a culture that enables individuals to contribute more than they ever thought possible — together.

Personal Courage and Conflict Resolution at Work

Why People Avoid Conflict Resolution?

Practicing personal courage is necessary if you want to really resolve conflicts at work. It is much easier and much safer to ignore the necessary conflict and play ostrich. Unfortunately, an unresolved conflict tends to escalate. It never really disappears because it simmers just below the surface. Think of water that is coming to a boil. It burbles up in the pot sporadically and then finally reaches the boiling temperature. At that point, a full blown rolling, constant boiling is seen on the surface of the water.

Conflict behaves similarly. The water may seem calm, but every once in awhile, usually at the worst possible times, the conflict burbles up to the surface once again. Unresolved conflict does not go away; unresolved conflict can turn into a full boil at any time.

Many people are afraid of conflict resolution. They feel threatened by conflict resolution because they may not get what they want if the other party gets what it wants. Even in the best circumstances, conflict resolution is uncomfortable because people are usually unskilled at conflict resolution. Finally, people can get hurt in a conflict and, at work, they are still expected to work together effectively every day.

❖ The Benefits of Conflict Resolution

This century's workplace makes conflict resolution more important, but also, more difficult. Team or work cell environments create more conflict as people with different opinions must choose to work together, often in close quarters.

Empowering work environments, in which the traditional reliance on a manager to solve conflicts and make decisions, bring coworkers into more frequent conflict, as they must work issues out for themselves. Conflict resolution also:

- Causes people to listen to and consider different ideas.
- Enables people to increase their alternatives and potential paths.
- Results in increased participation and more ownership of and commitment to the decisions and goals of the group or person.

The goal of the people or the team is not to eliminate conflict but to learn how to manage conflict constructively.

Conflict Resolution Steps

You've decided resolving the conflict is more important than all of the reasons why people avoid conflict. Here are tips to help you practice less scary, less intimidating, more effective and successful conflict resolution, with an individual or a team.

- Create an environment that is conducive to successful conflict resolution. Quiet, private settings work the best. Agree prior to sitting down together that the purpose of the meeting is to resolve the conflict. When you make this agreement, all parties arrive prepared.
- Determine what outcomes you'd like to see as a result of the discussion. A better working relationship? A better solution to the problem? Increased alternatives for successful projects? A broadened understanding of each person's needs and wants? Thoughtful solutions and outcomes are infinite if you are creative.
- Begin by allowing each party to express their point of view.
- The purpose of the exchange is to make sure both parties clearly understand the viewpoint of the other. Make sure each party ties their opinions to real performance data and other facts, where possible. This is not the time to discuss; it is the time to ask questions, clarify points for better understanding and truly hear the other's viewpoint.
- Agree on the difference in the points of view. You must agree on the problem together to begin to search for a solution. Often, problems are simply misunderstandings. Clarification can end the need for conflict resolution. Try to focus on the issues, not the personalities of the participants. Don't "you" each other as in, "You always ..."
- Explore and discuss potential solutions and alternatives. Try to focus on both your individual needs and wants and those of the other party. After all, if one party 'wins,' that means the other party 'loses.' People who feel as if they have

lost, are not effective coworkers. They harbour resentment and may even sabotage your project or relationship. Make sure you discuss the positive and negative possibilities of each suggestion, before you reject any suggested solutions. Build a discussion that is positive and powerful for all parties.

- Agree on a plan that meets the needs of all parties and the organization. Agree on follow-up steps, as necessary, to make the plan work. Agree on what each person will do to solve the conflict. Set clear goals and know how you will measure success.
- Do what you agreed to do.

With more experience in conflict resolution, you will grow more comfortable with conflict resolution. That's a positive outcome for the workplace. It will foster idea generation, help people get along, minimize negative behaviours and promote the success of all in placing their attention where it belongs — on the customer.

Establishing Truly Peak Performing Teams – Beyond Metaphoric Challenges

The term "Team Building" has a number of varying interpretations in various organizations and between individuals within these organizations. Adventure team building became popular in the 80s, where it was seen as a new commercial venture for those fast enough to jump onto the band wagon, and seen as the "in thing" for organizations that wanted to be perceived as being ahead with their personnel development policies and practices.

A Good Time was had by All

For those of us that have been there, this often amounted to an opportunity to get out of the office, to play with ropes and bridges and boats and sorts (without the kids!), to let one's hair down with colleagues, or to finally strike up that affair that's been brewing the last six months! We were all told that Together Everyone Achieves More, and that the reason we're in this team is that we share common goals linked to a common purpose in line with the company's mission, so let's have fun together! You get the picture. That's what we now call unstructured team building. Although this approach is great for building an *esprit de corps*, rewarding staff and generating short-term gratification, it doesn't really build the team. In the late 80s and early 90s, organizations realized that the unstructured team building approach, while it has its place, was a relatively expensive exercise, the outcome of which could be achieved at a staff lunch or a game of ten pin bowling. Real problems or challenges associated with the team dynamics were still overlooked. This realization gave birth to structured team building.

Structured Team Building

In structured team building, the activities are geared to achieving a specific problem or addressing a specific challenge, reinforced by experiential learning. Prior to "the day", the team is briefed on the purpose and nature of the team building exercise. A good facilitator will ensure that he/she understands the business objective of the event, and plans accordingly to achieve this with the team. Here, the facilitator works with the group dynamics of the team and uses experiential exercises as a metaphor to reinforce the learning experience. Examples are drawn from the work environment to enable the team to identify with the learning experiences, and all the exercises are geared towards achieving the business objective, e.g. improved communication, achieving sales targets and problem solving techniques. Generally, the cost of this exercise is not much more than that of the unstructured event, but the value added is substantially greater.

The structured team building industry is still thriving, and most companies feel that their investment in these activities still pays off – but only in the short term. These activities are still not geared to achieving sustainable outcomes.

Integrated Process Teams

In the mid to late 1990s, business process re-engineering became the fixation. At the same time, labour practice laws dictated more freedom and flexibility in favour of employees in the work place, and Information Technology provided greater opportunities for change and transformation than ever before. Gone are the days of homogenous teams operating in functional silos. Companies moved from an analogue to a digital organizational structure. Teams were reorganized all over the place to affect the new integrated business processes. Teams are now heterogeneous, dynamic, multifunctional and multicultural. We are told, rightly so, that diversified teams have a greater propensity for high performance than those with a single minded groupthink. The top management consultancies preached Change Management to soothe the pains of this transformation. "Team Building" was bandied about as a critical activity, part of the Change Management programme. What happened? Business processes were changed, new technology that no one understood was implemented, people were reorganized… and then sent on a team building event so that they could all work together as a high performance team in a land where Peter Pan really does fly. Sarcasm aside, most programmes were properly addressed as a structured team building event with stated objectives, but were the real issues identified and addressed? If so, then why do statistics show abnormally high staff turnover levels in most organizations shortly after a major transformation exercise?

The answer is that there was not matching of the psychology with change and technology. The softer issues around the people element of these transformation exercises were not diagnosed and treated – the process looked good on paper, but short cuts were taken.

True Coalescence for Sustainable Peak Performance

Marcus Evans professional training's associate trainers at Peak Performance, a management consultancy in the UK specializing in peak performance for business and individuals, have taken structured team building a level further by going back to basics, using common sense best practices to achieve sustainable outcomes by matching team psychology with change and technology. Whatever the objective of a structured team building event, whether before, during or post a business transformation exercise, the overriding objective is to *improve the performance of the team*. This can only be truly affected if your performance goals are measurable and achievable. To do this, they say, you need to know your performance levels today so that they can be measured in the future to confirm performance improvement. The Peak Performance Continuum™ is a framework to plot an individual and team's performance in line with global best practice standards.

This model addresses the traditional notion of team building as a process, a Coalescence Programme, rather than a once-off activity. It recommends the following 7 steps to building a sustainable peak performance team.

Step 1: Confirm the Business Objective: Ask questions like, What is the business purpose of the coalescence programme? How is this aligned to the overall company value proposition? What would make this a high performance team? Why? Is the coalescence programme taking place before, during or after a change process?

Step 2: Establish Team Metanoia: The Peak Performance definition of Metanoia is 'awareness with understanding'. At the start of most coalescence programmes, staff are told of the journey they are about to embark upon (awareness), but very seldom have a true appreciation for why and how this will affect them in the short and medium term (understanding). This step also includes identifying and recording any perceived problems/issues that may need to be addressed.

Step 3: Conduct Individual and Team Behavioural Profiling: This activity is crucial prior to executing the experiential learning. Without first having a good understanding of the individual and team profile, key issues may be ignored and left to fester. This step involves assessing all the personalities in the team in terms of their transactional styles, leadership styles, learning and thinking styles, conflict resolution styles, stressors and value systems. The consolidation of this information provides a team profile, which is then mapped to the department/company culture. If this mapping reflects a large gap, coalescence and team-building is premature and there are bigger issues to deal with.

Step 4: Prepare Experiential Learning Event Schedule: Given the facilitator's knowledge of the business objective (Step 1), perceived problems/issues (Step 2) and the individual and team profiles (Step 3), a schedule of discussion topics, experiential learning exercises, metaphoric challenges, management feedback, etc. is prepared.

Step 5: Experiential Learning: This is where the structured team building concept is executed. Using the cornerstones of building trust, respect, open communication and interdependency, the facilitator executes the Experiential Learning Event Schedule. The "wrap-up" part of this step includes recording what was learnt, expected benefits (quantitative and qualitative) and an action plan to address any issues identified in the programme to date.

Step 6: Establish Peak Performance Map: Whatever programme you are using, this 'map' should reflect a baseline benchmark of the individual and team performance prior to the coalescence programme, the revised positioning after the coalescence programme (where relevant), and a realistic improved positioning that the team needs to achieve, say, within six months. The map also indicates specific performance improvement activities, and Key Performance Indicators (measurables) to gauge performance.

Step 7: Benefits Realization: After an agreed period of time, typically six months, the team should workshop (preferably with the same facilitator), where they are on the Peak Performance Map. Successes should be celebrated and failures should be understood, revisited and addressed.

❖ Summary

To coalesce means to unite, to combine, to join together, gel together. Traditional structured team-building approaches can certainly achieve this on the day, and perhaps the effects are lasting for a short period back in the office. However, an approach to performance improvement that treats it as a process with enthusiasm, energy, momentum and integrity has longer lasting effects for cost-justifiable, sustainable outcomes.

WHAT IS A HIGH PERFORMANCE TEAM?

Synergism and the High performance Team

Synergism is the simultaneous actions of separate entitles which together have greater total effect than the sum of their individual effects.

In other words, synergism is focusing a group's efforts so that 2+2=5. Have you ever been part of a high performance team and experienced this synergism? Take a few minutes and write down some words to describe this experience.

You probably experienced exhilaration, stimulation, satisfaction, a sense of challenge and purpose, a natural high.

Also recall some examples of synergism and high performance teams in your everyday life, either your personal life or work related examples.

Athletics provides a multitude of examples, particularly team sports such as basketball, football, soccer, rowing, relay races, hockey, etc. It is not only the individual athlete abilities, but their work as a team that produces winners.

Other good examples of synergism come from the music world. Recall the power and energy produced by a top-notch marching band or symphony orchestra. It is up to each individual to know his or her part. There may be some solos, but ultimately what is important is how it all sounds together. Is the whole greater than the sum of its parts?

Business, too, abounds with examples of synergism. Bennis and Nanus, in '*Leaders*' cite the example of a famous city planner and developer.

> *When he was dissatisfied with the looks of some housing in his Columbia, Maryland, project, he tried to influence the next design by nagging and correcting his team of architects. He got nowhere. Then he decided to stop 'correcting' them and tried to influence them by sending them to look at the world's best, demonstrating what he wanted, what he was for. Inspired by Rouse's vision, the architects went on to create some of the most eye catching and functional housing in the country.*
>
> — **James Rouse**

Or consider what typically happens on a broader scale when starting a new business. One critical function often 'champions' the new opportunity: marketing because of a customer, research because of a new idea, or manufacturing because of production capability. True synergism, however, exists when people from all three functions agree on the new business target. Invariably, in this case, the energy of the team and the pace of commercialization accelerates and the odds of success of the new business venture increase.

The challenge is to create a situation where you and your work unit function as a team to achieve more than each can be individuals. In fact, the real payoff — the most important contribution you can make as a manager — is to produce synergy in your work unit. An important starting point for examining high performing teams and how to produce synergy is to look at your role as an Energy Manager.

Kinds of Energy

Your employees bring four different forms of human energy to their jobs: physical, mental, emotional, and energy of the spirit.

Physical Energy is the energy expended doing muscular work, working standing for long periods, playing games, exercising.

Mental Energy is the energy consumed in brainwork — reading, writing, talking with people, sitting in conferences and meetings, struggling with problems, planning.

Emotional Energy is the energy that helps keep a person's physical and mental machinery in momentum. This form of energy is, to a great extent, responsible for accomplishments from hour to hour and day to day.

Energy of the spirit is the form of energy that might be likened to electricity. When it flows through you, it sparks your spirits, gives you a sense of buoyancy. You are confident and resourceful. You work with decision, enjoy your work, are alive. Energy of the spirit is what allows people to spark one another and creates synergism. This powerful form of energy helps everyone do hard tasks easily, to put spirit into doing the most humdrum jobs, to go through the day with spring in their steps, and to work long hours without weariness.

How Managers learn to Man?

Most managers work their way up to their position. They begin as doers. The Management vs. Doer diagram illustrates the typical upward progression of the doers in an organization.

Managers of Managers	O	O	O	O	O	O	O	O	O	
Managers of Supervisor	O	O	O	O	O	O	O	X	X	X
Supervisors	O	O	O	O	O	X	X	X	X	X
Section Leaders	O	O	O	X	X	X	X	X	X	X
Doers	O	X	X	X	X	X	X	X	X	X

FIGURE 3.1 **Management vs. Doer**

A doer is anyone in a non supervisory capacity, as, for example, engineers, clerical workers, sales representatives, assemblers, testers secretaries. The X's indicate that their day is taken up totally with doer activities. In many cases, people are promoted because they are the best working in their particular function. When they become a section head or supervisor, they begin to take on more management activities, but continue to spend a large part of their time with tasks they used to perform as doers. What is that so? Consider your own situation; if you came up the ranks as a doer, how did you respond and think?

At the lower levels of management, when the pressure is on to get something done, the tendency is to continue to think and react as a doer and get it done rather than to reach the members of the work unit to do it.

As managers continue to rise in the organization, they find themselves spending more and more time on management activities, represented by O's, and less and less time in doer activities. They usually learn management activities from watching others, from modelling their bosses or through trial and error.

Advantages in learning to manage this way are that there is consistency of thinking and, if the model is good, the learners learn the right things. In addition, doing as well as managing becomes part of the managers reward system and is what will likely get further promotions. It also enhances the manager's comfort level knowing that the employee depends on him.

Unfortunately, learning to manage in this manner also has negative consequences. One problem is that this approach tends to perpetuate the way managers who preceded the new managers managed, which may work for some people, but not for others. This approach tends to foster a closed system as well as dependence on doing. Given the changes occurring in the world and in the workplace, this approach to the management issue needs to be reexamined.

While it is understandable that managers who are former doers probably rely on a one-to-one approach, and that this approach doers have its value, does it accomplish work the most effective, efficient way? Do managers have the time and energy to deal with all employees one-to-one? Does the size of the work unit realistically allow this? Take a few minutes to answer these questions.

Eight Attributes of the High-performing Team

Wilson research has identified eight attributes typically present in teams that perform in the zone of inspirations.

(i) *Participative leadership:* Creating an interdependency by empowering, freeing up and serving others.

(ii) *Shared responsibility:* Establishing an environment in which all team members feel as responsible as the manager for the performance of the work unit.

(iii) ***Aligned on purpose:*** Having a sense of common purpose about why the team exists and the function it serves.

(iv) ***High Communication***: Creating a climate of trust and open, honest communication.

(v) ***Future focused:*** Seeing change as an opportunity for growth.

(vi) ***Focused on task:*** Keeping meetings focused on results.

(vii) ***Creative talents***: Applying individual talents and creativity.

(viii) ***Rapid response***: Identifying and acting on opportunities.

You may be thinking this is common sense. And that's the good news. As Thomas Edison astutely observed, 'Common sense is genius in its working clothes'. You already know how important these eight attributes are, but are you using them or simply paying lip service to them as you manage your work unit? The rest of this book will take you step by step through each attribute, help you assess whether it is present in your work unit, and, if it is not present, offer suggestions about how you can go about developing it.

An important aspect of how you apply the specific attributes is to consider how teams develop. They don't happen overnight, but rather go through developmental stages.

Three Phases of Team Development

Establishing a high performance team is a developmental process. That is, a work unit must go through several phases of growth and change to become a high performance team. Most work units go through three phases, but all groups are not alike. Each passes through the phases at different rates and exhibits different patterns of interaction at each phase. Some indicators of team development, however, transcend these differences. You, as a manager, should consider these indicators, as you assess your team's development.

❖ Phase-I: Collection of Individuals

When people are asked to work together, they initially form a collection of individuals. This first phase gives individuals the opportunity to form identities within the work unit. Phase-I teams tend to be individual-centered, have individual goals rather than group goals, do not share responsibility, avoid changes, and do not deal with conflict. Members begin to define their purpose and responsibilities, identify the skills of other members, and develop norms for working with one another.

❖ Phase-2: Groups

In the second developmental phase, work units begin forming groups. Members develop a group identity, define their roles, clarify their purpose, and establish norms for working together. However, groups tend to be leader-centered; the leader provides direction, assigns tasks, reviews performance, and is the primary focus of communication.

❖ Phase-3: Team

The final phase, and difficult to attain, is that of an actual high performance team, a team able to focus energy, respond rapidly to opportunities, and share both responsibilities and rewards. Teams are purpose-centered; members not only understand the purpose but are committed to it and use the purpose to guide actions and decisions

How to Build and Maintain High Performance Team?

Understand Groups as Teams and Individuals Team Members

One of the ways to get higher performance from your people is to make sure that they work together as a team. Groups that work as teams have strengths that are missing from collections of individuals. Particularly in changing or unpredictable situations. But how do you tell when the group that you are managing has become a team? It doesn't happen simply because organizationally they all report to you, or because they happen to work near each other, or are friendly in their relationship. Team-sense requires more than organizational structure, or personal proximity, or good social relationships.

❖ Features of a Team

If you think about any group of people with whom you have worked, or that you have been able to observe, which you regard as being an effective team, you will probably find that it demonstrated seven characteristics features:

1. Its members share a strong sense of common purpose. But the team's idea of its goals develops within the team as a whole, it can't be imposed by you or altered by outsiders.

2. The members of the team interact to achieve their purpose. They discuss ideas with each other, offer and accept suggestions about each other's work, and take decisions together on anything that is important to the team's success.
3. Each member has a strong sense of the team's identity. They are very aware of themselves as a group. Over time, they develop a feeling of belonging together, as they get to know each other and learn about each other's capabilities and foibles. They think in terms of 'insiders' and 'outsiders', of 'us' and 'them'. This sense of group identity includes the team's leader. In fact, he is very much at the centre of it. A formal boss who is not 'one of us' becomes just another part of the team's external environment rather than a source of internal influence. This strong group identity means that the team is more likely to compete than to collaborate with other teams. Properly managed, this attitude can result in fruitful interteam competition and constructive rivalry. Badly managed, or not managed at all, it can cause interteam hostility and destructive 'one-upmanship' games.
4. A team is small enough to be self-coordinating. Each member has to be able to maintain a continuous awareness of how his actions affect the other members, and vice-versa. This really limits the group's size to between three and twelve members. Fewer than three lack strength as a group, but with more than a dozen the group begins to fragment: either smaller cliques develop within it, or team sense is lost altogether and coordination has to fall back on formal organization links.
5. A team has its own internal code of behaviour (an important part of the working atmosphere that we have seen affects the performance of each of its members). They not only conform to this code but act as a group to enforce it upon any out-of-line members. A variety of disciplinary sanctions may be applied, not just by the team's leader but by the team as a whole. They may range from a raised eyebrow to a Kangaroo court: from a certain quality of laughter in the group to outright expulsion (a member being sent to Coventry'). The team's behaviour code doesn't necessarily match the ethics of the world outside – nor even the personal ethics of every individual member. Sometimes it may fly in the face of external realities, although here the leader can play a key role in getting the group to adjust its code for the sake of its self-respect or self-preservation. The team's effectiveness within the organization depends very much on whether this behaviour code is positive, neutral or negative toward the organization's general interests.
6. Members of a team afford each other a high level of mutual support. There is a bond of loyalty within a team. The members are more concerned for the team's interests than for those of the wider organization, or for their own personal interests. Frequently, they will set aside private advantage for what they see as

the team's advantage. In return, the team protects its members from external pressures or threats. It closes ranks against anything the members regard as an attack on an individual member or on the group as a whole. Whether it is a workforce group or a management group, it practices solidarity.

7. The team has an internal structure which has little to do with the organization chart. The members adopt roles that are quite different in nature from the formal functions described by their job titles or job descriptions. These roles evolve out of the different personalities, temperaments and aptitudes of the members, and the" way they relate to one another. Usually, these roles are not consciously adopted, although objective analysis would reveal that members are in fact operating within them. This seems to be intuitively perceived rather than openly declared. The key role is that of the leader. This is the individual member who is recognized by the team as having the greatest influence on their opinions, attitudes and behaviour. He is the member accepted by the others as best able to guide an integrate the team's efforts. This is a practical working role, not a status position. The leader doesn't stand on his authority, he doesn't need to, in fact. The rest accept him instinctively as the natural leader. He may not be the formally appointed head of the team! This role can in fact be shared by more than one team member. Although it is a crucial role, it by no means the only one which is important to the team's success.

What are the Essential Qualities of an Effective Team Leader?

One of the chief fruits of good leadership is a good team & vice versa. That principle seems universal in human society, and relevant, too, to the creatures who serve man. Studies of dog teams, for example, show that Siberian huskies can reach and sustain a speed of about 20 mph provided they have a good lead dog. That is a parable, if you like, for human teams.

The characteristics of the leader and the outcomes are related. They can be tabled as follows:

TABLE 3.1 Characteristics and outcomes of a leader

Characteristics	Outcomes
• Enthuser	• People are purposefully busy and everyone has a basis on which to judge priorities
• Lives his values, such as integrity	• Sense of excitement. People willing to take on high work loads. Feelings of achievement

Contd...

• Leads by example	• Consistency. Followers know leader's values
• Generates good leaders from his followers	• Is trusted by his followers
• Aware of his own behaviour and his	• People aspire to be leader's environment example.
• Intellect to meet the needs of his job	
• Aware of the needs of the group he is leading and the needs of individuals	• The led begin to lead. Leader becomes less indispensable. People are delegated to, coached and supported
• Exhibits trust in his followers	
• Able to represent the organization to his people to the organization	• Followers feel they have some his people contribution to aims and are committed to them

CASE STUDY

Defining the Manager-Leader

Imperial Chemical Industries made (ICI) a profit of two billion pounds in 2005. the first British Manufacturing co. to do so. Five years previously one of their nine divisions was losing $200 million a year and two others were also in the red. The company put the development of management leadership as top of their personal priorities. For ICI believed that if leadership is effective, people will:

- Have a clear sense of direction and work hard and effectively
- Have confidence in their ability to achieve specific challenging objectives
- Believe in and be identified with the organization
- Hold together when the going is rough
- Have respect for and trust in managers
- Adapt to the changing world.

ICI's divisions mounted a number of management development courses which put emphasis on what the manager does in order to achieve the task, build the team and develop individuals. How the leader does the necessary functions – style – is less important and varies from individual to individual. The management leader must:

- Feel personally responsible for his resources – human, financial and material. (Feeling and caring: a sense of responsibility).
- Be active in setting direction and accepting the risks of leadership (being out in front).

Contd...

- Be able to articulate direction and objectives clearly and keep his people in the picture.
- Use the most appropriate behaviour and methods to gain commitment to achievement of specific objectives (leaders don't stick to one style).
- Maintain high standards of personal performance and demand high standards of performance from others.

In the context of teambuilding, knowing your own strengths and weaknesses will ensure that you compensate for what you lack. It is fatal to select people to work with you who are clones of yourself. You should deliberately choose individuals who have strengths, knowledge and experience which you do not possess in considerable measure. Humility in this sense is a leadership asset.

How to build a High performance Team?

How Teams are Built?

With a clear understanding of the features of a team and of the roles which may have to be filled within it, you are now better equipped to turn your group of subordinates into a cohesive, effective team. Probably the first place to start is with a hard look at the organization a structure.

You have to develop, as far as you can, structures that satisfy both the needs of the work and the requirements of team-groupings. This is often difficult in industries where people customarily work in large numbers without any identification in small work groups, such as production line work or large administrative offices. The problems are not only in how to divide the work, although this is a considerable task in itself. You may also have to overcome suspicion in the workforce and resentment by the shop-floor leaders, who have already created their own groupings — union interest groups rather than task groups. Rightly, they will see the motivational power of work teams as competition to that of their own groupings. Many managers also misunderstand the nature of team groupings. Applying the principles we outlined in the section on organisation of work, they may come up with an organisation chart that looks not unlike this:

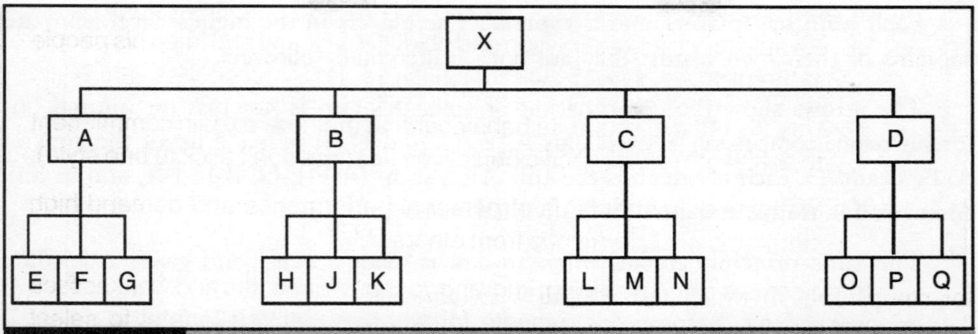

FIGURE 3.2 **Team Positioning Strategy**

Many a manager in this position sees this as one team rather than as four – and himself as having sixteen subordinates rather than being the leader of a team of five (the X-A-B-C-D) team. As a result he fails to create clearly differentiated responsibilities for his four subordinates and to delegate full authority to them. So they are not able to play effective leadership roles, and he is likely to play an 'external boss' role than that of a leader integrated with his team.

❖ Organising for Cooperation

Organisation charts serve a useful purpose by showing the formal relationship of jobs and responsibilities. What they do not necessarily create, however, is the sense of purposeful teamwork, without which the organisation structure remains sterile and lifeless. This can't be illustrated by means of a chart. The idea of organisation would be far better represented by a very different sort of picture – one which turns the impersonal structure of jobs into a series of teams, bound together by coordinated aims.

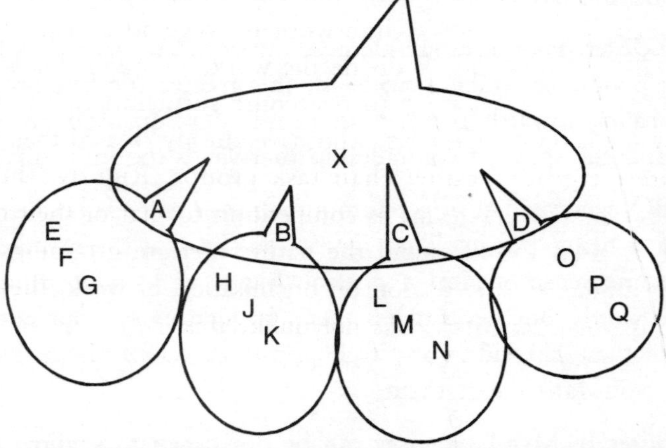

FIGURE 3.3 **Organisation of Team for Cooperation**

Each team has 'players' and a 'captain'. The players in the higher- level team are captains of their own teams: they are both leaders and followers.

The arrows show the coordination of aims. X's aim is not just for himself but for his team, comprising himself plus A, B, C, and D. It is made up of the aims of A, B, C and D, each of which is the aim of his team (A-E-F-G, B-H-J-K, and so on). Aims are for teams, not just for individual managers.

The same principle applies when an aim is made specific and given a deadline for completion, in which case we call it an objective.

❖ Joint Objective-setting

The concept of 'Management by Objectives', so popular only a few years ago, suggests that objectives are for individuals to achieve, by their own ability and wit. This, in fact, destroys a sense of leadership and team achievement. And it wasn't what the originator of the phrase meant by it at all.

For effective team building, objectives are objectives for the whole team. They have to be discussed within the team and jointly clarified and agreed. As leader, you play a prime role in doing this. But you recognise (and get your team to recognise) that the objectives are the team's, not just yours: you also get them to recognise that their objectives must interlock with the objectives of other teams in the organisation (both the lateral teams and the 'superior' team, of which you are one of the members).

The clearer your aims, better the start you have in working out where your priorities lie. How you can best use your time and other resources. Which particular skills and abilities you need to develop, what you need not concern yourself with. And similarly for your people, you may be efficient without clear, constructive aims, but you can't be effective.

The more closely your aims are identified with those personal skills and abilities you and your people can take a pride in, the greater the human stimulus they provide. In striving towards them, your people develop high morale, a sense of commitment and the spirit of comradeship that welds the individuals into a team.

Many MBO exercises fail to get commitment — perhaps because the objectives are thought of as being 'put in'. They ignore the fact that the members of the team already have some sense of aims – possibly vague and uncoordinated and never sharpened into words, but nevertheless there. In identifying your aims, you should try to draw out these hazy ideas and feelings and crystallize them. You realise what your aims are, you don't create them.

Other failures in MBO exercises can be put down to shallow thinking. The objectives given are unimaginative statements of the obvious — so obvious indeed that they serve little useful purpose in improving the way the job is run. (Anyway the obvious is often wrong: profit objectives for example. For anyone but a shareholder, profit is a convenient yardstick of progress, not the progress itself.) The act of thinking through the aims should give your team a better understanding of what their job is essentially about. The result should be a set of constructive ideas on improvement, and this must cost you some hard but stimulating mental effort. Good aims are never easy to realise in words.

Yet another reason for the failure of MBO — perhaps the key reason -is that the objectives are not thought of as the aims of people. Instead we have aims of 'positions', 'functions', or 'departments' – all obstructions. The reality is people. Ultimately an aim is a self-guidance mechanism in a human brain. If it is to influence human behaviour, it must become the personal property of the team members.

How to Maintain a High Performance Team?

Teams/Work groups can be divided into temporary and permanent. A temporary or ad hoc team or group is formed for a specific purpose and then disbands when that is accomplished. 'Task forces' and project groups belong to this category. A permanent or standing team continues in existence, with gaps in membership made up by new recruits. Committees can belong to either category.

- Why do we exist, what are we here for?
- What and who would be affected if we went out of existence?
- Are there more cost – effective ways our purpose and aim could be achieved than having this team?
- Has there been a significant change in our mission as a team?
- Have we perceived – or been given – new responsibilities?
- Are we still the right people to be tackling this work? Does it still need a team effort?

Remember that groups have a tendency to want to perpetuate themselves. The instinct for survival comes into play. We are here because we are here. Any move to disband the group can be perceived as a threat to unity. The desire for self-perpetuation regardless of task has taken over. The group has become a family, not a team.

Therefore, as leader you must reassure yourself (if not others) at intervals that there still is a real task for this group to perform and that it still requires the degree of teamwork you are seeking to build and maintain.

Maintaining Standards

Standards, you recall, are the group norms – usually unwritten – which largely determine the corporate behaviour of the group. There may be, for example, a high standard of attentiveness to each other in one group while in another you may notice that no one is listening to their neighbour or anyone else.

Standards are technical as well as interpersonal. Ideally, groups should set themselves, with some direction from their leader, standards of performance which they think they can attain. These should be neither too high nor too low, but sufficiently stretching or challenging to grip interest and – when achieved – to pay a dividend in a sense of achievement.

Over a period, however, two things can happen. First, the team's standards can slip. Idleness, indifference or that disease of success called complacency set in. These malaises introduce a general feeling of 'anything goes here'.

Secondly, the world outside the organisation changes. Standards in your given field or industry are constantly rising. What seemed to be high performance, high productivity or good sense to the customer ten years ago now seems mediocre judged from an impartial standpoint.

One first-aid remedy for declining standards is to generate a sense of competition. The fat and lazy manager entered for a marathon has some incentive to become lean and active. So it is with groups and organisations. The first step for you as leader is to bring home to the team that good though its performance is, it is no longer good enough. "Good enough for what?" asks the anxious team members. "Good enough to beat the competition", you reply.

Competition, you recall, deals with relative positions on a league table. But the true end of competing with others is not the transitory pleasures of winning. The true end of striving against competitors is to raise your standards against some absolute scale of value. That goal is summed up by the word 'excellence'. To compete means literally to seek something together. Actual competitions should be regarded as incentives, milestones, even games, but not the real object of the exercise.

It is not much good holding up absolute values like 'excellence' to a team with slipping standards. Your words will sound like 'motherhood' – abstract and banal. But tell the team or organisation where it stands in relation to the competition as factually as possible. Invite them to tell you why they are so low on the scale. Formulate with them some plans which will take you further up the leader within a given time.

CASE STUDY

Team Building

When Julian Pritchard became chief executive of Penleys Bank, it was like taking over a national institution. Penleys had been established in 1762. The Penley family provided a notable line of bankers until after the 1974 oil crisis. In the ensuing more difficult economic conditions, the Penleys and their friends on the board eventually found themselves presiding over declining profitability. For the first time the family bank, which prided itself on being a large family, had to declare redundancies. Pritchard was brought in from another more successful bank in 1984. "Look", he told his executive committee of directors, "we are in the middle of a revolution in the City of London, not to mention new competition from American and other foreign banks. At present Penleys is about third or fourth in the second division of merchant banks. My aim is to get it up into the first division within three years. That means that we have to raise our standards of technical performance, profitability and customer service. Could I have your views please?"

You can see what Pritchard is doing. He is using the language of the football league table to express in shorthand his resolve to transform the standards of Penleys Bank. In order to stand still, let alone to reach the top three places in the 'first division' of merchant banks, those standards have to be much higher. In the climate of modern banking, where tasks are increasingly complex and interrelated, that is going to require a higher quality of teamwork in Penleys between departments who have hitherto, seen themselves in separate boxes. Standards of presentation to potential clients will have to go up to the aftercare services of the backroom; technical and administrative staff need to be of a high order. It is vital that these people doing routine and relatively unexciting office functions feel themselves as much a part of the team as the 'star players' in Penleys corporate finance division. Julian Pritchard has a formidable leadership challenge in front of him. What do you think his next steps should be?

From this case study, you can see why I prefer the term teambuilding to team maintenance. If a human group resembled a machine, perhaps maintenance – replacing parts, oiling and greasing – would be the right word. You can maintain a machine or a house in its present state. But a leader is unlikely to be satisfied with any such present state. To repeat, you should never finish building your team. As a living entity, it is either growing or fading, never standing still. To maintain standards, you must aim for higher standards.

What are the Roles of Team Members for Effective Team Work?

Recent research has shown that members of a management team can contribute in two ways: in functional roles defined by their technical or professional abilities, and in team roles defined by the kind of contribution each member makes to the internal working of the team. It also appears that certain roles recur time and again in different teams. They seem to be necessary components of effective teamwork. These team roles define for each member his most effective way to contribute. Most people have a natural primary role, one they usually play in whatever teams they join. Many also have secondary roles they can play if these roles are not filled by other team members, or if their own primary role is more effectively filled by another member. In a small team they may play a combination of roles.

The role that each person finds it most natural to adopt will depend on a number of psychological traits: the degree to which he is introvert or extrovert, the degree to which he is calm or highly strung, the degree to which he is dominant or submissive, and his level of intelligence. Other aspects of the individual will also have an influence: his maturity, his instinct to trust or suspect others, his tolerance of uncertainty, and so on.

The long-term research project which has identified these team roles has been run at the Administrative Staff College at Henley by Dr. Melville Belbin. As his test-bed, he used teams formed during Henley courses to work on management exercises. He used psychometric tests to establish individual's traits and formed teams accordingly. The following are the eight most typical roles identified, under the titles Dr. Belbin gave them. Neither the roles nor the personal traits that go with them are rigid; no one will approximate closely to your 'preferred role' – the one in which you are most effective as a team member.

The 'chairman' is the team's natural leader – whether he is its formal head or not.

His concern is for purposeful, effective teamwork. He clarifies team aims and priorities and coordinates its resources to achieve external goals. He has a clear perception of members' strengths and limitations and focuses each on what he/she does best.

He establishes roles, work boundaries and communication channels, sees gaps and takes steps to fill them.

He tends to be extrovert and calm. He 'has character and integrity; possesses commonsense rather than a brilliant or creative intelligence; is dominant but not domineering. His natural authority is expressed in a relaxed unassertive way. He is trusting unless someone is proved untrustworthy, singularly free from jealousy, talks easily and is easy to talk to. In discussions he asks questions, listens and sums up group feelings or verdicts. He takes decisions firmly after all have had their say.

The 'shaper' is the team's action man and often its formal head.

His concern is for action and results. He shapes team effort towards specific task aims. In discussions, his compulsive drive is directed to objectives: he tries to unite ideas, needs and practical considerations into a single feasible project – which he pushes forward urgently to decision and action.

He tends to be extrovert and outgoing. Highly strung, nervily energetic, impulsive and impatient. He seems confident but is easily frustrated; only results reassure him. He is dominant, sees the team as an extension of his own ego; is competitive and quick to offer or accept a challenge. He may steamroller discussions. He is short-tempered but rows are quickly over without grudges. He is quick to sense a slight or suspect a conspiracy; intolerant of woolly thinking; may seem arrogant or abrasive. He can make the team uncomfortable, but he makes things happen.

The 'plant' is the team's idea man – the type to 'plant' in an ineffective team.

His concern is for major issues and fundamentals. He provides the most original suggestions and proposals, radical approaches to problems and obstacles and creative insights into existing lines of action. But he may miss detail or make careless mistakes. He can waste energy on irrelevancies and over-theoretical ideas.

He tends to be introvert, yet thrustful and uninhibited. Dominant and highly strung, he can be prickly if his ideas are criticised.

The most imaginative and intelligent member of the team, he criticizes other's ideas to clear the ground for his own counterproposals. He may do this tactlessly and cause offence. He may sulk if his own ideas are rejected. To get the best from him may require judicious flattery and careful handling – usually best provided by the 'Chairman'.

The 'resource investigator' is the team's contact man – its diplomat, salesman and liaison officer.

His concern is for exploring possibilities in the world outside. He keeps the team from stagnating or losing touch with reality. He lacks original ideas himself, but encourages innovation – is quick to see the relevance of new ideas. Within the team he is a good improviser, but he can waste time on irrelevancies that catch his fancy.

He tends to be extrovert, sociable, gregarious and dominant. He has an easily aroused interest. His response is enthusiastic but shortlived. He fails to follow through. The most active external communicator, he makes friends easily and has many contacts outside the team. He is in his office rarely – and then is probably on the phone. Without the stimulus of other people he becomes bored, demoralized, ineffective. Not someone for a solitary job.

The 'company worker' is the team's practical organizer.

His concern is for feasible action plans. He turns decisions and strategies into defined tasks that people can get on with. Give him a decision – he will make a schedule; give him a group of people – he'll make an organization chart. He needs settled plans with which to operate. He flounders in uncertain or rapidly changing situations.

He tends to be controlled and calm. He has 'character' integrity, and a disciplined approach, is not easily deflated or discouraged. He's efficient and methodical, but a bit inflexible. He is sincere and trusting towards others and will trim and adapt his schedules to fit agreed lines of action, but is unresponsive to ideas if not immediately practicable. He can be negative and unconstructive towards others' ideas, but is their best informant on what has been agreed and what each is to do.

The 'Finisher' is the team's checker lines and fulfiller of schedules.

His concern is for what might go wrong. He's never at ease unless he has personally checked every detail to ensure everything has been done, nothing overlooked. He's preoccupied with order, can get bogged down in detail and lose sight of objectives. His great asset to the team is his relentless follow-through.

He tends to be introvert, highly strung, anxious, obsessive and impatient. He has strength of character and self-control, low dominance and is rather unassertive. He keeps the team constantly aware of the need for urgency and attention to detail. He is intolerant of the more casual and slapdash members. This can be morale-lowering and depressing for the rest of the team.

The 'Monitor evaluator' is the team's judge – its most objective, un-involved member.

His concern is for cool, sound judgements. He provides dispassionate analysis, unclouded by ego-involvement, interpreting and evaluating large volumes of complex information; in analysing problems; in assessing others' contributions. He projects the team from committing itself to misguided projects or ideas. He likes time to mull things over.

He tends to be introvert and lack jollity, warmth, spontaneity. He has little enthusiasm or euphoria but is calm and dependable. He has a high IQ, but low drive, is unambitious. He has a serious and unexciting manner – a bit of a 'cold fish'. He may be fair-minded and open to change, but is often depressingly negative and unreceptive. He may be tactless and disparaging, and can lower team morale by damping at the wrong time.

The 'team worker' is the team's harmonizer – the 'cement' of the team.

His concern is for team unity and good spirit. He's aware of others' needs and worries, knows most about their private lives and family affairs, has the clearest perception of the emotional undercurrents in the team. Normally, his contribution isn't very visible. But when pressures threaten to disrupt the team, his loyalty, sympathy and support is invaluable.

He tends to be extrovert and calm. He has low dominance, is uncompetitive, soft and indecisive. He is the .most sensitive of member of the feelings of others. He is the most active internal communicator. Likeable, popular and unassertive, a good listener, he builds on others' ideas rather than producing his own rival ideas. He dislikes confrontation and tries to avoid or defuse it. He's loyal to the team as a unit and supportive to all its members.

From all this, Belbin concludes that the effectiveness of a team depends on how far its members recognize each others' abilities in specific team roles and adjust their own contributions to suit. Personal characteristics fit each member for some team roles, and make it less likely he will succeed in others. About 70% of people seem to be capable of playing an effective role in a team. The rest tend to perform as make-weights, or to be non-team people.

A team can deploy its members' technical or professional abilities to best effect only when its membership provides an appropriate balance of team roles. There is no single 'best' pattern of roles within a team. The ideal pattern differs from team to team, depending on the team's purpose and its environment. To create an effective team for a particular task, the required team roles have to be selected from a common inventory (i.e., the eight roles described), and the people who can play these roles have then to be drawn into the team. Most people's repertoire of roles can be extended through counselling and training.

This may be rather sophisticated stuff for the average middle manager or supervisor. Certainly, if you're managing a team of shop-floor operatives or clerical workers it has a limited application. However, apart from the fact that it's one of the most interesting pieces of new thinking about the human factors in management in recent years, it may be of value to you in recognising and fulfilling your role as a member of your management team, rather than as a leader. As you rise in the management hierarchy, this kind of thinking will become progressively more relevant and necessary.

ENGAGING EMPLOYEES: PRACTICES IN MICROSOFT

Microsoft India GTSC believes that employee engagement should revolve around a holistic value proposition and not just be limited to monetary benefits. The 'You & Microsoft' *Programme translates this belief into reality.*

Established in October 2003 in Bangalore, Microsoft India Global Technical Support Centre (GTSC) provides technical resolution services to global giant Microsoft's English speaking customers and partners across the globe. Microsoft GTSC is a part of a global network that supports millions of users and provides services customer segments.

Microsoft GTSC has developed a cohesive employee engagement programme termed "You & Microsoft "designed to connect employees psychologically and intellectually to the organization. Explaining the essence of the programme, Manish Sinha, Managing Director, Asia Pacific and India, customer service and support, Microsoft Corporation says, "We believe that organizational strategies and initiatives that fuel employee engagement should revolve around a holistic value proposition and not just be limited to compensation and monetary benefits. Our approach to building this engagement entails aligning the employee with the organizational culture and vision while recognizing and respecting his socio-cultural background and enabling him to blend in with the organization."

'You & Microsoft' programme is based on the premise that employee motivation is a function of multiple factors that go far beyond just tangible benefits. Microsoft India GTSC has identified eight critical needs that employees value and has integrated these in its programme to ensure that employees are satisfied with their work and with the organization.

Making a difference through work: Understanding the impact of employees' work and constantly asking the question whether they are making a difference through their work, accountability for the work that is done and rewarding their performance at work are critical elements of this. GTSC engineers receive appreciation e-mails from CIOs or eros of large enterprises when they successfully solve a problem.

Recognition: This comprises of both monetary and non-monetary rewards. Most of the time, it is the non-monetary aspect that is more impactful and will give an immense boost to the employees confidence when he or she is felicitated in a team meeting for his achievements. For example, the India GTSC organizes the ACE Awards (Architects of Excellence), which is given to individual engineers and teams, who go the extra mile to facilitate optimal use of Microsoft technology and drive customer satisfaction. Every quarter at MS India GTSC, all the people who have made a huge impact are brought together; this is about 70 - 80 people. An external speaker is brought to speak about experiences that have motivated them. The employees spend time with the speaker and their achievements are recognized.

Career growth: Microsoft GTSC employees are provided with avenues to grow within the organization, few regions outside the US to have all six business divisions, research, development, testing, consulting, sales and marketing and support. So If an employee is interested in pursuing research, he can move to Microsoft research, for development, the employee can move to Microsoft IDC. There are also additional technical roles within GTSC such as escalation engineers, technical leads. Additionally, mentoring is an extremely beneficial tool in deciding career path and provides employees with exposure to multiple parts of the business. GTSC engineers are mentored by senior employees within Microsoft, across the globe any line of work.

Fun: At Microsoft India GTSC, having fun while working on cutting edge technologies is a critical element. Events such as sports day, adventure tours, family days are organized at regular intervals for Microsoft India GTSC employees.

Environment: Excellent facilities and infrastructure are provided to employees ensuring productivity at work. Microsoft India GTSC in Bangalore has a high tech Xbox room, which has been set up to provide employees with a 24/7 virtual recreational space. Quiet room dorms are also provided for employees to relax during the course of the day. A flexible and relaxed dress code is in place to ensure that employees are comfortable at work. At Microsoft India GTSC, employees are part of interest groups such as cricket groups, dance groups etc. to enable their all-round development. All employees at Microsoft India GTSC actively participate in Corporate Social Responsibility (CSR) initiatives that provide them with opportunities to work closely with the underserved communities in India. For example, the Dream a Dream programme that recently concluded had active participation from GTSC employees. A painting competition was organized for underprivileged children at the GTSC campus. These paintings were then bought by Microsoft India GTSC and now adorn the walls of the GTSC office.

Care: Employees of Microsoft GTSC are provided with many benefits, an example that the company cares for their well-being. The medical benefits provided to every employee of Microsoft India GTSC are designed to keep employees healthy, happy, and moving ahead at optimal speed. Employee assistance programmes such as tuition assistance are open to all employees of Microsoft GTSC. Employees are given the opportunity to pursue higher education while working. Microsoft also supports employees by helping them with their tuition fees.

Technology: Engineers at Microsoft India GTSC have the opportunity to work on the latest cutting edge technologies. An example of this is that, about 50 percent of GTSC engineers were trained to work on SQL Server 2005 much before its launch in the market. Engineers at Microsoft India GTSC are given the opportunity to work closely with product development teams in Redmond, thereby helping in innovating and creating new products. These engineers are also actively involved in beta support projects to understand and anticipate the support environment for customers, for the latest technologies and products that are launched at Microsoft.

Money: Other than pay packages which are one of the best in the industry, flexible pay is available to all employees. Regular industry mapping of compensation ensures that the compensation packages are in line with industry standards.

By devoting equal attention to all elements holding significance for employees, Microsoft India GTSC has succeeded in demonstrating that sometimes money just ain't enough!

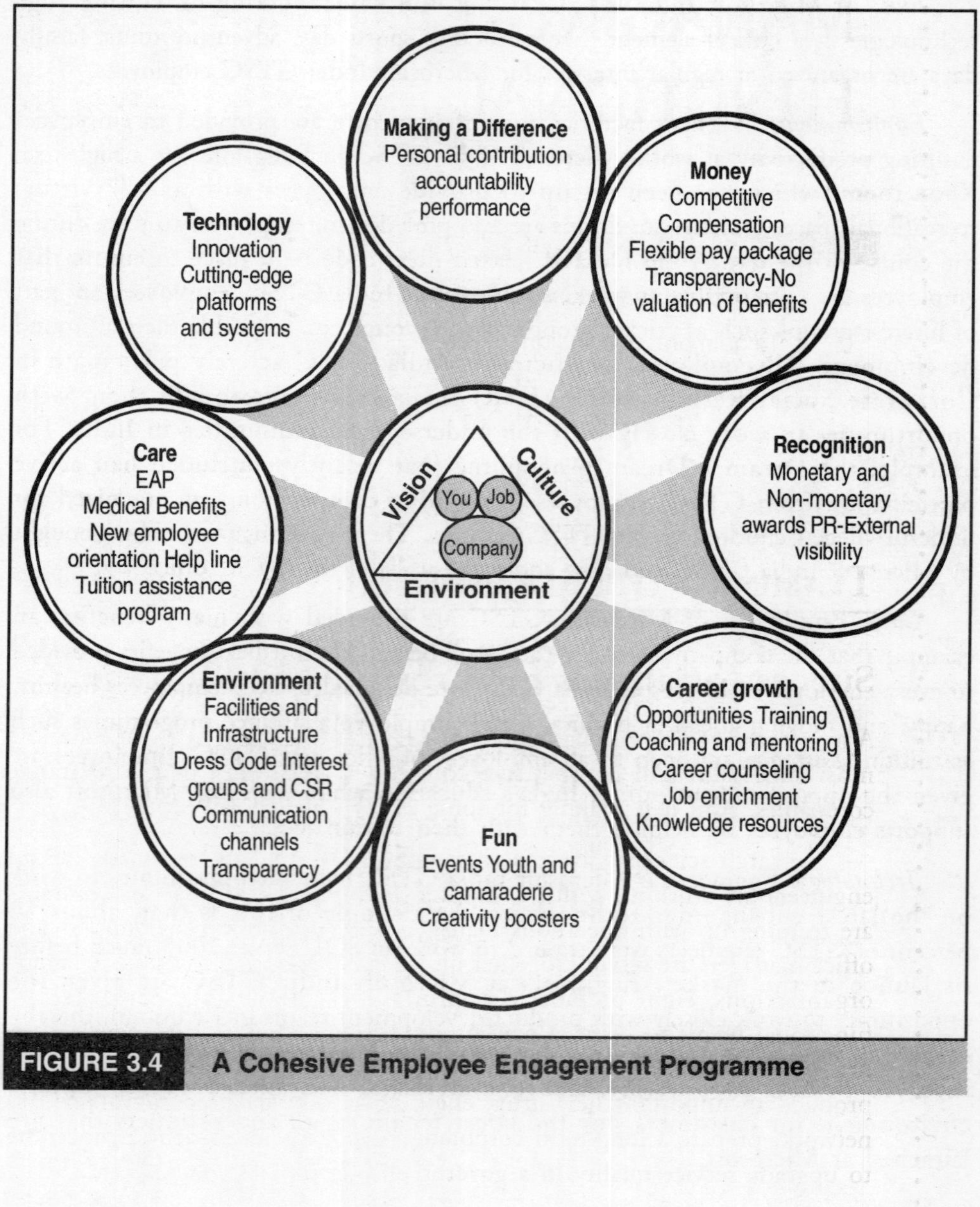

FIGURE 3.4 **A Cohesive Employee Engagement Programme**

CHAPTER 4

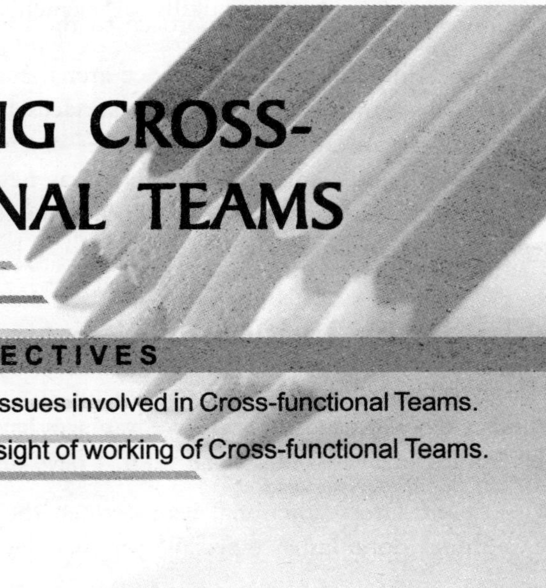

MANAGING CROSS-FUNCTIONAL TEAMS

LEARNING OBJECTIVES

- To understand the issues involved in Cross-functional Teams.
- To gain practical insight of working of Cross-functional Teams.

TEAMING WITH STRANGERS

Success Strategies for Cross-functional Teams

A new form of teamwork has quietly become a key factor in many of America's most successful and competitive companies, including many insurance companies. And it is making for some strange bedfellows.

Research scientists are meeting with marketing professionals; design engineers are working with purchasing department staff; cost accountants are teaming up with operations managers; and computer programmers and office managers are serving together on systems development teams. In many organizations, eight or more disciplines are working together on cross-functional teams to bring a new product to the marketplace, develop the next generation computer system, design a new layout for a factory floor, produce an important new drug, engineer a complex telecommunications network, prepare a long-term corporate strategy, or implement a procedure to upgrade service quality in a government agency.

In some property and casualty insurance companies, the functional silos have given away to cross-functional account teams that consist of home office and field personnel such as underwriters, account claim executives, account engineering executives and people with skills in pricing, billing, credit and customer service. The outcome is a seamless approach to the total customer relationship.

In the life and health insurance arena, some companies have reorganized the field sales support or policyholder services functions into a team-based, cross-functional organization. In essence, this means going from a service mode where one person handles one function, such as new applications, to a team approach where every team member can handle any request. Once again, the field sales representative or direct customer is the focal point of the collaborative process.

Why is the Industry Using Cross-functional Teams?

Effective cross-functional teams have many advantages. While some of the pluses apply to other types of teams, too, these advantages have a unique flavor when played out in the context of a cross-functional team. I have found six competitive advantages.

- ***Speed:*** Cross-functional teams, when they are appropriately empowered, get things done faster, especially product development and customer service.
- ***Complexity:*** Cross-functional teams improve an organization's ability to solve complex problems because they bring together people with different skill sets, experiences, perceptions and styles.
- ***Creativity:*** New product and service breakthroughs come from the clash of ideas, not from interactions among people with similar views.
- ***Customer focus.*** Cross-functional teams focus all of the organization's efforts on satisfying a specific internal or external customer or group of customers.
- ***Organizational learning:*** Team members pick up technical and professional skills more easily, gain important knowledge about other areas of the organization and learn how to work with people with different styles and cultural backgrounds.
- ***Single point of contact:*** The team promotes more effective and efficient teaming by identifying one place to go for information and decisions about a project or customer.

Success Strategies

On the face of it, cross-functional teams look like a great idea. Just get together a group of people from different parts of the organization, sit them down in a room and good things will happen. Not! There are some obstacles that must be addressed if the benefits of cross-functional teaming are to be realized in your organization.

- ***The team leader must have both technical and process skills:*** The leader must have the technical background to understand the subject of the team's work and to recognize the potential contributions of people from a wide variety of backgrounds. The leader must also have the interpersonal skills to facilitate a diverse group of people with little, no or even negative experiences in working together.
- ***The team must be empowered to act decisively:*** The senior management sponsors of the team must clarify the limits of authority available to the team. I recommend that the sponsor provide the vision, overarching goal or general set of expectations which the team, in turn, translates into specific objectives and a detailed plan. Once the objectives and plan are approved by the sponsor, the team should be empowered "to do whatever it takes to accomplish the objectives and implement the plan."
- ***Team objectives should be clear and specific:*** If there is one thing everyone is clear about, it is that successful, high performing teams have clear performance objectives and unsuccessful teams do not. Objectives are the "scoreboard" against which teams measure their progress and objectives are the "unifying force" that brings together the diverse members and stakeholders represented on a cross-functional team.
- ***Cross-functional teams need positive relationships with key stakeholders:*** Senior management, functional department heads, support groups, suppliers, customers and regulatory bodies (e.g., insurance commissions) are among the key people who can provide either pathways or barriers for a cross-functional team. "No team is an island" and, therefore, building effective external relationship is a critical success factor.
- ***Team members want "credit" for their performance on the team:*** Companies need to examine their performance management system to see whether team behaviours are taken into account and department heads incorporate team member performance data into their appraisals. Some department managers ask team leaders to complete the performance appraisal form for the people who serve on that team while other companies are experimenting with a team member peer review process.
- ***Companies should consider project team rewards and member recognition:*** In a team-based organization, companies need to develop a programme that rewards a team if it achieves a preannounced objective (e.g., bring a new product to the market by a certain date; increase customer satisfaction by X%). Individual recognition should go to people who are effective team players—people who

increase the effectiveness of the team by doing such things as sharing their expertise, pitching in when needed, facilitating meetings and asking the tough, but necessary questions.

- *Cross-functional teams should be small:* Many organizations make the mistake of including everyone with some connection to the task. As a result, cross-functional teams are often too large to be effective. We know, and many studies in group psychology confirm, that when a team gets too large, communications and productivity suffer because members feel less accountable and, as a result, their participation decreases. The ideal team has four to seven members—certainly no more than 10 members. If your team is too large, consider simply decreasing the membership, using a core team to make the key decisions or creating small task teams to do the bulk of the work.
- *Positive interpersonal relationships are essential:* The diverse nature of cross-functional teams usually means that lack of trust, poor interpersonal relationship and conflict are endemic. Therefore, it is important that the organization provide training and consulting designed to develop positive norms, conflict resolution tools, consensus building techniques and an appreciation of diverse team player styles.
- *Management must support the team process:* All the good work to create, develop and train teams can be sabotaged by key management stakeholders who do not cooperate or worse, undermine the team process. The senior management team and team sponsors must:
    - provide resources such as time, training, funds, people and equipment,
    - "talk and walk" teamwork in everything they do,
    - recognize and reward teams and team players,
    - communicate a set of expectations or overarching goals to the team,
    - break down barriers such as old paradigms and procedures and
    - model teamwork by participating in team building and operating as an effective team.
- *Front-end training is a real plus:* I recommend a kick-off launch session followed quickly by at least two days of basic team training. The launch meeting should include the team sponsor who presents management's expectations or goals and addresses all concerns and questions about the team process. The start-up training addresses such areas as team player skills, establishing norms, meetings management, external relationships and communications.

The insurance industry is making use of cross-functional teams to manage accounts, develop new products and provide customer service. The key to success is to eliminate the barriers by providing the training, consulting and other supports that maximize the benefits.

READ THE PULSE OF INDIAN CORPORATES ON CROSS-FUNCTIONAL TEAMS

Conventional teams – static, steady, intact, long-term, bound by geographies and shared functions. Not any more. With boundaries of and time fading into oblivion, the meaning and purpose of teaming in the business setting has evolved beyond imagination. So we have traditional teams rewrapped and reborn in contemporary avatars – the distributed, the global, the virtual and the cross-functional!

Cross-functional teams have always evinced interest because of their special composition. A group of co-workers, handpicked from varied functions, locations, levels, skills and backgrounds, and thrown together as a multihued mishmash. The agenda: a short-term project or assignment that requires a mixed bag of knowledge, skills, experience and expertise or solution to a problem that impacts on multiple parts of the organization, perhaps an improved work process, a product launch or a company-wide technology initiative.

Why Cross-functional Teams?

Traditionally, people have been accustomed to being responsible for their own results and their own people, functions, departments or business units. But now, organizations are trying to instill into teams the importance of seeing the bigger picture and fitting into it. Even research affirms that it is more important for an organization to be cross-functionally excellent than functionally excellent. There is enough evidence to prove that cross-functional teams lead towards path-breaking organizational change and innovation.

Cross-functional teams are not new to the corporate world. Examples abound in traditional and function-based organizations, including several manufacturing and automobile companies. The reason, shares Varda Pendse, Director, Cerebrus Consultants, is that typically in these organizations, each function operates in silos and the interdependence between each needs to be emphasized through external team formation. However, as modern organizations become process driven, flat and with matrix reporting structures, cross-functional teams are becoming part and parcel of the work culture and are not formed separately. "The cross-functional approach to problem solving and implementation is an ongoing process. In such organizations, the emphasis is on identifying the process, rather than the mere formation of a team", she explains.

The success of cross-functional teams in manufacturing set-ups offers learning points for the fast changing, competitive and cost conscious companies of today. As Pendse says, today many organizations prefer to use cross-functional teams or 'crack teams' for key initiatives. Such teams ensures that all interests are represented and views shared to ensure that there is limited scope for failure and high probability of ensuring that the cross-functional team is able to achieve its objective. Even for HR initiatives like performance management or career planning or competency building, organizations often form cross-functional teams to ensure effective implementation. The cross-functional teams are formed right at the design or feasibility stage itself to ensure that the buy-in exists for effective implementation.

Gautam Ghosh, training development specialist at Hewlett Packard Services, Bangalore is of the opinion that businesses are increasingly facing problems that are not pliable to 'simple' solutions. One factor, according to him is that businesses themselves see opportunities not in silos but in systems thinking. So a recruitment advertisement, is not just a recruitment advertisement anymore, it is also an opportunity to build the organization's brand! Therefore, it becomes imperative for the recruitment team to link up with the branding or marketing team and the corporate communications team. "Going forward, we will see a whole lot of cross-functional work being done by people," Ghosh predicts. Many agree that most critical problems in business are rarely just functional in nature – they are all cross-functional. "Given that most delays and bottlenecks in organization's responses happen at the functional boundaries, a cross-functional way of working definitely has its advantages," feels Professor Madhukar Shukla, XLRI Jamshedpur.

Escotel Mobile Communications is a good case in point. The company saved 25 crores in 2002-03 with the support of various cross-functional initiatives across functions and levels. Escotel believes that cross-functional teams reduce stress level in the organization, people enjoy getting things done, and are able to learn beyond their limited circles of influence. A feeling of commandership gets internalized in the company, making the culture participative, conducive to new thinking, innovations without inhibitions.

Rajan Dutta, Chief of HR and TQM, Escotel, feels that in today's fierce competitive business scenario, where the customer is not willing to pay for delays, gaps, and rework in an organization, cross-functional team functioning has become a mandate. "Cross-functional teams are no more limited to project work. The focus is on building innovation, creativity and value in the products and services, as well as evolving flawless, cost effective, timely and customer focused outputs. Every back-end process like recruitment, MIS, financial process and project management demands cross-functional thinking and functioning. I have had experience of cross-functional teams working in the areas of employees satisfaction, sales and marketing, technology, and customers are issues. The power of group work or team think-tank has been enormous, as these teams have come up with great ideas and recommendations and in some situations, excellent example of excellence in execution," he says.

Adds S. Ramesh Shankar, general manager, corporate human resources, Eicher Goodearth Ltd. "Cross-functional teams enable the organization to cut across the functional levels and look at issues in a holistic manner. They enable business solutions at a faster speed and make the organization flexible and agile to customer needs. They also enable the organization to conceptualize and deliver products faster and much closer to what the customer wants. They help in breaking hierarchy, bureaucracy and non-value added paperwork within the organization, and this is a very important new product development process."

Productivity and the bottom line... sure! But the icing on the cake is the special feeling of glory that comes with part of a 'chosen one' on a critical project. As Pendse puts it, "Membership to such teams is a corporate signal to the employee that he is being viewed as a 'hi-pot' or 'star' and his participation in the team is just another way of building competencies in cross-functional appreciation and business acumen." This in itself acts as a strong motivator for members and pushes them to work together and ensure achievement of the team objective.

❖ The Right Mix for Right Impact

- Select members with perfect mix of skills and expertise required for the project.
- Clarify the common aims and objectives that the team has to achieve.
- Identify the distinct roles and responsibilities of each team member.
- Use knowledge of entire team to determine strategies and solutions.
- Determine specific time lines and action plans needed to reach the goal.
- Train team members in team skills like communicating, listening, and facilitating.
- Periodically evaluate the functioning of the team and monitor effectiveness.

Tackling the Softer Issues

Managing teams is no cakewalk... especially when it comes to cross-functional teams. Tackling individual egos; breaking functional blocks in thinking and action; enabling people to work in teams to which they do not naturally belong; and growing beyond boundaries... the human angles are complex and varied.

One key concern, as Shukla says, is the ability of people to work together. "Unlike typically structured departmental teams, here the members would bring in different lenses to view the problem and different language to talk about it. The understanding and approach of a finance person to the problem would necessarily be different than how a sales professional would view it. For instance, one may look at the bottomline implications, while the other may focus on market share," he explains. While such diversity has the advantage of creating a more holistic understanding of the issues, it also places greater demand for adjustments on the members.

Functional and departmental pulls are another factor worth considering, Dutta points out. "At times, functional heads feel as if they are losing power if people from other functions start revising, making suggestions, taking actions under their circle of influence." Yet another critical aspect relates to the question of 'what is in it for me'... in other words, expectations of the team members with respect to their extra efforts and contributions. Also, cross-functional teams feel they are only a recommendatory body and do not have the power to implement. This makes them apprehensive of their ideas getting implemented. The challenge, Dutta stresses, is to keep cross-functional team continuously excited, focused and motivated to a goal, as their primary functional areas are different.

Another typical blocking experience – the ability of the team leader to manage the conflicts within the team and to convey with effectiveness to the senior management, the views of the team.

"When the team leader is perceived to be ineffective, the team members operate on cross-purposes. This is a surefire method to guarantee that the team will not meet its objective," Pendse cautions.

According to Ghosh, the issues with cross-functional teams are that the barriers are built over time. "We study in MBA that the functions are 'silos' but the reality does not sink in for a long time. We continue looking at imaginary barriers like 'us' and 'them' and I think that a 'silo mentality' is the greatest barrier to the success of a cross-functional team. Throw in the complexity of people working from across cultures in a globalized world under stringent deadlines – the challenges could not be greater," he says.

Success at Hand

So what makes all the pieces fit in neatly? Experts outline four key ingredients for success of cross-functional teams. To begin with, it is important to establish common goals, objectives and outcomes for the team. Then comes clarity of roles of individual team members and clear commitment by each team member to those goals. And finally, nothing to beat a well-defined measurement process to determine quantum and quality of success.

And naturally enough, the barriers to cross-functional team success are: unclear and frequently changing objectives, lack of management support for the team's assignment, and ambiguous roles of team members. The most effective cross-functional teams have committed team leaders who realize the role of constantly reinforcing and clarifying the goal and mission of the group. Pendse confirms that the success and effectiveness of a cross-functional team's performance is driven by the organizational culture, effectiveness of the team leader, the creditability of the team members and the support provided by the senior management to the team members. Absence of any of these impacts the effectiveness of the team and its performance. "Typically, after the cross-functional team is formed, one finds that the members do not find time to attend the meetings either due to lack of personal initiative or support from the bosses. Another typical experience is the ability of the team leader to manage the conflicts within the team as also to convey with effectiveness to the senior management the views of the team. If the team leader is perceived to be ineffective, the team members operate on cross-purposes and thereby ensuring that the cross-functional team will surely not meet its objective.

Often organizations make a mistake of taking teaming and team skills for granted. Bunching a group of unfamiliar faces and expecting them to naturally slide into synergy is unrealistic. The experience can actually be unnerving for some. This is where team leader's expertise comes into play. By creating a safe environment where one can raise issues of differences, he can facilitate conflict resolution before things get out of hand. While team results take the top slot, the leader also needs to recognize individual differences and contributions. Team members may have different levels of education, work experience, skills, approaches and perspectives, and each may add value to the project in his special way.

Whatever be the nature of the project, the success of the cross-functional team is ultimately measured by one basic fact... was the goal achieved? A simple, effective tool to ensure goal achievement is to organize periodic, brief meetings where the team members can brainstorm introspect and deliberate on the progress of the project... and this is especially useful in the case of slow-moving, long-term projects. Pendse recommends that the performance of the cross-functional team be reviewed and monitored on a regular basis at a managerial level and corrective action taken at the right time. She also suggests that the team must identify an owner. "After the successful accomplishment of their objective, it is important that the team needs to be felicitated and rewarded publicly. "As the cross-functional approach matures within the company, the reward and recognition programme must be built into the performance management and reward and recognition system. This will ensure that employees perceive the cross-functional as a way of working and aspire to work harmoniously and efficiently 'with passion' is offered a membership in such a team," she explains.

Dutta's preferred approach: create forums where small groups, entities and network get established around themes and objectives, solve problems, generate possible solutions or recommendations and implement them. The advantage: each team member gets an opportunity to learn, contribute and get rewarded and recognized. In this process, the company also benefits substantially.

Positive strokes go a long way, insist behavioural scientists and team performance experts agree. Celebrating small successes reaffirms what the cross-functional group is supposed to be doing, and gives specific indications of desired progress. Even seemingly insignificant gestures of appreciation can act as powerful tools to communicate mission, purpose and desired behaviours.

Many organizations have found that symbols of team identity like T-shirts and caps with inscribed team logos make a world of difference in boosting team morale. It's easy to understand why. Such symbols make a public statement of the team's shared purpose, and to some extent, push members towards achievement.

Two factors which enhance the cross-functional way of working, according to Shukla are: making the team accountable to a team goal; sometimes, even linking the variable rewards to the accomplishment of the team, and secondly, training of members not just in team skills but also in developing business perspective. "It is important to appreciate that teams are relationships, not systems. Systems can be implemented, while relationships develop over time", he affirms. Shukla believes that many organizations try to 'implement' cross-functional teams, which invariably results in failure to achieve desired results. "Just as it happens in any relationship, it takes time for people to warm-up to each other, to appreciate each other's viewpoint, and to develop a mutual understanding and respect. This process can be accelerated, but can't be ignored", he adds.

Steps to managing CFTs are as follows:

1. Ensure that each individual team member's talent and contributions are publicly recognized.
2. Keep team members consistently focused on the goals, while ensuring clarity and awareness of the measurement criteria.
3. Facilitate sensitivity to individual differences, but also emphasize interdependence and cooperation among the team members.
4. Build in elements of empowerment and allow decision making so that the team can be truly accountable for its results.
5. Help the team realize that they are an instrument to ongoing change and improvement in the organization.

A Way of Life

"Cross-functional teams should become a way of life in organizations," says Ramesh Shankar, "but organizations must ensure that they don't turn into routine, lifeless systems that lose their sheen with time. His advice: build process based organization structures to facilitate Cross-functional teams; create small teams for specific issues; break teams as soon as the issue is resolved (they should not last for more than three to five months); rotate members to create cross-functional mindset; enable members to play leadership roles by rotation.

Cross-functional teams are also more likely to be successful if a cross-functional culture is nurtured and bred within the organization. As Shukla puts it, "It would be difficult for people to adjust to demands of working with people from other functions, if they don't feel comfortable with them, and respect their contributions. Creating such a culture is a key role for human resources." The essential systems of job rotation and cross-functional informal interactions, which will provide the foundations and prepare people to work a cross-functional boundaries.

Pendse stresses that when cross-functional teams are introduced for the first time in an organization, training needs to be provided on team working, managing cross-functional teams and managing conflicts to the members. On an ongoing basis, typically, companies would then need to then train their employees on cross-functional teams as a work culture. "If the concept of cross-functional teams has to be kept alive as part and parcel of work culture then it is essential that it be woven in the fibre of all HR initiatives across all levels. In organizations where cross-functional teams are part of work culture, the competency of ability to work effectively in a cross-functional team is captured in the performance management system, succession planning, training need identification, or leadership development etc.," she shares.

As they say, two heads are most certainly better than one. Imagine the unending possibilities when multiple and diverse approaches come together to solve a problem. Truly, cross-functional teaming can work magic in the corporate setting, provided it has the right foundations, well-designed systems of ongoing support and a rewarding environment that nurtures and helps it flourish and achieve determined results. As Dutta rightly concludes, "Human beings have tremendous capacity to think and ideas have no individual proprietorship. In today's competitive business world, only those corporations will prosper which are able to manage and effectively implement human ideas."

❖ Challenges Abound

- Managing across geographical **distances** and time zones.
- Defining **norms** for the team appropriate to its determined mission.

- Inadequate **flow** of information and communication.
- Lack of **commitment** from top management and senior leaders.
- Inadequate HR systems and processes for **rewarding** team behaviour.
- Ambiguity, **boundarylessness** and lack of structure.
- Awareness and sensitivity to **cultural** differences.

CHAPTER

5

MANAGING DIVERSE AND VIRTUAL TEAMS

LEARNING OBJECTIVES

- To understand the issues involved in teams with Diversity and Virtual Teams.
- To gain a global perspective to Diverse and Virtual Teams.

Managing Teams with Diversity

We just didn't connect at all. I got my sales pitch ready based on the little bit I knew about the buyer. It was a woman in a Turkish company and I convinced myself I knew what was needed. A Turkish company? I thought 'low-tech, not very sophisticated'. A woman buyer? I thought 'she'll be focused on our customer service, not much interested in technology'. I only got through the first minute or two of the sales pitch before she stopped me and said "look, what I really need to know is what's different about your technical solution and what makes it the best fit with our needs". As I quickly discovered – all my assumptions were wrong and so was the sales pitch. The buyer was a leader in research and development and the company was putting together really sophisticated technical solutions for their own clients. The whole thing was a disaster. She wasn't convinced that we had good enough technology and looking back, I think she felt insulted by my approach.

Not long ago, I was told this story by a rather humbled salesman. It illustrated how easily our assumptions about different individuals, cultures or organizations can stop us creating effective and profitable connections. This is a powerful, business-focused way to look at diversity.

❖ What Connections Deliver to a Business?

It is through effective connections that we respond to the needs of diverse customers, attract recruits in the face of fierce competition, motivate and retain different employees, form joint ventures which deliver value, source and lead successful teams, leverage information and talent globally, and move into new host communities easily and confidently.

All these outcomes (and many more) rely on interactions between individuals, teams or organizations. Every connection is unique. Not only because the purpose may be different but also because of the diversity (differences) among those who need to be connected. Businesses that excel in connecting diverse stakeholders will have a sharp competitive edge. This level of performance will not be achieved without considering the powerful effects which differences among stakeholders can have.

A Working Definition of Diversity

Diversity has often been seen as a US-only issue, driven by concerns about legal compliance and focused on gender and race. Many leading global organizations are now using a far broader definition of diversity. They recognize that all kinds of individual, cultural or organizational differences affect the connections that deliver their business results. This is true wherever they operate. For them, managing diversity is not an optional aspect of business leadership – it is an everyday requirement.

Examples of the kinds of difference that need to be considered are:

Individual – gender, thinking style, role preference, experience, education

Cultural – how conflict is managed, different traditions and customs, the nature of business relationships, time management

Organizational – how people are rewarded and for what, decision-making processes, whether and how authority is delegated.

Bringing together diversity of particular kinds can help generate better solutions and increase capabilities in a business. Differences can also create barriers between individuals, teams and organizations. With two sides to the diversity story, we begin to see the management of diversity as a drive to optimize the impact of differences.

We are discussing some practical examples of business impact. Diversity is impacting business processes in every industry sector. Some situations are more sensitive to differences than others, is impacting but the impact is always there.

A few illustrative examples are shown below. This is by no means an exhaustive list, providing customer service: To provide effective after sales support for global customers, we need to consider differences in language, physical ability, location and time zone, cultural norms, access to technology, communication preferences and so on. Failure to assess and respond to these differences excludes some of the customer base from effective support.

Such exclusion can be costly and here is one example. Experts estimate that there/at/least 600 million people with disabilities worldwide. Perhaps as many as 1 in 3 people either have a disability or are close to someone who has. Surveys in some markets show that this group prefers to spend with companies providing good service to people with disabilities. Are you confident that you understand the issues of customers and employees with disabilities? Are you connecting effectively with them? Delivering innovative products and services, innovation as a business process is highly dependent on creating connections between individuals and/or organizations. But the formula for using connections and ideas to deliver innovative products and services is complex. Both diversity and inclusion have potentially high impact. This is true in every facet of the process from identifying client needs, through developing potential solutions and ultimately delivering a valuable innovation. One of/many examples is highlighted below.

Diversity in teams of problem solvers provides opportunities for breakthrough thinking. However, the potential benefits of such diversity are untapped if we lack the inclusive attitudes and practices to combine them. A study of corporate R&D teams showed performance (patents and products developed) was improved by diversity among the members. In this case, the diversity with impact was the length of time people had worked for the company. The positive impact was only seen when inclusive practices enabled the sharing of ideas among the 'generations' of researchers.

Leaders of Innovation can ask some simple strategic questions about diversity and inclusion. Who in my organization has the inclusive mindset and behaviours to excel at listening to potential customers, whoever they are? What kinds of diversity might contribute most to finding potential solutions to this need? How do we tap into that diversity, wherever it is and avoid the "not invented here" syndrome? How do we create an inclusive culture that really optimizes the flow and active consideration of different ideas?

Building productive teams: When surveying groups about how frequently diversity can cause 'broken' connections within their teams, I have found up to 60% answering "at least once a week". Diversity will only create these barriers to productivity when it is poorly understood and managed. This is an avoidable waste of productive time. Helping people identify and bridge their own, often hidden, differences is a good practice when new teams are formed.

An inclusive, unifying culture is also crucial and as part of that, I encourage people to think about the role of trust and the giving and receiving of feedback. How often have your behaviours been perceived as exclusive or disrespectful by other people when you never intended that to be the case? It happens a lot. Unless teams have a culture of trust where it is safe to provide feedback, patterns of exclusive behaviour persist. The impact on connections among peers and their productivity can be severe, even more so if the exclusive behaviours are demonstrated by the team leader.

Building Market Share in Diverse Customer Segments

Winning and serving diverse customers is a strong and obvious reason to develop diversity strategies and to build diversity in an organization.

Why should customers choose to connect with you rather than the competition? Creating a brand strategy which connects each potentially important customer groups to a business is highly dependent on understanding diversity of needs and ambitions. In India, this creates an interesting opportunity. Many organizations have relatively few women in their marketing and sales functions. Employers who can change this picture and utilise the life experiences and perspectives of more women should be able to deliver products and services more attractive to women customers.

In Europe and the US, financial service providers are continuing to develop products and service offerings aimed specifically at women. One key driver is the high number of small and medium-sized enterprises started by women. Becoming "the bank of choice" for these entrepreneurs is a highly attractive business opportunity. There are many other countries, including India, where this focus on women entrepreneurs could also be profitable. What are the ways in which an organization can position itself to capture that market? Attracting and retaining talent – competition for talent is ferocious in countries like India and China. Attrition rates for many employers are high, adding costs in terms of talent replacement, loss of experience and potential impact on business continuity. How do organizations get connected to the talent they need and maintain those connections?

In India, for example, it is clear that companies can connect to a substantial pool of female talent if they have the right mindset and practices to make it work.

Some enduring stereotypes impact women, which limit their potential contribution to the success of organizations in India, particularly larger ones. Progressive employers are making their working arrangements more attractive to certain groups of women. Part time working, flexible work schedules and telecommuting are all practices being used to lure experienced women back to work after they have had children.

In a talent-limited market, employers need to understand the differing needs and ambitions of each important pool of talent and be able to respond flexibly. What connects a company to its traditional workforce may not be effective with other groups. What talent pools do you need to connect with and what will that take?

Forming Joint Ventures that Work

For many Western multinationals, joint venture (JV) formation has been an essential part of gaining access to resources and markets in places like China, the Middle East and Russia. Now, an increasing number of JVs are being driven by the growth strategies of companies headquartered in India, China and other capital-rich countries.

Connecting people from different organizations for sustained, profitable JV activity is challenging. Differences in national and organizational cultures will impact how effectively people come together to build a new unit. Even within the same industry sector, companies have radically different cultures and common practices. One simple example is performance management processes. The venture partners may value different competencies and behaviours. Who ensures that the performance criteria selected for the JV will be understood and considered fair by all employees? Will the choices made motivate and retain all the key talent required by the JV? Good practice organizations are investing more time in the early stages of JV formation to do two things:

- Map out the differences which could have greatest impact and put in place mechanisms by which they are discussed and managed.
- Create an identity and expectations for the JV with the power to unify employees across the differences they bring with them.

Inclusive Leaders are the Key to Success

Leaders can optimize the impact of diversity in an organization. They do this by adopting an inclusive approach. They need to act both as a strategist and a role model. Inclusive leaders can start integrating diversity into their business thinking simply by asking good questions.

- What connections are most important to delivering success in this business?
- Externally (customers, communities, recruits, partners)
- Internally (employees, team members, business segments, functions)
- How might those connections be affected by diversity or exclusive attitudes? What kinds of difference will potentially be the most helpful or perhaps create the biggest barriers?

- What is the actual impact of diversity today versus what it could I should be in terms of Positive contributions to the business?
- Barriers to business performance, individual contribution, team cohesion or employee satisfaction? Are we excluding potentially important people or groups from our business?
- What could be done to optimise the situation?
- It can be helpful to provide leaders with a process to help them develop and answer the right questions for their specific situation. This is especially true in the early days of integrating inclusion and diversity into the business.

Leaders have a dramatic impact when they role model inclusive attitudes, practices and behaviours. This requires a high level of self awareness and honesty in response to some key questions including for example:

- Do I really demonstrate inclusive attitudes? For instance, would people say that I am open to ideas from any source?
- What biases and assumptions are impacting my ability to lead and connect with others?
- Do the common practices in my team allow everyone to contribute what they can and feel they are being treated fairly?
- Do my day-to-day behaviours make people feel valued and respected, whatever their level and role?

Leading companies are now integrating inclusive leadership practices into employee engagement surveys as well as tools used for performance management and leadership development.

Building a Culture of Employee Diversity: Looking through a Global Window

For an increasing number of forward thinking organizations, a focus on diversity has always been a core value until now. Diversity is being viewed in a new light it has actually evolved into a business imperative. Consider these workforce statistics. The U.S. Census Bureau predicts that by the year 2010, non-white ethnic people will represent more than one-third of the U.S. population and the Hispanic-American population will be the largest minority group in the continent. Organizations are realizing that to seek competitive advantage, they will need to understand customers, clients and employees from all such diverse groups and create an organizational climate conducive to all, disregarding ethnicity, colour, gender, sexual orientation, religion, socio economic class, household composition, age, disability and other demographic factors. And why just the U.S.? The same logic applies as well to Indian corporations, feels Tracy Ann Curtis, Director, Diversity, Cisco, Asia-Pacific, "Given the competition for talent in India, companies will need to seek talent wherever available. They cannot afford to close the doors based on any immaterial criterion like age or gender," she asserts. Anita S. Guha, Diversity Leader, IBM India agrees completely. "Increased competition and the impending talent crunch have placed 'equal opportunity at workplace' as a need of the hour globally. In view of the impending talent crunch, it is essential to identify and nurture every avenue of potential talent in the marketplace."

But talent sourcing apart, organizations are finding several other points in favour of a diverse workforce. Cisco, for instance, firmly believes that a workforce of inclusion allows it to be well positioned to anticipate important market changes, be responsive to customer needs, and build a solid foundation for the future. Meeting business objectives directly relates to the advantage of having an inclusive workforce and a diverse group of employees and suppliers. Says Curtis, "A workforce of inclusion brings a wealth of ideas, innovation and drive to the organization. This positions us to anticipate important market changes, be responsive to customer needs, and build a solid foundation for future needs."

Ingraining Diversity into Organization Culture

Recognized worldwide for its commitment to fostering equal opportunity at workplace, IBM has had a formal Equal Opportunity Policy for over 50 years. Dating back to IBM's legendary association with promoting diversity and equal opportunity at workplace; IBM hired women and blacks in 1899 – 20 years before women were given the right to vote up to 10 years before the National Association for the 'Advancement of Colored People was founded. IBM also hired its first employee with disability in 1914, 76 years before the Americans with Disabilities Act; and it was the first company to support the United Negro College Fund in 1944. Moving to more recent stats, over 40% of IBM's total employee population globally consists of women. In India, over 26% of IBM's total population consist of women employees.

"We have zero tolerance for any discrimination or harassment at the workplace" Guha states categorically. So how did exactly IBM go about building an inclusive work culture? "It's been a journey that began with compliance, grew from tolerance to commitment and finally business leverage. The journey certainly leads us to encounter rigid mindsets and sometimes it is not easy to get around them. Although changing rigid mindsets is a good aspirational goal, influencing behaviour in the workplace is something that can be more practically observed and measured" she shares.

IBM's manager feedback process has key questions around inclusive leadership; manager rewards are tied to the results of this survey – just one example of reinforcing the behaviours sought by the organization. There are a host of state-of-the-art training programs designed by our Center for Advanced Learning to help managers embrace their responsibility as inclusive leaders. The organization's rich heritage of diversity (IBM has hired women before the 1900s and the first person with disability was on board in 1914), the example of senior executives who role model positive leadership behaviours, reinforcement of diversity as a business imperative (and not only the socially responsible thing to do) – all help to foster inclusiveness at IBM.

Building a culture that is inclusive of diversity and the advancement of women is an ongoing focus and is largely driven through education programs like 'Mindset, which is a half day workshop for men and women. This workshop engages men and women to devise action plans that would build a more inclusive culture for women in their respective business units. 'Diversity and Inclusive Leadership' is a two day workshop targeted at managers across business units. This workshop trains managers to recognize and leverage individual differences at the workplace to a competitive advantage by capitalizing on cross-fertilization of ideas that entail when diverse employees work together to brainstorm on problems.

Cisco has a Gender Diversity Council which oversees hiring, development and advancement, retention, and culture initiatives throughout the company. During the fiscal 2006, 50 percent of new hires in finance and corporate communications were female, nearly 40 percent of new hires in operations and marketing were female and approximately 25 percent of total new hires were female.

Cisco Employee Networks help colleagues connect with others who share a similar culture, identity, or career goal (an example of a network is the Women's Action Network (WAN). This has been very active in India for the past two years). Through such networks, Cisco employees can celebrate and share diverse cultures and commonalities, cultivate career and professional growth, advance the success of Cisco business initiatives, and volunteer to join projects that benefit the community.

The mentoring programmes offered within the employee networks are often cited as one of the primary benefits of membership. In the past year, Cisco ethnic employee networks joined forces and launched a joint mentoring programme to increase participation and talent across the employee networks. Employees gain exposure to new experiences and professional skills to advance their careers; mentors build leadership and coaching skills; and Cisco gains a more enthusiastic workforce that can better focused on customer needs.

Cisco employee networks are supported and recognized as critical to the foundation of an inclusive organizational culture. Employee networks provide excellent structures and environments for facilitating career development, formal and informal mentoring, and social interaction.

In addition, Cisco sponsors diversity and inclusion efforts which provide awareness and educational resources to managers and all employees. "In Asia Pacific and across India, we have a commitment to have all of our managers attend a half day awareness workshop on diversity and inclusion with the intention to help foster a stronger and healthier work environment where all employees have an equal opportunity to succeed and reach their full potential", explains Curtis. Employees, on their own, can also sign up for instructor-led courses or watch videos on the Cisco intranet at their convenience. Some of the videos available on demand include professional development presentations from employee networks meetings, the annual Women's Leadership Offsite, and more.

There are various other examples of educational resources available to employees. 'Micro Inequities: The Power of Small TM' developed by Insight Educations Systems, is an instructor-led training available to Cisco employees. This 4-hour workshop is focused on raising awareness and driving behaviour change to raise business diversity performance and promote a culture of inclusion. It is hosted by a Cisco Vice President, who opens the session with an overview of Cisco's commitment to diversity, followed by the Micro lnequities training, and closing with an overview of their diversity plans. Many Cisco business groups have rolled this training out to their management teams and are now starting to deliver it to other employees. 'Diversions' is an electronic comic strip that presents the philosophy of diversity and inclusion at Cisco as well as practical tips for creating a more inclusive work environment. In the strip, a recurring cast of characters representing a multicultural team faces everyday challenges of diversity and inclusion in the workplace. Each episode features a theme related to the company calendar to make the content timely and includes issues focusing on women in the workplace. The intention is to take advantage of the historic impact of cartooning, particularly political cartooning and the rising popularity of contemporary animated films, to communicate complicated messages in an entertaining and fun medium. 'GlobeStnart' (developed by MeridianEaton Global), offered to all employees, is a Web-based tool that provides quick and easy access to extensive knowledge on how to conduct business effectively with people from countries around the world. Information is provided on more than 40 countries across a wide range of topics.

❖ The Way Forward...

Cisco and IBM have translated their diversity programmes into living realities. While they may have started with a formal policy, the initiative has not remained just that... it has actually infiltrated down the line, across the entire organization. People revel in its true spirit and believe in its essence.

But a majority of Indian companies have a long way to go before achieving milestones in the area of employee diversity initiatives. For example, in a 2005 study conducted by the Confederation of Indian Industry on women empowerment in the workplace revealed that women make up a mere 6% of India's workforce. What's more, there are only 4% women at senior management levels in the corporate sector.

So, does that mean we need a push in the shape of an equal opportunity employment law? Curtis thinks not. "I believe the market dynamics are a better imperative to ensure equal opportunity. We have enough laws already," she says.

Diversity Programmes at IBM

IBM India Women Leaders Council: Formed in March 2005, the council consists of 16 women leaders selected from different business units, selected by the Business Unit leaders. The objective of the Council is to enhance the technical, professional and personal development of women in IBM India by designing and developing key development as well as retention programmes. IBM has selected a cross-section of women from various locations and businesses across India. The role of the Council is to understand women's perceptions of issues and barriers to their advancement, develop recommendations to address issues/barriers, enhance networking opportunities for women, serve as visible role models for women, and provide insight to senior management on issues related to women.

Women in Technology Initiatives: aims to support the advancement and recognition of IBM's female technical talent; attract and recruit more qualified technical women to IBM; enhance IBM's image regarding women in technology; and working with outside organizations to influence the decisions of girls and young women to pursue education and careers in science and technology. WIT volunteers are involved in EX.I.T.E. (Exploring Interests in Technology and Engineering) Camps and K-12 programs for girls to build the pipeline of women in technology.

Development Programmes for Women: Programmes to build leadership and networking skills among women to encourage more women to take on leadership positions are also available for women top talent in particular. Women Leadership Development, a two day workshop is targeted at 'women on top' talent. The workshop addresses the challenges women in leadership roles face and collectively devise solutions to overcome these challenges. Taking the Stage – it is a video based 1.5 hour series of 4 workshops that is run with groups of women to enhance their networking and leadership skills. Senior women leaders facilitate these workshops across multiple locations. Women's Leadership Conference is an annual event over the last two years – when selected women on IBM's top talent are invited to an event that recognizes their contribution and encourages them further into leadership at IBM.

Working with people with disabilities: More than one billion people across the globe have a disability and as the world's population ages, this number is expected to grow significantly. IBM hired its first person with disability in 1914. With almost a 100 year heritage of commitment, IBM's Policy for People with Disabilities (PwDs) has since revolved around 3 As:

- *Accommodation:* Facilities that IBM provides to enable employees to work more independently and productively. Examples include physical improvements such as ramps, Braille signage in elevators, lowered water fountains, wide doors and the like. In India, all new locations are equipped with the standard requirements for people with disabilities and older facilities are being upgraded to conform to the same standards.
- *Accessibility:* Providing individual people with disabilities the technology tools in the workplace and in the marketplace, such as voice recognition software, HomePage reader, and the like. Currently, there are 9 Accessibility centers in IBM worldwide, each focusing on designing and deploying products appropriate for people with disabilities.
- *Attitude:* Changing the values and beliefs that some people have regarding people with disabilities. IBM actively recruits, hires and promotes people with disabilities. IBM helps promote an attitude of non-discrimination and offers opportunities to deserving individuals. In India, in addition to e-learning resources that focus specifically on building commitment to people with disability, IBM has a face to face Diversity and Inclusive leadership training programme that is aimed to promote an inclusive workplace. IBM also has plans to design some education around people with disabilities and are scouting for local service providers who can fulfill this need.

In India, IBM has undertaken several initiatives to increase visibility and access of people with disabilities at the workplace. In addition to providing accessibility products for PwDs, IBM has initiated Round-Table meetings with PwD employees to understand and address their unique concerns. They have established a voluntary PwD Network – EnABLErs at IBM – which is a great forum in which PwD joinees can participate, especially when they are new to IBM. The organization has also empaneled NGOs who are working to supply qualified PwD candidates. In 2006, IBM conducted IT Camps for children with disability to expose students to the exciting world of information technology, and to provide a scholarship fund for PwD candidates in an educational institute of repute. PwDs are employed in a variety of roles at IBM, India, including Project Management, Programming, Consulting, Operations Quality Assurance, Human Resources, and more. There is a conscious attempt not to classify certain jobs as fit only for people with disabilities – on the contrary, PwDs can contribute in a range of 'mainstream' roles.

Gender Diversity at Cummins

Cummins India has achieved remarkable success in increasing the number of women employed in all parts of the company including the shop floor. Cummins in India set out to employ women on the shop floor many years ago, following success of this initiative in the US and Europe. The advantages of employing women in all sections of the company including the shop floor have been accepted since.

The orientation programme for every employee includes a four hour module on Spectrum diversity – an awareness module. Additionally, 'treatment of each other at work' policy training is conducted as part of the orientation, to proactively avoid any instances of sexual harassment. Cummins also has a whistleblower policy and any employee, not only the affected, can report his / her grievance on a toll free number.

Employees who are identified for leadership training undertake a special course entitled 'Making Our Differences Work: Unleashing the Power of Inclusion.

Women Affinity Group (WAG) of Cummins actively engages women employees across Business Units and advises them on Career development, Work-Life Balance and Feminine Health through various interactive sessions.

Cummins College of Engineering for Women – an early initiative of Cummins India Foundation, was the first Engineering College in India for Women established in 1991 with a view to provide higher education to girls. The college was formed under the aegis of the 125 year old Maharshi Karve Stree Shikshan Samstha to bring about upliftment of girl child and help socially destitute women. The College is affiliated to Pune University and is approved by the Directorate of Technical Education. The College has been accredited for its quality by the Govt. of Maharashtra as well as by the National Board of Accreditation (NBA). It has received excellent grades from both these organizations. All students are well-placed and many have made remarkable progress in their careers. Each year the college sends two of its most meritorious students for higher education to the Rosc Hulman Institute of Technology, USA. The college also offers scholarships to both students and faculty alike for best project and leadership quality. Cummins College of Engineering for Women in partnership with the Maharshi Karve Stree Shikshan Sansthan plans to introduce the Mechanical Curriculum to fulfill the demand of Women Mechanical Engineers in Cummins and the industry.

The Five Cs of Managing Virtual Teams

Your face to face kick off meeting has just been deemed non essential travel by the powers that be. The project, however, is just as essential as ever. The team members are scattered in offices all over the country. They've never met, seen, or heard/each other, but they need to work as a unit. Getting them to gel together is your challenge.

Even managers who excel at team building in a live environment can find themselves frustrated when faced with a virtual team; yet, fostering strong team dynamics among people who never meet face to face is fast becoming a necessary skill. These five essential best practices will help you do it.

❖ Communicate

Communication is the most basic of management tools, and you probably think you have this one down. You know you need to include your team in project planning. You know you need to give timely feedback and immediate updates. But whatever your normal level of communication is, double it with your virtual team.

Clarity, frequency, and responsiveness are the keys. Experts will tell you that anywhere from 65-95 percent of communication is nonverbal. Yet for virtual team members, your words are often most or all of what they have to go on; they don't necessarily have the opportunity to pick up on the non-verbal cues that make up so much of your message. So make sure your words are clear, and deliver them often. Because their isolation prevents them from coming across information in less formal ways, regular meetings via conference call or other technology are essential for virtual teams. Have them weekly, and keep the appointment, even if you don't have any big news to report. Keep the agenda posted electronically in an area the whole team can access, and encourage them to add to it. Finally, make answering your virtual team members' emails and phone calls a priority to make up for the fact that they can't drop by your desk or catch you in the hall with a quick question.

❖ Chat

This is not the same as communication. Communication is professional. Chatting is personal. If you don't think personal communication is part of your business life, ask yourself if you've ever had lunch with a colleague, or stopped to ask how somebody was doing at the water cooler, or looked at the pictures on somebody's desk. Although your team members hardly need to be kindred spirits to work well together, some level of personal interaction is crucial for team bonding. Virtual teams don't have lunches together. They don't share water coolers. They can't see each other's desks. Chat cannot easily happen organically, so you need to provide a mechanism for it. Have a virtual pizza party: send a pizza to each location at the same time, and get together in an internet chat session or conference call to gab. Call your team members once in a while just to catch up. There are countless creative ways to introduce chat into your team dynamics; but you must make a conscious effort to do so.

❖ Change it up

It's the wealth of technology that we have at our fingertips that makes virtual teaming possible. Telephone and email are far from the only tools at your disposal. Instant messaging systems, collaboration software, group bulletin boards or discussion areas, and chat rooms are all useful for working and meeting together. Many of these tools can be obtained inexpensively or free. Learn what's out there, and use it all. Vary your methods of communicating, and learn which methods work best for which team members. Some people love email; others prefer the phone. Finally, make sure you are using each type of technology appropriately for the purpose it's best suited to. If one email has been forwarded and replied to several times among several people, you'd be better off moving the issue to a conference call or online discussion.

❖ Cut out

One of the most often neglected pieces to building a virtual team is providing a safe place for interaction and discussion without the manager. Whether it's a regular conference call, a bulletin board, or a chat session, your team needs a "staff room" that isn't accessible to you. Your live teams can take advantage of their proximity to have discussions about issues without you there, and in doing so they often develop ideas they might not feel comfortable bringing up and working through in your presence. Your virtual team needs the same opportunity. Some managers are uncomfortable creating a space that they can't get into, but if you ignore this need you not only eliminate a chance for a more free change of ideas, you risk ending up with a team that's bonded well with you, but not with one another.

❖ Conclusion

Just because you aren't there to take your team members out to lunch or just stop by to thank them for a job well done, doesn't mean that everything you know about rewards and recognition doesn't apply. Accomplishments must be acknowledged and celebrated, as a group when possible and appropriate. There are literally hundreds of ways to achieve this. Take the time to create a periodic newsletter and email or post it; be sure to have a section in it for accolades. Institute a peer-to-peer award system. Send virtual greeting cards or gift certificates from any of the dozens of websites dedicated to these purposes. Send them each a jar of jam when you reach a milestone. However you do it, just make sure you do.

The principles of managing virtual teams in good way are not much different from the principles of managing anybody or anything well. Apply two more C's to these five: consistent and conscious. Practice them that way, and it can be virtually painless.

CHAPTER

6

SELF-MANAGED TEAMS

LEARNING OBJECTIVES

- To understand the concept and requirements of Self-managed Teams.
- To gain practical insight into working of Self-managed Teams.

SELF-MANAGED TEAMS

The origin of the word 'team' can be traced back to the Anglo-Saxon word for 'family' which referred to harnessed animals to pull a load thereby implying common goals and cooperation. With time, the concept of teamwork gained importance with organizations taking measures to ensure that a team is equipped and empowered enough to function on its own. This situation today is perhaps best described by the term 'self-managed teams'.

Eric Trist and Fred Emery (England) discovered in the 1960s that coal miners gave a high output when organized in cross-functional and self-managed teams. Their productivity went down when they were arranged in conventional structures with hierarchical supervision. Consequently, they started experimenting with team structures and work arrangements. Every time they were led to a self-managed team, which would be self-sufficient in all the skills and resources needed for the job.

In the era of globalization, where technology, skills, and processes are not markedly differentiable, organizations are moving towards looking at different ways of organizing work, personnel and the organization structure. *Fortune* magazine called self-directed or self-managed teams as "the productivity breakthrough of the 90's". Self-managed teams are closely associated with the concept of employee empowerment, which entails the employee to have the requisite authority and resources required by him to carry out his responsibilities. A self-managed team differs from a normal work team or group in one essential way that the processes or the means to achieve the team goal are designed and decided by the team itself. Given the stiff competition at the global level, all organizations have been forced to focus on developing their human capital. With several organizational development interventions doing the rounds of HR corridors these days, this article aims to look at self-managed teams as a concept, what benefits they bring to the organization and associated challenges. The SMT implementation in the Pepsi plant at Palakkad, as observed by a group of XLRI students during their visit to the facility, has been cited as a case in point.

What are Self-managed Teams?

Self-managed teams are groups of employees who have the responsibility and authority to manage the work they do. The typical responsibilities of a self-managed team are planning, scheduling, assigning responsibilities among members, ensuring product quality, ordering material, taking decisions and problem-solving. The teams are also responsible for handling their inter-personal issues within themselves and work without any direct supervision. Self-managed teams are responsible for an end product or a specific deliverable. Knowledge sharing and extensive communication between members is central to the working of any self-managed team. Also, multi-skilling is a typical characteristic of self-managed teams.

How are Self-managed Teams Different from Quality Circles?

Self-managed teams differ from other employee participation methods like quality circles in the respect that unlike quality circles where the employees voluntary come together to suggest or develop quality improvements, in self-managed teams, the entire work process is structured around teamwork, with the team taking critical decisions. Also, a quality circle may or may not be empowered by the upper management but the empowerment is built into the very concept of self-managed teams. Self-managed teams unlike quality circles are not managed by an external supervisor, personnel manager, administrator or a quality manager but rather facilitated by a team leader from within the team. He is either chosen by the team members or appointed based on experience or skills.

Structure and Levels of a Self-managed Team

Though there is no official classification for self-managed teams, they can be broadly classified into three levels based on the degree of empowerment or authority vested in them:

- Basic level of empowerment,
- Intermediate level of empowerment and
- Advanced level of empowerment.

Basic level empowered teams are usually authorized to take decisions which involve low risk and do not involve much strategic thinking. These are typically decisions like solving of interpersonal team conflicts, task assignment among team members, modularizing team goals into individual member tasks etc.

Intermediate level empowered teams have higher authority. They are actively involved in work scheduling, leave management, directing and implementing process improvements, maintenance, purchase decisions, safety and housekeeping activities and small budget expenditures like team outings etc.

Advanced level empowered teams are highly empowered and work as strategic business partners. They can be involved in compensation, recruitment and termination decisions. They handle the performance management and appraisal process within the team and can even go on to make financial decisions and work in collaboration with other stakeholders like customers and suppliers.

In an ideal state, an organization having self-managed team structure would not require managers at all since all the decisions would be taken and implemented by the workers themselves.

Qualities of Successful Self-managed Teams

Some characteristics common to most successful self-managed teams are:

- ***Small team size:*** A successful self-managed team in most organizations usually comprises of 5-20 members, since a small team translates to higher cohesion among the team members and ease in pinpointing the accountability of members.
- ***Multi-skilling and multitasking:*** Most self-managed teams place great emphasis on cross-functional training and multitasking where team members can take each other's tasks and thus reduce the dependability on any one individual. This enhances the flexibility of the team and helps in better management of work in case one or more members leave the team. For example, the top management at Tektronix believes that the growth and development of individual employees is the primary vehicle of advancing company's long-

term interests. Harley-Davidson created the Harley-Davidson Learning Center. This is a facility dedicated to lifelong learning. Its primary role is to serve employees who want to keep their skills updated.

- *Commitment from top management:* It has been seen that self-managed teams can sustain themselves in organizations where the top management is actively involved in driving the initiative and willing to commit time, effort and resources to develop teams. The top management must be able to trust the team and be ready for initial setbacks in terms of productivity and committing financial resources till the team processes stabilize.
- ***Clearly defined team goals, key result areas (KRAs) and alignment of team objectives with the organization's objectives:*** Clearly set goals and KRAs imply that the team members are able to foresee the purpose of their work and how it contributes to the organization's goals at large. This enhances the work ownership amongst the employees and sets clear accountability levels in the organization. For example, Teerlink, Harley-Davidson's ex-CEO, said that total employee involvement (El) cannot exist until management and labour can agree that they have a mutual goal: the long-term success of the company. In Harley-Davidson, under this joint process, joint union-management study groups identify issues or problems and then research all possible solutions.
- *Diversity:* Diversity amongst team members implies diversity of thought which comes through members belonging to different backgrounds and functional areas. Member diversity improves the quality of team by bringing in the power of diverse and innovative thinking into the group.
- *Information sharing:* A well-developed information system in the organization ensures that timely and required information is available to team members. Information availability helps the self-managed team to arrive at informed and quality decisions.
- *Egalitarian culture:* The organizations aiming at empowering their teams should ensure that the culture of the organization supports team structure by bringing in egalitarian work policies and treating their mangers and workers alike. Most organizations which have successful self-managed teams ensure that there is a common dress code, dining areas and meeting rooms for its workers and managers. For example, at Honda's U.S. plant, everyone including the plant superintendent wears the uniform. At other sites, no one wears ties, special badges or any other sign of power.

Why Self-managed Teams?

When employees are completely in-charge of their job, it is likely to create a greater interest and attachment to job. This also means that the managers can devote their time in innovation and process improvement rather than monitoring the employees. Also, since the employees are the frontliners, their tacit knowledge of even the most miniscule aspect of the job is utilized when they are given the responsibility of the quality and end result. As self-managed teams require constant exchange of information, it leads to breaking of communication barriers between groups of employees. Other reported benefits of self-managed teams include: reduced absenteeism, increased productivity and increased employee satisfaction.

Self-managed Teams in India

Though self-managed teams have been successful to varying extent in the world, most organizations operating in India have not been able to implement self-managed teams. Only a handful of companies like Dr. Reddy's Laboratories, Pepsi (Palakkad), the Indian arm of the US-based Tech Books (printing and publishing solutions provider) have been successful in their attempt. Even these attempts have been far and few and limited to one or two locations or departments within these organizations.

One of the factors for this might be the traditional patronizing attitude of management and government in Indian context, which has prevented the unionized environment from becoming matured. Low literacy levels amongst workers and lack of requisite skills also play a role. Another major reason could be popularity of contract labour in India, which encourages most organizations to hire temporary workers from a low cost unorganized labour pool. Self-managed teams need time and effort to develop, which is not possible in case of a whole of contract workforce. Another reason is lack of dignity of labour in India or, rather, the South Asia, which translates into lack of trust by the management in the worker capability.

❖ Conclusion

Though it has been seen that self-managed teams enhance the productivity and efficiency in organizations, they can be detrimental to an organization's success if not implemented properly. Self-managed teams should not be looked at as a means of reducing costs by removing a layer of supervisors. It is not a quick fix solution but rather a long term way of increasing organizational effectiveness. Improved work quality and empowered employees through proper implementation of self-managed teams and top management commitment gives an organization a definite edge over its competitors.

CASE STUDY

Self-managed Teams at Pepsi, Palakkad

Pepsi's Palakkad plant started in the highly unionized environment of Kerala in 2001. While the original plant was planned in Coimbatore, license issues with the Tamil Nadu government and the simultaneous SOPs extended by the Kerala government led to the plant site in Palakkad. The potential human capital challenges in the state made Pepsi consider several options, which finally led to the decision of implementing self-managed teams in the plant which would hire a young educated workforce. While on one hand, the entire top management of Pepsi was enthused about this initiative, the employees took some time to be convinced that self-managed teams was not just another management fad, but a culture that was here to stay.

To begin with, all the employees were imparted training on self-managed teams and then divided into three self-managed teams. Each team had several positions like HR captains, quality captains and team leaders. Members occupy these positions on a rotational basis. The interactions with the members revealed that they enjoyed the independence they were given in this plant and felt that they had a far greater opportunity to enhance their skills in this system as they could even choose which machine they wanted to operate. They also felt that they received more respect here and that they were more confident of handling responsibility and resolving inter-personal issues because of being a part of self-managed teams. The employees were of the view that the quality levels had improved and they were resolving employee grievances on their own. Also, there was no unionization among the plant employees.

The various practices which ensure the continuity of self-managed teams in the plant include inter-shift meetings between the teams (space meetings), salary discussions between the management and the teams (open house), members conducting the first two rounds for the selection of new employees, members planning and organizing various functions in the plants, members handling their leaves and resolving grievances and team members being consulted for the preparation of the annual budget.

One roadblock in the implementation of the self-managed teams has been the high attrition rate of employees who are being poached by firms in the Middle East. This requires continuous training of the new employees, which might become difficult during peak production season. Pepsi will have to devise methods to cope with this challenge to sustain the existing level of self-managed team implementation and also to progress to the next level.

CHAPTER

7

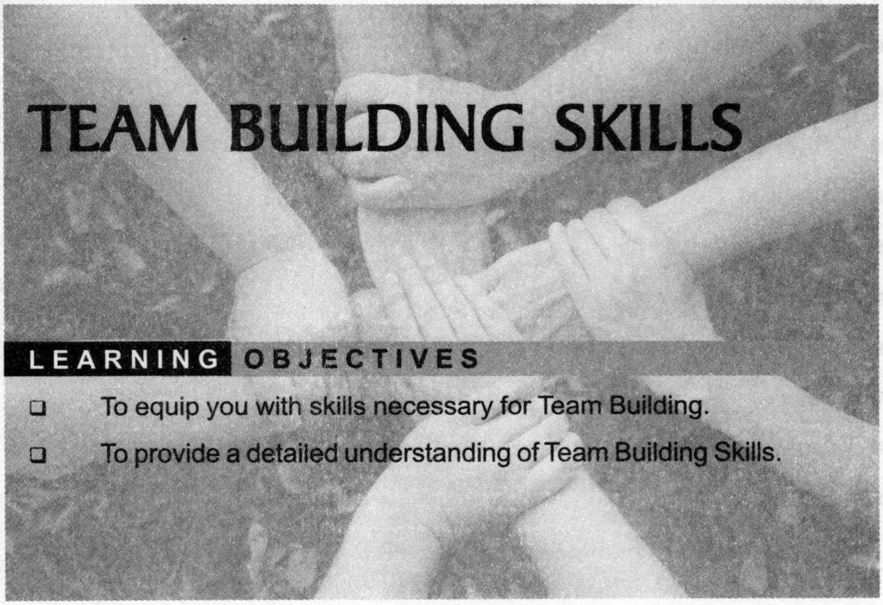

TEAM BUILDING SKILLS

LEARNING OBJECTIVES

- To equip you with skills necessary for Team Building.
- To provide a detailed understanding of Team Building Skills.

Team Building Skills: Effective Leadership

In many ways, good leadership is hard to define. It can't be directly measured. There's no leadership 'score' or report card. In fact often the measure of leadership is qualitative rather than quantitative although quantitative results always follow. So, the question remains, ***how can you tell if your leadership skills are effective***?

Plain and simple, leadership is about getting others to take action. If leadership effectiveness is lacking, less than best effort is put forth. The better the leadership, the better the effort. **Exceptional leadership inspires the best effort in others.**

Effective leadership is a function of both individual competencies and organizational culture. What are some signs that leadership isn't as effective as it could be? There are a number of them. They are indications that something is missing in the leadership equation.

- Inability to Motivate People
- Difficulty Attracting/Retaining the Right People

- Low Productivity
- Poor Customer Orientation
- High Stress
- Isolation
- Declining Profits
- Ineffective Delegation
- Lack of Creativity
- Lack of Initiative
- Ineffective Teams
- Poor Communications
- Lack of Vision
- Diminishing Revenues
- High Turnover

What can be done to improve leadership effectiveness? The answer is simple to understand and yet not so simple to implement. It starts with understanding the foundations of what makes someone an effective leader and what kind of organizational culture is most effective.

Effective Personal Leadership

When I ask workshop participants about characteristics of both good and bad leaders, ***the list never includes issues of intelligence, technical skills, or effective decision making***! Instead, the list is full of people-related traits – good listener, respectful, good communicator, develops others.

Effective personal leadership can be summarized as being competent in these skill sets:

- Becoming Influential
- Facilitating Teamwork and Collaboration
- Being a Catalyst for Change
- Managing Conflict
- Developing Others
- Having and Communicating a Compelling Vision

Unfortunately, improving one's competency in these areas is often a challenge. Let me explain why…

Unlike factual information, which gets processed in the neocortex of the brain, people related skills are processed in part of the brain called the amygdala. This portion of the brain regulates emotional insights and responses rather than logical insights and responses.

Improving the leadership skills set forth above requires one to break old habits/responses and form new ones, and we aren't able to do this simply by learning and acquiring knowledge. That's the difference between the neocortex and the amygdala.

There are a couple of inherent challenges with this process. Pretty much everyone acknowledges that they have room for improvement. The first challenge is knowing which areas to improve. We all have blind spots. We're aware of some of our shortcomings, but usually not all of them. Secondly, breaking habits and forming new ones requires commitment, persistence, and time. It usually takes support from others – people who can point out when you've acted in a way contradictory to your intent. It's important to use a reliable assessment to identify areas of growth opportunity. From those results, we can develop a plan of development which bolsters weaker areas and leverages stronger areas. The final aspect of a successful personal development plan relies on having one or more people who can support you, give unbiased, non-judgmental feedback, and help you make course corrections.

Organizational Culture

The foundations of a strong organization are:

1. Developing a clear and compelling **Purpose**
2. Identifying the organization's **Mission** to achieve the Purpose
3. Agreeing on a set of **Values** by which to carry out the Mission
4. Adopting a **Servant Leader** attitude throughout the organization.

An organization's **Purpose** is the 'Why' of its existence. It's not what it does as much as what it is striving to accomplish. It is a statement of the greater good it is attempting to achieve. It answers the question: "Why are we here?" and helps give clarity and focus to each person in the organization. It is the yardstick by which decisions are measured.

An organization's **Mission** is the "What" of an organization. It is a definition of what the company does to achieve its stated **Purpose**. It begins to define the core proficiencies of a business and helps keep it focused on achieving its purpose.

An organization's set of **Values** is the 'How' of an organization. It defines what an organization most values in the execution of its **Mission**. It's not an all encompassing list of possible values as much as a statement of what the organization most values in its people and their conduct. It defines behaviours and culture within an organization. It helps set the guidelines of what is and is not acceptable.

At the core of **Servant Leadership** is the premise that the customer is the most important person to the organization. As a consequence of that premise, it only follows that the most important people to the customer are the frontline staff. They're the people who customers interact with on a daily basis. This understanding leads to the philosophy that the job of the manager of the frontline people is to make their jobs as easy and effective as possible so the customer has the best experience possible. The result is an organizational chart that looks like an inverted pyramid. This servant attitude focuses leaders on developing those around them. It leads to people working together in a collaborative, solution-oriented environment.

How does one go about developing Purpose, Mission, and Values? Falling back on our understanding of Servant Leadership and the importance of everyone in the organization, the creation of Purpose, Mission and Values requires input from people in all areas of the company. They (the Purpose, Mission, and Values) need to be relevant to all involved, they need to be consistent with one another, and they need to be used consistently as a yardstick for decisions and policies. There's nothing worse than developing values and just paying them lip-service by not living them day-to-day. A practice like that lacks integrity and actually becomes a demoralizer.

In summary, when we combine personal competency in all areas of leadership skills with an organizational culture which supports people, their development, and their success, we end up with exceptional leadership which, in turn, inspires the best effort in others.

Building a Company of Great Leaders

❖ Starting from Scratch

All successful programmes and initiatives for developing leadership talent within an organization are created for one single purpose to support important business needs. These programmes are an integral part of running the day-to-day business of the company. They fuel growth while fulfilling the needs of human capital and leadership.

Most companies are not sure where to begin, others don't believe they can build leadership from scratch. Yet others start from scratch, launch costly initiatives with a variety of programmes, but with no real plan to build a system that will sustain good leadership.

The truth is: great leadership programmes are not programmes at all. They are essential processes for driving the business.

Everything in leadership begins and ends with business. A leadership strategy needs to define how you will support your business strategy. It is a fundamental part of running the business and needs to run across selecting, developing, assessing and compensating your leaders.

❖ Identifying Critical Capabilities

First, you need to identify the critical capabilities you will need in your leaders so that you realize your long-term business goals. Each organization is different and these differences will dictate a different and unique competency model. However, while good processes allow executive teams to assess their needs and rethink their strategy, they need to be kept in perspective.

A good competency model is a starting place for a dialogue and discussion of what's required and its sole function should be to add clarity to expectations. You need to then choose the critical behaviours that will define the success of your leaders, which will create clarity of what's really important for your business and industry.

Two factors decide how well a leader fits with his or her role: the business strategy and the amount of change in the environment.

❖ Business Strategy

There is no universal best leader model that describes ideal leadership characteristics and strategies. Business strategy can be broadly classified into two – growth strategy and return strategy. Having a growth strategy means you pursue profits primarily by expanding sales, while having a return strategy means you will compete on the basis of having a more efficient organization than your competitors. Both these strategies require different sets of skills and capabilities from the leadership team.

❖ Change in the Environment

The amount of change an organization will experience during the next few years can be measured on a scale ranging from transactional to transformational. Today, the pace of change is predictable and transactional change is only the first in a series of situations and business environments that show more dramatic change – like large acquisitions, industry transformations, financial crises. This kind of transformational change requires leaders with charisma, great communication capabilities and most importantly, strong vision.

Just like leaders need to have a fit with your business strategy, they also need to be comfortable with, and capable of dealing with, different degrees of change.

❖ The First Step...

Defining the capabilities required of your leaders is only the first step. To actually grow and reinforce their capabilities, you need to actually promote their growth through right sourcing, aligning, developing and rewarding. You need to identify the gaps between what you have and what you need.

Starting from scratch isn't easy, but it can be done. Sometimes, it's easier to start from scratch than to dismantle bad processes and then work out a new strategy.

Finding and developing leaders will become more challenging in the future than it is today. The future poses new challenges and greater speed and complexity, but also opportunities to develop leadership capability more effectively. The great companies of the future will be those who recognize the new challenges early and respond aggressively with the help of a strong senior team, a focus on their best talent and doing the right programmes the right way.

The Place for Passion in Leadership

Company performance depends on successful selling, followed by solid delivery, in line with strategic goals. But clients have a choice in who they buy from, and employees' commitment to producing quality products is impacted by a whole range of diverse, sometimes conflicting, demands – both personal and work related. Combining appropriate levels of passion, at the right times, with strong leadership – offering visibility of personal belief – inspires clients, staff and even suppliers to demonstrate the loyalty necessary to ensure ongoing corporate profitability and growth.

Requirements of Leadership

Much has been written about the requirements of leadership, and how to meet these requirements. In summary, four fundamental tasks have to be addressed: formulation of a vision of business success; development of a strategy for achieving this vision; definition of a pathway that will take an organisation from its current position to alignment with a new strategy; provision of support to ensure that this pathway is travelled, efficiently and effectively. Ultimately, organisational success can only be attained through accomplishment of the final task – which, as a consequence of recent social changes, is now a days recognised as demanding highly tuned soft skills.

While managers maintain the status quo, working with existing practices, a leader's role is to bring about change. This starts with crafting a new vision and defining clear targets. Focus, detachment and objectivity are essential at this stage. Strategy formulation is strongly associated with traditional 'hard skills', such as financial analysis, planning and identification of risks, and is best undertaken without emotion. 'Soft skills' begin to play an increasing part as activities move on to setting a new direction and detailing the pathway for attaining restated organisational aims. As results are largely achieved through people, true leadership qualities are called upon when, with a route to success mapped out, staff need to be coaxed and encouraged to undertake the required journey.

Though the majority of business heads possess excellent visioning and strategising abilities, many find the switch to 'people skills' more demanding, and indeed at odds with the very qualities essential for other aspects of their role. To accomplish a new company mission, willing, committed followers must be brought onboard. Working from the top, down through all levels of his organisation, a leader must build teams, and draw all parties to share appropriate common goals. He has to stimulate, influence and persuade his workforce. Even once employees are suitably motivated, clients too have to be won over, which involves all the same tactics and attributes.

A whole range of leadership styles have been defined, and can be adopted, to assist in developing loyalty from commanding to democratic, transactional to transformational but the application of sensitive relationship management is certain to have greatest positive effect. Those possessing high emotional intelligence are most likely to find relationship management within their capabilities, being more self and socially aware.

Why Followers Stray

Successful leaders need steadfast followers. But followers stray if they don't understand, or buy into, the corporate vision. Equally, they drift away if they don't have confidence in the person creating and selling the vision.

Employees cannot be expected to instinctively know of, or appreciate the reasons for, a new vision or strategy. Unless these are clearly communicated, with a thorough explanation of benefits at all levels, a workforce is highly likely to resist. Changes have to be sold to those they affect, and messages reinforced over and over again, particularly when they are radical.

Where direction is unclear or the vision not bought into or future benefits not seen, individuals will not follow a leader. To allow them selves to be led, staff must understand and accept a vision, seeing their own role within the bigger picture; they must feel cared about and a necessary part of what is happening. Yet, too often, messages are heard second-hand or watered down. At best, this leaves recipients unmoved or confused; at worst, it has significant negative impact. Equally, if new pressures conflict with personal values, placing opposing demands, workers will be reluctant to stay on the ordained path.

A workforce unaligned to organisational ambitions is often a symptom of applying the wrong leadership style for a given situation. Change invariably calls for a transformational style, with its focus on selling ideas and providing guidance, not commanding (do as I say) or transactional (do this and you'll be rewarded with that). Individuals grow under good leadership; under bad leadership they degenerate and quickly lose the will to be led.

People will only go along with someone who they respect and by whom they feel respected. They have to accept his authority to make decisions on their behalf. He has to be seen as competent, credible and trustworthy, operating non-politically and not in self-interest. Without these credentials, a leader's behaviour has a negative effect on stakeholders: employees, clients and suppliers alike.

So followers are lost, or perhaps never engaged, if they fail to be convinced by the vision or the leader. Non-followers have a number of choices, including ongoing demotivation, leaving an organisation or establishing their own direction of travel; all such outcomes are far from optimal. Better that everyone agrees to be led to a shared goal. And *passion* is a potentially powerful tool that can be used in the conversion of strays.

How Passion Helps?

Employees need to be enthused and energised to achieve corporate targets. Leaders who are passionate in their beliefs inspire those around them, building motivational forces and awakening workers to the possibilities of what they, their teams and the organisation can accomplish.

References define *passion* as: 'strong feelings', 'boundless enthusiasm', 'something that is desired intensely', 'devotion to a cause and tireless diligence to its furtherance' and 'in passion mode, one releases one's energy boundlessly, downward and outward'. It almost goes without saying that anyone driven by, and exhibiting passion will infect those around them with their enthusiasm – converting and exciting others, who feel injected with energy.

To witness the passionate selling of messages and ideas is an uplifting experience for staff. Demonstrable support for a vision, by those most involved in formulating it, creates firm faith in an organisation's directors. And by sharing his passion – using his valuable time and resources to communicate with the workforce – a leader is showing confidence that success is achievable through his people. In response, employees feel empowered and encouraged and, as objectives are met, deem that they themselves, with their teams, brought about improvements. Thus a positive spiral of accomplishment is generated.

Having convincingly imparted his vision, a leader must establish the path for change, so that willing followers can realise the required outcome. Sometimes the pathway isn't clear – help is needed in seeking the way. Where workers have been persuaded of the rightness of the undertaking, won over by fervour, they will readily join the exploration for the most suitable direction and means of travel. And, with the road ahead identified and clear, a passionately driven leader will expend time guiding and coaxing others, wherever necessary, to make the journey. He will continually check for alignment with the route to attaining targets, thus keeping the whole organisation moving forward. This keenness to embrace everyone in the company, from top to bottom, to contribute to bringing about success, gives a sense of worth and an investment stake in a perceived partnership. Thus inspired, staff will give their very best for the cause.

It is not unusual for business heads to be seen as distant and cold, lacking empathy. In such circumstances, it can prove difficult for subordinates to develop the enthusiasm required to pursue corporate goals. By contrast, displaying passionate behaviour makes a leader appear real. He emerges as courageous, standing up for what he believes in, driving from the front. The natural response to such voluntary exposure is to feel supportive, wanting to offer personal commitment to assist. In a time when automatic respect for authority is decreasing, the honesty of more emotional behaviour produces followers and, importantly, ones who recognise the imperfections of their leader, as well as his strengths. And such realistic appreciation and trust proves essential if dark times are encountered, with planned paths ending in blind alleys or strategies seeming unachievable. When things don't go to plan and extra drive is called for to face new challenges, the candor of bonds based on real human emotions is most likely to sustain the workforce through a difficult period.

Demonstrating Passion

A leader's confidence in a company vision is demonstrated by his desire to articulate the mission, endlessly explaining its benefits at every level, such that the follower base grows in number and drive. With the aim of establishing a common dream, about which everyone feels passionate, a leader must display integrity, empathy and courage. He builds mutual trust and respect through tireless communications, from exciting presentations down to one-to-one coaching sessions.

So, a key initial focus for a corporate crusade is countering the negatives that make followers stray. The starting point for this has to be clearly conveying and selling the vision, particularly where new ideas are more radical. Successfully promoting a fresh future, and the strategic journey required to reach it, takes passion – transferring one's own enthusiasm and belief to others, until they adopt the vision as their own. Only when employees truly understand the benefits attainable will they share in a leader's dream, not blindly following, but actively cutting a road to achievement of the sought after outcomes. This desired state is reached when those at the top of an organisation display a strong conviction for the mission, explaining in simple terms why it is preferable to the present state and adding vibrancy to the tasks ahead. Wanting people to understand why a message is important, wanting them to be as keen as you, honestly describing problems that may be encountered – all these things connect with, and influence, in a very positive way.

Communicating expectations of employees, and a confidence in their ability to meet these, resonates constructively, creating strong bonds. So also does empathy. Showing an understanding of others viewpoints and concerns – being attuned to their thinking – earns trust and support. And passion so naturally carries empathy with it, bringing to each individual's level the message 'I want you to share my beliefs because they're so important to me' and 'I need you to back me and help me to achieve my goals'. Shared values are tapped into, to reveal aims as collective. Leaders, thus, demonstrate respect for followers so that, by reflection, mutual trust and comfort is built. Out of this grows real, unswerving commitment and boosted morale.

Setting oneself up as sincere, accountable, open and of high integrity, is taking a significant risk. Prospects for failing, at some point, against such high standards are considerable. Keeping promises isn't always easy when buffeted by the demands of external forces. But it is this very vulnerability that captures and holds the loyalty of others. On the one hand being tough and reliable-feet firmly on the ground, especially through periods of most change and uncertainty, while on the other hand accepting challenge and admitting mistakes, portrays the type of honesty and realism that employees seek. Accepting shortcomings is evidence of humility and humility is ultimately a sign of strength, not weakness. It is the mix of drive and aspirations, with acknowledgement of flaws, which describes successful leadership.

With passion inside, how then can a leader instill like-mindedness in his staff? The start point is usually group presentations, reaching large numbers of people and boldly 'nailing one's colours to the mast' for all to see. Appropriate degrees of charisma are required, with gesticulation, movement and a range of tones of voice. Passion is active, not passive. Lively presentation skills may come naturally but, for most business leaders, calm restraint has become a way of life, so some acting skills might be called upon. And while every presenter has a personal style, inventing a manner that suits the company and the audience is vital, reflecting organisational culture.

Presentation content and how it is packaged is equally important. Listeners need to feel that the message matters, such that their belief and involvement also matters. Whilst it may seem a cheap trick, tugging at emotional heart-strings can be very effective, leaving a lasting impression. Contrast the impact, to a conference of software testers, between a presentation that starts "Software testing is important", and one starting with "I read in the paper yesterday of a little old lady in Scotland who, on receiving a huge electricity bill that she couldn't hope to pay, wandered out into the winter snows, confused and worried, and died of hypothermia; the bill was quite incorrect – the result of a software bug; don't you think we, the software industry, should all feel a sense of responsibility?". Add some pregnant pauses ar d some pacing up and down, and the result is a mesmerized audience.

Using rhetoric questions, pensively pausing on "That concerns me", sharing what appears to be inner thoughts – all these emotive tactics are effective. A leader showing that he has human feelings will never seem too detached from reality. Explaining visions and strategies in terms of how they provide outcomes to address minor concerns, is a powerful mix of 'big picture' and fine detail, answering every level of question in one hit. Demonstrating an ability to understand the trivial worries troubling followers, but moving these up to a higher plain; dealing with issues that listeners hadn't even thought of; pumping up small successes to show progress – each of these approaches impress and encourage.

Not only large presentations, but all communications, need to be undertaken with the same enthusiasm. Any manner of forums should be used – and opportunities created – to share and sell messages. 'Walking the floor' demonstrates involved interest; one-to-one and group coaching strengthens personal bonds, soothing and calming those fearful of change; actively listening. These behaviours subtly show, and build, commitment. And the theme of every interaction is always the same: to tie personal aspirations and values to corporate goals and visions – to exhibit passionate belief.

The actions described above are natural for transformational leaders, though less easy for others. For those who struggle to display a suitably convincing level of feeling, relying on their executive team for support is a good idea; indeed group leadership can increase effectiveness, through the appearance of a united front and a spread of faith, using a variety of communication styles.

But a set of important rules apply: don't command, don't demand too much (followers do not have the same volume of energy as leaders), don't be defensive or blame others, don't brag or be arrogant. Even dynamic presentations are not about being 'larger than life' or about self-promotion. Never reveal negative emotions – like anger. Effective passion is positive, inclusive and requesting, offering promise and drawing people in.

❖ Passionate Leadership Produces Committed Followers

Business success requires a loyal workforce, committed to achieving organisational goals. Leaders who exhibit passion – "devotion to a cause and tireless diligence to its furtherance – releasing energy boundlessly" – inspire those around them; employees and clients alike become partners, with the leader, enthused and energised to realise a shared dream.

TEAM BUILDING SKILLS: COMMUNICATION

The issue of communication is a vital one for any organization. It is worth considering for a moment what is the meaning of so important a concept.

What is Communication?

Communication is the process of creating, transmitting and interpreting, ideas, facts, and opinions and feeling it is a process that is essentially a sharing one – a mutual interchange between two or more persons. In organizations, communication is generally thought of in terms of:

1. The media of communication, e.g., memos, reports, letters etc.
2. The skills of communication, e.g., giving instructions, interviewing, chairing meetings etc., and
3. The organization of communications, e.g., the chain of command, briefing groups, committees etc.

❖ Formal Communication/Official Communication

These three aspects sum up the formal communication present within the organization, and must be distinguished from the informal aspects of communication, such as the so called 'grapevine' (rumour, gossip etc).

❖ Informal Communication

Formal communication must be distinguished from the informal aspects of communication, such as the so called 'grapevine' (rumour, gossip etc).

❖ Importance of Formal Communication

The rest of this lesson is concerned with formal, or official communication. Particular topics to be examined include communication flows, communication media, barriers to communication and the use of committees. In effect, the lesson deals with the communications questions that face practically every organization:

- What do we need to communicate?
- When should we communicate?
- To whom should we communicate?
- How should we communicate?

❖ The Flow of Communications in Organisations

The communication network of most organizations consists of vertical lines of communication providing upward and downward means of transmitting information, with a few integration mechanisms such as committees built across these lines. Some organizations also provide lateral lines of communication, which are seen as having equal importance with the vertical.

Mechanistic (Bureaucratic) Organizations

As we saw earlier, mechanistic (bureaucratic) organisations tend to adopt vertical lines of communication and interaction.

Organic organizations

Organic organisations are those that tend to adopt lateral lines.

Matrix structured organizations

We saw, also, that matrix-type structures contains both vertical and lateral lines of communication.

What is Vertical Communication?

The greatest tendency in most organisations is for communication to be thought of in terms of vertical interaction.

❖ Vertical Communication Process

Downward communication: In particular, management communicates policies, plans, information and instructions downwards.

Upward communication: Employees communicate ideas, suggestions, comments and complaints upwards. The downwards communication is achieved by means of the management chain, while the upwards communication is achieved by work-group meetings, by joint consultation machinery and by grievance procedures.

Vertical communication tends to be dominated by the flow in the downward direction.

❖ What is Lateral Communication?

The flow of information across the organisation is rarely comparable with the vertical flow. However, every organisation has to make *some* arrangements for coordinating the efforts of more than one department or section, and this may be done by means of interdepartmental meetings or committees. This is a rational and controlled approach to the problem of integration. It represents about the least that organisations can do to set up lateral lines of communication. Where an organisation is more organic in its operation, it tends to make greater use of lateral flows of information between people in the same specialism or working on similar tasks, for example. Much of the information flowing between such groups is highly technical or task-orientated and facilitates cooperation between groups. Such information in only passed up the line if it is of particular significance, or where it comes under the category of "need to know" for the manager concerned. Organisations which operate a system of 'management by exception' are able to make wider use of lateral forms of communication compared with organisations whose management insist on being kept fully in the picture all the time.

Managing by exception implies a high degree of delegation, where, once responsibilities have been fixed and standards of performance agreed, the managers concerned will only ask for information if (a) there is a problem or (b) it is time for a periodic review of progress.

Centralised (leader-dominated) channels of communication: Research work that has been carried out on groups at work suggests that, for simple problems, the quickest and most accurate results will be obtained by means of centralised (leader-dominated) channels of communication.

Decentralised communication channels: Conversely, for complex problems, the most acceptable are likely to come from decentralised communication channels, where there is greater encouragement to share facts, views and feelings.

Different Communication Media

The media of communication help to answer the question how should we communicate? The media can be divided into two main groups: (1) **written methods** and (2) **oral methods.**

❖ Written Methods

These are principally:

1. Letters
2. Memos
3. Reports
4. Notices, and
5. Printouts

Advantages: In comparison with oral methods, the written word is more permanent and less liable to misinterpretation. It also encourages the sender of a message to think about it before dispatch.

Disadvantages: The disadvantages are that written communication takes longer to effect than oral methods, and is still liable to misinterpretation despite the efforts of the writer to be clear and logical.

❖ Oral Methods

These are usually:

1. Meetings of one kind or another, and
2. Telephonic conversations.

Advantages and disadvantages: Oral communication may often lack the considered nature of written communication, but it does have the advantage of being reinforced by various forms of non-verbal behaviour such as facial expressions, gestures and body posture. One of the major difficulties associated with oral communication is its transience, the spoken work is a sound, and lasts only so long as it takes to pronounce it. Thus people are often able to deny, or to qualify what they have, in fact, said. This is one of the main reasons for the importance of minutes at a committee meeting – to provide a true and correct record. It also explains the growing use of audiovisual methods to capture spoken words and accompanying expressions every bit as much as the written word.

In practical business, there are two examples of communication methods which are especially widely used, and deserve further comment now:

1. Written reports, and
2. Talks or presentations.

Meetings, and in particular committee meetings, will be looked at later in the lesson.

1. *Reports:* A written report is basically the outcome of a study of the facts and implications of a particular situation. It is intended to summarise the facts of the situation, relate them to what the organisation is currently doing, draw appropriate conclusions and make useful recommendations. Reports can range from the short one page summary to the detailed work running into several thousand words. Whether long or short, a report is usually set out in the following format:
   - Title of Report
   - Terms of Reference
   - Introductory Comments
   - Findings
   - Implications for the Organisation

- Conclusions
- Recommendations or Proposals
- Name of Author(s)
- Date
- Appendices (longer reports only)

Typical report layout: Layouts such as above enable report writers to assemble their data and their ideas into a logical order. This is an important point for any report, as is clarity and conciseness of expression. A clear, well-argued report will stand a far higher possibility of acceptance than one which is rambling and verbose, however relevant its content.

2. ***Presentations:*** Most managers are called upon from time to time to make a presentation to their colleagues or their superiors. Presentations are widely used in selling situations, and in management planning exercises; they are also used when formally introducing major reports or when introducing new ideas or proposals to colleagues.

There are three key elements in any presentation:

- Preparation
- Content
- Delivery

Preparation: Preparation is a vital prerequisite for any presentation. The person making the presentation needs to consider the content of his talk and its delivery.

Content: So far as content is concerned, this is primarily a question of considering what to include and what to leave out, taking into account the needs and prior knowledge of the audience. Top management groups, or example, are mainly interested in the salient features of an idea or proposal, together with a summary of its principal benefits and disadvantages.

Operational levels of management generally require more detailed information and will respond to a more technical approach than their senior counterparts.

Delivery: The question of how to deliver the presentation again depends largely on the nature of the audience. Some groups will not be satisfied with anything less than a brilliant display of wit and ingenuity, others will be quite satisfied with a low-key, but extremely relevant, demonstration. **One point that is always helpful, whatever the audience, is the use of visual aids.** There is hardly a presentation that does not benefit enormously from visual illustration.

Visual aids that are most frequently employed include:

1. Flip Charts
2. Overhead Transparencies
3. Films (Video and Cine), and
4. Models, or
5. Physical examples of an item.

A code of good practice in the making of presentations could be as follows:

1. Consider your audience and their needs
2. Assemble your facts and ideas in the light of (1) above and taking account of the complexity of the material
3. Develop sufficient and suitable visual aids
4. Consider what other information should be made available (drawings, specifications, reports etc.)
5. Tell your audience what you are going to tell them, and then tell them what you have told them
6. Be enthusiastic about the subject (unless this would be completely inappropriate, e.g. the announcement of a new redundancy plan)
7. Be natural, i.e. if you are a quiet person, then be quietly enthusiastic
8. Maintain eye contact with your audience
9. Be prepared for questions both during and at the end of your presentation.

Barriers to Effective Communication

There are numerous barriers to communications, and some of the most important ones are discussed briefly below:

1. ***Individual bias and selectivity:*** We hear or read what we want to hear or see. People are often unaware of their bias until it is brought to their attention. Much of the bias is to do with cultural background and personal value systems.
2. ***Status differences***: Subordinates may well read more than what was intended into a superior's message. By contrast, superiors may listen less carefully to information passed up the line by subordinates. People at all levels may be reserved about passing information upwards, in case they incur criticism. One of the reasons for the relative failure of the "open door' policy of communication

adopted by many managers is that it relies on subordinates overcoming both their natural reserve and the status barriers of the organisation.

3. ***Fear and other emotional overtones can cloud the communication message:*** If a person has bad news to pass on, which is almost certain to upset the recipient, they will tend to avoid the whole truth and be content to pass on part of the message only. This issue of emotional barriers is particularly relevant in the handling of grievances. Angry people do not make good listeners, and thus any manager dealing with a deeply-felt grievance must allow for a period of 'cooling off" before expecting to make any headway with a solution. Indeed, it is now recognized that it is precisely in the area of the emotions that human beings appear to be worst at sharing, i.e. communicating. Not surprisingly, this is an area of attention in Organisation Development programmes, especially in relation to how conflict can be handled in a team.

4. ***Lack of trust is another important barrier to effective communication:*** If we are not sure of someone, we tend to hold back in our communication with that person. His mistrust may arise because of doubts about the recipient's motives or his ability to grasp what is being said.

5. ***Verbal difficulties are a frequent source of confusion and misunderstanding:*** These may arise because of the sheer lack of fluency on the part of the sender, or because of the use of jargon (specific application of words in technical and professional contexts), or perhaps because of pitching the message at too high a level of understanding. In terms of written words, the barriers are usually those associated with long-windedness, i.e. a failure to get to the point quickly and concisely.

6. ***Other important barriers to communication include information overload:*** (where a person is overloaded with memos, reports, letters, telephone messages etc.), inadequate machinery for communication (committees, briefing groups, joint consultation meetings etc) and sheer lack of practices in the skills of communicating.

   Overcoming, or at least reducing the effects of barriers to communication mainly consists in finding answers to the issues raised in the paragraph above.

Improvements in Communication by Adopting Strategies

(i) Ensuring that employees are made aware of communication problems

(ii) Setting up appropriate machinery for communication (upwards, downwards and laterally), and

(iii) Training employees in relevant techniques of communication.

Particular mechanisms which have been widely adopted include:

❖ Downward Communication

- Briefing Groups (where team leaders brief their immediate staff events)
- Staff Meetings (where all staff in one unit from one site are brought together)
- Bulletins, Notices and Circulars

❖ Upwards Communication

- Joint consultation committee (where management and staff meet to consult about issues)
- Suggestions schemes
- Trade union channels (via shop stewards, negotiating committees etc.)
- Grievance procedure

❖ Lateral Communication

- Interdepartmental Committees
- Special Project Groups
- Coordinating Committees

Operation of the Committee as a Communication Medium

Committees are found in practically every kind of organization. They are an integral part of the operation of every public sector organization, and are almost as popular in the private sector.

❖ What are Committees?

The first thing that can be said about them is that they are formal groups with a chairman, an agenda and rules of conduct. Committees invariably have a specific task or set of tasks to achieve. These tasks are frequently, although not always, associated with decision-making. In fact, many committees are expressly forbidden from reaching decisions, e.g., joint consultative committees and advisory committees. Some committees meet regularly, e.g., monthly senior officers committee in a public authority or quarterly planning committees of enquiry set up by Parliament or steering committee set up to monitor short-term projects.

As was stated above, committees are formal groups. The formality of a committee is expressed by the following features:

A chairman (or chairperson): Who is responsible for ensuring (a) that the committee is conducted in accordance with the rules, and (b) that it is supplied with the necessary resources, particularly with the written information it requires to carry out its work effectively.

A secretary: Who is the person responsible for taking the minutes of meetings, sending out the agenda and other papers, and generally acting as the administrative link with the members.

An agenda: Which sets out the agreed subject matter of the meeting. Part of the chairman's job before the meeting is to approve the agenda, over which he or she usually has the final word. The agenda enables committee members to know what is to be discussed and in what order, and this enables them in turn to prepare adequately before the meeting.

The minutes of the meeting: The official record of what has taken place. They serve to remind members of important issues or decisions that were debated at the time. Since they have to be agreed by the members as a true and correct record, they are a reliable source of information both to members and outsiders alike. In local authority committees and joint union management committees, for example, the minutes are made public for the benefit of ratepayers or union members, as the case may be.

Committee Papers and Reports: Which provide the committee with the quality of information, which will enable it to make well informed decisions or proposals. Reports, for example, may be purely factual, or both factual and analytical. Yet others may be innovative and imaginative. Whatever their contents and presentation, their aim is the same, i.e.: to provide relevant information, ideas and suggestions as the focal points for discussion of/agenda items.

Rules of procedure: Which are designed to promote the smooth running of a committee and to ensure that consistency and fair play are maintained. Such rules include procedures for:

- Speaking in a debate
- Proposing motions
- Voting
- Adding emergency items to the agenda, and
- Other issues relating to the operation of the committee as a communication medium

Advantages and Disadvantages of Committees

The advantages can be summarized as follows:

❖ Advantages

- Because they are organized groups, committees can undertake a larger volume of work than individuals or very small groups working in isolation
- Decision or proposals are based on a group assessment of facts and ideas, and not just on one powerful individual's preferences
- Committees can encourage the pooling of special know-how and talents possessed by individual members
- Committees act as a useful focal point for information and action within organisations.

These advantages are particularly important in two respects. Firstly, the sheer size and complexity of modern organisation make it increasingly impossible for isolated individual or small groups to meet the decision-demands of their organisations. Secondly, the growing pressures from all sections of the workforce for greater say in the decision making processes of their organisation are creating expectation that decision making will become more open and democratic. Committees are likely to be even more in demand as a result of these two factors.

However, it would be unrealistic to gloss over the disadvantages of committees as communication media.

The main disadvantages are as follows:

❖ Disadvantages

- Decision making is an altogether slower process when dominated by committees. It is also true that committee decisions may often represent compromise solutions rather than optimum solutions.
- Managers may be tempted to hide behind committee decisions, where these have proved unpopular and thus abdicate their personal responsibility.
- Committees sometime have tendency to get bogged down in procedural matters, which reduces the time available for the discussion of substantive issues.
- Committee work demands certain skills.
- Committees do not exist between meetings, and thus cannot act quickly and flexibly to meet sudden changes in a situation.

On balance, committees are probably best suited to large-scale bureaucracies and organisations which have a high degree of public accountability. Smaller-scale enterprises, on the other hand, would probably benefit more from the greater flexibility obtainable from less formal processes of decision making, such as informal management meeting and temporary project groups.

How to be an Effective Communicator

A young man whom I had known since he was in high school stopped by to see me and proudly displayed his recent MBA degree.

"I know a master's degree alone doesn't guarantee success," he said. "What do you think is the most important quality for someone who wants to become a business leader?"

I answered without hesitation, the ability to communicate.

Individuals who communicate effectively with people at all levels, of both genders, and from a variety of cultures and backgrounds are today's pacesetters.

In the old style hierarchical, authoritarian setting, communication is relatively simple. The top person tells the underlings to jump, and the underlings need only ask, "How high?"

In a modern organization, communication requires more finesse. The leader is not a transmitter of commands but a creator of motivational environments.

The workers are not robots responding to switches and levers, but thinking individuals pouring their ingenuity into the corporate purpose.

The corporate ideal is not mechanical stability, but dynamic, innovative, continuous change.

The leader who can't communicate can't create the conditions that motivate. The genius who can't communicate is intellectually impotent. The organization that can't communicate can't change, and the corporation that can't change is dead.

The good news is that anyone can become an effective communicator. The door to effective communication will open to anyone who uses these five keys:

Desire

Human infants have an inborn desire to communicate, and that desire enables them to pick up words quickly and to enlarge their vocabularies continuously.

That same kind of desire can enable you to enlarge your stock of words and improve your skill in employing them. Demosthenes, the Greek orator, had a desire to achieve eloquence after he was hissed and booed off the platform in Athens.

He cultivated the art of speech writing, then went to the shores of the Aegean Sea, where he strengthened his voice by shouting into the wind for hours at a time.

To improve his diction, he practiced speaking with pebbles in his mouth. To overcome his fear, he practiced with a sword hanging over his head. To clarify his presentation, he studied the techniques of the masters.

Today, more than 2,000 years later, the name Demosthenes is synonymous with oratorical eloquence.

Understanding the Process

Reduced to basics, communication consists of sending and receiving messages.

Language is the primary conveyer of thoughts and ideas. It turns abstract concepts into words that symbolize those thoughts. Those words take the form of spoken sounds or written symbols.

If the mind can immediately translate the sounds and symbols into mental pictures, communication becomes much more vivid and much more meaningful. If I say "I want a desk for my office," my listener has only a vague and general idea of what I want. If I say "I want a brown walnut desk," the listener has a more vivid mental picture.

The more skillful you become at conveying images, the more effective your communication will be.

Master the Basic Skills

Some people think the first requisite for good communication is an exhaustive vocabulary. Some people think it's impossible to communicate well without first absorbing a heavy dose of grammar, then memorizing a dictionary of English usage.

Words are important. Good grammar is important. And yes, it helps to know which words and expressions are considered standard and which are considered substandard among educated people.

But slavish allegiance to the rules of grammar can actually impede communication. People will sometimes go to great lengths to avoid usage that somebody has pronounced "ungrammatical" or "substandard." In the process, they forget the most important rule of communication: make it clear and understandable.

The vocabulary you use in every day speech has probably served you well. You use the words that you understand. Chances are, they're the words your friends, colleagues and employees understand.

If you try to use words beyond the vocabularies of the people you're trying to communicate with, you're not communicating; you're showing off.

Read the Gettysburgh Address, the Sermon on the Mount or Robert Frost's poetry. The communications that endure are written in plain, simple language.

Practice

I remember a story that gave me inspiration. A young musician had listened with awe as a piano virtuoso poured all his love and all his skill into a complex selection of great compositions.

"It must be great to have all the practicing behind you and be able to sit down and play like that," he said..."Oh," said the master musician, "I still practice eight hours every day."

"But why?" asked the astounded young man. "You're already so good!"

"I want to become superb," replied the older man.

I teach communication skills to thousands of people each year, through seminars, audio tapes, videotapes and books. Most of the people I reach are content to become good. Few are willing to invest the extra effort to become superb.

To become superb, you have to practice. It isn't enough to know what it takes to connect with people, to influence their behaviour, to create a motivational environment for them, to help them to identify with your message. The techniques of communication have to become part of your daily activity, so that they are as natural to you as swimming is to a duck. The more you practice these techniques, the easier you'll find it to connect with people, whether you're dealing with individuals one-on-one or with a group of thousands.

Patience

Nobody becomes a polished, professional communicator on the first try. It takes patience. A few years ago, William White, a journalism and English instructor, edited a book of early writings by Ernest Hemingway. The young Hemingway was a reporter for a Toronto newspaper, and this book was a collection of his articles written between 1920 and 1924.

The writing was good, but it was not superb. It gave a faint foregleam of the masterful storyteller who would emerge in "The old man and the sea" but it wasn't the Hemingway of literary legend.

What was lacking?

It was experience. The genius was there all along, but it needed to incubate. The sands of time can abrade or polish. It depends on whether you use your time purposely or let it pass haphazardly.

Acquiring skill as a communicator requires constant, careful, loving attention to the craft. The cub reporter didn't transform himself into a successful novelist through one blinding flash of literary insight. Like most people, he progressed from the "good" to the "superb" through hundreds of tiny improvements from day to day.

Communicating Assertively in the Workplace

Getting Started

Do you find that people get the better of you at work, that you're always the one that gets pushed around and ends up doing things that you'd rather not do? Does this make you resentful or unhappy because you feel helpless and unable to represent yourself strongly enough in the way you communicate?

Assertiveness is an attitude that honours your choices as well as those of the person with whom you are communicating. It's not about being aggressive and steamrolling your co-worker into submission. Rather, it's about seeking and exchanging opinions, developing a full understanding of the situation, and negotiating a win-win situation. Ask yourself these questions to determine your level of assertiveness:

- Do you feel "put upon" or ignored in your exchanges with coworkers?
- Are you unable to speak your mind and request what you want?
- Do you find it difficult to stand up for yourself in a discussion?
- Are you inordinately grateful when someone seeks your opinion and takes it into account?

If you answer 'yes' to most of these questions, you may need to consider becoming more assertive.

FAQs

Frequently Asked Questions are as follows:

Won't people think me aggressive if I change my communication style?

There are four types of communication style:

- aggressive—where you win and everyone else loses
- passive—where you lose and everyone else wins
- passive/aggressive—where you lose and do everything you can (without being too obvious) to make others lose too
- assertive—where everyone wins

If you become more assertive, people won't necessarily think that you've become more aggressive because their needs are met too. All that will happen is that your communication style becomes more effective.

I have had a lifetime of being passive. How can I change that now?

If you don't change what you do, you'll never change what you get. All it takes to change is a decision. Once you've made that decision, you'll naturally observe yourself in situations, notice what you do and don't do well, and then you can try out new behaviours to see what works for you.

I just don't have the confidence to confront people. Will becoming assertive help me?

This is a bit like the "chicken and egg." Once you become assertive, your confidence level will be boosted, yet you need to have sufficient levels of confidence to try it in the first place. Just try the technique out in a safe environment first so that you get used to how it feels, then you can use it more widely.

It's all right for people who have presence, but I'm small so I'm often overlooked. How can I become assertive?

Many of the most successful people, in business and in entertainment, are physically quite small. Adopting an assertive communication style and body language has the effect of making you look more imposing. Assume you have impact, visualize it, feel it, breathe it, be it.

I Find it hard to say 'No' to people. How can I change this?

Until you get used to being assertive, you may find this difficult. However, one useful technique is to say, "I'd like to think about this first. I'll get back to you shortly." Giving yourself time and space to rehearse your response can be really helpful.

Making it Happen

❖ Choose the Right Approach

Becoming assertive is all about making choices that meet your needs and the needs of the situation. Sometimes it's appropriate to be passive. If you were facing a snarling dog, you might not want to provoke an attack by looking for a win-win situation! There may be other occasions when aggression is the answer. However, this is still assertive behaviour as *you*, rather than other people or situations, are in control of how you react.

You may find it helpful to investigate some specially tailored training courses so that you can try out some approaches before taking on a coworker or manager in a 'live' situation. This sort of thing takes practice.

❖ Practice Projecting a Positive Image

Use 'winning' language. Rather than saying "I always seem to get the bum deal!" say "I've learned a great deal from doing lots of different things in my career. I'm now ready to move on." This is the beginning of taking control in your life. Visualize what you wish to become, make the image as real as possible, and feel the sensation of being in control.

Perhaps there have been moments in your life when you naturally felt like this, a time when you've excelled. Recapture that moment and 'live' it again. Imagine how it would be if you felt like that elsewhere in your life. Determine to make this your goal and recall this powerful image or feeling when you're getting disheartened. It will reenergize you and keep you on track.

❖ Creating a Positive Impression Prompts others to Take you Seriously

This can be done through nonverbal as well as verbal communication. If someone is talking over you and you're finding it difficult to get a word in edgewise, you can hold up your hand signaling 'stop' as you begin to speak. "I hear what you're saying but I would like to put forward an alternative viewpoint…" Always take responsibility for your communication. Use the "I" word. "I would like…," "I don't agree…," "I am uncomfortable with this…" Being aware of nonverbal communication signals can also help you build rapport. If you mirror what others are doing when they're communicating with you, it will help you get a sense of where they're coming from and how to respond in the most helpful way.

❖ Use Positive Body Language

Stand tall, breathe deeply, and look people in the eye when you speak to them. Instead of anticipating a negative outcome, expect something positive. Listen actively to the other party and try putting yourself in their shoes so that you have a better chance of seeking the solution that works for you both. Inquire about their thoughts and feelings by using "open" questions, that allow them to give you a full response rather than just "yes" or "no." Examples include: "Tell me more about why…," "How do you see this working out?", and so forth.

Assertiveness also helps you learn to deal with people who have different communication styles. If you're dealing with someone behaving in a passive/aggressive manner, you can handle it by exposing what he or she is doing. "I get the feeling you're not happy about this decision" or "It appears you have something to say on this; would you like to share your views now?" In this way, they either have to deny their passive/aggressive stance or they have to disclose their motivations. Either way, you're left in the driver's seat.

If you're dealing with a passive person, rather than let them be silent, encourage them to contribute so that they can't put the blame for their discontent on someone else.

The aggressive communicator may need confronting but do it carefully; you don't want things to escalate out of control. One option is to start by saying "I'd like to think about it first": this gives you time to gather your thoughts and the other person time to calm down. When you're feeling put upon, it's important to remember that you have as much right as anyone to speak up and be heard.

Conflict is notorious for bringing out aggression in people, but it's still possible to be assertive in this context. You may need to show that you're taking them seriously by reflecting their energy. To do this, you could raise your voice to match the volume of theirs, then bring the volume down as you start to explore what would lead to a win-win solution. "I CAN SEE THAT YOU ARE UPSET and I would feel exactly the same if I were you…however…" Then you can establish the desired outcome for both of you.

Common Mistakes

You go too far at first

Many people, when trying out assertive behaviour for the first time, find that they "go too far" and become aggressive. Remember that you're looking for a win-win, not a you win and they lose situation. Take your time. Observe yourself in action. Practice and ask for feedback from trusted friends or colleagues.

Others react negatively to your assertiveness

Your familiar circle of friends will be used to you the way you were, not the way you want to become. They may try and make things difficult for you. With your new assertive behaviour, this won't be possible unless you let them get away with it. If you find you're in this situation, try explaining what you're trying to do and ask for their support. If they aren't prepared to help you, you may choose to let them go from your circle of friends.

You bite off more than you can chew and get yourself into situations that are difficult to manage

If this happens to you, find a good way of backing down, go away and reflect on what went wrong, rehearse an assertive response, and forgive yourself for not getting it right every time. The more you rehearse the more assertive responses you'll have in your tool kit when you need them.

Checklists for Upward and Downward Communications

The importance of free-flowing forthright communications, both downward from management to employees and upward from employees to management, can hardly be overemphasized. Whether it's to support morale and productivity among the workforce or to assure that management takes advantage of employee input, good communications are essential. Where downward communication is poor, rumours and misinformation will fill the vacuum. Where upward communication is poor, employee grievances will fester driving down morale and productivity and increasing vulnerability to union organizing.

The following checklists of suggested vehicles for upward and downward communication can help you gauge whether your organization is performing as well as it might with respect to internal communication.

Upward Communications

- ***General manager's routine staff meeting with supervisors:*** In addition to production issues, these staff meetings should also include topics of interest to employees with respect to business developments, company affairs, that and any other topics that should be communicated by supervisors to rank and file.
- ***General manager's routine meeting with non-supervisory employees:*** In addition to production issues, these meetings should emphasize issues that involve pay and benefits, problems, complaints, rumours, and questions.

- ***Supervisor's routine meeting with employees:*** Upper management should ensure that supervisors have routine meetings that cover topics beyond production that are of interest to employees. In many environments, there is a tendency for supervisors to overlook these important communications vehicles while under pressure to produce.
- ***Employee newsletter for home delivery:*** The spouse should become involved in events and conditions to give the entire family a stake in and appreciation of the employee's job.
- ***Newsletters for supervisors:*** Subscriptions to appropriate newsletters that provide supervisors with information on how to do their jobs better and how to handling employees and job problems, or create a regular supervisor newsletter internally.
- ***Bulletin board programme:*** Every attempt should be made to make the bulletin board a viable source of information—in most cases, bulletin boards fall into disuse.
- ***Employee handbook:*** Handbooks should be published in an attractive, easy-to-use format so that they are readily usable by employees as a source of information.
- ***Supervisor's handbook:*** This document can serve as a training aid as well as communication tool.

Downward Communications

- ***Routine discussion meetings between employees and their supervisors:*** Supervisors should be trained in techniques for generating discussion among employees and in how to feed the information "up the line" on a routine basis. (Supervisors also need to be trained to feed information back down to employees.)
- ***Supervisor's appraisal of individual employees:*** Periodic appraisal by each supervisor on each employee under his or her supervision, including specific and focused questions which the supervisor must answer about each employee with a method for passing this information "up the line" in order to fix a "status appraisal" on each employee.
- ***Manager's appraisal of individual supervisors:*** Again, use focused, specific questions, recognizing that weak, arbitrary, unfair, or excessively harsh supervisors are a prime cause of employee discontent and acting out; be sure this information goes "up the line" in order to correct supervisory problems.
- ***Attitude surveys:*** Annual, anonymous questionnaires given to employees; use customized, specific questions that will alert management to trouble spots.

- *Employee suggestion programme:* For employees and family members, give monetary awards or other forms of recognition for accepted suggestions.
- *Grievance procedure:* Have a non-adversarial system where employees feel uninhibited in bringing their complaints and grievances past their immediate supervisors.
- *Open door policy:* Encourage employees to ask questions and take their concerns to anyone in the company.
- *Exit interviews:* Every employee who leaves the company should be interviewed and their comments on working conditions and morale recorded.

❖ Conclusion

All the above vehicles are effective. But more important than any specific vehicle for upward or downward communication is the commitment by top management and the supervisory staff to the ongoing importance of communication to the success of the business mission. This must be implemented through regular, consistent effort by management at all levels.

TEAM BUILDING SKILLS: EFFECTIVE LISTENING

Listening is an important part of the communication process. Recent studies on the communication process across a wide cross-section of people shows that, on an average, approximately 9 percent of the time is spent in writing, 16 percent of the time is spent on reading, 30 percent of time is spent on speaking, and 45 percent of the time is spent in listening.

Listening can be more tiring than talking. It demands intellectual, perhaps even emotional effort and total concentration It is a key factor in understanding others. Unfortunately, most of us are not very good listeners. Immediately after listening to a 10-minute speech, we typically remember only half of what has been said. After a few days, we've forgotten three-quarters of the message. Listening heads the list of essential skills, but it is not simple and few people think of developing it. It is such a routine activity that most people give it much thought. Yet, it can have a tremendous impact on success in your personal and business life.

What is Listening

Listening is a process involving five related activities:

1. *Sensing:* Physically hearing the message and taking a note of it. Reception can be blocked by interfering noises or impaired hearing.

2. *Interpreting:* Decoding and absorbing what you hear. The speaker's frame of reference may be quite different from yours, so you must try to determine what the speaker really means. Paying attention to non-verbal cues often increases the accuracy of your interpretation.

3. *Evaluating:* Forming an opinion about the message. Sorting through the speaker's remarks requires a good deal of effort. It is also tempting to dismiss ideas offered by people who are unattractive or abrasive and to embrace ideas by charismatic speakers.

4. *Remembering:* Storing a message for future reference. To retain what you hear, you must take notes or make a mental outline of the speaker's key points.

5. *Responding:* Acknowledging the message by reacting to the speaker in some fashion.

Types of Listening

❖ Various Situations Call for different Listening Skills

1. *Content listening:* The goal is to understand and retain information imparted by the speaker. The objective here would be to identify the key points of the message. In your mind, you create an outline of the speaker's remarks; afterward, you silently review what you have learnt. It doesn't matter whether you agree or disagree, approve – or disapprove – only that you understand. A typical case can be of a school teacher teaching students.

2. *Empathic listening:* The goal is to understand the speaker's feelings, needs and wants in order to help solve the problem. By listening, you help the individual vent the emotions that are preventing him or her from dealing dispassionately with the problem. This is the listening technique typically used by psychoanalysts.

3. *Active listening:* This calls for active participation from the listener who asks questions to clarify his understanding. The goal is to appreciate the other person's point of view, whether or not you agree. Hence the questions must be worded so as to clarify without offending the speaker.

4. *Critical listening:* The goal is to evaluate the message at several levels:

   - The logic of the argument
   - Strength of evidence
   - Validity of conclusions
   - The implications of the message for you

- The speaker's intentions and motives and
- The omission of any important and relevant point.

❖ A Good Listener

Some characteristics of a good listener are:

- Asks "What's in it for me?"
- Judges content; skips over delivery errors.
- Doesn't judge until comprehension is complete; interrupts only to clarify.
- Listens for ideas/central themes.
- Takes fewer notes and continues eye contact.
- Works hard at listening, exhibiting positive signs like leaning forward, clarifying doubts etc.,
- Avoids distractions.
- Exercises his/her mind.
- Keeps his mind open.

In order to listen effectively, a certain amount of discipline is needed. Practice the following:

- Stop talking to others and yourself. Learn to still the voice within.
- Imagine the other person's viewpoint.
- Look, act and be interested.
- Observe non-verbal behaviour.
- Don't interrupt.
- Listen between lines.
- Speak only affirmatively while speaking.
- Rephrase what the other person has just told you.

❖ Barriers to Listening

Under certain circumstances, there are barriers to listening which hinder the communication process. One should work at keeping these at bay. Typical are:

1. ***Boredom:*** I have heard that before, What is new? What a monotonous tone!

2. *Environment:* So noisy! Too many distractions.
3. *Preconceived ideas:* I know it all, I don't believe it.
4. *Tiredness:* Can't concentrate, I'm worried.
5. *The urge to speak and respond:* Jumping to conclusions, I believe you mean this. If you consciously avoid the above barriers and inculcate the traits of a good listener, then listening would become another important skill in your repertoire.

❖ Active Listening

In this tutorial, the reader can learn how to improve their listening skills by using Active Listening.

We spend up to 80 percent of our conscious hours using four basic communication skills:

- Writing
- Reading
- Speaking
- Listening

Listening accounts for more than 50 percent of that time, so we're actually spending 40 percent of our conscious time just listening. We tend to give little attention to the listening part of the communication process, which is amazing considering the facts stated here.

On average, people retain only 25 percent of what they hear. There are many reasons why this is the case:

- We perceive listening as a passive activity and find the prolonged concentration required impossible to maintain.
- The average person speaks at about 130 words per minute, whereas our thinking speed is about 500 words per minute. Consequently, we are continually jumping ahead of what is actually being said. We often, therefore, go on "mental walk-about", thinking of other things.
- We don't clear our minds beforehand so the "noise in our system" shuts out or distorts what is being said.
- The listener is tense with emotion so that his or her ability to listen is seriously impaired.

- We are concerned with our reply so that the concentration is on this rather than what is being said to us.
- The perception of the listener may so differ from the perception of the talker that a totally different interpretation of the information may occur.

How can We improve Our Listening?

Quite simply, by getting the sender of the message involved with the receiver to create a two-way communication. The technique of making the process of communication two-way is called **Active Listening**, which, as the name suggests is an active not a passive process.

❖ Active Listening Steps

The steps in active listening are:

- A sends a message.
- B receives a message. This involves concentrating fully on what is being said.
- B states what s(he) has understood but **makes no evaluations.**
- A either agrees with B's interpretation or, if not, sends the message again.
- This process is continually repeated until understanding by both parties has been achieved.

❖ Active Listening Techniques

Two techniques that can help us become more competent at active listening are **Summarising** and **Reflecting**.

❖ Summarising

This is concerned with the factual side of the message and involves stating back to the speaker the listener's understanding of the information. This paraphrasing should take place at regular intervals and has the advantage of:

- Checking understanding.
- Offering opportunities for clarification.
- Showing the speaker that you have been listening to what has been said, thus demonstrating your interest.
- Giving the speaker feedback on how well the message has been expressed

Useful phrases are:

- "As I understand it, what you are saying is ...."
- "So your point is that ...."

TEAM BUILDING SKILLS: COORDINATING

Coordinating-'achieving unity of effort', in Urwick's phrase is not a separate function of a manager. As Sune Carlson wrote, "The concept of coordination does not describe a *particular* set of operations but *all* operations which lead to a certain result."

Coordination is required because individual actions need to be synchronized. Some activities must follow one another in sequence. Others must go on at the same time and in the same direction in order to finish together.

How to coordinate?

Obviously, you can get good coordination if you get people to work will together. This means integrating their activities, communicating well, exercising leadership, and team building. You should also pay attention the specific techniques discussed below:

❖ Planning

Coordination should take place before the event rather than after it. Planning is the first step. This means deciding what should be done and when. It is a process of dividing the total task into a number of sequenced or related subtasks. Then you work out priorities and time scales.

❖ Organizing

You know what should be done. You then decide who does it. When you divide work between people, you should avoid breaking apart those tasks which are linked together and which you cannot separate cleanly from each other.

Your biggest problem will be deciding where the boundaries between distinct but related activities should be. If the boundary is either too rigid or insufficiently well defined, you may have coordination problems. Don't rely too much upon the formal organization as defined in job descriptions, charts and manuals. If you do, you will induce inflexibility and set up communication barriers, and these are fatal to coordination.

The informal organization which exists in all companies can help coordination. When people work together they develop a system of social relationships which cut across formal organizational boundaries. They create a network of informal groups which tend to discipline themselves. This frees management from detailed supervision and control and leaves it more time for planning, problem solving and the overall monitoring of performance.

❖ Delegating

The informal organization can help, but you still need to delegate work to individuals in a way that ensures they know what is expected of them and are aware of the need to liaise with others to achieve a coordinated result.

The art is to make everyone concerned understand the points on which they must link up with other people and the time in which such actions have to be completed. You should not have to tell people to coordinate, they should coordinate almost automatically. They will do this if you delegate not only specific tasks but also the job of working with others.

❖ Communicating

You should not only communicate clearly what you want done, you should also encourage people to communicate with one another.

Avoid situations in which people can say: 'Why didn't someone tell me about this? If they had, I could have told them how to get out of the difficulty.' Nobody should be allowed to resort to James Forsyte's excuse that 'no one tells me anything'. It is up to people to find out what they need to know and not wait to be told.

❖ Controlling

If you use the processes described above, and they work, theoretically you will not have to worry any more about coordination. But of course, life is not like that. You must monitor actions and results, spot problems and take swift corrective action when necessary. Coordination doesn't just happen. It has to be worked at, but avoid getting too involved. Allow people as much freedom as possible to develop horizontal relationships. These can facilitate coordination far more effectively than rigid and authoritarian control from above.

CASE STUDY

Coordinating

There is no one right way of coordinating a number of activities. It all depends on the nature of those activities and the circumstances in which they are carried out; for example, the present organization structure, the existence of coordinating committees and the facility with which communication can take place between those involved. Ultimately, good coordination depends upon the will of everyone concerned – to coordinate or be coordinated. Mechanical devices such as committees will not necessarily do the trick.

An example of good coordination took place in a company which was developing a new product in a new market. Neither the product nor the market fitted conveniently into the existing divisional structure and it was therefore decided to appoint one man as project manager to get the product launched. He would have a staff of two – a brand manager and a secretary. The work of development, production, marketing, selling and customer servicing would be carried out by the relevant departments in various divisions of the company.

The project manager had the status and authority to get things done by each department. The board was right behind the project and had allocated the priorities and resources required. But the different activities had to be coordinated and only the project manager could do it.

The easy way out would have been to set up a massive coordinating committee and leave it at that. This would have failed. Projects of this complexity cannot be coordinated just by creating a committee.

The project manager developed a different approach, which proved to be highly successful. His first objective was to make everyone concerned enthusiastic about the project. He wanted them to believe in its importance so that they would be committed to working closely with the other departments involved.

His next step was to hold separate discussions with each departmental head so that he completely understood the programme of work required in each area. With the help of a project planner, he then drew up a chart showing the key events and activities, and the relationships between them, and the sequence in which they needed to take place in order to complete the project. This chart was distributed to all the departmental heads supplemented by an explanatory brief on the work required at each stage of the programme. Only then did he call a meeting to iron out difficulties and to ensure that everyone knew what had to be done and when.

He set up a system of progress reports and held progress meetings with departmental heads. But these were only held as necessary and he did not rely upon them to achieve coordination. He depended much more on

Contd...

personal contacts with individual managers, reviewing problems, noting where adjustments to the programme were needed, and stimulating the managers to even greater efforts when required. It was time consuming, but it kept him closely in touch so that he could anticipate any likely delays, setbacks or failures in communication, and be in a position to take action. He used the chart as his main instrument for checking that the critical events took place as planned.

The successful coordination and completion of the project were not achieved by one method but by the judicious use of a combination of techniques relevant to the situation: motivating, team building, planning, integrating, monitoring and controlling.

TEAM-BUILDING SKILLS: COUNSELLING

People Problems

As a manager, you will constantly be faced with people's problems. They come to you with their troubles or you become aware that all is not well and something must be done about it.

❖ Dealing with Problems

The four styles that can be adopted to deal with these problems are:

1. *Tell:* You solve the problem for them. You are the expert. You are the person in authority. You pronounce. They listen. Theirs is not to reason why.

   This is the authoritarian approach. The individuals may or may not obey, but even if they do as they are told, they won't know why and they will not know how to cope next time.

2. *Manipulate:* You know best, or think you do. You realize that a 'telling' approach is crude and that more will be achieved if the individuals feel that what they are going to do is what they wanted to do.

   Manipulators steer people in the direction in which they, the manipulators, want them to go. They do not care about the real needs of the individuals concerned, they only offer help and advice which further their own interests and increase their power.

   Manipulators have a poor opinion of the people they are manipulating. They want to change them to the sort of people the manipulator wants them to be. Such men are dangerous, although if they are seen through – and they often are – their efforts will be counterproductive and will only reflect badly on themselves.

3. *Advise:* When you give advice you get the individuals with problems involved in solving them. You are not exactly telling them what to do, instead, you are jointly analysing the situation against the background of their own needs, expectations, hopes and fears.

   Advisers can help their clients to learn not only how to solve the current problem but also how to cope with it if it arises again. Good advisers will get their clients involved in discussing alternative solutions to the problem, leaving them to make the final choice. But there is the danger that as experts, advisers will so weigh the pros and cons of each alternative in favour of their preferred solution that their clients are left with little real choice.

   This is one of the reasons why good advice is not always taken. What may appear to you as good advice is not perceived as good advice by the recipients. They may agree at the time because of your authority but, deep inside; they see it differently. You may feel that you have passed the problem and its solution over to them but you may well have been in effect saying, 'Which of my ideas appeals to you?' They are not truly involved, and because of this, a joint understanding of the roots of the problem will not have been achieved. A superficial solution may well emerge which, on reflection, the individual feels uncomfortable about implementing.

4. *Counsel:* If you adopt a counselling style you are more concerned with the individual than the problem. You genuinely want to get involvement in solving it, not by presenting a choice of solutions from on high, but by getting the individual to decide for himself, with your help, what the best solution would be for him. The strength of the counselling approach over any other is that people will become more truly committed to do something if they can 'own' the problem and its solution. And they do this if they have made up their own minds and personally believe it is the right thing to do. Telling, manipulating, even advising, can each put pressure on people to which they can react negatively.

Why Counsel?

As a manager, you may often have to tell people what to do when you want to get them into action and there will be many occasions when you may believe that the right thing to do is to give someone advice because you genuinely feel that you know best.

But advice is often not taken and you should always consider when faced with people problems whether a counselling approach will produce better results. It takes time and trouble, but if someone is really worth saving, then your time would have been well spent.

How to Counsel?

There are two difficulties you have to overcome if you want to counsel effectively. First, you have to help the individuals to identify the real, 'core' problem, and this is hard because they may not be able to do this for themselves, let alone you. Second, you have to get the issue out into the open. This means dealing with feelings that people might not wish to reveal, especially to their boss. Personal problems can be compounded if people cannot talk about them and, somehow, the counsellor has to break through this barrier.

There is no formula for overcoming these difficulties. All you can do is to adopt a flexible approach which can be modified to fit individual circumstances, as described below.

1. *Listen actively:* Active listening means more than simply not talking. The counsellor has to show interest and attention so that the person being counselled thinks that he or she is the only one that matters. Plenty of eye contact is needed, coupled with words of encouragement when the individual opens up. People should not be led, but can be helped to develop a theme beneficially.
2. *Observe:* Observe as well as listen. Oral communication can be clumsy and full of hidden meanings. Take note of gestures (body language), manner, tone and expression as well as listening to the words. Use imagination to evoke meaning.
3. *Question:* The counsellor helps people to understand and define the problem by asking pertinent, open-ended questions, pertinent in the sense that they emerge from the information which the individual is giving during the session, open-ended in the sense that they are non-directive-; they do not suggest the answers you want. Questions are the starting point to get individuals to explore and clarify the problem and their feelings about it so that they can develop possible solutions for themselves.

The sort of questions you can ask are:

- What do *you* think? What is happening?
- How does this problem affect *you?*
- When did *you* first become aware of this difficulty?
- Where have *you* come across this problem?
- Who else is involved?
- Why do *you* think the problem has arisen?
- What do *you* feel should be done about it?

Don't tumble out the questions, especially the last one. They should emerge naturally during the course of the session, providing linking points or stepping stones to a further exploration of the problem, its causes and its solution.

4. ***Recognize feelings:*** The problem, unless it is purely technical, will involve feelings. You have to allow them to be expressed. In fact, by so doing, you may well help individuals by getting them to unburden themselves and release their emotions about the situation. You may be able to help a lot simply by letting these feelings come out and by listening to them sympathetically and without comment. All you need to do from time to time is to 'reflect' feelings. This means feeding back a remark in your own words such as 'so you feel that 'which either demonstrates that you understand or gives people a chance to restate their case.

5. ***Define the problem:*** This is the challenge. Individuals may define their problem in very broad terms, testing the water to find out if you are likely to respond in an understanding way. To get to the root of the matter you have to look for clues and help individuals to explore issues in greater depth so that they can define the problem for themselves with the aid of sympathetic listening and brief, well-directed questions. A considerable amount of both listening and questioning may be necessary before the point becomes clear, since strong emotions and clarity of expression seldom go together. When you think you under-stand the individual's viewpoint, it is often helpful to ask a summarizing question such as, 'Is this what you mean?' without passing any moral judgment.

   You should gradually form a hypothesis about the problem as the session continues. Do not reveal it to the individual. Instead, explore views, opinions, reactions and feelings in order to test the hypothesis and adopt, modify or replace it. This hypothesis will be your guide on how to help the individual to come to terms with the problem and deal with it. But you should not prejudge the issue. The hypothesis should emerge from what you hear and see, and you should be prepared to change it if new information becomes available.

   Above all, do not reveal that you think you have the answer. Your hypothesis is just used to indicate the direction that is most likely to lead to a resolution of the problem and your aim is to get the individual to work this out.

6. ***Explore solutions:*** Start from the hypothesis of why the problem exists—as defined by the individual, who should then be encouraged to suggest alternative ways of dealing with it. While you should make encouraging noises, you should not specifically approve or disapprove of anything. Simply get the individual to go through the pros and cons and come to a decision, unaided by you, on the best course of action. So long as you are certain that this solution will not harm the individual or anyone else, you can go along with it. But do not get

over-enthusiastic. Content yourself with a calm, even a cool statement, to the effect that you believe that the individual will provide the support needed to implement it. If you believe the solution is harmful, you have to try to get the individual to recognize this. Only suggest that further consideration is required, if you know that the solution cannot be implemented, because it fundamentally contravenes company policy or because you are convinced that the effect will be detrimental to the individual or others.

7. *Implement:* If you are asked to provide specific help with implementation, you should do so. Otherwise, let the individual carry on, but be ready to provide additional counselling if things look as if they are going wrong.

When to Counsel?

As a manager, you should be prepared to use the counselling approach if a member of your staff has a personal problem which is affecting his work. You are not there to pry into personal affairs but if you can help someone to get over a hang up you thereby achieve a change in behaviour which results in improved performance, the time given to counselling may well prove worthwhile and, of course, the more valuable a member of your staff is, the more time you should be prepared to spend on their problems.

Counselling, however, is not always the appropriate technique. You have to flex your management style to cope with different situations and there will be occasions when to deal with a problem member of your staff, you have to be more directive. But before taking this route, you should always consider whether in the longer run a counselling approach would be more beneficial not only for the individual but also for yourself as their manager.

Team Building Skills: Developing People

Investing in People

The chairman of an advertising firm once said that his "inventory goes up and down in the lift". His prime resource, his working capital, was people. The same applies in any other sort of organization. Money matters, but the human beings who work there matter even more.

If you want to take a pragmatic view of people, regard them as an investment. They cost money to acquire and maintain and they should provide a return on that outlay; their value increases as they become more effective in their jobs and capable of taking on greater responsibility. In accounting terms, people may be treated like any other asset on the balance sheet, taking into account acquisition costs and their increasing value as they gain experience.

The Learning Curve

The rate at which the value of staff increases is related to their natural ability, their motivation and the opportunities they have to get jobs or to achieve promotion. Developing people is about accelerating the rate of this increase at minimum cost. It always takes a period of time to become effective in a job. This process can be represented by a 'learning curve', thus:

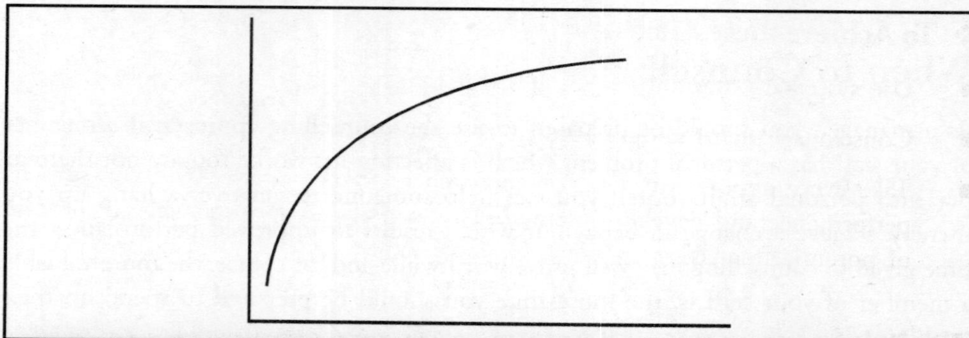

FIGURE 7.1 **A Learning Curve**

A career is often a sequence of learning curves, which could be re-presented thus (where x=promotion):

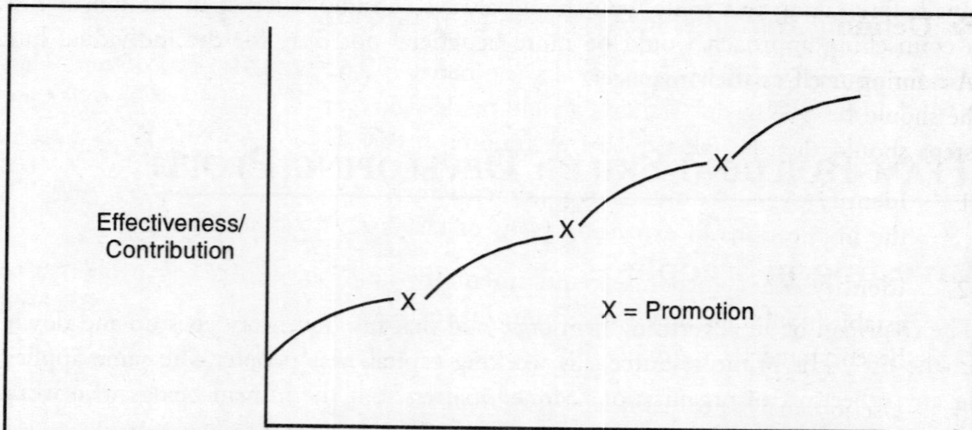

FIGURE. 7.2 **A Sequence of Learning Curves**

Development Aims

❖ Your Aims Should Be

1. Steepen the learning curve, i.e. to reduce the time taken to become effective.
2. Minimize learning costs-the opportunity costs of what people could do if they were fully trained, and the actual cost of training them.
3. Improve performance in the existing job, thus developing potential for the future.

❖ To Achieve these Aims

- Use systematic training techniques (for the manual and clerical jobs).
- Consciously plan the development of your present and future managers.
- Take every opportunity you can to coach your staff to improve their present performance and develop potential. This is particularly important in the case of potential management material.

Training

Start by defining training needs, and on the basis of this definition decide how and where training is to be carried out.

❖ Defining Training Needs

A training need exists where there is a gap between what someone can do and what he should be able to do. Training should be de-signed to fill that gap. The following steps should then be taken to define training needs:

1. Identify overall corporate requirements for manpower and skills by studying the implications of expansion plans or changes in technology.
2. Identify other corporate requirements by analysing operating problems to establish whether they result from inadequacies in performance which would be corrected by training.
3. Use job analysis to define the requirements of individual jobs in terms of skills and knowledge.
4. Use performance assessment to measure the extent to which individuals or groups of individuals have gaps in knowledge or skills which could be corrected by training.

5. Determine individual training needs on the basis of performance appraisal and study the results of such appraisals to identify common training needs.
6. Carry out assessments of management succession requirements and the potential of individuals for promotion.

How to train Manual and Clerical Staff?

For manual and clerical jobs where knowledge and skill requirements are not too complex, job instruction techniques should be used. These should be based on job analysis, which breaks the job into stages, listing at each stage the operations that have to be performed and the skills and knowledge required. The key points to be learned should be emphasized, including special points of difficulty, safety factors and exceptions to the normal routines.

From this analysis, you should draw up an instruction plan consisting of the following:

1. Put the trainee at ease and create interest by explaining why training is going to take place, what is going to be done and how the trainee will benefit from it.
2. Check on what the trainee already knows or can do.
3. Explain and, wherever possible, demonstrate what has to be done and how. Take one step at a time and only move on to the next step when you are sure the trainee has absorbed what has been taught. Stress key points and say and show everything clearly.
4. Check understanding at each stage. Make the trainee do the work or explain to you what needs to be done.
5. Make the trainee practise each stage until the required standards of accuracy and speed are reached. It is some-times best to do this progressively. Thus when any two successive stages can be done separately at the required standard, get the trainee to practise them jointly until the standard for both stages together is reached. Then a third part is added and so on until the whole job is learned.
6. Put the trainee to work, but check, evaluate and retrain as necessary.

Remember that the basic purpose of training is the transfer of skills from those who have them to those who do not. Just having the skills is not enough to be an effective trainer. Anyone responsible for training should understand how best to impart knowledge or skills using the techniques described above.

Remember also that when you are training someone, the person under instruction does not necessarily want to learn, and may even be frightened of learning. Hence the importance of putting trainees at ease and creating their interest in learning. They have to see it as something that will benefit them as well as the company. They must not feel threatened.

Where to train?

Robert Townsend's approach to training in *Up the Organization* is simple: "The only way I know to get somebody trained is on the job."

This statement expresses a fundamental truth. People learn best by doing. Training off the job is too often irrelevant and there is always the problem of transferring what is learned on a course back to the workplace. Effective transfer of learning is possible if the off-the-job training simulates working conditions with a reasonable degree of precision, but this is often difficult to accomplish.

Training off the job is, however, appropriate in some circumstances. For example, it is often quicker and cheaper to train fitters and machinists in their basic skills in a separate workshop. And some knowledge, for example, of how to operate a new machine, may only be obtainable outside the organization.

But the fact remains that most learning takes place on the job, and its effectiveness depends on whether managers and supervisors are able to carry out training as one of their key responsibilities.

How to train Managers?

Off-the-job training can be of benefit to managers and supervisors. Action-centred techniques which involve trainees directly in real work problems, while providing them with the help and guidance of external tutors, have proved effective.

Managers can also benefit from the broadening effect of an external course which enables them to reflect and build upon their own experience and, more importantly, to meet and talk with other managers. Don't worry if they come back and say they learned more in the bar than in the classroom. It's what they learn that matters, not how they learn it.

Nevertheless, on-the-job training is still the best way of developing managers, especially if it is properly organized. Use planned experience and coaching as described below.

Management Development

Management development is about improving the performance of existing managers, giving them opportunities for growth and development, and ensuring, as far as possible, that management succession is provided for.

Managers need to be given the opportunity to develop themselves. As Peter Drucker wrote:

> *Development is always self-development. Nothing could be more absurd than for the enterprise to assume responsibility for the development of a man. The responsibility rests with the individual, his abilities, his efforts... Every manager in a business has the opportunity to encourage self-development or to stifle it, to direct it or to misdirect it. He should be specifically assigned the responsibility for helping all men working with him to focus, direct and apply their self-development efforts productively. And every company can provide systematic development challenges to its managers.*

In Douglas McGregor's phrase, managers are grown — they are neither born nor made. And your role is to provide conditions favourable to faster growth. As McGregor wrote:

> *The job environment of the individual is the most important variable affecting his development. Unless that environment is conducive to his growth, none of the other things we do to him or for him will be effective. That is why the 'agricultural' approach to management development is preferable to the 'manufacturing' approach. The latter leads, among other things, to the unrealistic expectations that we can create and develop managers in the classroom.*

There are three main activities in management development performance appraisal and management by objectives.

❖ Planned Experience

People learn mainly through experience. Surely, therefore, it is worth spending a little of your time planning the experience of any one with potential for development.

Planning someone's experience means giving him extra tasks to do which provide a challenge or extend him into a new area. It could be a project which he has to complete himself or he could be included in a project team looking at a new development or problem which cuts across organizational boundaries. Projects which enlarge experience in unfamiliar areas; for example, a marketing executive in finance or vice versa, are particularly useful. Planned experience will work better if it is accompanied by coaching so that those undergoing it can receive the maximum benefit from expert advice.

❖ Coaching

The best way to learn how to manage is to manage, under the guidance of a good manager. Coaching is an informal but deliberate way of providing this guidance. It should be linked to performance appraisal and the counselling that takes place as part of the appraisal procedure.

But coaching is a more continuous process. Every time you delegate a task to someone and discuss the outcome, you are presented with a coaching opportunity. When you delegate you can provide guidance on how the job should be done. When you discuss progress with your subordinate or when he reports back to you, you can ask questions on how well he has thought through what he is doing, suggest alternative ways of looking at a problem (do not provide the solution) and provide constructive criticism if things are not going right.

You can help to develop people by discussing higher-level problems with them, involving them in your decisions and increasing their understanding of how to tackle a job senior to the areas for which they are responsible.

Every contact you have with a subordinate provides you with a coaching opportunity. Without too much effort, you can contribute significantly to his improvement and growth by making the most of the chances offered to you.

TEAM-BUILDING SKILLS: CONDUCTING MEETINGS

❖ Down with Meetings

Meetings bloody meetings, the title of a well-known training film, strikes a familiar chord with us all. When you think how many committees exist and how many meetings are held in any organization, it is remarkable how hard it is to find anyone who has a good word to say for them.

It has been said that committees are made up of the unfit appointed by the incompetent to do the unnecessary, and, again, that the camel is a horse designed by a committee. Experience of badly organized and pointless meetings is so widespread that, for many people, these cynical comments come very close to the truth.

❖ What's Wrong with Meetings?

Meetings are criticized because they:

- Waste time-too many people talk too much.
- Fail to produce decisions and can be slow, exasperating and frustrating; they legitimize procrastination and indecisiveness.

- Tend to be dominated by a few people with strong personalities.
- Make lowest common denominator recommendations.
- Encourage political decisions where vested interests can prevail by means of lobbying and pressure.
- Dilute responsibility
- Are costly in time and money
- Concentrate on trivialities they cannot grasp big issues beyond their scope. Northcote Parkinson cited as an example of this, a committee which approved a £1 million capital development project (which it couldn't properly understand) in ten minutes flat yet spent two hours arguing about a new cycle shed costing £800.

❖ What's Right with Meetings?

Meetings tend to incite such criticism because they are not properly organized. Many of the criticisms leveled at meetings are really criticisms of their misuse, not their proper use. A well-organized meeting held at the right time for the right reasons can bring a number of benefits. It can:

- Ensure that important matters get proper consideration from all involved.
- Clarify thinking in that members have to justify their positions before the others present.
- Ensure that different viewpoints are aired.
- Act as a medium for the exchange of information.
- Save time by getting a number of people together.
- Promote coordination.
- Create something as a group which the individuals could not have achieved working separately, this is the process of synergy, where the whole is greater than the parts. To make meetings work, there are three things that must happen:
    - They should be set up properly
    - There should be a good chairman
    - The members should be able to participate effectively.

BOX 7.1 Do's and Don'ts of Meetings

Dos	Don'ts
Use a meeting if the information or the judgement is too great for one man.	Use a meeting if one can do the job better.
Set up committees only when it is essential to assemble people with different viewpoints in one place at one time.	Set up a committee if you want sharp, clear responsibility.
Appoint a chairman who is going to be able to control the meeting and get the best out of it.	Use a committee to administrate anything.
Put people with different backgrounds on the committee who can contribute Ideas.	Use a meeting or committee if you need speedy action.
Tell committee what they are to do and what their authority is.	Appoint a bigger committee than you need – over ten people can become unwieldy.
Be explicit about when you want the meeting to report back	Hold unnecessary meetings – it may be a good thing to meet regularly on the first Friday of every month but it may be an even better thing to meet only when you have something to discuss.
Use meetings where they work best – reviewing or developing policies, coordinating decisions, ensuring that all concerned with a programme are consulted and kept informed.	
Wind up committees as soon as they have served their purpose.	

Chairmanship

The success or failure of a meeting largely depends on the chairman. If you are chairing a meeting this is what you must do.

❖ Prior to the Meeting

Before the meeting starts, ensure that it has proper terms of reference and that the members are briefed on what to expect and what they should be prepared to contribute. Plan the agenda to provide for a structured meeting, covering all the issues in a logical order. Prepare and issue briefing papers, which will structure the meeting and spell out the background, thus saving time going into detail or reviewing purely factual information during the meeting.

❖ During the Meeting

1. Start by clearly defining the objective of the meeting, setting a time-scale which you intend to keep.
2. Go through each item of the agenda in turn ensuring that a firm conclusion is reached and recorded.
3. Initiate the discussion on each item by setting the scene very briefly and asking for contributions – ask for answers to specific questions (which you should have prepared in advance) or you may refer the matter first to a member of the meeting who can make the best initial contribution (ideally you should have briefed that individual in advance).
4. Invite contributions from other members of the meeting, taking care not to allow anyone to dominate the discussions.
5. Bring people back to order if they drift from the point.
6. If there is too much talk, remind members that they are there to make progress.
7. Encourage the expression of different points of view and avoid crushing anyone too obviously if he has not made a sensible comment.
8. Allow disagreement between members of the meeting but step in smartly if the atmosphere becomes too contentious.
9. Chip in with questions or brief comments from time to time, but do not dominate the discussion.
10. At appropriate moments during the meeting summarize the discussion, express views on where the committee has got to and outline your perception of the interim or final decision that has been made. Then check that the meeting agrees, amending the conclusion as necessary and ensure that the decision is recorded exactly as made.
11. Summarize what has been achieved at the end of the meeting, indicating who has to do what by when.
12. If a further meeting is needed, agree to the purpose of the meeting and what has to be done by those present before it takes place.

Members

If you are a member of a meeting you should:

1. Prepare thoroughly, have all the facts at your fingertips, with any supporting data you need.

2. Make your points clearly, succinctly and positively, try to resist the temptation of talking too much.
3. Remain silent if you have nothing to say.
4. Keep your powder dry if you are not leading the discussion or if it is a subject you are not knowledgeable about. Listen, observe and save your arguments until you can make a really telling point. Don't plunge in too quickly or comprehensively–there may be other compelling arguments.
5. If you are not too sure of your ground, avoid making statements such as 'I think we must do this'. Instead, pose question to the chairman or other member of the meeting such as, 'Do you think there is a case for doing this?'
6. Be prepared to argue your case firmly, but don't persist in fighting for a lost cause. Don't retire in a sulk because you cannot get your own way; accept defeat gracefully.
7. Remember that if you are defeated in committee, there may still be a chance for you to fight another day in a different setting.

THE MORNING MEETING RITUAL

Is your organization plagued by inefficient communications, finger pointing, and lack of accountability? Get all key decision makers to the table—same time, every day. Welcome to Marty Linsky's The Morning Meeting. From *Harvard Management Communication Letter.*

A global petrochemical company struggling to create a coherent strategy after a merger with a very different kind of firm. A small advertising and design house trying to manage itself during a time of rapid growth. A public agency facing a series of budget cuts that threaten core services and deeply held values. An established bank losing market share to new boutique players coming into its market and cherry picking high margin products. As diverse as the challenges facing these organizations seemed, when my colleagues and I looked closely, we recognized that they shared two closely linked underlying causes: chronic communication problems within the executive team and a lack of shared accountability.

When communication is stifled and turf protection the order of the day, an organization's senior leadership team is less than the sum of its parts and cannot grapple with strategic and operational challenges most effectively. Expertise and energy go untapped: less than frank communication sometimes means that team members do not know the full extent of one another's issue; and a lack of shared accountability leads some to think, "Hey, that's his problem and he's got to fix it."

In contrast, two qualities characterize high-functioning leadership teams:

1. Hard conversations happen—difficult issues move quickly from people's heads to the conference table.
2. Accountability is shared—individuals on the top team feel a responsibility to the organization as a whole, not just for their piece of the action.

To take senior teams to a new level of leadership, we have put together a model of top team communication that we call The Morning Meeting (TMM). It's a deceptively simple name for an intricately ritualized event that has delivered significant payoffs to the organizations that have put it into practice: Backbiting and turf protection are dramatically reduced. Tough problems are addressed while they are still manageable. Issues cannot be covered over, and people can no longer hide. Ownership increases.

What TMM Looks Like

The genesis for the TMM model was an organization we worked with where the top team met every morning, every day, at the same time. Because this meeting was where the big decisions got made, admittance was a highly valued privilege. Executives who were on the road called in, unless time zone differences made such virtual attendance impossible.

Here's how TMM in its purest form works: Every day, at the same time, the top team—numbering between six and fifteen people, both staff and line—assembles around a conference table, either in person or virtually. Also at the table are one or two others who either are responsible for an important current initiative or are valued for their area of expertise. There's no preset agenda. While the CEO sits at the head of the table, if there is such a spot, he does not run the meeting, and everyone sits in the same place each day.

Around the conference table on folding chairs, in a sort of gallery, are a handful of deputies and executive assistants to the principals at the table. Sometimes the CEO will have an issue or two to begin the meeting. More often, the CEO defers to the person seated to his left, the No. 2 person—the chief of staff, deputy CEO, or COO—who starts things off and runs the meeting. When No. 2's issues are fully discussed, the person seated to the left raises any issues of concern, and so on, clockwise around the table, full circle to the CEO. Once everyone at the table has had an opportunity to speak, everyone in the gallery leaves and the top team gets a chance to go around the table again. In this second phase of the meeting, executives discuss highly sensitive issues, such as legal and personnel matters, that demand a higher level of confidentiality. Depending on the size of the group and the complexity and number of issues, the entire meeting can take as little as 15 minutes or as long as two hours.

❖ The Ground Rules

- Anyone can put anything on the table for discussion; it doesn't have to be related to one's own area of responsibility. All are expected to be willing to comment on every issue raised, even those that lie beyond their technical expertise or area of responsibility.
- These are decision meetings, but issues do not just get raised and resolved. Implementation plans are broadly outlined and agreed upon, and internal and external communication strategies often are considered. Sometimes, with particularly sensitive issues, the exact language that everyone around the table is going to use is hammered out.
- Once an issue is fully vetted, the CEO determines the decision rule that will govern it. He decides whether he'll be the one to make the final call, whether a particular individual or subgroup will make it, or whether it will be made by group consensus.
- Changing one's mind, even in the middle of the conversation, is OK, even respected. Not having an opinion is not.
- There are no arguments about fact questions. Participants are to get the facts and raise the subject at the next meeting. Keep in mind, however, that fact questions are sometimes masks for deeper value-laden issues. An argument about the cost of opening a remote office might mask strategic concerns about whether expansion is a good idea.

Making it Work in Your Organization

When we try to introduce some variant of TMM into an organization, there is often resistance: "We can't do that here." "We're too busy." "How can so many senior people keep their schedules so flexible every day?"

Our experience, however, is that the resistance is often a mask for anxiety about leaving a familiar if dysfunctional mode of operating. (Being "too busy" is a way of feeling valuable.) Members of the top team have grown comfortable with the autonomy they have, with their one-on-one relationship with the CEO and with other team members, and with not having the responsibility of worrying about the organization as a whole. Having those conversations around the coffee machine sometimes feels safer than having them in a formal meeting.

That said, the TMM model is a flexible one. Not all executive teams will need to institute it daily to see benefits; one firm we worked with has had considerable success with a weekly meeting. During a crisis or during organization-wide change initiatives, we advise holding the meeting daily. When things are running smoothly, meeting less frequently can deliver positive results.

Of course, complexity and challenge do not exist solely within the upper reaches of an organization. Division and unit heads can adapt the model to foster better decision making and execution within their teams.

On the surface, TMM is about communication, but imbedded within it are norms and values that are critical for organizations that must deal with difficult issues and adapt nimbly to new situations: an openness to considering multiple perspectives, a willingness to share responsibility for finding creative solutions, and the discipline to move consistently from strategy to execution.

Surviving the Storm

By now, many HR professionals and team leads are familiar enough with team dynamics to start teams out on the right foot. Teams are kicked into gear with a team formation exercise or chartering session that lets all members know what they're expected to accomplish together and how much empowerment they have for getting there. Despite this important groundwork, teams usually hit rough spots as individuals clash and pressure to perform builds. With some teams, members will stop attending meetings altogether or attack personalities instead of positions – even the quiet ones! The team leaders complain that their members are trying to take over and that they (the leaders) are trying to do the best that they can. What can be done to help teams get over these growing pains and back on track?

Team theorists call this second stage of team development, the 'storming' phase – I, call it 'puberty'. It's like we're dealing with some unruly teenagers who are trying to make their statement in the world with 'attitude.' At the same time, the team leaders have to manage this behaviour and be prepared to deal with conflict and frustration.

I believe at this point it's important that the teams stop what they're doing and regroup. Take a half-day for members and the lead to vent and get all the issues out on the table, followed by structured problem solving and action planning exercises. This process of identifying and solving issues is the third phase of team development, referred to as 'norming.' It's a quick, transitional step that helps teams get back on track and enter into Stage four, 'performing.'

Here's the meeting process that I would recommend:

❖ Step 1

First, get all your teams in one room for this meeting as there may be issues that are similar at the team, leadership, managerial, departmental and/or organizational levels. Having everyone present enhances the energy level identifies overall trends and validates concerns as part of a normal developmental process. Have each team sit together during the event and have their team leaders act as the facilitators. To start off the meeting event, review definitions of a high-performance team. This sets a context for the upcoming discussion. Ask for additional input from the participants.

❖ Step 2

In my experience, there are always some positives that seem to get pushed aside when the negatives become so pervasive. So to ensure both the positives and negatives of teaming come out, I suggest doing a 'Forcefield Analysis' – a Star Trek name for a very simple, practical tool. This tool fleshes out the good and the bad (and sometimes the 'ugly'!). Divide a flip chart in half. As the header of one column, scribe 'What currently is helping us achieve high performance as a team?' In the other column, scribe 'What currently is not helping us achieve high performance as a team?' Have the team leaders help their team prioritize the most urgent and high impact issues that the team has some control over versus low impact, externally controlled issues (i.e. 'ineffective meetings' versus 'departmental budgets').

❖ Step 3

Once the issues have been prioritized, have each team pick what they perceive to be their number one issue (usually the 'easiest' to solve and has the greatest impact on helping the team become more high performing). Start brainstorming solutions. Make sure the team leaders encourage creativity and monitor any members' attempts to 'yeah but' or invalidate another member's idea. Sometimes members may feel insecure in putting forth their issues because they don't want to feel singled out. When anonymity is required, have members write their ideas down, one per post-it note. Throw the papers in a pile and redistribute them randomly for presentation and scribing purposes.

❖ Step 4

From the array of solutions have members then determine the easy from the not-so-easy solutions to implement. Once the easy solutions have been identified, start to action plan. My favourite format for action planning includes:

- What the solution/activity is?
- How we're going to go about doing it?
- Who's responsible?
- What resources are required to successfully complete the action?
- When will it be complete?
- What will the results look like?
- Who's going to monitor this plan to ensure it gets done?

Make sure that the team leaders challenge the 'doability' of the prescribed actions. Nothing enhances poor morale like having a team go through an action planning session to end up with tasks that prove impossible to complete.

❖ Step 5

If time permits, have the teams go on to their second highest priority issue. If no time is left, these issues then become the immediate focus of upcoming meetings. At the very least, once the plans are made, have the teams present their issue/action plan to the other teams for feedback and validation (i.e. *'this is what we liked about your solution(s)'* and *'this is what we think you could improve on'*). This process helps the teams feel part of the bigger 'departmental' picture. It provides better objective input to solutions that may be unrealistic or require additional information that only other teams may be able to provide.

As the manager, make sure that the teams feel your support for these non-task activities. Too often, management has teams facilitate the 'norming' event, but is then unwilling to help the teams with the necessary resources to help them get back on their feet (i.e. time, coaching, team leader training, etc.). What you've noticed already are the consequences of not maintaining the team process which, when avoided, significantly impact all task related activities.

You may even want to have your senior manager attend the action planning stage for the purposes of positive support and confirmation of the team process. This is where 'challenging up' becomes necessary and demonstrates your commitment to the team initiative.

My experience is that this 'norming' process should occur quite frequently as teams, especially in this day and age, will regress back to 'storming' as a result of any organizational changes (i.e. new team leader, new team member, new mandate, etc.) So be prepared to do the above activity a number of times. Good luck!

TEAM BUILDING SKILLS: MENTORING

In business, it is often said that the best form of management development is self-development. It is also said that you learn your job by doing it, not by being taught how to do it. But these sayings are only half-truths. People do not always know the way to go, neither do they always know the right way to get there. Guidance is necessary.

Traditionally, guidance is provided by the boss, and he is usually the best person to do it. He is, however, naturally inclined to be more concerned with getting the job done (job-orientated) rather than looking after the development of his staff (people-orientated). And this tendency will always be present when managers are under pressure, as they usually are. They know they ought to spend more time coaching their staff because they know that eventually they will get better results that way, but they also know that they must respond quickly to their work demands, so these will come first.

Training managers and the growing profession of career development managers can teach skills or advise on career steps, but they cannot provide much help with the day-to-day job and short-term development needs. Neither are they readily available to give immediate advice. This is where mentoring comes in.

What is Mentoring?

A mentor is defined by the *Oxford English Dictionary* as an experienced and trusted adviser. The word is Greek. The first known person who carried out this role was Mentor, adviser of the young Telemachus in Homer's *Odyssey.*

This process of mentoring goes on in all organizations on an informal basis, but there are considerable benefits from formalizing the system. This means appointing and training mentors who provide their advice to specified individuals and whose mentoring activities are coordinated by someone with authority in the organization, possibly the career development executive.

The Roles of A Mentor

Mentors play four roles that are as follows:

1. *Coach:* Mentors help the individuals assigned to them (sometimes called mentees) to analyse how they are doing their work and to define or redefine their aspirations. The mentor creates an atmosphere in which people can openly discuss and discover what counts for them. Self-assessment of how problems are being tackled by individuals in their job is encouraged and people are also stimulated into deciding for themselves what they need to learn and do to improve performance and prepare themselves for greater responsibility.

2. *Teachers:* As teachers, mentors provide direct guidance on how the individual's work problems can be solved. In giving this guidance, however, a good mentor will ensure that learning takes place. In other words, individuals will know how to tackle the problem themselves next time it arises.

   Mentors can also teach skills more directly by holding 'what if' sessions, in which they present problems to the individual in the form of 'what if the situation arises, how would you deal with it?' Mentors encourage and train the people they deal with to use analytical problem-solving techniques—getting the facts, defining the problem, reviewing alternative solutions, and evaluating each alternative before making a decision.

Trainees of any kind can benefit from having a mentor to whom they can go for advice on their course, the technical problems they are meeting, what they should be learning and how to get the most out of their experiences.

Mentors can also help people to learn about the organization's culture which determines 'the way things are done about here'. Every enterprise has its special ways of doing things and to fit into the organization and to progress within it, people have to learn about the behaviour that is felt to be consistent with the culture. They need to know the basic beliefs and assumptions that govern organizational behaviour, and they will be helped to do this if they know something of the traditions, folklore and legends that exist in all organizations. Individuals can find out these things themselves, but mentors can informally help them to speed up the process simply by discussing why things are done in certain ways.

3. *Sponsor:* Mentors create opportunities for their clients to prove themselves to demonstrate what they have to offer. They will get their 'mentees' on to project teams and advise them on the network they must build up, to assist them to develop an idea and get it accepted. Within organizations, so called 'intrapreneurs' who are involved in innovation will benefit from the sponsoring activities of mentors.

   In their sponsoring role, mentors will provide direct support as an advocate for the individuals they are helping. They will talk to their bosses and their colleagues in order to give them help and encouragement and, eventually, accept the proposals they put forward.

4. ***Devil's advocate:*** In this role, mentors challenge and confront their clients. They give them practice in presenting their arguments, handling counter-arguments and persuading others to accept their views. The mentor will provide guidance on what works and what doesn't and will help to increase the individual's confidence in dealing with higher management or sceptical colleagues.

Setting up a Mentoring Programme

The steps you should take to set up a mentoring programme are to:

1. ***Sell the scheme to management:*** They must know what is going to happen, why it is going to happen and what the benefits will be to them as managers and to the organization as a whole.

2. *Appoint a coordinator:* You need someone who will carry out the detailed work of setting up the system, training and guiding mentors (the mentors' mentor) and monitoring progress.

3. *Identify who would benefit from having a mentor:* New employees, trainees, individuals marked for promotion, or innovators.

4. *Select mentors:* Mentors should be volunteers, but you have to encourage the right people to volunteer and gently dissuade those who do not have the qualities required. Mentors need broad knowledge of the organization and its culture, a high level of technical, professional or managerial expertise, a real interest in people with the ability to empathize with their problems and aspirations, and actual or potential skills as a coach or teacher.

5. *Train mentors:* Ensure that mentors understand their role and know how to carry it out. This means appreciating that they can only guide or persuade, they cannot command and they must not cut across the normal lines of authority. Training in coaching and counselling techniques is particularly important. But the training should not produce a rigid approach to mentoring. Rules should be minimized and mentors should be given the maximum freedom to operate them in the way that suits them best.

6. *Allocate individuals to mentors:* Take care to link mentors to members of staff who will benefit from their mentor's particular skills and methods. Agree allocations with managers first.

7. *Enlist and maintain the support of managers:* Managers can feel squeezed out by the activities of mentors. It is important to ensure that managers do not feel threatened in any way and that they will provide backing to any mentors who are guiding members of their staff. Mentors must avoid at all costs undermining the authority of managers.

8. *Monitor the programme:* Get mentors to prepare progress reports and to bring to the coordinator any problems they are meeting. Encourage mentors who are having difficulties, and step in quickly to overcome adverse reactions from managers.

9. *Publicize benefits:* Make sure that everyone knows about the benefits of the mentoring system.

10. *Recognize mentors:* Mentoring is a demanding task which has to be done as an extra duty. Mentors should receive recognition for carrying out this work. They should know that their contributions are appreciated and that they are taken into account when reviewing their rewards and promotion prospects.

Build a Mentoring Culture – People Management

The People in your organizations train for years and go into debt for college. People work late nights and weekends. People spend the entire day taking phone calls when they're supposed to be on vacation. And people generate ideas and create the solutions that your organizations need.

People do these things. The people you have working for you today and the people you may hire tomorrow. And, the people who may resign because no one has recognized their abilities.

Yet, clearly, organizations do not do a good enough job developing and promoting their most important resource – their people.

What does it take to develop your people?

It takes more than writing "equal opportunity" into your organization's mission statement.

It takes more than sending someone to a training class. It takes more than hard work on the part of your employees. What development takes is people – from the CEO's office to the mailroom – people who are willing to listen and to help their colleagues. Development takes coaches; it takes guide; it takes advocates.

Development depends on mentors.

Time after time, successful people I talk to say that one of the most important keys to their success is having a mentor. It is hard to make it without a mentor and it takes too much time without a mentor.

But often there is no mentor around when you need one and especially when you face "particular challenges." What do I mean when I talk about the "particular challenges" that people in organizations face?

Challenges that Need Mentoring

Let me give you a few examples of some challenges we working people all deal with. Imagine that you are facing these situations. How would you react?

First scenario. You've been working in a staff job and a line job opens up in another city. It would be a perfect career move for you but the company fills the job without even asking if you're interested. They don't ask because they assume your spouse wouldn't want to leave his or her job to relocate. What would you do?

Or imagine this. You're in a meeting. It's your opportunity to shine in front of upper management. You've got an important point to make and you start to talk. Someone cuts you off. What would you do?

Or let's say you make that important point—and no one says a word about it. But five minutes later, a guy at the other end of the table says the same thing you did. This time it's a brilliant idea, and he gets all the credit. What would you do?

You're in another meeting — there's always another meeting — and one of your bosses tells a demeaning joke about the Pope — you are Catholic, and everyone knows it. What would you do?

Or a joke about gays — which you are, and maybe no one knows it. Or a joke about women — which you're not, but some of your colleagues sitting right next to you are. What would you do?

My point is not so much whether you or I know how to react in each of these situations

❖ Why does Mentoring work?

My point is really that we need to recognize that there are people in every organization — whether they're men or women, minorities, or people who grew up without any business role models in their lives — who don't know how to react in these situations.

And it's our responsibility to teach them.

Organizations are only as successful as the men and women who make them work.

So, if we care about our organizations and our people, we have to share our knowledge of the organizational culture; we have to share our wisdom; we have to mentor.

Mentoring Best Practices

If you want to establish a mentoring culture within your organization, here are some mentoring best practices.

- Set organizational goals. Don't establish a mentoring programme just because it is a good business practice. Develop a mentoring programme based on solid business goals such as increasing diversity or making your organization a better place to work
- Find out why the talented employees you wanted to keep left you.
- McKinsey and Co. asked top people what they look for when deciding which company to join and stay with. The answer: a great company and a great job. Talented employees want exciting challenges and great development opportunities. They leave because they are bored. Mentoring is a key to attracting and retaining talented employees.

- Develop people to their fullest potential. In order to develop your people, provide training opportunities, challenging projects and assignments, feedback, coaching and mentoring. In one study with people who had experienced real mentors, half of them said the mentoring experience "changed my life." Those are powerful words.
- Foster mentoring for women and minorities. Ten years ago, when I began a new job, I sat with female colleagues during company presentations, and wondered, "Why are the guys up there and we're not?" One of my first job assignments was to develop and manage a mentoring programme. We included a special group mentoring programme for women. Today, many of the young women I knew ten years ago at that company, have, in fact, climbed onto the stage themselves. Mentoring helped move women into the ranks of vice president, senior vice-president and division president.
- Point to the money. Losing talented employees and wasting talent costs companies money.

And remember, whatever programmes you design; they won't be effective unless there is commitment from the top. Visible, daily commitment.

Team Building Skills: Coaching

Coaching Techniques for Dealing with Underperformers

People do not perform at their job for one of two reasons: either they can't or they won't. Think about that for a minute. There is a world of difference between the two reasons.

If they can't do their job, it likely indicates a simple lack of skills or knowledge. This type of employee is coachable and usually easy to work with.

The second type of employee is the one we will address in this article—the employee who chooses not to do his or her job for whatever reason. These employees are either unsure of what is expected of them, or they refuse to do the job. The former situation is easier to address; the latter is a candidate for progressive discipline, which we will discuss later in this article.

Why are employees who refuse to do their jobs so tough to deal with? As managers, we:

- Expect them to read our minds and know what is acceptable
- Expect people to change on their own

- Expect them to look around and see what others are doing
- Cross our fingers and hope they just "get it."

As managers, what might we be doing wrong? We may be:

- Unsure of our own standards
- Unclear in our expectations and consequences of not following through
- Afraid of what Human Resources (HR) might say
- Afraid the employee will get upset and turn it into a confrontation
- Not sure what to say or how to say it.

How, then, do we deal fairly and firmly with underperforming employees? The secret is to give effective feedback on a regular basis, link that feedback to a 6–12 month coaching plan, link individual coaching plans to your company's performance review process (if you have one), and, if the situation warrants, link that to progressive discipline.

First of all, let's be clear on what you can and cannot address as a manager. You have the right to address employee behaviour and performance at work as often as you want and whenever warranted. Why employees behave a certain way or choose to perform at a certain level is their choice, but there are consequences to these choices. But we are not psychiatrists, and why people behave outside what is acceptable at work should be left to the experts to address. We can, however, expect and demand acceptable behaviour and performance at work.

How to give Feedback to an Underperforming Employee?

Feedback takes many forms. There is the written, formal feedback that takes place once or twice a year; informal feedback, like a thank you for a job well done; and behavioural feedback meant to improve employee performance, which we will address.

The objective of behavioural feedback is to let employees know the impact of their behaviour on the workplace, the team, or customers. Positive feedback is given when employees are doing a great job; corrective feedback is given when they are not. If we intend to give either type of feedback to employees, we need to ensure that we are being as clear as possible.

Examples of ineffective ways to give feedback include:

- Being personal
- Giving feedback in public

- Not being factual
- Giving a subjective opinion
- Waiting until weeks or months after the fact
- Not being specific
- Providing feedback on issues over which the employee has no control
- Verbally attacking the employee

Examples of effective ways to give feedback include:

- Keeping the feedback to behavioural issues
- Giving it in private
- Providing it with the intent for improvement
- Giving it in a timely manner
- Being specific
- Keeping the content to issues the employee can control

How do we give corrective feedback to underperforming employees so that we get their buy-in and do not put them on the defensive? The next section provides a four-step model for doing just that.

A Four-step Model for Giving Corrective Feedback

Just the facts – Give a clear behaviour description

A behaviour description is simply stating exactly what you saw or heard: just the facts. It is very difficult to argue with a good behaviour description since you will be stating exactly what was said or done without giving any judgment or conclusion.

For example, imagine you have an employee who is constantly late for meetings. If you were to say "You are always late for meetings, and I want it to stop," the employee would likely respond with something like, "No, I'm not, I was on time two weeks ago." Before you know it, you're into an argument and off-track.

A much better approach might be to say, "I noticed that you were 15 minutes late last Friday, you were 10 minutes late Tuesday, and you were 15 minutes late today." If true, it is impossible to argue with. The employee might try to justify why he or she was late but cannot argue with the facts. This approach separates the behaviour from the person and makes the discussion more impersonal.

Two key benefits to sticking to observable facts are that the approach 1) is much less confrontational and avoids putting the employee on the defensive, and 2) ensures that there is no misunderstanding around your concern.

Your reaction – How does the behaviour make you feel as the manager?

How, as a manager, does the behaviour make you feel? Are you happy, frustrated, angry, embarrassed, or thrilled? It is important that your employees know how you feel; you are the boss. They may have no idea that you are upset or angry about a certain behaviour until you tell them. They may try to dismiss the concern, but they cannot argue with how you feel.

Impact – What is the impact of the behaviour on the larger picture?

What is the impact on morale, the team, customers, and the company? Some employees may be shocked by the impact their behaviour has on other people. By describing the impact, you are giving the behaviour importance.

Request – What do you want to see happen?

Make your request a question, not an order, since having the employee come up with the solution will result in much better buy-in. Also, if the employee does not follow through and change, you have every right to challenge them. It's quite difficult for an employee to explain why they did not follow through on their own plan. Two examples of the four-step model follow.

Example 1

"Jared, let me tell you what I've heard. Yesterday I overheard you telling a customer on the phone that they were wrong, and just now I heard you tell a customer to call back because you are busy (**facts**). I'm concerned about company image (**reaction**). Talking like that to customers will give a poor service image and likely lead to complaints to management (**impact**). What do you suggest you do to address it?" (**request**)

Example 2

"Bernice, we need to talk about what I just saw. I saw you yelling at Tammy in the project meeting, and you also told her to stay out of the project finances (**facts**). I'm upset (**reaction**). Acting like this in meetings causes tension within the team, and I'm concerned the team will shut down and not give ideas in the future (**impact**). What can we do to resolve this?" (**request**)

Tips on giving feedback:

1. Practice first with someone you trust in order to get feedback on your feedback. Ask them to argue, make excuses, and play "what if" games.
2. Write down what you are going to say.
3. Don't allow yourself to get sidetracked from your objective of coming up with a plan to correct negative behaviour. It is very easy to get into problem solving technical issues, exploring excuses for behaviour, or being put on the defensive

yourself. Some employees will take the approach of "the best defense is a good offense" and try to argue their way out of it. Keep your objective in mind!

How to negotiate Coaching Plans with All Employees

❖ What is Coaching?

Coaching is a process that involves working with someone on a one-to-one basis to help that person achieve a desired result. It is the skill of providing feedback, direction, and support. The goal of coaching is to help the person develop the skills necessary to resolve their own problems in order to build self-esteem and confidence.

Managers should negotiate coaching plans with each employee and link these coaching plans directly to performance reviews so that there will be no surprises come performance review time.

By taking the role of a coach, you tap into the self-motivation of the employees to become part of the solution; coaches collaborate with others to develop their potential, thus building employees' self-confidence.

Some managers avoid the coaching approach because it takes time, while others simply do not see that developing others is their job. Ultimately, the consequence of not coaching is that employees never reach their potential, and the organization suffers as a result.

❖ Why Coach?

You coach employees to develop them or to correct a problem. Underperformers fall into the second category.

Advantages of coaching

Coaching...

- Tests employee potential
- Increases confidence
- Allows managers to delegate
- Ensures that your standards are met
- Develops your staff
- Corrects a problem

Disadvantage of coaching

Coaching takes time and effort.

Key Steps in becoming an Effective Coach

Know yourself and others

We are all different. One of the greatest challenges that faces us today is to recognize strengths and weaknesses in each person and adjust accordingly. Some people are quiet and more introspective, while others are more gregarious; some are very open and confident, while others are defensive and harder to deal with. Recognizing these differences will help the coach adjust and adopt his or her approach. Remember, the goal of coaching is to create a climate that encourages a change in performance. Employees all learn and absorb information differently. It is for this reason that they must be involved in deciding what works best for them.

Describe the performance gap and its consequences

Highlighting one specific area at a time so that the person does not feel overwhelmed. Be specific about the behaviour or performance area you want to discuss and why you think it will benefit the person's development. Let the employee know clearly what any consequences of his or her behaviour could be.

Give initial feedback

It is important that you are clear, specific, and behavioural. Use the feedback approach described previously.

Involve the employee in determining a solution

We are more committed to solutions into which we have input. It is for this reason that you need to be open to involving the employee in the solution. The solution may be painfully obvious to you, but let it come from them.

Coaching opportunities grow out of relationships that are built on mutual trust and respect. This does not happen by accident. This may not be present in the case of underperforming or difficult employees, so you must set clear expectations and deadlines and use necessary resources. Establish trust and respect by giving ongoing feedback and personally recognizing and reinforcing well-done work.

Encourage and express confidence

Remember, the overall purpose of coaching is to engage employees in a process of striving toward optimal performance that will benefit the organization as well as themselves. Your confidence in them will build their own confidence. By closing on a positive note of support, you help motivate people to succeed.

Give ongoing feedback

Employees who receive consistent support from others respond more positively to developmental feedback when it becomes necessary. As a coach, you use your feedback skills to teach, guide, encourage, and refocus your employees. It is important to constantly encourage and reinforce the attempt to change performance. Your employees deserve an honest reaction from you. As a coach, you need to guide them back onto the right track if they lose their focus. Without ongoing recognition, they could lose heart and give up before they have changed for the positive.

Follow up

This is a formal process that involves a meeting with the person to review and summarize the initial performance gap, how it has been resolved, and the effect it has had on them as well as the organization. This confirms that your coaching effort was not just lip service—you take this seriously. And it also sends a clear message that you do expect to see your standards met in the organization and are committed to working with others to ensure that this happens.

Preparing for a Coaching Meeting

- Know your standards and expectations
- Determine any skill or knowledge gaps between what you expect to see and the actual performance
- Try to determine the cause of the problem.

Conducting the Coaching Meeting

- Be sure that the employee knows this is a development opportunity, not punishment
- Give feedback on performance
- Have the employee come up with proposed solutions
- Listen carefully
- Settle on a plan and set small goals

After the Meeting

- Follow up regularly
- Give ongoing feedback
- Possibly set up a buddy system with an experienced team member

When to move to Progressive Discipline?

In some cases, employees refuse to get on board despite your best efforts. If you have been clear in your standards and your expectations, and the employee still refuses to cooperate or alter his or her behaviour and performance, then they have made his or her choice. Employees are adults, and as adults we all make choices, sometimes to our own demise. The reality is that some employees will never meet your standards, and you must deal with it.

Some reasons for progressive discipline are as follows:

- Tardiness
- Absenteeism
- Poor performance
- Stealing
- Lying
- Breach of confidentially
- Inappropriate dress
- Inappropriate language
- Credit card abuse
- Fraud
- Internet abuse
- Conducting personal business at work
- Telephone abuse

You will have discretion in how to deal with some infractions; others will be completely out of your hands. Breaches such as stealing, lying, fraud, violence, dress, and harassment will be dealt with by HR and the organization, since most companies have clear policies on such infractions.

For some infractions, such as instances of consistent underperformance, tardiness, and language, you will have considerable latitude, and, as a manager, you are expected to deal with them yourself.

The following is a four-step progressive discipline approach to dealing with such infractions.

1. ***An off-the-record chat:*** This is not the typical first step of progressive discipline, but you may find that, after a clear chat with a problem employee, the behaviour ends immediately and you may not need to go to the next steps.

   For an off-the-record chat, bring the employee into your office and close the door. This alone will send a clear message that you mean business.

The tone of the meeting can be light to very stern, depending on the situation, but at a minimum, you must discuss and get clear understanding on three things. First, be specific about the problem behaviour using your behaviour description techniques. Second, set very clear expectations. Third, be clear on the consequences if the behaviour continues. If you are unsure of the company's position on consequences, have an off-the-record talk with HR. (Give HR and your boss a heads-up that you are having this chat.)

Note that "off-the-record" does not mean undocumented. Be sure to write down everything that was discussed and when and what, specifically, was agreed upon. In the uncomfortable event that the legal department and the courts eventually get involved (not likely, but be safe just in case), take detailed, specific notes. Put them in a file and hope you never have to see them again.

2. *Verbal warning:* If your off-the-record chat does not work and the employee is not improving, then you need to get HR involved and move to the first formal step of discipline: a verbal warning. Many companies have verbal warning forms for this purpose. HR will explain the steps and will likely run the meeting with the employee and you. Verbal warning forms go into the employee's file and are signed by all parties. If the employee refuses to sign, this can be noted on the form.

3. *Written warning:* If the problem stays the same or worsens, you move to the written warning stage. Similar to the verbal warning, written warning forms are handled by HR, go in the employee's file, and specify what is expected regarding behaviour and performance as well as the consequences of not improving.

4. *Suspension or termination:* The last step is letting the employee go. Some infractions bypass the first three steps and call for immediate suspension or termination, such as violence, stealing, or lying. HR manages this, and company security or the police may be involved. By this time, the problem is clearly out of your hands, except for providing evidence or information.

❖ Summary

We have seen when, why, and how to give feedback to underperformers and how to link daily feedback to your coaching plans. We have seen how and when to act as a coach. If employees choose not to meet minimum standards and perform adequately, then we need to take progressive steps to protect the organization and other employees.

We have seen that managing employee performance and behaviour is your responsibility, but responsibility for following it through rests with the employee. As the old saying goes, "You can lead a horse to water, but you can't make him drink." Employees make choices about their behaviour and performance, and if they choose not to live within the boundaries set by you and the organization, then you need to cut your losses and find an employee who will. After all, there are plenty of good, ethical people out there who would go to work every day wanting to do a good job for you.

Coaching — A Powerful Catalyst for Transforming Performance

When we were at school, perhaps the least useful criticism a teacher could offer us was to write 'could do better' at the end of our work. It was hardly a helpful remark because, unadorned, it told you nothing other than that the teacher didn't like your work very much and wasn't even sufficiently inspired to offer suggestions for how you could actually do better.

As adults, we feel entitled to receive constructive comments about our work or our overall performance. Yet no matter how constructive these comments might be, the truth of the matter is that today, in the real world of business, all of us, without exception, could indeed do better.

Or at least we could, if only we knew how.

The purpose of coaching in business is precisely that: to empower you to do better and to show you how you can do better. Learning how to do better is not an easy task. As children we are more open to having our personalities guided and our performances prodded and improved than we are as adults. By the time we reach adulthood, our experiences of life, combined with our genetic heritage, leave most of us feeling that our personalities are fully formed and that we're not really open to making changes in our attitude or behaviour.

You hear the consequences of this all the time. 'I am what I am', people say. 'Take me or leave me', they proclaim. 'It's too late for me to change' is another comment beloved of those who do indeed feel that it is too late for them to change.

The trouble is, though, that people who make these kinds of proclamations do in fact very rarely perform to the top of their potential. They might do well, perhaps even very well, but even if this is so, you can be sure that, yes, they could do better.

But if they are going to do better, two basic factors need to feature within their attitude towards their performance.

The first factor is a willingness to change. Fortunately, this is a diminishing obstacle in today's business world. Coaching is maturing as a concept and people are getting accustomed to the idea that coaching is not just a remedial intervention for people who aren't doing well, but rather a means of helping people who are already doing well to do even better.

The second factor is a willingness to find out what you need to do in order to change for the better. Add those two factors together and you have an irresistible formula for being more successful in the future. For the truth is that whatever level of performance we reach, there is always going to be an 'increment of improvement' available to us.

Just as professional sportsmen and women take for granted the need to probe every aspect of their performance to make it even better, anybody in business — no matter how much they have achieved to date — should surely do the same. They must, in short, accept the role that coaching can play in maximizing their own performance and helping them strive for a stratospheric level of achievement.

In broad terms, business coaching should be directed at all of the following objectives:

1. Amplifying an individual's own knowledge and thought processes.
2. Improving the individual's self-awareness and facilitating the winning of detailed insight into how the individual may be perceived by others.
3. Creating a supportive, helpful yet demanding environment in which the individual's crucial thinking skills, ideas and behaviours, are challenged and developed.

The Specifics of Coaching

Business coaching today covers a wide range of areas of human expertise. Some coaching is directed at improving important niche skills such as writing a marketing plan or even a press release. On the other hand, coaching can also involve psychological interventions that address very fundamental personal issues, preconceptions and attitudes the individual brings to the workplace.

Not every kind of psychological intervention is coaching, however. For example, psychotherapy and counselling, powerful as they can be as tools, are directed more at helping individuals understand themselves better in a personal context and cope with and enjoy life more.

Business coaching is focused on business, and in particular on how individuals can be helped to perform better at the organizations that employ them. In practice, some of the issues addressed by business coaching, psychotherapy and counselling may be quite similar, but there is a significant difference in that business coaching is ultimately about helping the individual to perform at a maximum level within a particular organization.

Another significant difference between business coaching and psychotherapy/ counselling is that business coaching tends to be focused around a very specific problem or challenge identified by the individual being coached or by the organization that employs him or her. This means that business coaching is usually limited in duration, and will always focus on the problem in hand. Psychotherapy or counselling, on the other hand, involve going into aspects of the 'private self' and can last for a long time, even many years.

What Sort of Person should be a Business Coach?

When a particular professional or technical skill is being taught, an experienced practitioner in that area of expertise is likely to be the best coach. But when a more psychological type of intervention is required, such as when a behavioural issue is being scrutinized in the coaching process, a trained psychologist with experience of the real world of business is most likely to be suited to the demanding needs of the assignment.

"Business psychologists need to be good at spotting the positive aspects of an individual's psychological make-up".

Indeed, if a proper psychologist is not used, there is a serious danger that the intervention may be unskilled or superficial, and may perhaps cause more problems that it solves. Business psychologists, however, bring to their work an in-depth understanding of human behaviour, thought processes and other manifestations of personal psychology in the business world.

Business psychologists need to be good at spotting the positive aspects of an individual's psychological make-up that are responsible for successful performance. But in many ways, the most important contribution business psychologists can make to the coaching process is to be able to identify problems that are inhibiting the individual's performance or preventing the individual from really fulfilling their potential.

This last point is particularly important. As human beings, we are at one level, simply highly sophisticated types of biochemical machines. And like any other machine, it is all too easy for our capabilities to be massively undermined by a spanner in the works. The spanner might be something easily identifiable through just one or two coaching sessions, or it might be something buried deep down in the individual's make-up: something that needs unearthing by a business coach carrying out a fairly detailed and in-depth investigation into their psychological background.

A high-performer, for example, who refuses to delegate authority even to highly able and dedicated colleagues, may have a simple but not immediately obvious personal reason for being like this. These personal reasons often turn out to originate in the individual's childhood. It's not necessarily the case that the individual doesn't perform well, but rather that the individual will never be all they can be until the problem is identified and recognized. This may be solved in just one session, or it may take many months. But when a cause of negative behaviour is identified and its potency diminished, the sky can be the limit as far as individual and corporate performance is concerned.

Because coaching is essentially a psychological intervention, it's easy to assume that the benefits it yields will themselves be psychological and relatively intangible. But this is not the case at all. There is abundant evidence that coaching can be a highly effective process at a commercial level.

Benefits to organizations providing coaching can include the following:

1. Improvement in company revenues and profits
2. Enhancement in operational efficiency
3. Development in employee morale and motivation
4. Increased employee productivity particularly through developing soft skills
5. The provision of clear thinking space to gain clarity and fresh perspectives
6. The leveraging of organizational culture change
7. Better career progression and succession planning
8. The creation of cultures and environments which promote loyalty and reduce staff turnover.

There's no doubt that coaching is already recognized as a major resource for businesses in the UK. According to recent research undertaken by the Chartered Institute of Personnel and Development (CIPD), around 87 percent of UK companies make use of some form of coaching to develop their staff.

Business coaching can take place on a one-to-one or team basis. The crucial point is that either individual executives or the team of executives shall be given access to one or more professional specialist coaches who are solely motivated by the desire to help the coached person succeed. The coach will be or should be immune from company dynamics and politics, while also being aware of them. The coach will take time to monitor, assist and guide the coached person without having any other personal or political agenda than the success of the individual.

Today, there is a boom in business coaching. The reason is not hard to find: it can help an individual being coached make great strides in their personal performance, and the quality of this personal performance can also bring huge benefits to the organization employing the individual. There is a particular boom in one-to-one coaching, because this form of coaching is especially effective. Indeed, business executives are so much aware of this that increasingly the provision of a coach on an ongoing or periodic basis will be enshrined in employment contracts, especially for senior people.

❖ Finally, What about the Confidentiality Issue?

This is always a sensitive matter in business coaching because one principal purpose of the coaching activity is to unearth and identify issues that may be inhibiting the individual from performing to his or her fullest capability. To what extent should the organization who employed the coach (and most coaches are employed by the organization rather than the individual) be made aware of these issues?

The simple answer is that it is unethical for a coach to break confidence about sensitive matters. Coaches will therefore regard the coaching sessions with individuals as sacrosanct and private. However, they will certainly urge individuals to bring particularly difficult problems to the attention of the organization and may in certain circumstances ask the individual's permission to do this themselves. Furthermore, any really serious problem identified does need to be brought to the attention of the organization, but again, this must be done with the full consent of the person being coached. Unless confidentiality is in place, there is little chance of the individual approaching the coaching procedure with the level of frankness necessary for the process to be effective.

Team Building Skills: Persuading

A manager's job is 60 percent getting it right and 40 percent putting it across. Managers spend a lot of time persuading other people to accept their ideas and suggestions.

Persuasion is just another word for selling. You may feel that good ideas should sell themselves, but life is not like that. Every one resists change and anything new is certain to be treated with suspicion. So it's worth learning a few simple rules that will help you to sell your ideas more effectively.

Six Rules for Effective Persuasion

1. ***Define your objective and get the facts:*** Decide what you want to achieve and why. Assemble all the facts you need to support your case. Eliminate emotional arguments so that you and others can judge the proposition on the facts alone.

2. ***Find out what 'he' wants:*** Never underestimate a person's natural resistance to change. But bear in mind that such resistance is proportional, not to the total extent of the change, but to the extent to which it affects him personally. When asked to accept a proposition, the first questions people ask themselves

are: 'How does this affect me?' 'What do I stand to lose?' 'What do I stand to gain?' These questions must be answered before persuasion can start.

The key to all persuasion and selling is to see your proposition from the other man's point of view. If you can really put yourself into the other man's shoes, you will be able to foresee objections and present your ideas in the way most attractive to him.

You must find out how he looks at things, what he wants. Listen to what he has to say. Don't talk too much. Ask questions. If he asks you a question, reply with another question. Find out what he is after.

Then present your case in a way that highlights its benefits to him, or at least reduces his objections or fears.

3. ***Prepare a simple and attractive presentation:*** Your presentation should be as simple and straightforward as possible. Emphasize the benefits. Don't bury the selling points. Lead him in gently so there are no surprises. Anticipate objections.
4. ***Make him a party to your ideas:*** Get him to contribute, if at all possible. Find some common ground in order to start off with agreement. Don't antagonize him. Avoid defeating him in arguments. Help him to preserve his self-esteem. Always leave him a way out.
5. ***Positively sell the benefits:*** Show conviction. You are not going to sell anything if you don't believe in it and communicate that belief. To persuade effectively, you have to sell yourself. You must spell out the benefits. *What* you are proposing is of less interest to the individual concerned than the effects of that proposal on him.
6. ***Clinch and take action:*** Choose the right moment to clinch the proposal and get out. Make sure that you are not pushing too hard, but when you reach your objective don't stay and risk losing it. Take prompt follow-up action. There is no point in going to all the trouble of getting agreement if you let things slide afterwards.

Team Building Skills: Creating Shared Mindset

As we have learnt more about the intangibles of business—quality of leadership, the ability to make things happen quickly, a clear growth strategy, strong functional competencies, and brand recognition—we have seen that strong leaders and successful firms make choices that affect not only what happens inside their firm but also how investors value those decisions.

Intangibles become visible when they are actively understood and managed by leaders in an organization. When this is done, employee commitment, customer intimacy, and investor confidence rise. (For more information on managing intangibles, look for the paperback release of Dave Ulrich and Norm Smallwood's *How Leaders Create Value).* One intangible that many leaders rightly address in change efforts is organization culture, or shared mindset.

Shared Mindset creates Intangible Value

An organization begins to have a shared mindset when management approaches outlive any one executive and involve more than a single management practice, fad, or era. It represents an enduring thought pattern or framework that everyone in your organization brings to all activities. A shared mindset exists when customers and investors outside and employees inside have a common view of the organization's identity.

A shared mindset produces intangible value when it creates an identity or positive reputation in the mind of employees, customers, and investors that is tied not to a person or product but to the firm itself. Employee commitment, productivity, and behaviour both shape and are shaped by the identity of the firm. Investors also tend to be affected by the extent to which employees have a shared mindset. When every contact with a company reveals the same set of values and goals, it sends a powerful message.

We have worked with more than a hundred executive teams to create a desired identity or shared mindset. Regardless of scope, the process for crafting a shared mindset is similar.

❖ Phase 1: Create the Desired Identity

1. Ask each individual to write a response to the question: "What are the top three things we want to be known for by our best customers in the future?
2. Collect the responses and categorize them, sorting rigorously. At this point in the exercise, the goal is to see the extent to which a shared mindset exists among the top team, which requires exactness of language and ideas.
3. Add the total number of responses in the top three categories and divide by total responses for a rough measure of shared mindset. Our rule of thumb is that a desired level is 80 percent—rare in the first round.
4. Discuss themes by clustering and defining ideas that emerge from the responses. Redo the exercise until an 80 percent consensus on the top three items can be reached.

5. Put the themes into words that resonate with customers and then test the articulated mindset with customers in one-on-one meetings, focus groups, and other customer contact and research methods to make sure it is right. Ensuring that the words resonate with target customers is crucial, if the desired mindset will not influence buying choices, it is the wrong one.

❖ Phase 2: Determine How to make the Identity Real to Customers

Once you have the confidence your identity will have meaning and impact for target customers, you must find ways to make this identity real to those customers in their terms. This can be done by finding points of contact—touch points—between the firm and the target customer and creating ways to make the desired identity real in each one.

❖ Phase 3: Determine How to make the Identity Real to Employees

To make the identity real for customers, employees must reflect the shared mindset. To encourage this, companies must create plans and systems that ensure that employees' daily actions reflect the shared mindset. Several critical factors for leaders who want to make the mindset real to every employee include treatment of talent, reward systems, and training and development.

❖ Phase 4: Build an Action Plan for Implementation

Developing a shared mindset will change how employees, customers, and investors think and act. When your employees behave in ways that customers would like them to behave, employees, customers, and investors are all well-served. In the fourth phase, the ideas from preceding phases are translated to action. To be successful, action plans need to be specific, start small, and have leadership support.

Developing a shared mindset is just one example of how an intangible can add value to an organization. When leaders understand how they can build intangible value, they can begin to identity specific actions they can take to strengthen their firm brand and market value. Recent events illustrate how business leaders' impact on the market value of their companies can be a double-edged sword. Some executives inflated market value through deceit and manipulation and ultimately devastated their companies. Real leaders build tangible and intangible value and increased the market value of their businesses for the long term.

TEAM BUILDING SKILLS: MOTIVATING

In today's economy, more so in knowledge based industry — IT, ITES/BPO, the biggest task in front of a Manager is to motivate and retain employees. All the attempts made in this direction are big failure and no one knows what a route to employees' heart is. Here in this article, I have made an attempt to list some of the innovative ways to motivate an employee. Applying or implementing the below mentioned ideas is not an assurance that an employee will stick to you but still if done in a proper way, in a long run, these will surely be of benefit for the organization.

If your staff are going to achieve the results you are aiming at, they must be well motivated. That is, they must be made to want what you want them to want.

Ensuring that your staff is well motivated is essentially a matter of using the leadership skills and appropriate management style. An understanding of the process of motivation will greatly enhance your chances of success.

Understanding Motivation

Motivation is an organization's lifeblood; yet "motivation," as a business subject, is largely ignored. Even when not ignored, it certainly is not a focal point for strategic thinking.

Seldom is a clear, coherent, and overall approach taken to the challenge of motivating people. Most organizations don't give it much thought until something starts to go wrong. Pain gets people's attention.

❖ Four Reasons Explain this Fact of Life

1. Motivation is intangible.
2. Motivation drives all human action. It is the energy source. Those seeking to shape the behaviour ultimately wrestle with motivation.
3. With a bit of work, we can intuit our own motivation and monitories shifting nature and intensity. But we can only observe and measure the motivation of others indirectly.
4. Motivation is lost in a twilight zone.

Like a pop up fly ball which drops to the ground between a couple of confused fielders, motivation can fall into cracks. Everyone has an interest in motivation, but few, if any, know who is responsible for mapping the overall game plan.

Defining Motivation

Motivation has been defined as:

- The psychological process that gives behaviour purpose and direction (Kreitner, 1995);

- A predisposition to behave in a purposive manner to achieve specific, unmet needs (Buford, Bedeian, & Lindner, 1995);
- An internal drive to satisfy an unsatisfied need (Higgins, 1994);
- And the will to achieve (Bedeian, 1993). For this article, motivation is operationally defined as the inner force that drives individuals to accomplish personal and organizational goals.

❖ Why do we need Motivated Employees?

- Motivated employees are needed in our rapidly changing workplaces.
- Motivated employees help organizations survive.
- Motivated employees are more productive.

To be effective, managers need to understand what motivates employees within the context of the roles they perform. Of all the functions a manager performs, motivating employees is arguably the most complex. This is due, in part, to the fact that what motivates employee's changes constantly (Bowen & Radhakrishna, 1991).

Research suggests that as employees' income increases, money becomes less of a motivator (Kovach, 1987). Also, as employees get older, interesting work becomes more of a motivator.

Theories on Motivation

Understanding what motivated employees and how they were motivated was the focus of many researchers following the publication of the Hawthorne Study results (Terpstra, 1979).

Five major approaches that have led to our understanding of motivation are:

- Maslow's need hierarchy theory,
- Herzberg's two-factor theory,
- Vroom's expectancy theory,
- Adams' equity theory, and
- Skinner's reinforcement theory

Maslow's Theory states that employees have five levels of needs (Maslow, 1943): physiological, safety, social, ego, and self-actualizing. Maslow argued that lower level needs had to be satisfied before the next higher level need would motivate employees.

Herzberg's Theory categorized motivation into two factors: motivators and hygienes (Herzberg, Mausner, & Snyderman, 1959). Motivator or intrinsic factors, such as achievement and recognition, produce job satisfaction. Hygiene or extrinsic factors, such as pay and job security, produce job dissatisfaction.

Vroom's Theory is based on the belief that employee effort will lead to performance and performance will lead to rewards (Vroom, 1964). Rewards may be either positive or negative. The more positive the reward the more likely the employee will be highly motivated. Conversely, the more negative the reward the less likely the employee will be motivated.

Adams' Theory states that employees strive for equity between themselves and other workers. Equity is achieved when the ratio of employee outcomes over inputs is equal to other employee outcomes over inputs (Adams, 1965).

Skinner's Theory simply states those employees' behaviours that lead to positive outcomes will be repeated and behaviours that lead to negative outcomes will not be repeated (Skinner, 1953). Managers should positively reinforce employee behaviours that lead to positive outcomes. Managers should negatively reinforce employee behaviour that leads to negative outcomes.

Motivation and Needs

Motivation begins with the needs that exist within us all. If these are unsatisfied we establish a goal, consciously or unconsciously, and take action to achieve that goal. The basic motivation model therefore looks like this:

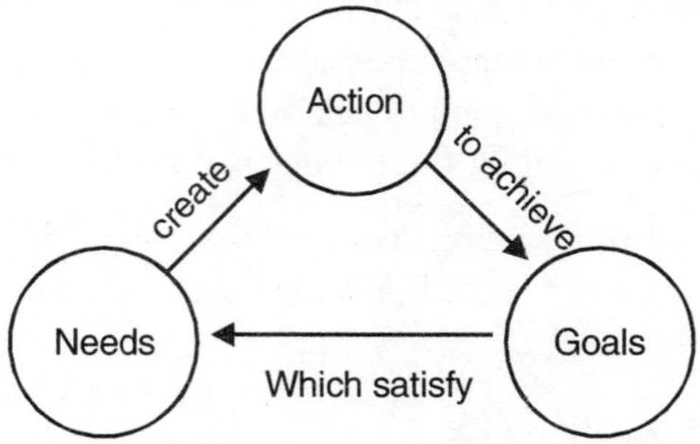

FIGURE 7.3 Basic Motivation Model

Most people make the mistake of trying to motivate others on the basis of faulty assumptions about their future behaviour". People's needs and the ways in which they are satisfied are much more complex than we tend to think. We observe behaviour and draw conclusions from it, but very often we do not really know what the motivating factor is.

The following is an example of how a superficial analysis of needs can lead a company astray:

The management of an aircraft assembly plant in the UK fell into this trap a few years ago when they were in the happy position of having a full order book and a shortage of skilled craftsmen. To achieve production deadlines, they recruited fitters from all parts of the country, promising help with settling in costs and removal expenses. Unfortunately, a very high proportion of the fitters (nearly 50 percent) left within three months when they were just beginning to become effective. Heavy recruitment costs had to be written off and production suffered.

The immediate reaction of the factory manager was that the newly engaged fitters needed more money. He could not alter basic rates but he encouraged his rate fixers to relax times and so increase bonus earnings. But labour turnover carried on at the same high rate, although earnings were increased all round.

The factory manager therefore asked the personnel manager to investigate the problem more thoroughly. The latter interviewed every fitter who was leaving and also a large sample of existing workers. He got the same story from everybody. Because this was the first production run, there were many modifications and design changes. This led to shortages of tools and parts. The fitters felt they were being messed about and were utterly frustrated by the constant interruptions and delays. Moreover, their earnings fluctuated considerably. They never knew what was going into their pay packets from one week to the next and this caused great difficulties with their wives, who were trying to adjust to new surroundings and expenditures.

Hardly any of the fitters complained about the level of earnings, it was their unpredictability that concerned them. Their basic needs were for a settled working environment and an end to wildly fluctuating pay packets, not extra cash.

To avoid this sort of problem you need to know more about the needs affecting motivation — how they are classified and how they operate.

Classification of Needs

The most famous classification of needs is the one formulated by Maslow. He suggested that there are five major need categories which apply to people in general, starting from the fundamental physiological needs and leading through a hierarchy of safety, social and esteem needs to the need for self-fulfillment, the highest need of all.

Another behavioural scientist, Frederick Herzberg, developed what he called a two factor model of human needs at work, on the basis of what some people regard as rather spurious research. One group of factors revolves around the need for people to develop in their job as a source of personal growth—it includes the needs for achievement, responsibility and recognition. The second group is associated with the needs for fair treatment in pay, supervision, working conditions and administrative practices.

How Needs Operate

According to Maslow, man is a wanting animal. It is unsatisfied needs that drive him forward. As one need is satisfied, the next one in the hierarchy emerges.

Herzberg looked at needs another way. He suggested that his first group of needs, those associated with the work itself: responsibility, achievement etc. are the real satisfiers because they seem to be effective in motivating the individual to superior performance and effort. The second group of needs, those associated with the environment in which work is carried out: pay, conditions etc. serve primarily to prevent job dissatisfaction, while having little effect on positive job attitudes. Herzberg christened this second group the 'hygiene' factors.

Herzberg and many others who have followed him thus distinguished between the *intrinsic* factors arising from the work itself, and the *extrinsic* factors provided by the employer, such as pay. The claim has been made that while extrinsic rewards can be important in increasing effort and minimizing dissatisfaction, intrinsic rewards relating to responsibility and achievement may have a longer and deeper effect in creating and increasing job satisfaction. The whole creed of 'job enrichment' (giving people more responsibility and scope in their jobs) has been founded on this belief.

While classifications of needs may be helpful, their use in understanding the complex nature of motivation is limited. For instance, even Herzberg had to admit that money 'takes on some of the properties of a motivator with dynamics similar to recognition for achievement', and neither he nor anyone else has been able to prove a significant relationship between satisfaction of needs and performance. We, therefore, need to look at other aspects of motivation.

The Relationship between Satisfaction and Performance

It is clearly simplistic to believe that a happy worker is a productive worker. There are some people who are quite happy to do nothing. But it could be equally simplistic to think that a satisfied worker is *necessarily* a productive worker. There is such a thing as being self-satisfied. Moreover, the numerous research projects on motivation carried out within factories and offices over the last fifty years have failed to produce convincing evidence that satisfaction leads to good performance. It has been shown that satisfaction explains less than 20 percent of variances in performance. Indeed, it is possible to say that it is not satisfaction that produces good performance, but good performance that produces satisfaction.

We must, therefore, reject the theory that passive and historical feelings of job satisfaction are the key motivators—an essentially static theory — and look at the more dynamic aspects of motivation in the shape of what people are seeking in the future – their expectations.

❖ The Role of Expectations

Motivation is a forward-looking process. The degree to which we are motivated depends very much on our perception of the likelihood that certain behaviour will achieve the results we want. Motivation is much more about expectations than about satisfactions. This concept of expectancy was formulated by Vroom, among others. He wrote:

> *Whenever an individual chooses between alternatives which involve certain outcomes, it seems clear that his behaviour is affected not only by his preference among these outcomes but also by the degree to which he believes these outcomes to be probable... An expectancy is defined as a momentary belief that a particular act will be followed by a particular outcome.*

Thus, in the case of the aircraft company mentioned earlier, the fitters were demotivated because their expectations about a steady flow of earnings were disappointed, not because they were not enough.

It follows from this commonsense proposition—people will only be motivated if they think they are going to get what they want (or avoid what they don't want)—that expectations about rewards have an important impact on motivation. We must therefore, consider the role of the reward system.

❖ The Reward System

It was suggested above that good performance causes satisfaction – a sense of achievement. Douglas McGregor said: "Commitment to objectives is a function of the rewards associated with their achievement."

If we want effort from the people who work for us, there are two factors we must consider:

- The value of the rewards to the individual in so far as they are likely to satisfy his needs for security, social esteem, and self-fulfilment
- The probability that rewards depend on effort, as perceived by the individual; in other words, his expectations about the relationship between his effort and his reward.

Thus, the greater the value of a set of rewards and the higher the probability that receiving each of these rewards depends upon effort, the greater the effort that will be made in a given situation.

The painstaking research of countless behavioural scientists seems, therefore, to have resulted in the 'discovery' that effort depends on the rewards people can expect to get — a fact which any sensible line manager knows without resorting to research. But effort is not enough. It has to be effective effort if it is to produce what we want. And there are a number of additional factors which affect motivation.

Other Factors Affecting Motivation

- *Ability:* The individual's intelligence, skills and know-how.
- *Perceptions about the job:* What the individual wants to do or thinks he is required to do. From the organization's point of view, it is desirable that the individual's perceptions should coincide with what it believes he ought to be doing.
- *Influence of other people:* The pressures exerted on a person by fellow employees, family and other social groups to which they belong. Group pressures are important because they affect social needs and the need for esteem.
- *The work itself:* The extent to which the work itself gives people an opportunity for achievement, responsibility and satisfaction. The following story is an example of how the quality of working life, resulting from the way jobs are designed, can affect performance.

In the new policies department of an insurance company, output, as measured by policies issued per clerk, was falling badly. A preliminary investigation suggested that high labour turnover was a major causal factor. A further investigation indicated that the nature of the work itself was the problem. The qualification level for new entrants was fairly high—four or more O levels. But the clerks were put on absolutely routine work. Each one dealt with a single stage in the process of dealing with new insurance policies. Their work was then checked by another section. Some people therefore spent their whole day checking or rechecking other people's work, a soul destroying occupation. If any interesting work needed to be done, it was hived off to a department of specialists. Only routine work went down, what was aptly called 'the pipeline'. The answer to the problem was to give each clerk whole segments of work, including the interesting bits. There was a significant reduction in staff turnover and improvement in performance.

These variables affecting performance can be expressed in the model shown in Figure 7.4, which is based on the important work of Lawler and Porter in this field.

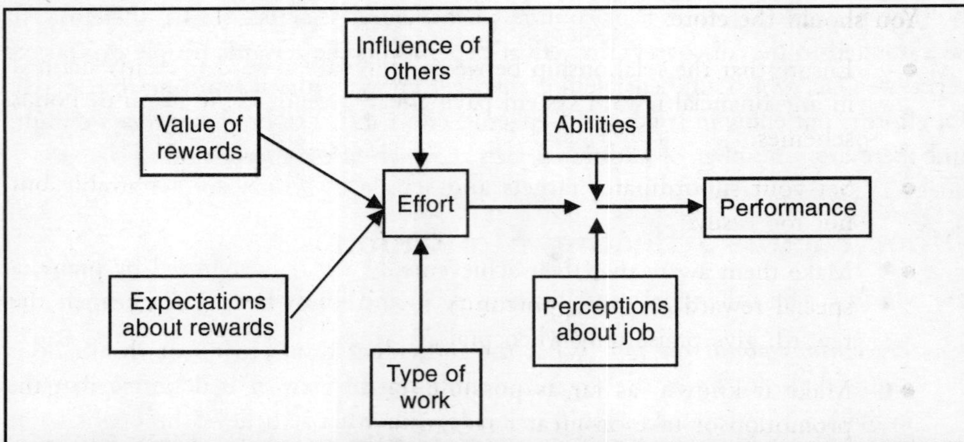

FIGURE 7.4 Variables Affecting Performance

Motivation in Practice

The analysis of the process of motivation in this chapter suggests certain things that you can do as a manager to improve your ability to motivate. These are as under:

1. Try to understand what the needs of your subordinates are in terms of Maslow's categories: security, social-esteem, self-fulfilment.
2. Find out not only what they need but also what they want. You may not be able to give it to them but you might at least be able to modify your approach to motivation in the light of this knowledge.
3. Use financial rewards as a prime motivator. Money is important because it satisfies so many needs — it provides what people want to increase their standard of living, but it also serves as the most effective way of recognizing achievement (self-fulfilment) and enabling people to demonstrate their achievement to others (esteem).
4. Bear in mind, however, that money is not the only reward that people need and want. They can also be motivated by recognition, praise, promotion and the work itself—the opportunity to achieve something extra or to take on greater responsibility. And this sort of reward can sometimes be more effective than money. It depends on their individual needs, and the reason you should try to identify these needs is that you can be more discriminating in the use of rewards.
5. Remember the importance of expectations as an influence on motivation. A reward will be much more effective when people know what they can get if they work hard and well enough.

You should therefore:

- Ensure that the relationship between effort and reward is clearly defined in any financial reward system payment by results, commission or bonus schemes.
- Set your subordinates targets and standards which are achievable but not too easily.
- Make them aware that their achievements will be recognized by praise, a special reward or the opportunity to do better but don't cheapen the reward, give praise only when praise is due.
- Make it known, as far as possible, what people have to do to gain promotion or take on greater responsibility.
- Spell out not only what they can get if they do well but also what they won't get if they do badly. This is not a crude carrot and stick tactic but a clarification of the fact that what they achieve or don't achieve is up to them.

6. Always keep in mind that your aim, as defined by Douglas McGregor, is the creation of conditions such that the members of the organization can achieve their own goals *best* by directing their efforts towards the success of the enterprise. Hence the value of:
   - Identifying people's needs, so that you can try to adjust rewards to meet those needs.
   - Getting people to think for themselves about what they can and should do and agreeing targets and standards with them.
7. Recognize the fact that people can be motivated by the work itself if it satisfies their needs for responsibility and achievement. Do this by using the following job enrichment techniques:
   - Increasing the responsibility of individuals (as in the insurance company case mentioned earlier).
   - Giving people more scope to vary the methods, sequence and pace of their work.
   - Giving a person or group a complete natural unit of work, thus reducing specialization.
   - Removing some controls from above while ensuring that individuals or groups are clearly accountable for achieving defined targets or standards.
   - Giving people the control information needed to monitor their own performance.

- Encouraging the participation of employees in planning work and innovating new techniques.
- Assigning projects to individuals or groups which give them more responsibility and help them to increase their expertise.

8. Remember that group pressures can affect motivation, for good or ill. Take steps to get groups on your side by involving them in key decisions which affect their work.

Motivating the Employees (Our Present Philosophy)

Employee motivation is enhanced most when organizations creatively and appropriately employ a multitude of motivators. We've profiled 10 areas that powerfully impact motivation.

Economic rewards: Money is a primary motivator. While base salary remains the largest share of the total cash pie, cash incentive plans continue to grow in popularity. Special achievement incentive rewards, spot bonuses, and cash equivalent rewards all play a role in the economic reward package. In many companies, stock based incentive plans, once limited to top executives, are offered to all employees. We are seeing an explosion of creative ideas in the realm of economic rewards, although not all approaches motivate people.

Promotions and transfers: While having economic value, promotions also carry crucial social and psychological meaning (recognition and sense of accomplishment) that, for many, far outweigh additional money or perquisites.

Opportunity to grow: The chance to improve one's self is an enormously important source of motivation. Organizations that offer this advantage are in a win-win partnership with their employees. The company creates and maintains a talented workforce to use as a competitive weapon, and the employees sharpen their own competitive edge as they self-actualize. Talk about synergy.

Challenging and stimulating work: The nature of work as a source of motivation varies with personality. For some, detailed work involving technical tasks can be a turn on; for others, fast-paced work with changing goals, roles and challenges is their dream job. But whatever the person-job match, the work itself proves every bit as important a motivator as economic rewards.

Autonomy: Freedom to take action, to make decisions, to work independently, is one of the factors most valued by people. Autonomy is crucial to achieving a sense of self-worth. Autonomy strongly influences the decision of individuals to join and stay with an organization.

Leadership: Leaders inspire people through their words and actions. By presenting a clear sense of purpose, offering a vision worth striving toward, and providing encouragement, leaders have the power to imbue people with hope, enthusiasm and determination.

Formal, psychic rewards: These rewards have symbolic significance. They spotlight individual or team achievement and outstanding contribution, giving people high visibility recognition that tends to be warmly remembered years after the event.

Informal psychic rewards: Positive feedback from a person's manager, peers, subordinates and others has a profound impact on motivation. Such informal psychic rewards are more than after-the-fact reinforcement; they are also an incentive that people seek to feel appreciated for what we do and who we are — our unique abilities, skills and knowledge.

Goals: Goals are powerful motivators. Goals give people a clear sense of what is expected of them, offering challenge and opportunity. They can energize and inspire exceptional effort.

Fun: Many work places are woefully devoid of smiles and laughter, yet a bit of humour goes a long way towards brightening the day and infusing spirit into the culture. Fun plays a vital role in motivation.

Motivating the Employees (Some Innovative Ways)

Get to know every employee

It is virtually impossible for a mid level manager to motivate his/her employees without getting to know them. Whenever starting a new job, all managers should make a point of having a one-on-one meeting with each member of their staff. Managers who do not know what makes each employee tick will find it very difficult to motivate them. Similarly, if the manager does not know an employee's strengths, he will be unlikely to find the right role for them. These one-on-one sessions are a great opportunity to encourage employees to contribute their ideas.

Show respect by asking employees for their feedback

When management doesn't ask employees for feedback, they are in essence saying, "We don't care what you think about how we treat you, and besides, we know what's best for you anyway." In contrast, when management asks employees for feedback about their management style and practices, they communicate respect and concern. In such an atmosphere, employees are more likely to feel committed to their work and the company.

Asking for feedback isn't just about communicating respect and concern, though. It's also about finding out what's working, and what isn't. Too often, we assume we know, when we don't. In one study, conducted by Kepner Tregoe, less than 1/3 of employees surveyed felt their manager knew what motivated them. Over ½ of the managers surveyed agreed.

Just as smart companies actively and continuously solicit feedback from their customers to find out how well they are meeting their needs, smart companies actively and continuously solicit this kind of feedback from their internal customers — their employees.

Give employees as much control as possible over their work

This strategy is related to the former one. The more control and autonomy employees have over their work, the more they're able to use their minds. The issue of control goes far beyond the intellectual realm, though. Decades of research shows that when people feel they don't have control, their intellectual functioning, interpersonal functioning, and behaviour deteriorate.

Feeling out of control creates tremendous stress and, if chronic, leads to the condition called Learnt Helplessness, which in turn leads to depression. When employees have a say in their work, and therefore feel in control, they become more energized, enthusiastic, and productive. (Important Note – the drive for control is so powerful that if employees aren't given opportunities for positive control, they will find ways of exerting negative control, such as calling in sick, engaging in work slow downs, illegitimately using short term disability, etc.).

Challenge them to improve the operation

One way for managers to make it clear that they welcome input and suggestions is to give each employee a clear mandate in their work requirements to take a hard look at the whole operation and make recommendations for improvements. This sets down a marker that all employees are expected to contribute their ideas. It is equally important to comment on each employee's efforts in this area at evaluation time.

Give employees who serve the customer, the power to please the customer

When organizations create policies and practices that hamstring the frontline service professional's ability to please the customer, they are virtually guaranteeing a demoralized, cynical workforce. Conversely, if frontline customer service professionals have the power to please the customer, the predominant tone of their interactions is one of appreciation and delighted surprise. This can't help but create a sense of pride and well-being — the emotional foundation of world class customer service.

"Customer for a Day"

Another mechanism manager can use to elicit suggestions is to have each employee be "Customer for a Day." In offices that have customers, whether they be internal or external, it can be quite enlightening to look at the operation from the client's point of view. The most engaged and creative employees (i.e. the "Master Sergeant Romeros" of the operation) will probably identify a long list of things that can be improved to make the customer's experience more comfortable, transparent and efficient. At a minimum, the experience will sensitize employees to any hardships experienced by the customer. (Note: Employees would not really be "Customer" for the whole day. But they should be given sufficient time to go all the way through the process, and then to write up their impressions and suggestions for the supervisor.)

Notice when employees do things right

Many managers unwittingly increase their own frustration, while creating a demoralized workforce, by always focusing on employee mistakes. Unfortunately, it's human nature to notice what's wrong more easily than what's right. Since we are all affected by how we are perceived, and since "what gets noticed, gets repeated," giving in to this natural tendency creates a downward spiral of increasing undesirable behaviours and decreasing morale. To prevent this from happening, provide managers with training and coaching about how to become a more consistent "good finder."

The great idea award

It is also important to find a way to reward or recognize employees whose suggestions help improve the operation. One option is to establish a Great Idea Award and give the recipient a customized certificate. Other options could be to give them a logo item, a cash award or even a day off (It will depend both on what the parent agency permits and what the employee values most). Managers at agencies that offer cash awards to employees who make money-saving suggestions should find out the procedures and use that mechanism whenever appropriate.

Don't force employees to check their brains at the door

Few things kill the spirit more quickly than mind-numbing work. Give employees the opportunity to think on the job. Encourage them to improve the work processes they're involved in. Not only does it make sense — people who do the work usually have the best ideas about how to do it better — it makes work more enjoyable and interesting.

In the customer service field, an excellent — and unfortunately underutilized — way to engage employees' minds, is to turn them into "customer service detectives." Create processes and rewards that encourage them to find out what customers want and then deliver this critical information to key decision makers.

Don't forget the implementation

A crucial part of this whole equation is the actual implementation of the great ideas generated by employees. Without follow-through, the organization simply ends up with a long list of unused suggestions and a lot of frustrated employees. To the extent possible, managers should put the person who suggested a great idea in charge of the actual implementation. The initiator of an innovative idea usually has a sense of ownership and is highly motivated to see their suggestion put into effect. Those managers who try to take the lead on all new initiatives will find themselves overworked and unable to accomplish everything they would like. By delegating the implementation, the managers can give their employees a terrific developmental opportunity, with the manager just needing to provide guidance and support.

❖ Conclusion

These are just a few suggested methods for encouraging employees to contribute their ideas for improving their organization. Implemented on their own, each of these practices would have limited impact. The key is to use a multifaceted approach that continually reinforces the fact that employees' ideas are welcome, valued, and rewarded. It would be awesome to see how much an organization's effectiveness could be improved if all managers were to systematically seek out and implement these kinds of suggestions from frontline employees. By helping your management team optimize employee emotions, you will be helping your organization make a significant impact on the primary sources of competitive advantage in today's marketplace.

TEAM BUILDING SKILLS: DELEGATION

You can't do everything yourself, so you have to delegate. At first sight delegation looks simple. Just tell someone what you want him to do and then let him do it. But there is more to it than that.

It may be that you would wish to delegate everything except what your subordinate cannot do. But you cannot then withdraw. You have arranged for someone else to do the job, but you have not passed on the responsibility for it. You are always accountable to your superior for what your subordinate does. Hence, as is often said, you can't delegate responsibility.

Delegation is difficult. It is perhaps the hardest thing that managers have to do. The problem is getting the balance light between delegating too much or too little and between over or under-supervision. When you give someone something to do, you have to make sure that it gets done. And you have to do that without breathing down his neck, wasting your time and his, and getting in the way. There has to be trust as well as guidance and supervision.

❖ Advantages of Delegation

- It relieves you of routine and less critical tasks.
- It frees you for more important work-planning, organizing, motivating and controlling.
- It extends your capacity to manage.
- It reduces delay in decision-making as long as authority is delegated close to the point of action.
- It allows decisions to be taken at the level where the details are known.
- It develops the capacity of staff to make decisions, get things done and take responsibility.

❖ When to Delegate?

You should delegate when:

- You have more work than you can effectively carry out yourself.
- You cannot allocate sufficient time to your priority tasks.
- You want to develop your subordinate.
- The job can be done adequately by your subordinate.

❖ How to Delegate?

When you delegate you have to decide:

- What to delegate.
- To whom you delegate-choosing who does the work.
- How to inform or brief your subordinate-giving out the work.
- How you will guide and develop your subordinate.
- How you will monitor his performance.

❖ What to Delegate?

You delegate tasks that you don't need to do yourself. You are not just ridding yourself of the difficult, tedious or unrewarding tasks. Neither are you trying to win for yourself an easier life. Delegation will, in fact, make your life more difficult, but also more rewarding.

Clearly, you delegate routine and repetitive tasks which you can not reasonably be expected to do yourself as long as you use the time you have won productively.

You also delegate specialist tasks to those who have the skills and know-how to do them. You cannot do it all yourself. Nor can you be expected to know it all yourself. You have to know how to select and use expertise. There will be no problem as long as you make it clear what you want from the experts and ask if necessary, force them to present it to you in a usable way. As a manager you must know what the specialist can do for you and you should be knowledgeable enough about the subject to understand whether or not what they produce is worth having.

Choosing who does the Work

Ideally, the person you choose to do the work should have the knowledge, skills, motivation and time needed to get it done to your complete satisfaction. Frequently, however, you will have to use someone who has less than ideal experience, knowledge or skills. In these cases you should try to select an individual who has intelligence, natural aptitude and, above all, willingness to learn how to do the job with help and guidance. This is how people develop, and the development of your staff should be your conscious aim whenever you delegate.

You are looking for someone you can trust. You don't want to over-supervise, so you have to believe that the person you select will get on with it and have the sense to come to you if he is stuck or before he makes a bad mistake.

How do you know whom you can trust? The best way is to try people out first on smaller and less important tasks, increasingly giving them more scope so that they learn how far they can go and you can observe how they do it. If they get on well, their sense of responsibility and powers of judgement will increase and improve and you will be able to trust them with more demanding and responsible tasks.

Giving out the Work

When you delegate you should ensure that your subordinate understands:

- Why the work needs to be done
- What he is expected to do
- The date by which he is expected to do it
- The authority he has to make decisions
- The problems he must refer back
- The progress or completion reports he should submit
- How you propose to guide and monitor him
- The resources and help he will have to get the work done.

Your subordinate may need guidance on how the work should be done. The extent to which you spell it out will clearly depend on how much he already knows about how to do the work. You don't want to give directions in such laborious detail that you run the risk of stifling your subordinate's initiative. As long as you are sure he will get the job done without breaking the law, exceeding his budget, embarrassing you or seriously upsetting people, let him get on with it. Follow Robert Heller's golden rule: "If you can't do something yourself, find someone who can — and then let him do it in his own sweet way."

You can make a distinction between *hard* and *soft* delegation. Hard delegation takes place when you tell someone exactly what to do, how to do it and when you want the results. You spell it out, confirm it in writing and make a note in your diary of the date when you expect the job to be completed. And then you follow up regularly.

Soft delegation takes place when you agree generally what has to be achieved and leave your subordinate to get on with it. You should still agree limits of authority, define the decisions to be referred to you, say what exception reports you want , and indicate when and how you will review progress. Then you sit back until the results are due and observe from afar, only coming closer for periodical progress meetings, or when the exception reports suggest that something needs looking into, or when a problem or decision is referred to you.

You should always delegate by the results you expect. Even if you do not need to specify *exactly* how the results should be achieved, it is a good idea when delegating a problem to ask your subordinate to tell you how he proposes to solve it. You then have the opportunity to provide guidance at the outset; guidance at a later stage may be seen as interference.

Guidance and Development

Delegation not only helps you to get your work done; it can be used to improve your subordinate's performance and therefore your trust in his ability to carry out more responsible work. Instruction, training and development are part of the process of delegation.

❖ Monitoring Performance

At first you may have to monitor a subordinate's performance carefully. But the sooner you can relax and watch progress informally the better.

You will have set target dates, and you should keep a reminder of these in your diary so that you can ensure they are achieved. Don't allow your subordinates to become careless about meeting deadlines.

Without being oppressive, you should ensure that progress reports are made when required and that you discuss deviations from the original plan in good time. You will have clearly indicated to your subordinate the extent of his authority to act without further reference to yourself. He must therefore expect to be reprimanded if on any occasion he exceeds his brief or fails to keep you informed. You don't want any surprises and your subordinate must understand that you will not tolerate being kept in the dark.

Try to restrain yourself from undue interference with the way the work is being done. It is, after all, the results that count. Of course, you must step in if there is any danger of things going off the rails. The Nelson touch is all right if your subordinate is a Nelson, but how many Nelsons have you got? Rash decisions, over-expenditure and ignoring defined and reasonable constraints and rules must be prevented.

There is a delicate balance to be achieved between hedging someone around with restrictions which may appear petty and allowing him licence to do what he likes. You must use your knowledge of the subordinate and the circumstances to decide where the balance should be struck. The best delegators are those who have a comprehensive understanding of the strengths and weaknesses of their staff and the situation in which they are working.

Above all, avoid 'river banking'. This happens when a boss gives his subordinate a task which is more or less impossible to do. As the subordinate is 'going down' for the third time his boss is observed in a remote and safe position on the river bank saying: "It's easy really, all you need to do is to try a bit harder."

The thoughts of Some Successful Delegators

John H. Johnson, editor and publisher of Johnson Publishing Company, Chief Executive Officer of Supreme Life Insurance Company and on the board of many large US corporations said of his delegation techniques: "I want to be big and I want to be bigger and I can't do it all by myself. So I try to do only those things that I can't get anyone else to do."

Franklin D. Roosevelt (late us President from 1933-1945) used a particularly ruthless technique based on competition, when he requested his aides to find some information. One of his aides told the story as follows: "He would call you in, and he'd ask you to get the story on some complicated business and you'd come back after a couple of days of hard labour and present the juicy morsel you'd uncovered under a stone some where and *then* you'd find out he knew all about it, along with something else you didn't know. Where he got this information from he wouldn't mention, usually, but after he had done this to you once or twice, you got damn careful about your information."

Robert Townsend's approach to delegation when he was chairman of Avis was to emphasize the need to delegate 'as many important matters as you can because that creates a climate in which people grow.'

Robert Magaven, when he started as the head of Safeway Food Stores told his division managers: "I don't know anything about the grocery business but you fellows do. From now on, you're running your division as if it were your own business. You don't take orders from anyone but me and I'm not going to give you orders. I'm going to hold you responsible."

Franklin Moore related the following example of strong delegation: Ralf Cordiner, the head of General Electric in the US for ten years had a vice president who wanted to see him urgently about a problem. The vice president explained his problem, and the choices he thought he had. 'Now, Mr. Cordiner,' he said, 'What should I do?' 'Do?' Cordiner answered, "You'd damn well better get on an airplane and get back to your office and decide. And if you can't decide we'd better get someone who can."

Peter Drucker, writing about responsibility, referred to a news-paper interview with a young American infantry captain in the Vietnam jungle. The reporter asked: "How, in this confused situation can you retain command?" The captain replied: "Around here, I am the only guy who is responsible. If these men don't know what to do when they run into an enemy in the jungle, I'm too far away to tell them. My job is to make sure they know. What they do depends on the situation which only they can judge. The responsibility is always mine, but the decision lies with whoever is on the spot."

CASE STUDY

Delegation

A group of researchers studying how managers delegate found that the following was happening in one of the companies they were studying:

In the situations in which the men we were interviewing found themselves, the boss was usually a hurried, and sometimes a harried, man. He gave out broad, briefly stated assignments, expecting his subordinates to make sense out of them. He also expected them to decide what information they needed, to get that information and then to go ahead and carry out their assignments. In the case of repetitive tasks, the typical boss assumed that after a few trials his subordinates would know for themselves when a job needed doing.

Frequently, the boss wasn't sure himself about which things needed attention in his department. And although he knew what eventually had to be accomplished, often he had lesser idea than his subordinates about the approaches to take. It wasn't unusual therefore for the boss to be vague or even impatient when approached with questions about the job while it was

Contd...

going on. Usually, he was much more assertive in describing what he wanted after a job was done than while it was in progress.

The production director came out of the board of directors' meeting where he had been roundly criticized for not getting the most out of his organization. He immediately called a meeting of his subordinates and told them: "I don't intend to subject myself to such humiliation again. You men are paid to do your jobs; it's not up to me to do them for you. I don't know how you spend your time and I don't intend to try to find out. You know your responsibilities, and these figures bear out that you haven't discharged them properly. If the next report doesn't show a marked improvement, there will be some new faces around here."

The Rules of Delegation

Delegation will always be one of the most important management skills and one of the easiest to get wrong. Good delegation saves you time, develops you people, grooms a successor, and motivates. Bad delegation will cause you frustration, demotivates and confuses the other person, and fails to achieve the task itself. Here are the simple steps to follow if you want to get delegation right, and the seven levels of delegation freedom you can offer.

A simple delegation rule is the acronym SMART. It's a quick checklist for proper delegation. Delegated tasks must be Specific, Measurable, Agreed, Realistic, and Time bound. If you can't check these points, don't delegate it. If you want to go one further, use SMARTER (same but with Exciting and Recorded).

The Steps of Successful Delegation

1. ***Define the task:*** Confirm in your own mind that the task is suitable to be delegated. Does it meet the criteria for delegating?
2. ***Select the individual:*** What are your reasons for delegating to this person? What are they going to get out of it? What are you going to get out of it?
3. ***Assess ability and training needs:*** Is the other person capable of doing the task? Do they understand what needs to be done. If not, you can't delegate.
4. ***Explain the reasons:*** You must explain why the job or responsibility is being delegated. And why to that person? What is its importance and relevance? Where does it fit in the overall scheme of things?
5. ***State required results:*** What must be achieved? Clarify understanding by getting feedback from the other person. How will the task be measured? Make sure they know how you intend to decide that the job is being successfully done.

6. *Consider resources required:* Discuss and agree what is required to get the job done. Consider people, location, premises, equipment, money, materials, other related activities and services.
7. *Agree deadlines:* When must the job be finished? Or if an ongoing duty, when are the review dates? When are the reports due? And if the task is complex and has parts or stages, what are the priorities?

   At this point you may need to confirm understanding with the other person of the previous points, getting ideas and interpretation. As well as showing you that the job can be done, this helps to reinforce commitment.

   Methods of checking and controlling must be agreed with the other person. Failing to agree this in advance will cause this monitoring to seem like interference or lack of trust.

8. *Support and communicate:* Think about who else needs to know what's going on, and inform them. Involve the other person in considering this so they can see beyond the issue at hand. Do not leave the person to inform your own peers of their new responsibility. Warn the person about any awkward matters of politics or protocol. Inform your own boss if the task is important, and of sufficient profile.
9. *Feedback on results:* It is essential to let the person know how they are doing, and whether they have achieved their aims. If not, you must review with them why things did not go to plan, and deal with the problems. You must absorb the consequences of failure, and pass on the credit for success.

The Seven Levels of Delegation

Delegation isn't just a matter of telling someone else what to do. There is a wide range of varying freedom that you can confer on the other person. The more experienced and reliable they are then the more freedom you can give. The more critical the task then the more cautious you need to be about extending a lot of freedom, especially if your job or reputation depends on getting a good result. Take care to choose the most appropriate style for each situation.

1. **"Wait to be told." or "Do exactly what I say."**

   No delegation at all.

2. **"Look into this and tell me what you come up with. I'll decide."**

   This is asking for investigation and analysis but no recommendation.

3. **"Give me your recommendation, and the other options with the pros and cons of each. I'll let you know whether you can go ahead."**

Asks for analysis and recommendation, but you will check the thinking before deciding.

4. **"Decide and let me know your decision, but wait for my go ahead."**

The other person needs approval but is trusted to judge the relative options.

5. **"Decide and let me know your decision, then go ahead unless I say not to."**

Now the other person begins to control the action. The subtle increase in responsibility saves time.

6. **"Decide and take action, but let me know what you did."**

Saves more time. Allows a quicker reaction to wrong decisions, not present in final level.

7. **"Decide and take action. You need not check back with me."**

The most freedom that we can give to the other person. A high level of confidence is necessary, and needs good controls to ensure mistakes are flagged.

TABLE 7.1 Empowerment: The Emperor's New Clothes

External Commitment	Internal Commitment
• Tasks are defined by others	• Individuals define tasks
• The behaviour required to perform tasks is defined by others	• Individuals define the behaviour required to perform tasks
• Performance goals are defined by management	• Management and individuals jointly define performance goals that are challenging for the individual
• The importance of the goal is defined by others	• Individuals define the importance of the goal

Remember, commitment is about generating human energy and activating the human mind.

External commitment: This is a contractual compliance. This commitment is external because all that is left for the employees is to do what is expected from them.

External commitment is a psychological survival mechanism for many employees – it is a form of adaptive behaviour that allows individuals to get by in most work environments. Prolonged external commitment makes internal commitment extremely unlikely, because a sense of empowerment must be learned, developed, and honed.

Internal commitment: Individuals are committed to a certain project, person, or programme based on their own reasons and motivations. By definition, internal commitment is participatory and very closely allied with empowerment.

The degree to which internal commitment is plausible in any organization is limited. Moreover, the extent of participation in corporate goals and aspirations will vary with each employee's wishes and intentions.

For top managers, the essential thing to know is that there are ***limits*** to internal commitment.

❖ How do you produce Internal Commitment?

- Pay, like other popular incentive schemes, often advances the idea external commitment while creating a bias against internal commitment.
- Many employees do not embrace the idea of empowerment with any more gusto than management does.

Recommendations for Managers

- Recognize that every company has both top-down controls and programmes that empower people, and that some inconsistencies are inevitable and must simply be managed. When these inner contradictions become apparent, encourage individuals to bring them to the surface; otherwise, a credibility gap will be created that can pollute the organization for many years to come;
- Don't undertake blatantly contradictory programmes. For instance, stop creating change programmes that are intended to expand internal commitment but are designed in ways that produce external commitment. Make sure that what is being espoused will not contradict what actually happens.
- Understand that empowerment has its limits. Know how much can be created and what can be accomplished. Know that empowerment is not a cure all. Do not evoke it needlessly. Once it has been created, do not misuse it.
- Realize that external and internal commitment can coexist in organizations but that how they do so is crucial to the ultimate success and failure of empowerment in the organization. For instance, external commitment is all it takes for performance in most routine jobs. Unnecessary attempts to increase empowerment only end up creating downward spirals of cynicism, disillusionment, and inefficiencies. As a first, precaution, distinguish between jobs that require internal commitment and those that do not.
- Establish working conditions to increase empowerment in the organization. If you want to help individuals move away from external commitment, encourage them to examine their own behaviour. Many employees are willing to become more personally committed if management is really sincere, if the work allows it, and if the rewards reinforce it.

- Calculate factors such as morale, satisfaction, and even commitment into your human relations policies, but do not make them the ultimate criteria. They are penultimate. The ultimate goal is performance. Individuals can be excellent performers and report low morale, yet it is performance and not morale that is paramount. When morale, satisfaction, and sense of empowerment are used as the ultimate criteria for success in organizations, they cover up many of the problems that organizations must overcome in the twenty-first century.
- Help employees understand the choices they make about their own level of commitment. One of the most helpful things we can do in organizations is to require that human beings not knowingly kid themselves about their effectiveness.
- Remember that empowerment can run contrary to human nature, and be realistic about how to achieve and use it.

Team Building Skills: Put Right People in Right Jobs

People who really know recruiting also know that the best way to understand the overall recruiting process is to visualize it as a subset of the common business practices of supply chain management, Six-Sigma quality and customer relationship management (CRM).

Recruiting cannot reach its optimal impact, nor can it help drive a firm's "performance mindset," if it views itself in isolation. Instead, it must view itself as part of the entire people/productivity process. It's not enough "just to recruit them," it's equally important to look at the next step, which is to ensure that top performers and new hires are continually placed in the right job. And after a period of time in any job, it's also important to continually redeploys your employees into other "more appropriate" jobs.

Unfortunately, we now know that two of the most common errors that managers make are 1) in placing the wrong people in the wrong jobs and 2) keeping them in these jobs for too long.

Right Person/Right Job for Top Performers

By "right person/right job" I don't mean the traditional "skill fit," but rather the underutilization of talent by putting top performers into inconsequential jobs and vice versa. Here's a list of the 16 most common errors managers make in how they treat and place their top performers. The common errors are listed in descending order of importance (in terms of business impact).

A placement error occurs if a manager...

1. Fails to identify a firm's "mission critical" positions, and then fails to focus their energies on these critical positions (10% of all jobs).
2. Fails to identify top performers, and then fails to treat them differently than the average worker.
3. Allows a mission critical position to be left open/vacant.
4. Allows a mission critical position to be filled with a non-top performer.
5. Allows a top performer to remain in a non-mission critical position (generally because they assume that top performers will move on their own).
6. Allows a top performer to have a "mediocre manager".
7. Allows a top performer to be 'stuck' in a mission critical position beyond their peak growth period.
8. Allows a "bottom performer" to remain on the same team as a top performer.

Other management failures include...

1. Providing little differentiation (less than 40%) in pay between the top and the average performers.
2. Allowing a low percentage of all employees' pay to be at risk (less than 20%), contingent on performance.
3. Not knowing specifically what motivates, challenges and frustrates every top performer.
4. Not providing every top performer with the resources they need to in order to succeed (great teammates, budget, a plan and learning opportunities).
5. Not providing every top performer with 'stretch' goals and enough on-the-job P&L opportunities to prove to themselves and others what they can do.
6. Allowing a top performer to get a better offer from another firm prior to getting a 'better' internal offer from their own firm.
7. Failing to continually 'challenge' any employee to the limit of their expectations.
8. Not measuring and rewarding their managers for doing each of the above things.

❖ Conclusion

"Place them and forget them" is a common approach to recruiting. But it is equally important to ensure that the right people are placed in the right positions, so that top performers can optimize their learning and growth. Unfortunately, many managers take a cavalier approach to placing workers, and as a result, they have top performers working in non-essential jobs. In addition to impacting their morale and retention, it also affects the firm's productivity, as well as its ability to maintain a competitive edge.

If you want your team to be productive, it's essential that you periodically conduct a "human capital audit" to ensure that the right people are placed in the right job!

31 Core Competencies for A Team Building

Major competencies for which employers look, along with some of the behaviours associated with each.

The following is a summarized list of the 31 competencies listed by 'cluster' (similar competencies related to a common skill set). Each competency includes a definition and the observable behaviours that may indicate the existence of a competency in a person.

Competencies Dealing with People

❖ The Leading Others Cluster

1. *Establishing focus:* The ability to develop and communicate goals in support of the business' mission.
    - Acts to align own unit's goals with the strategic direction of the business.
    - Ensures that people in the unit understand how their work relates to the business' mission.
    - Ensures that everyone understands and identifies with the unit's mission.
    - Ensures that the unit develops goals and a plan to help fulfill the business' mission.
2. *Providing motivational support:* The ability to enhance others' commitment to their work.
    - Recognizes and rewards people for their achievements.
    - Acknowledges and thanks people for their contributions.
    - Expresses pride in the group and encourages people to feel good about their accomplishments.

- Finds creative ways to make people's work rewarding.
- Signals own commitment to a process by being personally present and involved at key events.
- Identifies and promptly tackles morale problems.
- Gives talks or presentations that energize groups.

3. *Fostering teamwork:* As a team member, the ability and desire to work cooperatively with others on a team; as a team leader, the ability to demonstrate interest, skill, and success in getting groups to learn to work together.

Behaviours for team members

- Listens and responds constructively to other team members' ideas.
- Offers support for others' ideas and proposals.
- Is open with other team members about his/her concerns.
- Expresses disagreement constructively (e.g., by emphasizing points of agreement, suggesting alternatives that may be acceptable to the group).
- Reinforces team members for their contributions.
- Gives honest and constructive feedback to other team members.
- Provides assistance to others when they need it.
- Works for solutions that all team members can support.
- Shares his/her expertise with others.
- Seeks opportunities to work on teams as a means to develop experience, and knowledge.
- Provides assistance, information, or other support to others, to build or maintain relationships with them.

Behaviours for team leaders

- Provides opportunities for people to learn to work together as a team.
- Enlists the active participation of everyone.
- Promotes cooperation with other work units.
- Ensures that all team members are treated fairly.
- Recognizes and encourages the behaviours that contribute to teamwork.

4. *Empowering others:* The ability to convey confidence in employees' ability to be successful, especially at challenging new tasks; delegating significant

responsibility and authority; allowing employees freedom to decide how they will accomplish their goals and resolve issues.

- Gives people latitude to make decisions in their own sphere of work.
- Is able to let others make decisions and take charge.
- Encourages individuals and groups to set their own goals, consistent with business goals.
- Expresses confidence in the ability of others to be successful.
- Encourages groups to resolve problems on their own; avoids prescribing a solution.

5. *Managing change:* The ability to demonstrate support for innovation and for organizational changes needed to improve the organization's effectiveness; initiating, sponsoring, and implementing organizational change; helping others to successfully manage organizational change.

Employee behaviours

- Personally develops a new method or approach.
- Proposes new approaches, methods, or technologies.
- Develops better, faster, or less expensive ways to do things.

Manager/Leader behaviours

- Works cooperatively with others to produce innovative solutions.
- Takes the lead in setting new business directions, partnerships, policies or procedures.
- Seizes opportunities to influence the future direction of an organizational unit or the overall business.
- Helps employees to develop a clear understanding of what they will need to do differently, as a result of changes in the organization.
- Implements or supports various change management activities (e.g., communications, education, team development, coaching).
- Establishes structures and processes to plan and manage the orderly implementation of change.
- Helps individuals and groups manage the anxiety associated with significant change.
- Facilitates groups or teams through the problem solving and creative thinking processes leading to the development and implementation of new approaches, systems, structures, and methods.

6. ***Developing others:*** The ability to delegate responsibility and to work with others and coach them to develop their capabilities.

- Provides helpful, behaviorally specific feedback to others.
- Shares information, advice, and suggestions to help others to be more successful; provides effective coaching.
- Gives people assignments that will help develop their abilities.
- Regularly meets with employees to review their development progress.
- Recognizes and reinforces people's developmental efforts and improvements.
- Expresses confidence in others' ability to be successful.

7. ***Managing performance:*** The ability to take responsibility for one's own or one's employees' performance, by setting clear goals and expectations, tracking progress against the goals, ensuring feedback, and addressing performance problems and issues promptly.

Behaviours for employees

- With his/her manager, sets specific, measurable goals that are realistic but challenging, with dates for accomplishment.
- With his/her manager, clarifies expectations about what will be done and how.
- Enlists his/her manager's support in obtaining the information, resources, and training needed to accomplish his/her work effectively.
- Promptly notifies his/her manager about any problems that affect his/her ability to accomplish planned goals.
- Seeks performance feedback from his/her manager and from others with whom he/she interacts on the job.
- Prepares a personal development plan with specific goals and a timeline for their accomplishment.
- Takes significant action to develop skills needed for effectiveness in current or future job.

Behaviours for managers

- Ensures that employees have clear goals and responsibilities.
- Works with employees to set and communicate performance standards that are specific and measurable.

- Supports employees in their efforts to achieve job goals (e.g., by providing resources, removing obstacles, acting as a buffer).
- Stays informed about employees' progress and performance through both formal methods (e.g., status reports) and informal methods (e.g., management by walking around).
- Provides specific performance feedback, both positive and corrective, as soon as possible after an event.
- Deals firmly and promptly with performance problems; lets people know what is expected of them and when.

❖ Communication and Influencing Cluster

8. *Attention to communication:* The ability to ensure that information is passed on to others who should be kept informed.
   - Ensures that others involved in a project or effort are kept informed about developments and plans.
   - Ensures that important information from his/her management is shared with his/her employees and others as appropriate.
   - Shares ideas and information with others who might find them useful.
   - Uses multiple channels or means to communicate important messages (e.g., memos, newsletters, meetings, electronic mail).
   - Keeps his/her manager informed about progress and problems; avoids surprises.
   - Ensures that regular, consistent communication takes place.
9. *Oral communication:* The ability to express oneself clearly in conversations and interactions with others.
   - Speaks clearly and can be easily understood.
   - Tailors the content of speech to the level and experience of the audience.
   - Uses appropriate grammar and choice of words in oral speech.
   - Organizes ideas clearly in oral speech.
   - Expresses ideas concisely in oral speech.
   - Maintains eye contact when speaking with others.
   - Summarizes or paraphrases his/her understanding of what others have said to verify understanding and prevent miscommunication.

10. *Written communication:* The ability to express oneself clearly in business writing.
    - Expresses ideas clearly and concisely in writing.
    - Organizes written ideas clearly and signals the organization to the reader (e.g., through an introductory paragraph or through use of headings).
    - Tailors written communications to effectively reach an audience.
    - Uses graphics and other aids to clarify complex or technical information.
    - Spells correctly.
    - Writes using concrete, specific language.
    - Uses punctuation correctly.
    - Writes grammatically.
    - Uses an appropriate business writing style.
11. *Persuasive communication:* The ability to plan and deliver oral and written communications that make an impact and persuade their intended audiences.
    - Identifies and presents information or data that will have a strong effect on others.
    - Selects language and examples tailored to the level and experience of the audience.
    - Selects stories, analogies, or examples to illustrate a point.
    - Creates graphics, overheads, or slides that display information clearly and with high impact.
    - Presents several different arguments in support of a position.
12. *Interpersonal awareness:* The ability to notice, interpret, and anticipate others' concerns and feelings, and to communicate this awareness empathetically to others.
    - Understands the interests and important concerns of others.
    - Notices and accurately interprets what others are feeling, based on their choice of words, tone of voice, expressions, and other nonverbal behaviour.
    - Anticipates how others will react to a situation.
    - Listens attentively to people's ideas and concerns.
    - Understands both the strengths and weaknesses of others.
    - Understands the unspoken meaning in a situation.

- Says or does things to address others' concerns.
- Finds non-threatening ways to approach others about sensitive issues.
- Makes others feel comfortable by responding in ways that convey interest in what they have to say.

13. *Influencing others:* The ability to gain others' support for ideas, proposals, projects, and solutions.
    - Presents arguments that address others' most important concerns and issues and looks for win-win solutions.
    - Involves others in a process or decision to ensure their support.
    - Offers trade-offs or exchanges to gain commitment.
    - Identifies and proposes solutions that benefit all parties involved in a situation.
    - Enlists experts or third parties to influence others.
    - Develops other indirect strategies to influence others.
    - Knows when to escalate critical issues to own or others' management, if own efforts to enlist support have not succeeded.
    - Structures situations (e.g., the setting, persons present, sequence of events) to create a desired impact and to maximize the chances of a favorable outcome.
    - Works to make a particular impression on others.
    - Identifies and targets influence efforts at the real decision makers and those who can influence them.
    - Seeks out and builds relationships with others who can provide information, intelligence, career support, potential business, and other forms of help.
    - Takes a personal interest in others (e.g., by asking about their concerns, interests, family, friends, hobbies) to develop relationships.
    - Accurately anticipates the implications of events or decisions for various stakeholders in the organization and plans strategy accordingly.
14. *Building collaborative relationships:* The ability to develop, maintain, and strengthen partnerships with others inside or outside the organization who can provide information, assistance, and support.
    - Asks about the other person's personal experiences, interests, and family.

- Asks questions to identify shared interest, experiences, or other common ground.
- Shows an interest in what others have to say and acknowledges their perspectives and ideas.
- Recognizes the business concerns and perspectives of others.
- Expresses gratitude and appreciation to others who have provided information, assistance, or support.
- Takes time to get to know co-workers, to build rapport and establish a common bond.
- Tries to build relationships with people whose assistance, cooperation, and support may be needed.
- Provides assistance, information, and support to others to build a basis for future reciprocity.

15. *Customer orientation:* The ability to demonstrate concern for satisfying one's external and/or internal customers.
    - Quickly and effectively solves customer problems.
    - Talks to customers (internal or external) to find out what they want and how satisfied they are with what they are getting.
    - Lets customers know he/she is willing to work with them to meet their needs.
    - Finds ways to measure and track customer satisfaction.
    - Presents a cheerful, positive manner with customers.

Compentencies Dealing with Business

❖ The Preventing and Solving Problems Cluster

16. *Diagnostic information gathering:* The ability to identify the information needed to clarify a situation, seek that information from appropriate sources, and use skillful questioning to draw out the information, when others are reluctant to disclose it.
    - Identifies the specific information needed to clarify a situation or to make a decision.
    - Gets more complete and accurate information by checking multiple sources.

- Probes skillfully to get at the facts, when others are reluctant to provide full, detailed information.
- Routinely walks around to see how people are doing and to hear about any problems they are encountering.
- Questions others to assess whether they have thought through a plan of action.
- Questions others to assess their confidence in solving a problem or tackling a situation.
- Asks questions to clarify a situation.
- Seeks the perspective of everyone involved in a situation.
- Seeks out knowledgeable people to obtain information or clarify a problem.

17. *Analytical thinking:* The ability to tackle a problem by using a logical, systematic, sequential approach.
    - Makes a systematic comparison of two or more alternatives.
    - Notices discrepancies and inconsistencies in available information.
    - Identifies a set of features, parameters, or considerations to take into account, in analyzing a situation or making a decision.
    - Approaches a complex task or problem by breaking it down into its component parts and considering each part in detail.
    - Weighs the costs, benefits, risks, and chances for success, in making a decision.
    - Identifies many possible causes for a problem.
    - Carefully weighs the priority of things to be done.
18. *Forward thinking:* The ability to anticipate the implications and consequences of situations and take appropriate action to be prepared for possible contingencies.
    - Anticipates possible problems and develops contingency plans in advance.
    - Notices trends in the industry or marketplace and develops plans to prepare for opportunities or problems.
    - Anticipates the consequences of situations and plans accordingly.
    - Anticipates how individuals and groups will react to situations and information and plans accordingly.

19. *Conceptual thinking:* The ability to find effective solutions by taking a holistic, abstract, or theoretical perspective.
   - Notices similarities between different and apparently unrelated situations.
   - Quickly identifies the central or underlying issues in a complex situation.
   - Creates a graphic diagram showing a systems view of a situation.
   - Develops analogies or metaphors to explain a situation.
   - Applies a theoretical framework to understand a specific situation.
20. *Strategic thinking:* The ability to analyze the organization's competitive position by considering market and industry trends, existing and potential customers (internal and external), and strengths and weaknesses as compared to competitors.
   - Understands the organization's strengths and weaknesses as compared to competitors.
   - Understands industry and market trends affecting the organization's competitiveness.
   - Has an in-depth understanding of competitive products and services within the marketplace.
   - Develops and proposes a long-term (3-5 year) strategy for the organization based on an analysis of the industry and marketplace and the organization's current and potential capabilities as compared to competitors.
21. *Technical expertise:* The ability to demonstrate depth of knowledge and skill in a technical area.
   - Effectively applies technical knowledge to solve a range of problems.
   - Possesses an in-depth knowledge and skill in a technical area.
   - Develops technical solutions to new or highly complex problems that cannot be solved using existing methods or approaches.
   - Is sought out as an expert to provide advice or solutions in his/her technical area.
   - Keeps informed about cutting edge technology in his/her technical area.

❖ The Achieving Results Cluster

22. *Initiative:* Identifying what needs to be done and doing it before being asked or before the situation requires it.
   - Identifying what needs to be done and takes action before being asked or the situation requires it.

- Does more than what is normally required in a situation.
- Seeks out others involved in a situation to learn their perspectives.
- Takes independent action to change the direction of events.

23. ***Entrepreneurial orientation:*** The ability to look for and seize profitable business opportunities; willingness to take calculated risks to achieve business goals.
    - Notices and seizes profitable business opportunities.
    - Stays abreast of business, industry, and market information that may reveal business opportunities.
    - Demonstrates willingness to take calculated risks to achieve business goals.
    - Proposes innovative business deals to potential customers, suppliers, and business partners.
    - Encourages and supports entrepreneurial behaviour in others.
24. ***Fostering innovation:*** The ability to develop, sponsor, or support the introduction of new and improved method, products, procedures, or technologies.
    - Personally develops a new product or service.
    - Personally develops a new method or approach.
    - Sponsors the development of new products, services, methods, or procedures.
    - Proposes new approaches, methods, or technologies.
    - Develops better, faster, or less expensive ways to do things.
    - Works cooperatively with others to produce innovative solutions.
25. ***Result orientation:*** The ability to focus on the desired result of one's own or one's unit's work, setting challenging goals, focusing effort on the goals, and meeting or exceeding them.
    - Develops challenging but achievable goals.
    - Develops clear goals for meetings and projects.
    - Maintains commitment to goals in the face of obstacles and frustrations.
    - Finds or creates ways to measure performance against goals.
    - Exerts unusual effort over time to achieve a goal.
    - Has a strong sense of urgency about solving problems and getting work done.

26. *Thoroughness:* Ensuring that one's own and others' work and information are complete and accurate; carefully preparing for meetings and presentations; following up with others to ensure that agreements and commitments have been fulfilled.

- Sets up procedures to ensure high quality of work (e.g., review meetings).
- Monitors the quality of work.
- Verifies information.
- Checks the accuracy of own and others' work.
- Develops and uses systems to organize and keep track of information or work progress.
- Carefully prepares for meetings and presentations.
- Organizes information or materials for others.
- Carefully reviews and checks the accuracy of information in work reports (e.g., production, sales, financial performance) provided by management, management information systems, or other individuals and groups.

27. *Decisiveness:* The ability to make difficult decisions in a timely manner.

- Is willing to make decisions in difficult or ambiguous situations, when time is critical.
- Takes charge of a group when it is necessary to facilitate change, overcome an impasse, face issues, or ensure that decisions are made.
- Makes tough decisions (e.g., closing a facility, reducing staff, accepting or rejecting a high stakes deal).

Self-Management Competencies

28. *Self-confidence:* Faith in one's own ideas and capability to be successful; willingness to take an independent position in the face of opposition.

- Is confident of own ability to accomplish goals.
- Presents self crisply and impressively.
- Is willing to speak up to the right person or group at the right time, when he/she disagrees with a decision or strategy.
- Approaches challenging tasks with a "can do" attitude.

29. *Stress management:* The ability to keep functioning effectively when under pressure and maintain self control in the face of hostility or provocation.

- Remains calm under stress.
- Can effectively handle several problems or tasks at once.
- Controls his/her response when criticized, attacked or provoked.
- Maintains a sense of humour under difficult circumstances.
- Manages own behaviour to prevent or reduce feelings of stress.

30. *Personal credibility:* Demonstrated concern that can be perceived as responsible, reliable and trustworthy.
    - Does what he/she commits to doing.
    - Respects the confidentiality of information or concerns shared by others.
    - Is honest and forthright with people.
    - Carries his/her fair share of the workload.
    - Takes responsibility for own mistakes; does not blame others.
    - Conveys a command of the relevant facts and information.
31. *Flexibility:* Openness to different and new ways of doing things; willingness to modify one's preferred way of doing things.
    - Is able to see the merits of perspectives other than his/her own.
    - Demonstrates openness to new organizational structures, procedures, and technology.
    - Switches to a different strategy when an initially selected one is unsuccessful.
    - Demonstrates willingness to modify a strongly held position in the face of contrary evidence.

CHAPTER 8

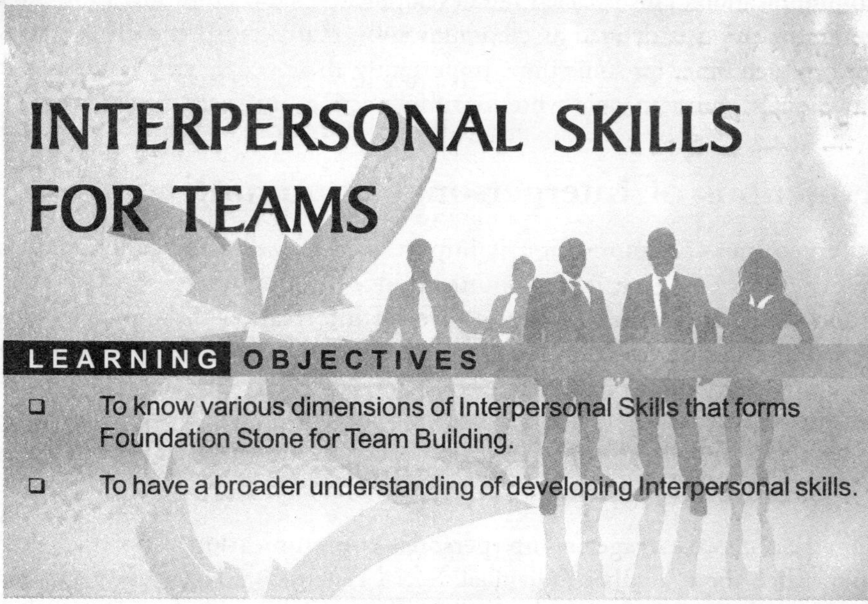

INTERPERSONAL SKILLS FOR TEAMS

LEARNING OBJECTIVES

- To know various dimensions of Interpersonal Skills that forms Foundation Stone for Team Building.
- To have a broader understanding of developing Interpersonal skills.

INTERPERSONAL SKILLS

The Contextual View

One way of defining interpersonal communication is to compare it to other forms of communication. In so doing, we would examine how many people are involved, how physically close they are to one another, how many sensory channels are used, and the feedback provided. Interpersonal communication differs from other forms of communication in that there are few participants involved, the interactants are in close physical proximity to each other, there are many sensory channels used, and feedback is immediate. An important point to note about the contextual definition is that it does not take into account the relationship between the interactants.

The Developmental View

We have many different relationships with people. Some researchers say that our definition of interpersonal communication must account for these differences. These researchers say that interacting with a sales clerk in a store is different than the relationship we have with our friends and family members. Thus, some researchers have proposed an alternative way of defining interpersonal communication. This is called the developmental view. From this view, interpersonal communication is defined as communication that occurs between people who have known each other for some time. Importantly, these people view each other as unique individuals, not as people who are simply acting out social situations.

Functions of Interpersonal Communication

Interpersonal communication is important because of the functions it achieves. Whenever we engage in communication with another person, we seek to gain information about them. We also give off information through a wide variety of verbal and non-verbal cues. Read more about the various functions of interpersonal communication and then complete the interactive activity and the quiz at the end of this unit.

❖ Gaining Information

One reason we engage in interpersonal communication is so that we can gain knowledge about another individual. Social Penetration Theory says that we attempt to gain information about others so that we can interact with them more effectively. We can better predict how they will think, feel, and act if we know who they are. We gain this information passively, by observing them; actively, by having others engage them; or interactively, by engaging them ourselves. Self-disclosure is often used to get information from another person. Self-disclosure is seen as a useful strategy for sharing information with others. By sharing information, we become more intimate with other people and our interpersonal relationship is strengthened. Read about self-disclosure and then complete the interactive activity and take a short quiz to test your understanding of the concept.

❖ Building a Context of Understanding

We also engage in interpersonal communication to help us better understand what someone says in a given context. The words we say can mean very different things depending on how they are said or in what context. **Content Messages** refer to the surface level meaning of a message.

❖ Relationship Messages

Refer to how a message is said. The two are sent simultaneously, but each affects the meaning assigned to the communication. Interpersonal communication helps us understand each other better.

❖ Establishing Identity

Another reason we engage in interpersonal communication is to establish an identity. The **roles** we play in our relationships help us establish identity. So too does the **face**, the public self-image we present to others. Both roles and face are constructed based on how we interact with others.

❖ Interpersonal Needs

Finally, we engage in interpersonal communication because we need to express and receive interpersonal needs. William Schutz has identified three such needs: inclusion, control, and affection.

- Inclusion is the need to establish identity with others.
- Control is the need to exercise leadership and prove one's abilities. Groups provide outlets for this need. Some individuals do not want to be a leader. For them, groups provide the necessary control over aspects of their lives.
- Affection is the need to develop relationships with people. Groups are an excellent way to make friends and establish relationships

Relationship Development

Researchers have studied relationships to understand how they develop. One of the most popular models for understanding relationship development is Mark Knapp's Relational Stages Model. Knapp's Model works well to describe many types of relationships: romantic couples, friends, business partners, roommates, etc. Other models have also been discussed. For instance, Stephen Duck's Relationship Filtering Model is another way of looking at how relationships begin. Read about these models and then complete an interactive activity and short quiz to test your knowledge.

❖ Knapp's Relationship Escalation Model

Initiation: This stage is very short, sometimes as short as 10-15 seconds. In this stage, interactants are concerned with making favorable impressions on each other. They may use standard greetings or observe each other's appearance or mannerisms.

Experimenting: In the next stage, individuals ask questions of each other in order to gain information about them and decide if they wish to continue the relationship. "Many relationships progress no further than this point".

Intensifying: Self-disclosure becomes more common in the intensifying stage. The relationship becomes less formal, the interactants begin to see each other as individuals, and statements are made about the level of commitment each has to the relationship.

Integrating: The individuals become a pair in the integrating stage. They begin to do things together and, importantly, others come to see them as a pair. A shared relational identity starts to form in this stage.

Bonding: During the bonding stage, a formal, sometimes legal, announcement of the relationship is made. Examples include a marriage, "best friend" ritual, or business partnership agreement. Few relationships reach this level.

❖ Duck's Relationship Filtering Model

Sociological/Incidental cues: Duck's model is a set of filters through which we make choices about the level of relationship we wish to pursue with others. The first filter, sociological/incidental cues, describes the constraints placed on our meeting people due to where we live or work. In other words, given our sociological location, there are some people we see a lot of and others we never meet.

Pre-interaction cues: Information we gain about people before we even interact with them leads us to exclude or include individuals with whom we wish to have a relationship. For instance, the appearance of some individuals will cause you to avoid or approach them.

Interaction cues: As we begin to interact with others, we make judgments about whether to include or exclude them from possible relationships.

Cognitive cues: At the deepest level, we make judgments about people based on their personality and the degree to which we think it will match ours. As others reach this level, we consider them "best friends."

❖ Knapp's Relationship Termination Model

Differentiating: In this stage, partners begin to stress the 'me' instead of the 'we.' In other words, the individuals begin to assert their independence. They may develop different hobbies or activities. The relationship may continue to dissolve, or this stage may be a warning sign that the couple needs to address their relationship status.

Circumscribing: Communication between the couple diminishes during this stage. They tend to avoid certain topics of discussion. Outwardly, the couple appears normal. At this stage, attempts can be made to discuss the relationship and return it to a positive state.

Stagnating: During the stagnating stage, the individuals avoid discussing the relationship because they think they know what the other will say. Others begin to take notice that something is wrong.

Avoiding: The pair begins to physically separate themselves during the avoiding stage. The individuals try to reduce the opportunities for discussion.

Terminating: This is the final stage of the relationship. Termination may come naturally, such as at the end of the semester when roommates move out, or arbitrarily, through divorce. Termination of the relationship can occur positively or negatively.

Relational Patterns

As relationships progress, patterns of interactions take shape that we may not recognize. This section describes some of these patterns. Complete the interactive activity at the end of the unit and then take a quiz to test your knowledge.

Rigid role relations: There are two basic types of behaviours in relationships: dominance and submissiveness. Dominance is often referred to as one-up, while submissiveness, one-down. In some relationships, the two are complementary—one individual is one-up, the other one-down—and the relationship is rewarding. Other relationships are symmetrical, where both parties are one-up or both are one-down. Problems can result when individuals feel trapped by their role as the dominant or submissive member of the relationship. Flexibility can help both partners enjoy the relationship.

Disconfirmations: Whenever we communicate with someone else, we open ourselves up for rejection. The other individual can accept what we say or reject what we say. Researcher Evelyn Sieburg has identified seven "disconfirming" responses that reject the other individual.

- *Impervious:* Failing to acknowledge the other person.
- *Interrupting:* Cutting the other's message short.
- *Irrelevant:* Giving a response that is unrelated to what the other has said.
- *Tangential:* Briefly responding to the other's message.
- *Impersonal:* Responding by using formal, jargon-laden language.
- *Incoherent:* Responding with a rambling, difficult to understand message.
- *Incongruous:* Giving contradictory verbal and non-verbal messages.

Spirals: A third type of relational pattern is a spiral. "In a spiral, one partner's behaviour intensifies that of the other". Spirals can be progressive, in which one partner's behaviour leads to increasing levels of satisfaction for the other. Spirals can also be regressive, where one partner's communication leads to increasing dissatisfaction. Stopping regressive spirals from getting out of control depends on the open communication between the two individuals.

Dependencies and counter dependencies: A final type of relational pattern is dependencies and counter dependencies. In a dependency relationship, one individual sees himself or herself relying on another person for something. Soon, he or she agrees with whatever the other says or does. In a counter dependency, one individual sees himself or herself as not being dependent on the other. Thus, he or she disagrees with the other quite frequently.

Interpersonal conflict: Conflict is a part of most every interpersonal relationship. Managing conflict, then, is important if the relationship is to be long-lasting and rewarding. Learn how to manage conflict in your relationships and then complete the activity.

Defining Conflict

Conflict has been defined as "an expressed struggle between at least two interdependent parties who perceive incompatible goals, scarce resources, and interference from the other party in achieving their goals". Important concepts in this definition include "expressed struggle," which means the two sides must communicate about the problem for there to be conflict. Another important idea is that conflict often involves perceptions. The two sides may only perceive that their goals, resources, and interference is incompatible with each other's.

Common Problems in Conflict Management

Researchers have identified several problems that typically arise in conflict situations. First, the parties will simply avoid the conflict. This can be damaging, because it can lead to greater problems in the future. It is usually best that the individuals discuss their differences. Second, individuals involved in conflict may blame the other individual. Often, individuals go beyond the specific behaviour in question and blame the character of the person. When people use words such as, "He's such a slob," they are engaging in blaming the other's behaviour. A final problem that is often encountered in conflict management is adopting a win-lose mentality. Focusing on each individual's goals/outcomes will help avoid using a win-lose strategy.

Defensive climate: The climate in which conflict is managed is important. Dyads should avoid a defensive climate, which is characterized by these qualities:

- ***Evaluation:*** Judging and criticizing other group members.
- ***Control:*** Imposing the will of one group member on the others.
- ***Strategy:*** Using hidden agendas.
- ***Neutrality:*** Demonstrating indifference and lack of commitment.

- *Superiority:* Expressing dominance.
- *Certainty:* Being rigid in one's willingness to listen to others.

Supportive climate: Instead, individuals should foster a supportive climate, marked by these traits:

- *Description:* Presenting ideas or opinions.
- *Problem orientation:* Focusing attention on the task.
- *Spontaneity:* Communicating openly and honestly.
- *Empathy:* Understanding another person's thoughts.
- *Equality:* Asking for opinions.
- *Provisionalism:* Expressing a willingness to listen the ideas of others.

Additional tips: A few final tips can help insure that conflict is successfully managed:

- *Conflict can be constructive:* Recognize that conflict can strengthen your relationships.
- *Be prepared*: Plan how you will communicate about conflict in order to create a supportive climate.
- *Be involved*: Do not withdraw from the conflict or avoid conflict situations.
- *Withhold quick retorts*: Be careful about what you say and how you say it.

Review: Summarize what you have discussed and make plans to continue the discussion and if time permits, immediate resolution.

Interpersonal Skills for Teams

Most executives assume they know who their "people" are: They're the team players, the ones who know what's going on in their colleagues' personal lives, the ones who can smooth over interpersonal conflicts. They're usually found in human resources or sales.

The truth, however, is much more nuanced than that. Interpersonal savvy is critical in almost every area of business, not just sales and HR. In fact, it comprises aptitudes that are more varied than a lot of people might think. Recently, we've conducted extensive research on the people side of doing business—what we call the relational factor. After more than eighteen years of studying how the deeply embedded life interests of business professionals develop into career roles, we know that individuals do their best work when it most closely matches their underlying interests. Managers, therefore, can boost productivity by using their employees' relational interests and skills to guide personnel choices, project assignments, and career development.

We've analyzed psychological tests of more than 7,000 business professionals, and our findings challenge the limited traditional notion of who "people" are. Using factor analysis, a method of statistical analysis, we have identified four distinct dimensions of relational work: influence, interpersonal facilitation, relational creativity, and team leadership. In this article, we'll explain each component and show how knowledge of all four can help managers hire the right employees, make the best work assignments, reward performance, and promote career development (others' and their own)

The Four Dimensions

To maximize the interpersonal capacity of your organization, you must understand all four areas of relational work, because when you match employees' interests and skills to their responsibilities, everybody gains.

❖ Influence

Professionals who earn a high score in this dimension enjoy developing and extending their sphere of interpersonal influence. They take pleasure in persuasion, negotiation, and the power of holding valuable information and ideas. This dimension of relational work is all about changing the point of view or the behaviour of others. An old expression, "He could talk a dog off a meat truck," aptly describes high scorers here. Whether to a customer or to a colleague—and whether they're talking about a product, a service, or an idea—these people live to sell. Think of the manager in your firm who is always able to get more resources for his projects than anyone else can. Or picture that former boss of yours who could always get people fired up for the next challenge, regardless of how tired they were from the last one.

While people who score high in influence can be found in any function and any industry, we've discovered that individuals with deal intensive roles in financial services and sales tend to stand out in this dimension. Jeffrey Manning (all names of people cited as examples in this article are pseudonyms), for instance, the managing partner of a very successful venture capital firm, was running his own fund at age thirty-one. Some would argue that his success was a function of good timing—he entered the world of high-technology investing in the mid-1990s—but those who have done business with him have a different explanation: Jeff is a natural at deal-intensive finance. He's a born networker. Whether he's on the golf course or at the annual dinner for a prominent charitable organization, his talent for meeting people and inspiring their confidence is indisputable. Jeff is not a salesperson, nor is he a team-focused manager. He's an alliance builder and negotiator. He can locate and gather key players to participate in deals that optimize value for all parties involved.

❖ Interpersonal Facilitation

This is the dimension many people first think of when they think "people person." Individuals with high scores here are keenly attuned to the interpersonal aspects of a work situation. They intuitively focus on others' experiences and usually work quietly behind the scenes to keep their colleagues committed and engaged so that projects don't get derailed. They naturally ask themselves questions like "What group will work together best to get this job done?" and "Why is Joe being overcritical in meetings and underperforming in general?" and "What sort of assignment does Miriam need to grow and feel more competent?" These types of issues rarely show up in reports, but as every seasoned manager knows, handling them effectively is essential to organizational success.

Consider Alicia DiGiavonni, the internal medicine unit manager at a Boston-area HMO. Alicia has an MBA and is a focused, task-oriented operating manager, but her success comes from her effectiveness as the organization's unofficial psychologist. Alicia has done more in the way of counseling, conflict resolution, coaching, and informal personality assessment than many of the therapists who work in the mental health unit. Staff members frequently confide in her when there is disabling friction within a work team, when they need career advice, or when they're struggling with personal issues. She is an expert at recognizing hidden agendas at meetings and identifying the problems that workers are reluctant to share with senior managers. She knows which combinations of people on a project team would yield great synergy and which would be disastrous. On countless occasions, Alicia has kept projects on track through skillful, behind-the-scenes interventions.

❖ Relational Creativity

At its core, this dimension is about forging connections with groups of people through visual and verbal imagery. This is the relational work being done when an advertising account team conceives of a campaign, when a marketing brand manager develops a strategy to reach a particular consumer segment, when a speech writer crafts the president's next address, and when a senior manager develops a motivational theme that will focus and inspire her employees.

Although relational creativity in business is most commonly used for persuading customers to buy and investors to invest, it is different from the influence dimension. Professionals skilled in influence convince others on a person-to-person basis, whereas people talented at relational creativity use images and words to arouse emotions and create relationships with groups. This dimension is not a measure of creativity in general—only in the interpersonal realm. Someone who's creative in an analytical area of business work (such as designing new investment instruments) can still have low interest in relational creativity; similarly, an artist (such as a composer or a painter) can lack skill in this domain.

Most of us don't have much occasion to interact with people who stand out in this dimension, although chances are we have co-workers with this strength that we don't know about because it has no outlet in their daily jobs. For an example of someone with outstanding skills in relational creativity, look at Diane Weiss, a senior editor for a major magazine. Whether the question is which illustration to use, how best to express data graphically, what title to give an article, or what image to put on the cover, Diane is the one to ask: She has an unerring sense of what will pull readers in. But she is not known for her easy management style or her ability to "read" people. In fact, even her most ardent fans will agree that she can be exceedingly difficult to work with. For understanding the masses, though, Diane is as good as you can get. She is a bona fide people-person—with the emphasis on the plural.

❖ Team Leadership

Individuals who score high in this dimension need to see and interact with other people very frequently to feel satisfied. Conversely, the more time they spend in front of a computer screen, the worse they feel and perform. Professionals with a high level of interest in team leadership love managing high-energy teams in busy service environments and enjoy working both with the team and with the customer. Their ideal job might be overseeing a busy resort or a retail store.

The difference between individuals who score high in team leadership and those who do so in the influence dimension is their interest in managing people. High scorers in team leadership always want to work through a group. They're the embodiment of the player-coach role. People who score high in influence are interested in the outcome of an interaction, the closed deal, whereas those scoring high in team leadership focus more on the interpersonal and managerial processes. Compare the managing director of mergers and acquisitions at an investment bank (excelling in influence) with the sales manager at a large automobile dealership (strong in team leadership). Not all team leaders even effective ones have high scores in this dimension, however. It is quite possible for team leaders in areas such as production, research and development, and information technology to show little interest in this particular relational skill. But we consistently see high scores here for leaders of teams that have a strong customer focus.

It's important to note that the four relational dimensions are not discrete types. A person can have great interest and skill in two or more of these areas or in none of them. And scoring high in more dimensions isn't necessarily better; some are irrelevant or even detrimental to certain types of work. Above, we've offered examples of people who are stars in one dimension, but some of them score high in other areas as well.

Clearly, 'people' and their relational talents are not interchangeable. Put Diane where you should have Alicia, and the results will be disastrous. That's why it's so important to align your employees' relational talents with their job responsibilities. Keep the four dimensions in mind when you're hiring new employees, assigning tasks, rewarding employees for their contributions, and developing the people in your organization, including yourself.

The Essentials of Compassionate Communication for Interpersonal Relations

Introduction

We have all been in situations where there were terrible misunderstandings. Either we have felt misunderstood or the other has. We often leave these situations mystified as to what had happened. How were we so misunderstood? What did I do wrong? Or, Why were they so stubborn? Couldn't they understand what I was trying to say?

This short tutorial highlights the main ways humans get into trouble trying to communicate, and describes effective new ways to communicate which avoids these pitfalls and brings people into a close understanding of one another.

First, we'll look at the things we do that get us into trouble. These fall into three groups:

1. Our tendency to add interpretations and judgements to what we observe.
2. Our tendency to blame or try to make another responsible for how we are feeling.
3. Our resistance to letting others know what we want, need or what's really important to us.

Marshall Rosenberg has studied communication styles around the world. He has discovered that when situations feel difficult, most people in the cultures of the world today drop into a rather unrefined and critical form of our language. And even when we are polite in difficult situations, we turn this kind of language in upon ourselves, with such statements as, "Why can't I do anything right."

As an easy to understand metaphor he has called this language 'Jackal.' It doesn't matter what your native language is, Jackal has become part of most every modern language. With Jackal, people say things like: "You should know better than that", "Why can't you keep your room clean?" "You are an idiot and a troublemaker." Jackal analyses people, judges them and labels them. It's not a very friendly language, and we've all learned to use it.

But Marshall discovered that not every culture spoke Jackal, there were a few peaceful cultures that had no wars and little conflict. They had a different way of looking at each other that was more compassionate, and the way they spoke demonstrated a desire to connect and understand, rather than analyse, correct or label.

He decided to call this type of language Giraffe, named for the animal with the biggest heart and the furthest vision. When we speak in Giraffe, we don't see any advantage in attacking, blaming or telling someone what he is with labels. We are much more interested in the other persons feelings, wants and needs. Giraffe is a language of the heart, a language that connects us; Jackal is a language that separates us.

So we are going to start learning this language of Giraffe. We will learn it by looking at what happens when we communicate, and doing entertaining exercises that show us clearly how we have been communicating up to now and what other options we have for communicating in a way that connects us.

The Skills of Compassionate Communication

Here is a list of some of the main skills involved in Compassionate Communication. These will be described in greater detail as we go on.

1. How to hear the underlying values, needs and desires of any person we are communicating with, even if they are not skilled at communicating these things, and to stay connected to them in this process, even if they are attacking or blaming us. This is called "Listening with Giraffe Ears."
2. How to identify the deeper needs, wants, desires or longings that are underneath our own upsets, confusions, complaints and blaming.
3. Noticing the subtle and often confusing differences between bodily or sensed feelings such as "I feel sad" and a feeling-interpretation mixture such as "I feel betrayed."
4. Noticing how humans usually interpret and analyse what we observe and then mistake that for the observation itself. We will learn how to state our observations and interpretations separately and how to simply observe without interpretation.
5. We will learn the subtle difference between a Request and a Demand, and how demands alienate us and requests connect us.

6. We will learn that to deeply understand what is important to another does not mean that we must DO what they want. Understanding them also does not mean that we have to agree with them. And understanding them does not mean that they are right and we are wrong. These erroneous beliefs are key reasons why we often won't let ourselves understand someone we are in conflict with.

❖ Listening with Giraffe Ears

The concept of Giraffe and Jackal ears is an important one.

If we are listening to others with our culturally trained 'Jackal' ears, we hear complaints, criticisms and attacks everywhere. It's easy in that case to respond with similar attacks or to feel defensive or to just leave feeling miserable and misunderstood.

When we wear Giraffe ears however, we have a powerful technology available to us. Think of Giraffe ears as a sophisticated translating device. When we decide to put on Giraffe ears, all the criticisms, blames and attacks of others are translated into simply their feelings and unmet wants and needs.

When we wear Giraffe ears we hear their pain but we don't take it personally. We can have empathy and feel connected to a person when we hear only their feelings and needs. It's as if they already spoke perfect Giraffe themselves.

As Marshall says, "Criticism, complaints, judgements and attacks are all just tragic expressions of difficult feelings and unmet needs".

❖ Empathy or "Being Heard and Understood"

An important fact about communication is that under stressful situations, we often can't hear much of what's going on with another until we feel the other has heard and understood us.

But when we really feel that the other has heard and understands what we want or need, then we relax and can hear what's important to them too.

In a conflict, if one person is upset and the other isn't, then it's usually easy for the non-upset one to listen and let the other one feel understood.

But if both people are very upset, then both want to be understood and can't hear what the other is saying.

So if we are both upset how do we get around this need to be heard and understood before we can hear the other? The answer is to find our own inner source of understanding that is not dependant on the other, what Marshall calls "Empathy for Oneself" or "Compassion For Oneself."

Empathy For Oneself is simply a term for an inner calmness and centredness, even if just a little bit, which allows us to see and hear the other clearly even when we have strong feelings inside. Those who have this skill are well respected, since it is a skill that not everyone has developed. But it is a skill which can be cultivated once one is aware of it and see's the usefulness in making one's life happier as well as making life more wonderful for all those around us.

The Four Steps of Compassionate Communication

Compassionate communication consists of 4 simple steps, that can be used in different ways. We will list them quickly here and then get into greater detail further on. The generic steps are:

1. To say what was observed happening (in a conflict it is usually what happened that upset us or the other.)
2. To say what the feelings are.
3. To say what the underlying wants, needs, values or importances are (usually what you wanted to happen or were afraid wouldn't happen).
4. (Optionally) To make a request of the other.

These four steps are used in two different ways depending on:

1. If we are trying to tell another honestly about what is happening with us, or
2. If we are trying to help another tell us what is happening with them.

    (a) Expressing myself with honesty

    Step 1: When I (saw, heard, etc.) ....(the observation).........................

    Step 2: I felt ...... (your feelings in a simple non evaluative way).............

    Step 3: Because I was wanting ....(your wants, needs, hopes etc.).....

    Step 4: And I would now like..................(a request, not a demand)..........

    (b) Hearing another with empathy*

    Step 1: When you (saw, heard, etc.) ....(the observation) ....

    Step 2: Did you feel ....(a guess of what they might feel) ....

---

* On side "B", when we are guessing another person's feelings or needs, we are not trying to tell them what they are feeling or needing, rather we are simply trying to hear them and make a first attempt to understand, and get them to tell us more correctly — and we expect them to correct our guesses. When they correct us we repeat what we have heard until they agree that we understand. This second side is about them and your needs and desires are not part of it or talked about at this time.

Step 3: Because you were wanting ....(guess their wants, needs, hopes etc.)...

Step 4: And would you now like...................(guess what they might request).......

Observations

"The ability to keep observation and evaluation separate is the highest form of human intelligence".

— **Jiddhu Krishnamurti**

❖ Some Common Types of Evaluations

- Judgements
- Analyses
- Interpretations
- Labels
- Projections

It's a simple fact that we all tend to habitually and automatically evaluate and interpret whatever we observe. This probably had survival benefits in the jungle by helping us predict what might be running after us on the trail. But when we are in non-threatening situations, this 'skill' of evaluating, interpreting and imagining often doesn't serve us at all instead it adds unfortunate, even poisonous meanings to what we observe. We often add information that is not actually there, usually by reaching into our past for similar situations, and then we can imagine that someone is saying something or meaning something that they are not. This is also the process that causes worry our uncontrollable imagining that undesirable things will occur. These imaginations and projections are one of the main causes of conflicts.

Most humans are not conscious of this process within themselves. When we see or hear something, instead of just noticing it for what it is, we often react — we worry about the implications of it by creating dire scenarios in our mind and then getting upset with them; we project out what we think the other person is 'really' doing or meaning and then we get angry about what we think; we go into our past to similar situations, but of course bad ones, and decide that "we've seen this before" and then judge what we are observing as bad. There are endless ways we use our mind to add more than what is really there and then to get upset about it. And to boot, we hold on dearly to what we imagine too, as though this creation of our mind is absolutely true, and we rarely think to verify it before we pronounce our judgement! We are very skilled at finding ways to get upset.

So the first skill in Compassionate Communication is to develop the more advanced skill of being aware of what we are observing and how we are adding our own extra content: our imaginations, worries, projections and interpreting, analysing, or labeling it. We simply want to bring this process into consciousness so that we can check to see if our thoughts about what we are observing is indeed correct or if we need to adjust it.

The simplest way to experience this is to imagine that you are a video camera. If there was an argument going on between two people, a video camera would report exactly what they said, and how loudly, and with what facial expressions. But it would not interpret it and say, "These two people fighting, and they are fighting because one of them is an idiot and the other is acting like a victim." Only humans would try to add that extra content, and interpret it that way and then start an argument about whether it is true or not. So let's practice for a bit being a video camera and see if we can just report the facts.

The Different Kinds of Feelings

What is the difference between someone saying "I feel rejected" and "I feel sad"?

When I say "I feel rejected," I am really making two statements, one is a statement that I have an undesirable or uncomfortable feeling, and the other is an accusation that someone else did something bad to me in this case, I am saying that they also rejected me. It's the same as saying "I feel miserable because you rejected me." The truth may really be that they were just late for a meeting and didn't have time to talk to me.

So the difference between "I feel rejected" and "I feel sad" is that the first one contains an interpretation which another might not agree with in this case, they say they didn't reject me, maybe they were just late for the meeting and couldn't talk.

But now the phrase "I feel sad" says something that no one can disagree with, because it's all about my inner experience, how I feel inside. Again this is the first source of conflicts and upsets — a disagreement about the interpretation of the facts.

Here's another example. If I say to another "I feel betrayed," they would probably feel like I just hit them with a brick. Even if they want to understand and empathize with my pain, they will have a hard time doing it because it sounds like an attack. To say "I feel betrayed" is the same as saying "I feel terrible because you betrayed me." It's true that I have a terrible feeling inside, but the other could easily disagree with how I've interpreted it.

So what do we do about this?

This is another example of Observations vs. Interpretations. We just need to take a closer look at how we really feel and then notice how we are attaching an interpretation to it.

Wants, Needs, Values, Desires, Importances, Longings, Hopes and Dreams

We cannot fully sense our own needs, wants or desires as long as we have any judgements about them — we also will never get another to share their deepest needs and desires as long as they sense we have any judgements about theirs.

All those words at the top of this page have an important relationship. They are all words that describe what's important to us and often what we live for.

As we go through life we are constantly noticing what attracts us and what we need to both survive and to be happy. These things range from the most basic needs such as food, water, safety and sleep, on to higher level needs such as love and a sense of belonging, and then others such as a sense of purpose and a desire to make the world a happier place.

Whenever we think that any of these very important wants and needs in our life are threatened, we automatically react, usually unconsciously, to protect that which we feel is so vital to us.

The truth is that usually we share most of the same needs and desires. But when we don't communicate them, we often don't work together to get them met, and we never find out that the other really does respect us and wants us to be happy.

Somehow these needs, wants and desires get buried inside us and we are only semiconscious of them. We often don't articulate them to others when we feel they are threatened. Also, because of our Jackal upbringing, we are often afraid to admit many of our wants, needs and desires — we have seen them judged so heavily.

In the language of Giraffe, we become more conscious of the needs we have that are feeling threatened, and we know that all needs, longings and desires come from the heart. So we bravely start articulating them and find a way to get our mutual needs and desires met without having to resort to violence or verbal fighting.

There are several synonyms for these basic values are very important to us. It's helpful to be aware of these different words for them so that we can pick the words which most accurately fit when we are trying to describe what is important to us. Some of these synonyms are in the title of this page.

Blames and Complaints

In many cultures, but not all, it's common to believe that when something goes wrong, someone must be to blame. It's a distortion of the concept of responsibility.

True responsibility has nothing to do with blame or fault. However, for many people these two ideas have been muddled beyond distinction.

And so when something goes wrong in our lives, and the frustration and feelings are very strong, we easily go back to the old strategy of blame. And this urge can be uncontrollable.

We are really looking for relief from our frustration or pain, and we think that venting these strong feeling somehow makes us feel better but it does only for a moment!

If there is no one else we can imagine blaming, we will instead blame ourselves. And if we can find someone else who has played even the slightest role in our dilemma, we will use them instead. We will blame the postman for our package being late, we will blame the government for us not having a good job, or we will blame our spouse for us not feeling loved the way we want.

If we look at the process of blaming from a distance, we can observe that as a strategy for handling our strong frustrations, it is not very effective. It seems effective in the first few moments of venting, but in the long run it make life more difficult. If we do get someone to change to make us happy, they will be resentful. In the long run, the cost is high in our relationships, since blaming separates us and causes fear, anger and pain.

And complaining is a relative of blaming, just less focused than blaming.

It's understandable that we want to free ourselves from powerful frustrations. And the most effective way is to do the normal steps of Compassionate Communication:

1. Observe clearly without evaluation what happened.
2. Experience and acknowledge our feelings.
3. Look for the values, desires, importances and needs that seemed to be threatened or shattered by the situation.

As this process becomes a natural part of our life, doing these steps will often resolve the desire to blame without even needing to talk to the others involved, but even when we do want to talk to them, we will be able to share our experience, taking complete responsibility for our feelings and not needing to accuse or blame another.

Another Level of Honesty Speaking Our Truth

We often say we are "speaking our truth" when we directly and bluntly tell someone the way we feel and the way we see things especially when we have strong feelings. Doing that can be an important step in our growth, especially for those of us who have been too polite and have hidden what we think and feel. Brad Blanton in his book "Radical Honesty" describes very well how we get into fear, shame and politeness traps, and how to break out of them; and his book is well worth reading.

But don't think that freely letting out our initial thoughts and feelings is the end of the road. Usually these first expressions are just our REACTIONS, not the real honest truth about what is going on inside us. These first reactions usually contain our judgements and projections and are mostly talking about the other person, and doesn't contain much insight into what the real disturbance inside us is about. Paul Lowe talks about this when he says:

> *"The only way to go beyond the restrictions of how we have lived as human beings is to be responsible for ourselves, at every level. That includes the willingness to go to the source of our disturbance instead of blaming someone else. In fact, it might just be the opposite — when we are disturbed, instead of blaming others, we would thank them for helping us to find that place in ourselves that was not in balance."*

So how is it that we can be FULLY HONEST and FULLY TELL OUR TRUTH. We do it by honestly owning our own interpretations, projections and judgements, as well as our feelings, wants and desires — and talking about that rather than about the other person — in other words, doing the steps of Compassionate Communication.

If we speak the full and honest truth about what has just happened within ourselves we are often amazed at how interested the other person is — rather than the usual defensiveness which appears when we try to talk about them or how they affected us. One key point that will help us remember this is: Be selfish! Use every upset or disturbance in life as an opportunity for our own growth. If I say I am telling another about them to help THEM, it is almost always a lie, a way to avoid dealing with my own issues and instead subtly trying to get another person to change so they don't trigger my neurosis. Instead I can selfishly share what's going on with me, about myself. In the process it is amazing to find that others are so inspired by this honesty that they change tool.

❖ A "Don't Want" is Hard to give

When stating our wants, needs, desires etc. it's valuable to try to state them in positive terms rather than negative terms. Let me give you an example.

We often hear statements like, "I don't want to live in a messy house." To understand that we really have to imagine what it is that you do want, especially because everyone's idea of "messy" is a bit different. If you said "I want to live in a clean house," or "I want to live in a house where the floors are clean," we have an easier time picturing that, but even then you could be more specific.

Marshall tells the story of a woman who told her husband, "I don't like you spending so much time at work." Thinking that she didn't want him to work so much, the next week he joined a bowling team. But that didn't make her any happier, what she really wanted was for him to spend more time with her. So being specific helps us in getting what we really want.

Now this is not a dogmatic statement, there will be sometimes that it takes a lot of thinking to say what you want without a negative in it, for example, You may say "I want to live in a house where there are not dirty clothes left laying around on the floor," and it takes some thought to realize what you want is "To live in a house that looks neat and orderly." But just give it a try and see how much different it feels to say what you want in positive language.

Requests versus Demands

Ask for 100% of what you want, and always be willing to hear a "NO"

Requests of others is a normal part of our everyday life. There are things we want and we need to communicate them if we are to have any chance of receiving them.

In addition to the everyday use of requests, it is also the fourth step of Compassionate Communication, but making a request is always optional and depends upon the situation. In fact once you learn CC well you will find yourself only using the steps you need in any situation.

The important thing to know about a request is that it is very different than a demand. Even a polite sounding 'request' is really a demand if we get angry or punish the other for not giving us what we ask for.

Making a demand will only get us what we want temporarily, because in the long run the person will resent us and distance from us for being forced to do as we want.

Another important aspect of requests is that it's often embarrassing to ask for what we want. And so when we do get enough courage together to do it, it's even more embarrassing if the other says "NO."

So a difficult part of making requests is to be able to make them and also be open to hearing a NO. When we hear a NO, it's important that we hear this as a statement about THE OTHER PERSON, and their feelings and needs, not as a statement about ourselves. If we think it is a judgement about ourselves, then we will get defensive and then loose our connection to the other.

Also, as with stating needs with a positive wording, Marshall uses the same idea when he talks about requests. Here he says it's important to use "Positive Action

Language." What that means is to ask for something that is an observable action, such as "I'd really like you to spend 2 or 3 nights a week with me." That is clear and can be done if it is agreeable. But it is difficult to give something which is vague and unconcrete like "I'd like you to want to spend more time with me," or "I'd like you to feel better about our relationship." Neither of those can be easily done or demonstrated.

More about Requests and Demands—How do we deal with our Hopes and Expectations?

> *"Most of our emotional pain comes from our expectations. We are constantly faced with a choice in life — to be right, or to be happy — we can't have both."*
>
> — **Ian Jampolski**

Most of our pain flows from our expectations. But the idea is not to be free of all expectations, but rather it is to be conscious of them and notice when they are causing us pain. At that moment we then have choices, either the choice to simply let go of the expectation for the moment and recentre ourselves, or perhaps simply to acknowledge that we have it. Sharing our experiences from this perspective allows others to connect with us and what we are going through, whereas unconscious blaming separates us.

Demands are closely related to expectations, and in CC we observe how demands alienate and separate us from those we care about.

If we want to be happy, it's important not to judge anyone's desires, needs or even their expectations, and that includes our own. We are more interested in accepting what we want in life and what others want in life, and finding the most effective ways of communicating them. We are then most likely to get what we want, and also remain closely connected to those we want these things from.

The happiest people are those who are the most flexible and have the ability to derive pleasure from a wide range of experiences, even ones they never expected. Since their expectations are not too strongly fixed, they are open to whatever comes, and find they can enjoy surprising occurrences as well as the things they told themselves they are hoping for.

In classical eastern spirituality, we could call an expectation just another form of attachment. But we do not need to judge attachments or expectations, we merely want to become aware of what we go through life expecting, and the ways we have tried to get those things for ourselves. We can then notice if the methods we are using result in our connections with others becoming closer or further apart.

Acknowledging Another's Wants and Needs

One of the biggest challenges to compassionate communication is to simply be able to ACKNOWLEDGE what another wants and needs without judgement. Often when we hear what another wants, we react by thinking or telling them: You don't need that, you shouldn't want that, it's not very evolved to want that, that's silly, unnecessary, inappropriate etc.

We feel that it's far easier to argue with them about the appropriateness of their desire than to deal with our inner disturbance about it.

This is related to the feeling that if we acknowledge their need or desire then we will have to meet it or do something about it, which we don't. We can simply hear it, understand it, and appreciate what this means for that person and not even try to imagine yet how they might be able to get what they want.

It's important to realize that accepting another's desires or needs doesn't mean that we have to do anything about it. It's far more important to all of us that our feelings, wants and needs are heard and understood! How they are ultimately met is really secondary — think about it.

The importance is the connection, and to stay connected we simply have to understand what it is they want. Once we are connected, and if we can't do what they would like, we may be able to help them find some other way to get that need or desire met.

Transactional Analysis for Interpersonal Relations

Transactional Analysis is a theory developed by Dr. Eric Berne in the 1950's. Originally trained in psychoanalysis, Berne wanted a theory which could be understood and available to everyone and began to develop what came to be called Transactional Analysis (TA). Transactional Analysis is a social psychology and a method to improve communication. The theory outlines how we have developed and treated ourselves, how we relate and communicate with others, and offers suggestions and interventions which will enable us to change and grow. Transactional Analysis is underpinned by the philosophy that:

- People can change.
- We all have a right to be in the world and be accepted.

Initially criticized by some as a simplistic model, Transactional Analysis is now gathering worldwide attention. It originally suffered much from the popularized writings in the 1960's. Also, summarized explanations, such as this, which can only touch on some of the concepts in Transactional Analysis, led their readers to believe that there was very little to it. Many did not appreciate the duration and complexity of the training.

Today, there is greater understanding of Transactional Analysis. More and more people are taking the four to five year part time training courses to qualify, and increasingly universities are accrediting these courses for master's degrees. Those taking training include psychiatrists, organizational and management consultants, teachers, social workers, designers, engineers and the clergy.

Today Transactional Analysis is used in psychotherapy, organizations, educational and religious settings. Books have been written for all ages, from children through to adults, by people all over the world. Transactional Analysis is truly an international theory relating to a diverse range of cultures.

Theoretical concepts within the Transactional Analysis world are constantly being challenged and developed making it a rich dynamic process. Berne died in July 1970 at the age of 60. However, Transactional Analysis has not stood still and continues to develop and change, paralleling the processes we encourage in ourselves and others.

There are some key concepts in Transactional Analysis which are outlined here for your information.

Transactional Analysis — Contracting

Transactional Analysis is a contractual approach. A contract is "an explicit bilateral commitment to a well-defined course of action" Berne E. (1966). Which means that all parties need to agree?

- why do they want to do something?
- with whom
- what they are going to do
- by when
- any fees, payment or exchanges there will be.

For example, we want the outside of our house painted, we need to find a person who will paint it and who will give us a quote for doing it. If we agree to the quote, and we like him or her enough, we will no doubt employ them. We will agree a date and time, perhaps check they are insured, and choose the colour of the paint and off they go.

Sometimes, contracts will be multi-handed with all parties to the contract having their own expectations. If these expectations are all congruent then fine, if not then discussing everyone's expectations will lead to greater understanding and therefore to a clear contract.

Contracts need to be outlined in positive words i.e. what is wanted, rather than what is not wanted. Our minds tend to focus on the negative and so this encourages failure. For example, how many times do we look round when someone says to us "Don't look now but.......", the same is true when we set up contracts which start "I don't want to do .... anymore".

We have contracts about employment, how much will we be paid and when, what holidays we are due, what deductions there will be etc. In order to ensure placements are effective then different, but similar, details are required. Naturally, these details will vary depending on the setting in which we work.

All parties need to state what are they are prepared to do. Are they able and willing to undertake what is being asked, is this appropriate? Does it fit within any statements of purpose and function? Is it legal? Do they have the competence to deliver this? Do they want to do? What does each party want of the others?

In summary, contracts need to be: measurable, manageable and motivational. Measurable means that the goals need to be tangible. That each party involved in the contract will be able to say in advance how they will know when the goal has been achieved. The goal will be specific and behavioural and clearly defined. The contract will also need to be manageable and feasible for all those concerned.

Transactional Analysis — Ego States

Transactional Analysis First Order Structural Model

Berne devised the concept of ego states to help explain how we are made up, and how we relate to others. These are drawn as three stacked circles and they are one of the building blocks of Transactional Analysis. They categorise the ways we think, feel and behave and are called Parent, Adult, and Child. Each ego state is given a capital letter to denote the difference between actual parents, adults and children.

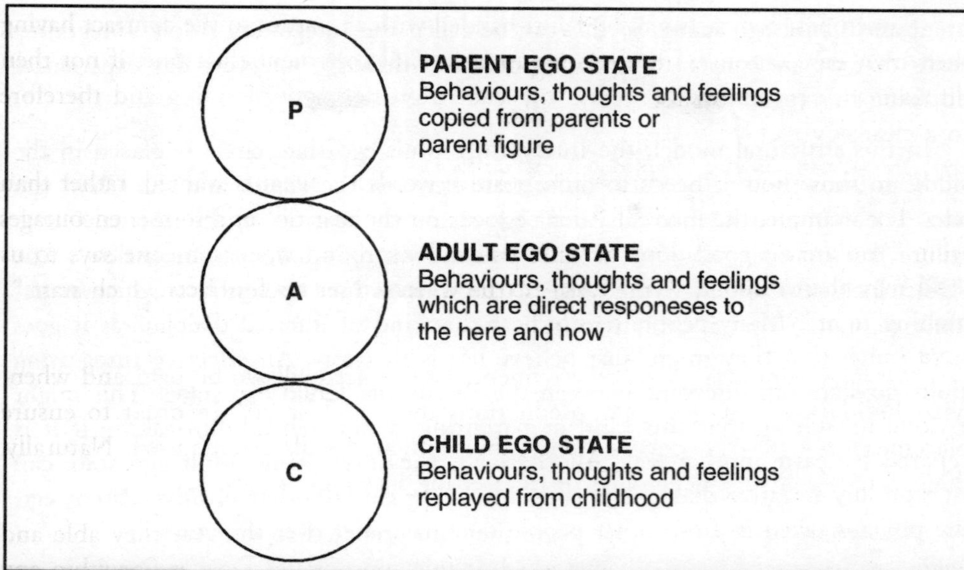

FIGURE 8.1 **Three Stacked Circles of Transactional Analysis**

Parent Ego State

This is a set of feelings, thinking and behaviour that we have copied from our parents and significant others.

As we grow up we take in ideas, beliefs, feelings and behaviours from our parents and caretakers. If we live in an extended family then there are more people to learn and take in from. When we do this, it is called introjecting and it is just as if we take in the whole of the caregiver. For example, we may notice that we are saying things just as our father, mother, grandmother may have done, even though, consciously, we don't want to. We do this as we have lived with this person so long that we automatically reproduce certain things that were said to us, or treat others as we might have been treated.

Adult Ego State

The adult ego state is about direct responses to the here and now. We deal with things that are going on today in ways that are not unhealthily influenced by our past.

The adult ego state is about being spontaneous and aware with the capacity for intimacy. When in our adult state we are able to see people as they are, rather than what we project onto them. We ask for information rather than stay scared and rather than make assumptions. Taking the best from the past and using it appropriately in the present is an integration of the positive aspects of both our

Parent and Child ego states. So this can be called the Integrating Adult. Integrating means that we are constantly updating ourselves through our every day experiences and using this to inform us.

In this structural model, the Integrating Adult ego state circle is placed in the middle to show how it needs to orchestrate between the Parent and the Child ego states. For example, the internal Parent ego state may beat up on the internal Child, saying "You are no good, look at what you did wrong again, you are useless". The Child may then respond with "I am no good, look how useless I am, I never get anything right". Many people hardly hear this kind of internal dialogue as it goes on so much that they might just believe life is this way. An effective Integrating Adult ego state can intervene between the Parent and Child ego states. This might be done by stating that this kind of parenting is not helpful and asking if it is prepared to learn another way. Alternatively, the Integrating Adult ego state can just stop any negative dialogue and decide to develop another positive Parent ego state perhaps taken in from other people they have met over the years.

Child Ego State

The Child ego state is a set of behaviours, thoughts and feelings which are replayed from our own childhood.

Perhaps the boss calls us into his or her office, we may immediately get a churning in our stomach and wonder what we have done wrong. If this were explored we might remember the time the head teacher called us in to tell us off. Of course, not everything in the Child ego state is negative. We might go into someone's house and smell a lovely smell and remember our grandmother's house when we were little, and all the same warm feelings we had at six year's of age may come flooding back.

Both the Parent and Child ego states are constantly being updated. For example, we may meet someone who gives us the permission we needed as a child, and did not get, to be fun and joyous. We may well use that person in our imagination when we are stressed to counteract our old ways of thinking that we must work longer and longer hours to keep up with everything. We might ask ourselves "I wonder what X would say now". Then on hearing the new permissions to relax and take some time out, do just that and then return to the work renewed and ready for the challenge. Subsequently, rather than beating up on ourselves for what we did or did not do, what tends to happen is we automatically start to give ourselves new permissions and take care of ourselves.

Alternatively, we might have had a traumatic experience yesterday which goes into the Child ego state as an archaic memory that hampers our growth. Positive experiences will also go into the Child ego state as archaic memories. The positive experiences can then be drawn on to remind us that positive things do happen.

The process of analysing personality in terms of ego states is called structural analysis. It is important to remember that ego states do not have an existence of their own, they are concepts to enable understanding. Therefore, it is important to say "I want some fun" rather than "My Child wants some fun". We may be in our Child ego state when we say this, but saying "I" reminds us to take responsibility for our actions.

Contamination of the Adult Ego State

The word contamination, for many conjured, up the idea of disease. For instance, we tend to use the word for when bacteria has gone into milk. Well, this is similar to the case with the contaminated Integrating Adult ego state. This occurs when we talk as if something is a fact or a reality, whereas this is actually a belief. Racism is an example of this. The Integrating Adult ego state is contaminated in this case by the Parent ego state. If we are white we might have lived with parents or significant others who said such things as "black people take our jobs". Growing up, it is likely, that having no real experience to go by, we believed this. We might also have been told that black people are aggressive. In our Child ego state may well lodge some scared feelings about black people and in this ego state we may start to believe "All Black people are scary". This would mean that there would be a double contamination of the Integrating Adult ego state. However, we would think that such statements were facts rather than beliefs and when this happens we say that this is Integrating Adult ego syntonic. That is, they fit with the Integrating Adult ego state and only those people outside of our situation and sometimes outside of our peer group or culture can see that, objectively, such beliefs are just that and therefore they can be changed.

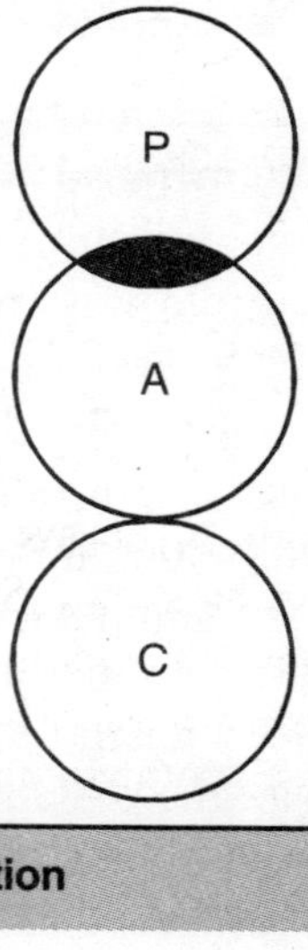

FIGURE 8.2 **Parent Contamination**

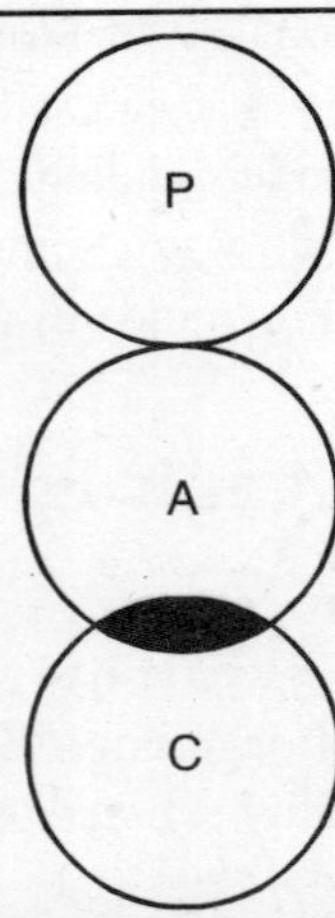

FIGURE 8.3 Child Contamination

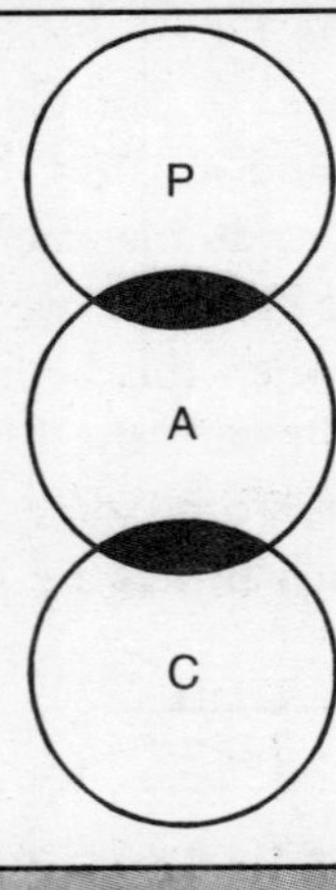

FIGURE 8.4 Double Contamination (Parent and Child)

TRANSACTIONAL ANALYSIS — THE DESCRIPTIVE MODEL

This model shows how we function or behave with others. The model used here is divided up into nine and we have used S. Temple's (1999) term "mode" as it differentiates it from the structural ego state model mentioned above. We colour the different modes in red and green for those who find colour helpful as a tool. Effective communication comes from the green modes, (just as with traffic lights we get the go ahead when the green light comes on), and ineffective communication come from the red modes (as with the red traffic light). When we come from the red modes we invite a negative response, and vice versa from the green modes.

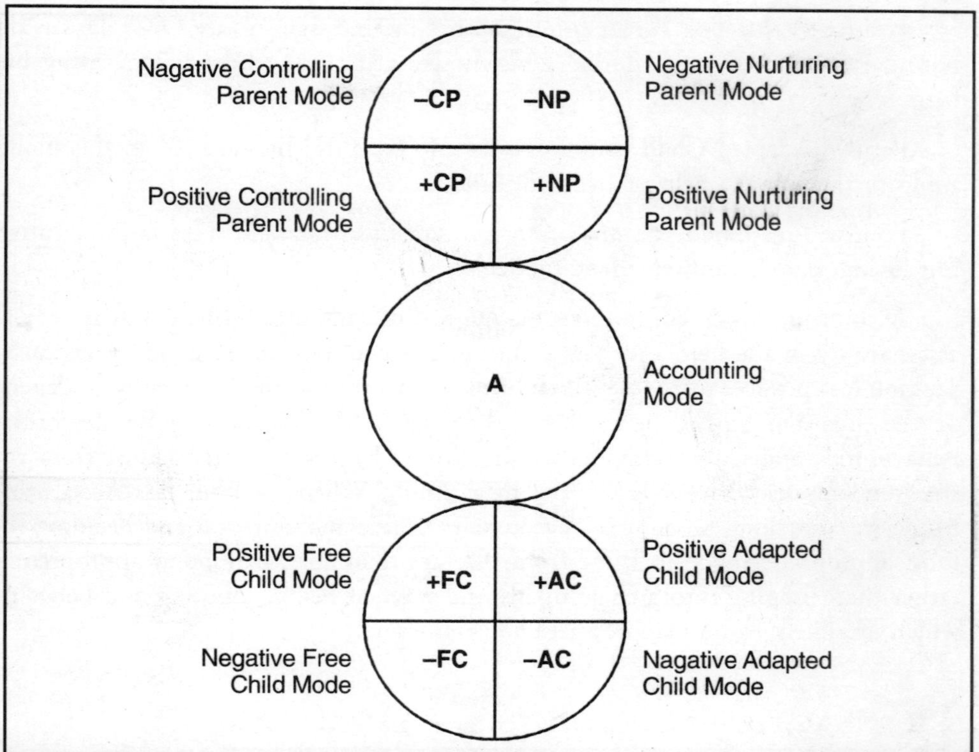

FIGURE 8.5 Transactional Analysis – The Descriptive Model

Ineffective Modes

Negative Controlling Parent communicates a "You're not OK" message, and is punitive.

Negative Nurturing Parent communicates a "You're not OK" message. When in this mode the person will often do things for others which they are capable of doing for themselves. When in this mode, the person is engulfing and overprotective.

Negative Adapted Child expresses an "I'm not OK" message. When in this mode the person over-adapts to others and tends to experience such emotions as depression, unrealistic fear and anxiety.

Negative Free Child in this mode the person runs wild with no restrictions or boundaries. In this mode they express a "You're not OK" message.

Effective Modes

Positive Nurturing Parent communicates the message "You're OK". When in this mode the person is caring and affirming.

Positive Controlling Parent communicates the message "You're OK". This is the boundary setting mode, offering constructive criticism, whilst being caring but firm.

Positive Adapted Child communicates an "I'm OK" message. From this mode, we learn the rules to help us live with others.

Positive Free Child communicates an "I'm OK" message. This is the creative, fun loving, curious and energetic mode.

Accounting mode communicates "We're OK" messages. The Adult is able to assess reality in the here and now. When the Accounting mode is in the executive position it is possible to choose which of the other effective modes to go into, depend on the situation. This is then called Accounting Mode. When using the descriptive behavioural model, the term Accounting Mode helps to differentiate it from the structural model where it is referred to as Adult. When stable in this Accounting Mode we are taking account of the present context and situation and deciding the most appropriate mode to come from. We are then able to respond appropriately rather than flipping into archaic or historic ways of being, thinking and behaving which are likely to be inappropriate and unhelpful.

Transactional Analysis – Diagnosis

It is helpful to be able to assess or diagnose which ego state in the structural model, or which mode in the descriptive model, somebody is in. In this way, we can respond appropriately as well as ensure which mode we are addressing.

However, when we work with other staff or are relating with young people, we are responding on the behavioural level. It is not always possible, or appropriate, to be undertaking more in-depth types of diagnosis. I have outlined them here though so that an understanding of the complexity of the process can be achieved.

❖ Behavioural Diagnosis

Words, tone, tempo of speech, expressions, postures, gestures, breathing, and muscle tone provide clues for diagnosing ego states.

Parent mode words typically contain value judgments, Adult words are clear and definable, and Free Child mode words are direct and spontaneous. For example, a person in Adapted Child mode may cry silently, whereas when in Free Child mode we are likely to make a lot of noise. 'You' or 'one' usually come from Parent. This can switch even mid-sentence. If we are leaning forward, it is likely we are in the posture of the Parent mode, whereas if we are in Adult mode we tend to be erect.

These are indicators not guarantees. Assessment needs to be supported by other methods of diagnosis.

❖ Social Diagnosis

Observation of the kinds of transactions a person is having with others. For example, if eliciting a response from someone's caretaking Parent it is likely that the stimulus is coming from Child, though not necessarily the Adapted Child mode. Our own responses to someone will often be a way of assessing which ego state or mode they are coming from.

❖ Historical Diagnosis

The person's past also provides important information. If, as a child we had feelings similar to those we are experiencing now, it is likely we are in Child ego state. If our mother or father behaved or talked in the same way that we are behaving or talking now then we are probably in a Parent ego state.

❖ Phenomenological Diagnosis

This occurs when we re-experience the past instead of just remembering it. This means that diagnosis is undertaken by self-examination. This is sometimes accurate and sometimes very inaccurate as the Child ego state may be afraid to allow our Adult to know what is going on.

Transactional Analysis – Strokes

In Transactional Analysis, we call compliments and general ways of giving recognition strokes. This name came from research which indicated that babies require touching in order to survive and grow. It apparently makes no difference whether the touching induces pain or pleasure — it is still important. On the whole, we prefer to receive negative strokes than no strokes at all, at least that way we know we exist and others know we exist.

We all have particular strokes we will accept and those we will reject. For example, if we have always been told we are clever, and our brother is creative, then we are likely to accept strokes for being clever, but not for being creative. From this frame of reference, only one person in the family can be the creative one and so on.

Stroking can be physical, verbal or non-verbal. It is likely that the great variety of stroke needs and styles present in the world results from differences in wealth, cultural mores, and methods of parenting.

The Stroke Economy

Claude Steiner suggests that, as children, we are all indoctrinated by our parents with five restrictive rules about stroking.

- don't give strokes when we have them to give
- don't ask for strokes when we need them
- don't accept strokes if we want them
- don't reject strokes when we don't want them
- don't give ourselves strokes

Together these five rules are the basis of what Steiner calls the stroke economy. By training children to obey these rules, says Steiner, parents ensure that "A situation in which strokes could be available in a limitless supply is transformed into a situation in which the supply is low and the price parents can extract for them is high."

We, therefore, need to change the restrictive rules to unrestrictive ones:

- give strokes when we have them to give
- ask for strokes when we want them
- accept strokes if we want them
- reject manipulative strokes
- give ourselves positive strokes

Strokes can be positive or negative:

1. "I like you"
2. "I don't like you".

Strokes can be unconditional or conditional. An unconditional stroke is a stroke for being whereas a conditional stroke is a stroke for doing. For instance:

"I like you" — unconditional

"I like you when you smile" — conditional

As negative strokes these might be:

"I don't like you" — negative unconditional

"I don't like you when you're sarcastic" — negative conditional.

People often have a stroke filter. They only let in strokes which they think they are allowed to let in. For instance, they allow themselves to receive strokes for being clever and keep out strokes for being good looking. One way to think about this to consider being out in the rain. The rain is the strokes that are available to us, both positive and negative. There is a hole in the umbrella and some of the strokes go through and we save them in a bucket to enjoy in lean times. Conversely, we might use them negatively to reinforce the negative strokes we give to ourselves. Of course, some just bounce off the umbrella and we might not accept the good strokes that are coming our way. Some might come in but fall straight onto the floor.

Transactional Analysis – Life Positions

Life positions are basic beliefs about self and others, which are used to justify decisions and behaviour.

When we are conceived we are hopefully at peace, waiting to emerge into the world once we have grown sufficiently to be able to survive in the outside of the womb. If nothing untoward happens we will emerge contented and relaxed. In this case, we are likely to perceive the world from the perspective of I am OK and You are OK.

However, perhaps our mother had some traumatic experiences, or the birth was difficult or even life threatening. This experience is likely to have an effect on the way we experience the world, even at the somatic level. In which case, we might emerge sensing that life is scary and might, for example, go into "I am not OK and You are not OK either".

Let's take it that the pregnancy went fine, and the birth was easy enough. What then? Well life experiences might reinforce our initial somatic level life position, or contradict it. If we were treated punitively, talked down to, and not held, we may begin to believe "I am not OK and You are OK". This might be the only sense we can make of our experiences.

Let's take another situation. Perhaps we were picked on and bullied as a child. We learnt that the way to get by was to bully others and that way we felt stronger and in control. Our behaviour then comes into the I am OK and You are not OK quadrant. Of course this may cover up our belief that we are really not OK, but nobody sees that. They just see our behaviour, and in fact we may have forgotten all about our negative feelings about ourselves as we have tried so hard to deny the pain of believing we are not OK.

These life positions are perceptions of the world. The reality is I just am and you just are, therefore how I view myself and others are just that "views" not fact. However, we tend to act as if they are a fact. Just like when somebody says "I can't do this, I'm useless". Rather than "I don't know how to do this. Will you show me?" The latter is staying with the fact that they do not yet know how to do it, whilst the former links being useless with not being able to do something.

There are a number of ways of diagramming the life positions. Franklyn Ernst (1971) the originator of the OK Corral drew it in quadrants, We have put these into red and green to show the effective and ineffective quadrants for communication and healthy relationships. By shading in the quadrants according to the amount of time we think we spend in each, we can get an idea of the amount of time we spend in each.

FIGURE 8.6 The Ok Corral

Berne talked about the life positions as existential positions, one of which we are more likely to go to under stress. This is significantly different to the concept Ernst uses, i.e. that we move around them all during the day. Whilst there is some truth in this, we could agree with Berne that there will be one major position we go into under stress, with perhaps another position underneath this one. These positions can change as we develop and grow. The difference between Berne and Ernst is important.

Chris Davidson (1999) writes about the three dimensional model of Okayness. All of the previous diagrams talk as if there were only one other person in the equation, when in reality there are often more. For example, the behaviour of young people in gangs may say that they believe they are okay and perhaps other gangs in their neighbourhood are okay, but an individual or gang from another neighbourhood are not okay. We often do this at work as well. We find other people who we like and then we gossip and put other people down. We are therefore saying that we believe we are okay but those others are awful (underneath this there may be a belief that we are not okay either but we feel better by putting someone else down). In this way, the two dimensional model of okayness i.e. that there are only two people involved, becomes three dimensional model where there can be three or more involved.

There is also the way in which we view life itself. If we consider that there is something wrong with us, and that others are not to be trusted and are not OK either, then the world would be a scary place and we are likely to experience life as tough and believe we will only be all right if we keep alert and on the look out for danger and difficulties.

Blame Model

The Transactional Analysis 'Okay Corral' can be linked to 'blame', for which Jim Davis TSTA developed this simple and helpful model. Commonly, when emotions are triggered, people adopt one of three attitudes relating to blame, which each correlate to a position on the Okay Corral:

- I'm to blame (You are okay and I'm not okay — 'helpless')
- You are to blame (I'm okay and you are not okay — 'angry')
- We are both to blame (I'm not okay and you are not okay — 'hopeless')

❖ None of These is a Healthy Position

Instead the healthy position is, and the mindset should be: "It's no-one's fault, blame isn't the issue — what matters is how we go forward and sort things out." (I'm okay and you are okay — 'happy') (With acknowledgements to Jim Davis TSTA)

Transactional Analysis – The Script

The script is a life plan, made when we are growing up. It is like having the script of a play in front of us — we read the lines and decide what will happen in each act and how the play will end. The script is developed from our early decisions based upon our life experience. We may not realise that we have set ourselves a plan but we can often find this out if we ask ourselves what our favorite childhood story was, who was our favourite character in the story and who do we identify with. Then consider the beginning, middle and end of the story. How is this story reflected in our life today?

Another way of getting to what script is may be to think about what we believe will happen when we are in old age. Do we believe we will be alive at 80 or 90 years old, be healthy, happy, and contented? What do we think will be on the headstone for our grave? What would we like to be on it?

Transactional Analysis – Driver Behaviour or Working Styles

These are ways in which we defend against the injunctions. These are very helpful to us and when we understand them, we can work to their strengths through choice, rather than because subconsciously we believe we have to do things this way to be okay. The names of five working styles have been developed, these are:

- Be perfect
- Be strong
- Try hard
- Please others
- Hurry up

The importance of recognising these in ourselves and others is that we can then work to the best of them rather than be driven by them.

The working style 'Be Perfect' means that we will be really good at doing accurate detailed reports, we will be neat in our appearance and our homes will be clean and tidy. If we have this style and are under stress it is likely that we would beat up on ourselves for not being good enough, for making a mistake, for something being out of place. Of course, we created the rule about what perfection is, and then we don't meet up to it we have a go at ourselves. This may also mean that we expect others to be perfect too which can be hard on the colleagues we work with.

If we have a Be Strong working style we will be great in a crisis. We can take control of situations and people will often feel safe around us. The difficulty is we may come across as aloof as we don't express feelings very often. For us, there is a tendency to say "it is" rather than "I am". The former phrase distances us from our feelings, enabling us to safe. We may stand apart from playful activities fearing we may look stupid. Instead of saying this however, it is likely that we condemn the activity as stupid and put down the person who suggested it.

If we have the Try Hard style we are great pioneers. We love new projects and new things to do. We probably have a great wealth of information as we like to gather different ideas together. We are best working under pressure. When stressed we may start too many things. We are more likely to start things but not finish them so celebrating achievements may not happen very often. We get sidetracked by starting to experiment with different ideas or ways to do things. We are likely to use phrases such as: "I'll try and do what we agreed" or "What I am trying to tell you is".

If we have the 'Please Others style' we will be a great team member. We like to please people without even asking them how we can do this as we prefer to guess. We can see both sides of an argument and attempt to calm things down. We will be keen to do things for others, often to the point of rescuing them. Decision-making is not our strong point and we may frustrate people by not expressing our own opinion. We prefer other people to determine priorities, not us. We worry about changing our behaviour in case others won't like us.

Those of us with the Hurry Up working style will get a great deal done in a short amount of time. If reports are wanted in on time, we are the person to do them. However, we tend to overload our time table and take on too much. This may mean that important aspects are overlooked. We are likely to be impatient with others and often finish their sentences for them. We make only superficial changes as we are so quick to get on with things and not take an in-depth perspective. We might select priorities so quickly that a significant area is overlooked. The way we structure our time is also influenced by our script.

Transactional Analysis — Time Structuring

The way in which we structure time is likely to reflect the different hungers. We all structure time in a variety of ways:

- Withdrawal
- Rituals
- Pastiming
- Activities
- Games
- Intimacy

Obtaining balance means ensuring that we have sufficient time for play and intimacy and if this does not occur then it would be beneficial to explore what we might be avoiding.

Transactional Analysis – Games

I am sure that every one of us must have been in the situation where we have said, "Why does this always keep happening to me" or "I always keep meeting people who hurt me and then go off and leave me". Sometimes it may be that we like to help people and then it goes wrong as the person we were trying to help says that we didn't do it well enough and that we got it wrong. We might think "Well, I was only trying to help" and feel got at.

When similar situations keep happening over and over again then the term Transactional Analysis uses for this is a game. A game is a familiar pattern of behaviour with a predictable outcome. Games are played outside Adult awareness and they are our best attempt to get our needs met — although of course we don't.

Games are learned patterns of behaviour, and most people play a small number of favourite games with a range of different people and in varying intensities.

First Degree games are played in social circles, generally leading to mild upsets not major traumas.

Second Degree games occur when the stakes may be higher. This usually occurs in more intimate circles, and ends up with an even greater negative payoff.

Third Degree games involve tissue damage and may end up in the jail, hospital or morgue.

Chris Davidson (2002) has argued that world politics can involve fourth degree games — where the outcomes involve whole communities, countries or even the world.

Games vary in the length of time that passes while they are being played. Some can take seconds or minutes while others take weeks, months or even years.

People play games for the following reasons:

- To structure time
- To acquire strokes
- To maintain the substitute feeling and the system of thinking, beliefs and actions that go with it
- To confirm parental injunctions and further the life script
- To maintain the person's life position by "proving" that self/others are not OK
- To provide a high level of stroke exchange while blocking intimacy and maintaining distance
- To make people predictable.

❖ Ways to deal with Games

There are various ways to stop a game, including the use of different options than the one automatically used. We can:

- cross the transaction by responding from a different ego state than the one the stimulus is designed to hook.

- pick up the ulterior rather than the social message e.g. when a person says "I can't do this, I'm useless". Rather than saying "Let me do this for you" instead say "It sounds like you have a problem. What do you want me to do about it?" (said from the Adult ego state)

- the opening message to the game always entails a discount. There are further discounts at each stage of the game. By detecting discounts we can identify game invitations and defuse them with options. (A discount is when we minimise, maximise or ignore some aspect of a problem which would assist us in resolving it. Such as saying in a whiny voice "This is too difficult for me to do", so we automatically help them).

- replace the game strokes. Loss of strokes to the Child ego state means a threat to survival. We get a great many strokes from games, even if they are negative. However, if we don't obtain sufficient positive strokes, or give ourselves positive strokes, we will go for quantity rather than quality of strokes and play games to get them. This loss of strokes is also a loss of excitement that the game has generated.

Another way to think about this is to consider the game role we or the other person is likely to take. One way to discover this is to ask the following questions:

1. What keeps happening over and over again?
2. How does it start?
3. What happens next?
4. And then what happens?
5. How does it end?
6. How do you feel after it ends? (John James, 1973)

We can then consider the reason we might have taken up a particular role, where we might switch to, and then consider how to do things differently. We need to consider what our own responsibility is in this — if the situation is too violent for us to get involved what options do we have? We could call for help, get others to come with us to intervene and so on. We need to choose the appropriate assistance and take the action required.

CHAPTER

9

FROM MANAGING TEAMS TO LEADING TEAMS

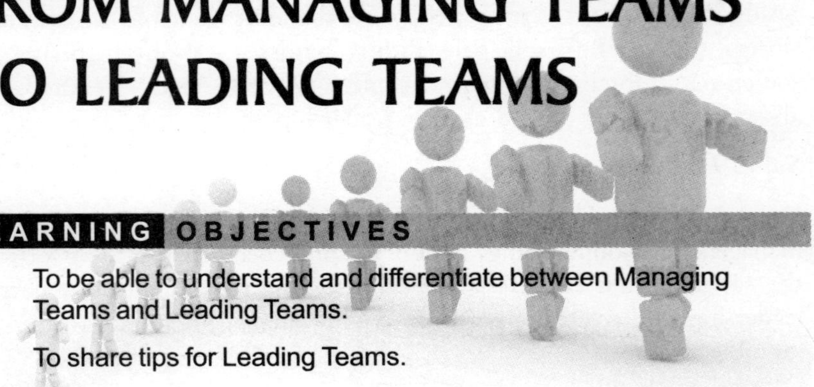

LEARNING OBJECTIVES

- To be able to understand and differentiate between Managing Teams and Leading Teams.
- To share tips for Leading Teams.

SHIFT FROM MANAGING TEAMS TO LEADING TEAMS

Leadership versus Management

❖ A Huge Difference

Do you want to be a leader or a manager? You need to make a choice as there is a huge difference. "The world is full of managers and desperately short of leaders — real leaders."

❖ Today's World Realities

The old ways of management no longer work and will never work again. The magnitude and pressure of environmental, competitive, and global market change we are experiencing is unprecedented. It's a very interesting and exciting world, but it's also volatile and chaotic. You cannot address these new challenges with more of the same management solutions — successful change requires leadership.

Psychological research has shown that "under circumstances of uncertainty or unusual challenge and difficulty, people look for help in understanding questions about what matters, what to do, what direction to take, and what they should not do. Providing people with the answers that help them with these difficult questions is the essence of leadership."

❖ Leading Change

Leadership is about getting people to abandon their old habits and achieve new things, and therefore largely about change — about inspiring, helping, and sometimes enforcing change in people. "While there can be effective management absent ideas, there can be no true leadership".

So, to lead or to manage?

You need both. The old proverb says that leadership is doing the right thing; management is doing things right. The difference between the two is not as sharp as the saying would suggest, and both are required for effective corporate growth: leadership risk creates opportunities while management strictness turns them into tangible results.

However, "if your organization is not on a journey, don't bother about leadership — just settle for management", advises John Adair.

"There is a direct correlation between the way people view their managers and the way they perform." Strong leadership is imperative for shaping a group of people into a force that serves as a competitive business advantage".

New Manager	
Classic Managerial Work	New Leadership
Planning	Creating Vision and Inspiring
Organizing and Hierarchy	Aligning the Web of Relations
Measuring and Controlling	Empowering and Coaching

❖ Synergy between your Leadership and Management Roles

- *Leadership role:* To provide inspiration, create opportunities, energize people, and make key choices
- *Management role:* To make things happen and keep work on track; to supervise endless details and engage in complex interactions that are routinely part of any development.

❖ What drives Others to carry out your Will

If you are a **manager**: WHAT you are

If you are a **leader**: WHO you are and what you DO

Leadership — Going Beyond Manager's Tasks

Manager's tasks:

- administrating
- planning
- controlling

Leader's extra tasks, in addition to manager's tasks:

- forming a vision which provides people with a bridge to the future
- inspiring, encouraging, and energizing people, arousing their willing and enthusiastic support to the common task at hand
- empowering people to pursue the common course of action

TABLE 9.1 Differences between what Leaders and Managers Do

Managers	Leaders
React	Create Opportunities
Control Risks	Seek Opportunities
Enforce Organizational Rules	Change Organizational Rules
Seek and then follow direction	Provide a vision to believe in and strategic alignment
Control people by pushing them in the right direction	Motivate people by satisfying basic human needs
Coordinate effort	Inspire achievement and energize people
Provide instructions	Coach followers, create self-leaders, empower them

On which side you're more comfortable when you're in Charge?

Management	Leadership
Restricting	Enabling
Controlling	Freeing
Playing safe	Risking
Molding	Releasing
Forcing	Enhancing
Regimenting	Challenging
Stifling	Participating
Rigid	Flexible
Autocratic	Democratic
Doing things right	***Doing right things***

Strategic Leadership

❖ Objective of Strategic Leadership

Strategic leadership provides the vision, direction, the purpose for growth, and context for the success of the corporation. It also initiates "outside-the-box" thinking to generate future growth. Strategic leadership is not about micromanaging business strategies. Rather, it provides the umbrella under which businesses devise appropriate strategies and create value.

In short, strategic leadership answers two questions:

- **What** — by providing the vision and direction, creating the context for growth, and
- **How** — by sketching out a road map for the organization that will allow it to unleash its full potential; by crafting the corporation's portfolio, determining what businesses should be there, what the performance requirements of the business are, and what types of alliances make sense; and by defining the means (the culture, values, and way of working together) needed to achieve corporate goals.

❖ The Distinguishing Characteristic

The distinguishing characteristic of the strategic leadership level — as compared with team level and operational level leadership — is that it implies responsibility for achieving the right balance between the whole, i.e. organizational needs, and the parts, be they large (functions) or small (teams or individuals).

❖ Setting the Right Direction

As a strategic leader responsible for the enterprise strategy development and implementation, your prime responsibility is to ensure that your organization is going in the right direction.

Seven Functions of Strategic Leadership

1. *Purpose/Vision:* to provide direction for the organization as a whole.
2. *Strategic thinking and planning:* to get strategy and policy right.
3. *Operational/Administration:* making it happen (overall executive responsibility).
4. *Organization fitness to situational requirement:* organizing or reorganizing (balance of whole and parts).

5. ***Energy, morale, confidence, espirit de corps:*** releasing the corporate spirit.
6. ***Allies and partners, stakeholders, political:*** relating the organization to other organizations and society as a whole.
7. ***Teaching and leading the learning by example:*** choosing today's leaders and developing tomorrow's leaders.

Result based Leadership

❖ What is Result based Leadership?

Results based leadership has relentless emphasis on results. It's simple equation:

Effective leadership = attributes × results.

This equation suggests that leaders must strive for excellence in both terms: that is, they must both demonstrate attributes and achieve results. Each term of the equation multiplies each other; they are not cumulative.

❖ Why Result based Leadership?

What is missing in most leadership related writings and teachings, is the lack of attention to results. Most of them focus on organizational capabilities such as adaptability, agility, mission-directed, or values based or on leadership competencies such as vision, character, trust, and other exemplary attributes, competencies and capabilities. All well and good, but what is seriously missing is the connection between these critical capabilities and results. And this is what results based leadership is all about: how organizational capabilities and leadership competencies lead to and are connected to desired results.

WHAT DESIRED RESULTS ARE AND HOW THEY ARE DEFINED AND MEASURED?

Effective Leadership Equation

Effective Leadership = Attributes × Results

Effective leaders must strive for excellence in both:

1. Demonstrating attributes, and
2. Achieving results

❖ Four Areas of Results

1. **Employee results** (human capital)
2. **Organization results** (learning, innovation)
3. **Customer results** (delight target customers)
4. **Investor results** (cash flow)

Volatility Leadership

❖ Why Volatility Leadership?

We are living in the new economy characterized by rapid unpredictable change and volatility. Volatility and chaos aren't bad or good — they are just realities. While associated with strife, hardship, and discontent, volatility and chaos are also synonyms for fundamental change, breakthroughs, discoveries, and optimist. "In this new world, leaders must anticipate, rush to think, reach out, build enduring bonds with customers and stakeholders, and get comfortable with leading at the edge of chaos." To guide your organization through volatile times, you must learn how to see the patterns in chaos and take charge, learn how to act boldly to safeguard your organization and lead it to a brighter future, and to alter your strategies to prepare for whatever the world may bring next.

❖ Ten Volatility Leadership Best Practices

The ten critical elements outlined below provide a process of stabilization that will help you harvest the benefits of the rapid change brought about by the volatile times, reduce the risk of volatility and the likelihood of crisis:

1. Make haste slowly
2. Partner with Customers
3. Build a culture of commitment
4. Put the right person, in the right place, right now
5. Maximize knowledge assets
6. Cut costs, not value
7. Out position your competitors
8. Stir, don't shake
9. Cut through the noise
10. Focus, or fail

"While the individual strategies provide proven solutions to specific challenges, their greatest value lies in the integrated protocol for leadership created by their fusion — a whole greater than the sum of its parts."

❖ To Lead in Volatile Times you Must

- learn to stay ahead of the volatility curve and its inherent dangers
- learn to manage rapid upturns as well as downturns
- learn to anticipate and prepare for volatility
- distinguish patterns and order amidst chaos

Entrepreneurial Leadership Defined

Entrepreneurial leadership involves instilling the confidence to think, behave and act with entrepreneurship in the interests of fully realizing the intended purpose of the organization to the beneficial growth of all stakeholders involved.

In the new era of rapid changes and knowledge based enterprises, managerial work becomes increasingly a leadership task. Leadership is the primary force behind successful change. Leaders empower employees to act on the vision. They execute through inspiration and develop implementation capacity networks through a complex web of aligned relationships.

Continuous Rewriting of Leadership Rules

"One of the key elements of highly effective leadership is the refusal to believe that a business model, however sound and well crafted, is ever good to run on autopilot. Recognizing this, the most successful leaders continuously improve their models by engaging in a perpetual process of interactive learning".

To change the company's culture and your own leadership style, get exposed to new challenging voices that would force you out of your comfort zone. Subject yourself to the 360 degree evaluation process: ask not only your supervisors, but also your employees, customers, and peers to rate your management performance. Promise anonymity to encourage honest opinions.

Leading Innovation

Leading innovation is a delicate and challenging process. You need to encourage expansive out-of-the-box thinking to generate new ideas, but also filter through these ideas to decide which to commercialize. Use a balanced "loose-tight" style of leadership for this purpose. "Loose-tight leadership alternates the creation of space for idea generation and free exploration with a deliberate tightening that selects and tests specific ideas for further investment and development". Looseness usually dominates the early stages of the innovation process; in the later stages, tightening becomes more important to scrutinize the concepts and bring the selected ones to the market.

A balanced approach is essential to loose-tight leadership. Those who remain loose too long generate plenty of ideas but have difficulty commercializing them. Those who lock into the tight mode choke off all but most obvious ideas, thus confining innovation to incremental line extensions of existing products that add little value.

❖ Leaders as Entrepreneurs: Ten Key Actions Roles

Leaders —

1. are persons who make a significant difference.
2. are creative and innovative.
3. spot and exploit opportunities.
4. find the resources and competencies required to exploit opportunities.
5. are good team-builders and networkers.
6. are determined in the face of adversity and competition.
7. manage change and risk.
8. have control of the business.
9. put the customer first.
10. create capital.

SITUATIONAL LEADERSHIP

Leadership Styles

Your leadership style is how you behave when you are trying to influence the performance of others. It is the way you supervise or work with someone.

There are four leadership styles (but there is no one best leadership style):

1. Directing
2. Coaching

3. Supporting
4. Delegating

Depending on your employees' competencies in their task areas and commitment to them, your leadership style may vary from one person to another. You may also lead the same person one way sometimes and another way at other times. Use a variety of leadership styles in directing and supporting the work of others and make them a second nature to you in your roles as a manager and as a parent.

❖ Using the Skill/Will Matrix

If you assigned a task to someone and the job does not quite get done well enough, one of the most likely reasons is that:

- you have delegated the task to someone who is unwilling or unable to complete the job, and have then remained relatively uninvolved or 'hands-off', or
- you may have been too directive or 'hands-on' with a capable person who was quite able to complete the assignment with little assistance from you; you just ended up demotivating him/her.

Consequently, whether you are managing, or leading or coaching, it is critical to match your style of interaction with the coachee's readiness for the task.

Don't work Harder, work Smarter

❖ Competence and Commitment Defined

- **Competence** is a function of knowledge and skills, which can be gained from education, training and/or experience.
- **Commitment** is a combination of confidence and motivation. Confidence is a measure of a person's self-assuredness — a feeling of being able to do a task without much supervision, whereas motivation is a person's interest in and enthusiasm for doing a task well.

❖ Leader's Behaviour

- **Directive Behaviour** involves clearly telling people what to do, how to do it, and when to do it, and then closely supervising their performance.
- **Supportive Behaviour** involves listening to people, providing support and encouragement for their efforts, and then facilitating their involvement in problem solving and decision making.

Super-leadership

❖ Why Super-leadership?

Super-leadership is a new form of leadership for the era of knowledge based enterprises distinguished by flat organizational structures and employee empowerment. A super-leader is one who leads others to lead themselves through designing and implementing the system that allows and teaches employees to be self-leaders.

"The function of leadership is to produce more leaders, not more followers."

— **Ralph Nader**

❖ Empowered Self-leadership

The best organizations have a theory and practice of leadership that subscribes to and promotes the concept that leadership exists at all levels within the organization. "Everyone provides leadership for those responsibilities that have been assigned to them. For the highest performing organizations, even the lowest ranked staff within an organization must assume leadership and attention to detail for their responsibilities in a manner similar to the most senior and powerful".

With super-leadership, followers are treated and become self-leaders.

❖ Key Benefits of Super-leadership

- high team performance and flexibility
- high follower development and self-confidence
- high team creativity and innovation
- high long-term performance
- high ability of the team to work independently in the absence of a leader

Values based Leadership

❖ What is Values based Leadership?

Leadership is not limited just to singular measure of effectiveness — it is a multidimensional phenomenon.

Values based leadership is different from other modes in that it includes all the three factors:

1. Effectiveness — measuring the achievement of the objectives

2. Morality — measuring how change affects concerned parties, and
3. Time — measuring the desirability of any goal over the long-term.

Values based leadership is not simply about style, how-to, following some recipe, or even mastering "the vision thing". Instead, it is about ideas and values. It is about understanding the different and conflicting needs of followers, energizing followers to pursue a goal than they had thought possible. "In practical business terms, it is about creating conditions under which all followers can perform independently and effectively toward a single objective."

❖ Why Values based Leadership?

Values based leadership is a must in modern flat organizations characterized by transparency and easy availability of information. As Steve Jobs, the co-founder of Apple Computer, put it, "The only thing that works is management by values. Find people who are competent and really bright, but more importantly, people who care exactly about the same things you care about."

❖ Leader's Ideas

Leadership is not about style, but about ideas. While there can be effective management absent ideas, there could be no true leadership. "Ultimately, it is ideas that motivate followers, and concepts powerful enough to energize people are typically broad, transcendent, even "philosophical" in nature".

❖ Leader's Beliefs and Attitudes

The primary determinant of a leader's success or failure is not a lack of know-how or style. "Instead, the key variables are the leader's beliefs and attitudes".

❖ Building Trust

Building relationships requires the building of trust. Trust is the expectancy of people that they can rely on your word. It is built through integrity and consistency in relationships.

"Trust elevates levels of commitment and sustains effort and performance without the need for management controls and close monitoring."

Principle-centered Leadership

❖ Principle-centered Leaders Defined

Principle-centered leaders are men and women of character who work on the basis of natural principles and build those principles into the center of their lives, into the center of their relationships with others, into the centre of their agreements and contracts, into their management processes, and into their mission statements.

❖ New Paradigm

Responding to classic dilemmas of modern living, principle-centered leadership presents a new way of thinking that is to help you to:

- achieve and maintain a wise and renewing balance between work and family, personal and professional ambitions, in the middle of constant crises and pressures.
- adhere to simplicity in the thick of increasing complexity.
- maintain a sense of direction in today's wilderness, where well-developed road maps (strategies and plans) are rendered useless by rapid change that often hits you from the blind side.
- look at human weaknesses with genuine compassion and understanding rather than accusation and self-justification.
- replace prejudice (the tendency to prejudge and categorize people in order to manipulate them) with a sense of reverence and discovery in order to promote learning, achievement, and excellence in people.
- get empowered (and empower other people) with confidence and competence to solve problems and seize opportunities — without being or fearing loose cannons.
- encourage the desire to change and improve without creating more pain from the gain.
- become a contributing member of a complementary team based on mutual respect and the valuing of diversity and pluralism.
- know where to start, when and how to recharge your batteries to maintain momentum for learning, growing and improving.

❖ Principles versus Practices

- *Practices — what to do's* — are specific activities or actions that work in one circumstance but not necessary in another.
- *Principles — why to do's* — have universal application; when principles are internalized into habits, they empower people to create a wide variety of practices to deal with different situations.

❖ Leading by Principles versus Leading by Practices

- *Leading by practices:* All the judgment and wisdom is provided in the form of rules and regulations; employees don't have to be the experts and don't have to exercise judgment.
- *Leading by principles:* These requires a different type of and more training, but the payoff is more expertise, creativity, and shared responsibility at all levels of the organization.

Principles-centered Leadership

❖ Four Levels of Practicing

Principles-centered leadership is practiced from the inside out on four levels:

1. *Personal:* your relationships with yourself.
2. *Interpersonal:* your relationships and interactions with others.
3. *Managerial:* your responsibility to get a job done from others.
4. *Organizational:* your need to organize people — to recruit them, train them, compensate them, build teams, solve problems, and create aligned structure, strategy and systems.

CHAPTER

10

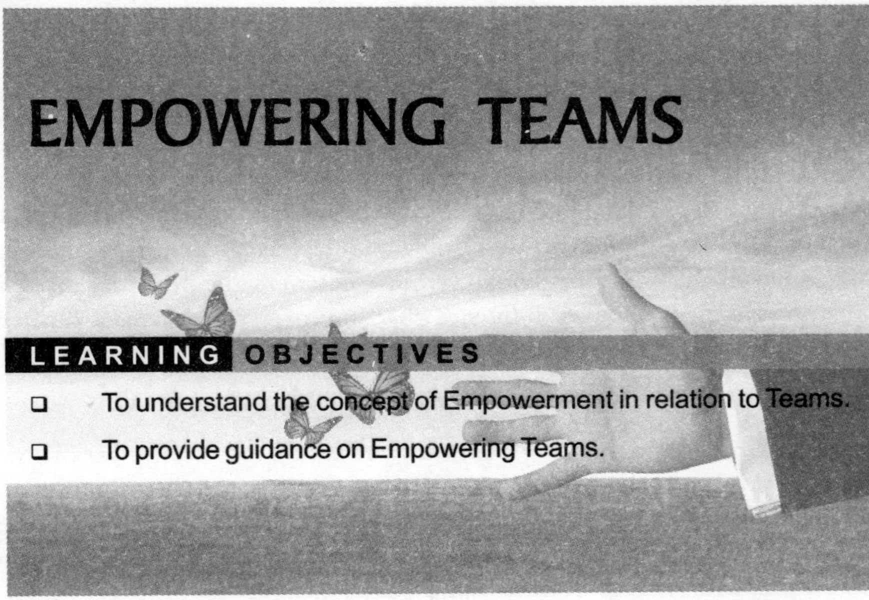

EMPOWERING TEAMS

LEARNING OBJECTIVES

- To understand the concept of Empowerment in relation to Teams.
- To provide guidance on Empowering Teams.

EMPOWERING TEAMS

Empowerment = Power × Information × Knowledge × Rewards

Empowerment, as a concept, has gained immense ground in recent years and we find many senior management teams grappling with the idea of creating an empowered organization. It is a mutually reinforcing process, where the individual and organization's gains are manifold. The process stems from the idea that if employees are given some degree of ownership over their jobs, they are likely to perform them well, at times much beyond the organization's expectations.

The case for empowerment in today's organization is understandable. With unrelenting competition, constantly changing external environment, an aggressive and demanding customer and need to take opportunities which are too local, too fleeting and too many in number, a centralized decision making process would prove to be a disaster. The pivotal question, in this context is: what decisions should be left for employees to take? And here, unfortunately, there are no straight answers.

It is now widely recognized that decisions concentrated at the top hampers flexibility and timely action at the lower levels. On the other hand, pushing down decision making at lower levels, may lead to chaos, conflicting decisions and a discernible lack of common purpose. The decision to take decisions or to push it upwards should be left to employee's discretion. The organization should develop the employees and also create a culture whereby an individual is the right judge to decide or push it up the hierarchy.

Empowerment is an interactive and interdependent process in which every individual and team gains in competence and enhance level of autonomy and control over their job. The true meaning of empowerment, however, is a process of increasing organizational effectiveness by developing and deploying competent influence. Being competent in the context of empowerment describes the potential that employees must possess for exercising influence that improves performance. Influence, in a similar context, implies competence in action.

Competent influence would imply three related elements viz.:

Commitment: Exhibiting commitment would necessarily mean using one's capability to improve performance. It has been found in several cases in the organizational context where employees shy away from taking action even when they can contribute significantly towards improving work processes or solving work related problems. It is so because over a period of time they have learnt that it is not wise to offer ideas, to get involved or take risks. The first element in competence, therefore, is commitment to demonstrate competence.

The challenge for the organizations, thus, is to create environments where employees are aware that demonstrating competence is the norm. It is equally important for employees to aggressively pursue the continuous development of their own competence by seeking new work experiences and taking learning initiatives. Also, employees need to be rewarded for developing their own competence and that of others.

Capable: Capable describes knowledge and skills possessed by employees in order to exercise competent influence. Capable employees would necessarily have three characteristics. They possess necessarily skills and knowledge that is required for making important/useful decisions, solving problems and creating new ideas. They are able to match their knowledge and skill to an appropriate outcome. They possess the necessary skill to influence others with their technical knowledge and skills.

Ethical: Being empowered means exercising competent influence, which may not be quite possible without a set of ethical norms. This would require an employee not to disguise what he does not know, to use his influence to make a positive effect on the organization's performance and to be accountable to the stake holders of the organization.

The advantages of creating an empowered organization cannot be overstated. In the present day environment, where the only competitive edge which an organization can derive is through its people, it becomes imperative to have an empowered workforce which can give peak level performance at all times.

Examples of how employees have used empowerment include hotel employees using their own cars to transport guests to airport during a taxi strike, repairing broken luggage for guests and carrying a sick guest to hospital at midnight. All of these guest empowerment actions created memorable guest experiences often leading to a return customer.

Some of the largest and most successful companies in the world have created an empowered workforce. Chairman of Texas Instruments, Mark Shephard, sees his employees as a "source of ideas, not just acting as a pair of hands ", while in retail giant Walmart, Sam Walter says, that "our best ideas come from clerks and stock boys". In Boeing, they are "proud of their ability to pull people from several layers down in the technical structures and put them in charge of major projects often with higher salaried and senior people reporting to them.

Another off quoted example of an empowered organization is Southwest Airlines. Southwest Airlines is the fifth largest airline company in America, operating more than 2100 flights per day and carrying over 44 million passengers a year to 50 different cities all over the United States. It was the first airline with a frequent flyer programme to give credit for the number of trips taken, not just the number of miles flown, and also pioneered senior discounts, Fun Fares, Fun Packs, a same day air freight delivery service, ticketless travel, and many other unique programs. To support their belief that people take better care of things they own, and that this special care is ultimately passed on to the customer, Southwest created a profit sharing programme and a broad-based stock option plan which allows employees to participate in the financial benefits of an ownership culture.

Ownership extends beyond just the financial benefits of profit sharing and stock option plans and is manifested in the priority they place on employee initiative and responsibility. Southwest is built on the principle that employees are expected to take on an entrepreneurial role in being proactive owners who are cognizant of corporate values and confident enough with their empowerment to participate in decision making and continuous improvement. This entrepreneurial spirit provides employees with the freedom and responsibility to take effective action and the financial participation through ownership which allows them to benefit from the company's overall performance.

What's unique about Southwest's employee involvement is that it has really empowered employees to take on responsibility for maintaining the high performance standards of the company with few complications. Southwest has the most productive workforce in the industry with 2400 customers served per employee annually, once again double its competitor's average. Southwest also has the lowest turnover rate among airlines, with less than 4.5% of employees leaving per year. There is also no retrenchment policy at Southwest, which has never permanently laid off an employee.

The concept of empowerment can be used in our day to day lives by teachers, parents and coaches. Svenlzoren Eriksson, the English Soccer Manager, is a promoter of the concept, which involves, listening to team members, encouraging dissent, slashing hierarchies, reaching decisions by consensus and above all empowering.

Studies have universally shown that empowerment can speed up decision-making and increase reaction times. It releases the creative and innovative capabilities of employees and leads to greater job satisfaction, motivation and commitment, while giving employees greater responsibility and a greater sense of achievement from their work. It reduces operational costs by eliminating unnecessary layers of management, along with reducing quality control and checking operations.

But are there any identifiable indications to suggest that the employees in an organization are empowered? Interaction between employees with customers, managers and each other could give a valuable insight into the level of empowerment. An empowered workforce needs to be aware of organization's vision and broad strategic goals. They try to move beyond their functional specialty and show interest in company's financials, competitive data, company publications and press reports. They analyze their job in terms of its relevance to the overall organization's mission, They hold themselves responsible for their performance and results. To this extent, they exhibit a fair degree of control over the outcomes of their work. They are always seeking feedback on their performance and feel a compelling need to improve it on a continuous basis. They set high standards for themselves and are always striving to achieve and surpass them. They take initiatives to help others in their area of work in order to improve overall organization's performance. They exhibit a win-win attitude where everyone is a winner and no one loses. They do not shy away from asking for additional resources when they do not have what they require to perform well.

A pertinent question facing the top management team is how to avoid these pitfalls and make empowerment seep through the cultural fabric of their organization. Here it is important to understand that the process of empowerment proceeds along formal as well as informal track. Top level commitment to empowerment and emphasizing its value throughout the organizational hierarchy helps in creating awareness and change in behavioral patterns, yet such informal processes cannot carry the phenomena enough. The support of formal structure and systems is mandatory to institutionalize and make it a part of the organizational fabric.

Feedback is the key. For empowerment to become a completely functioning condition, every individual and every work group within an organization requires constant feedback across all their performance connections. For feedback to become the backbone of the empowerment process, it needs to be self managed and structured.

Performance evaluation drawn from multiple sources: Empowerment of employees would involve decentralization which would entail making important decisions away from the boss's field of view. This would also involve greater interaction with internal and external customers, and developing cross-functional linkages. The performance feedback can be received from a variety of sources, apart from the boss, to ensure objectivity and relevance. 3600 appraisal is widely used in such organizations where an employee receives performance evaluation from a wide set of colleagues, subordinates and sometimes customers. Empowered teams also sometimes appraise their team members. Often, these inputs are combined with boss evaluation, in periodic evaluation meetings between the manager and employees.

Group incentives: The incentive schemes in empowered organizations need to be designed in a manner, by which cooperation and collaboration are rewarded. Most incentives encourage and reward individual performance. Individual competitiveness may thwart group performance and effectiveness. To promote a culture of empowerment, organizations need to augment individual reward scheme with group level rewards. These may take the form of gain sharing, profit sharing, bonus pool rewards, where awards available for individuals depend upon the performance of group as a whole.

Error tolerance: Empowering employees would also entail encouraging them to learn by making mistakes and experimenting. Unless the organization is tolerant of genuine mistakes, a culture of empowerment would never develop. If employees are not convinced that they can take risks, they will never innovate and learn.

Increased communication: Sound decision making requires information and since in an empowered organization, decision making is widely distributed, it becomes imperative for such an organization to develop widely distribution information systems. The presence of electronic mail, internal newsletter, rich library, regular staff and cross functional meetings signifies the organization's attempt to make information available.

Emphasis on generalists: The bureaucratic hierarchical structure lays immense emphasis on functional specialists as jobs are defined and well structured. The managers are expected to perform within the confines of their functional expertise and to that extent skill development is limited to their own specific complex workings.

Empowered organizations, in contrast, are loose with fluid functional boundaries and such prefer generalist managers who are at ease moving horizontally within an organization.

Emphasis on a learning culture: Since empowerment involves competency development, every effort is made by the organization to create a culture of continuous learning, which goes beyond formal training and development programs. Mentoring, coaching, learning through experimentation, self-learning as also e-Learning are important ways of fostering a culture of continuous learning.

It must be realized that empowerment as a process is time consuming, deliberate and requires continuous support and commitment from the top management. It is a philosophy which has to seep into the organization's culture and result in a change of management attitude and practices. The role of a boss experiences a shift from one of controlling and directing to a more nurturing role of a coach, mentor and facilitator.

At the heart of empowerment is trustworthiness which is a function of character and competence. Character is what we are; competence is what we can do. And both are necessary to create trustworthiness. Both character and competence are necessary to inspire trust. Character includes integrity and maturity, while competence includes technical competence, conceptual competence and interdependent competence.

The process of empowerment is an experience of an organization which invariably results in superior quality, better services and high morale and motivation within the organization. But as with all the good things in life, the process requires perseverance, patience and commitment.

ADVANTAGES OF EMPOWERMENT

- ***Customer Service:*** The employees would be able to render service to the customer which are spontaneous and appropriate and which would definitely give the impression to the customer that he is dealing with an employee who has influence in the organization.
- ***Flexibility:*** Empowered employees are ready to respond to changes and opportunities as they arise.
- ***Speed:*** This would be a definite outcome when employees realize that responsibility for action rests with them.
- ***Cross functional linkages:*** Horizontal linkages are likely to develop as they would facilitate qualitative and faster decision making. Cross functional teams can form and reform not necessarily at the instance of the higher management. Benefits accrue from what the team contributes to member's regular work. If a link ceases to add value, the participant will drop it.

- *Morale:* Empowerment is a definite morale booster, as employees feel good when they have greater control over their jobs. This also has an overall organization wide positive impact.
- *Changing job profile:* With majority of organizations going in for flatter organization structure, the employees are increasingly faced with limited promotions as career growth options. In this scenario, increased responsibility and authority span could serve as an attractive reward in lieu of promotion and subsequent monetary enhancement. It could also go a long way in building loyalty and prevent attrition in organization.

Empowerment: Myths and Misconceptions

- *Confusion with socio/political meaning of empowerment:* The purpose of extending the power of people in organizations should be to ensure individual and organizational growth. When organizations uncritically take on the political and social meaning of empowerment, they fail to stay single minded in their pursuit of improved performance. They will tend to concentrate on redistributing power which may or may not improve performance.
- *It is not about delegation:* Equating delegation with empowerment does not come close to capturing its full meaning. Empowerment may include delegation, but it includes a lot more. It implies new ways of structuring an organization, developing and using teams, new ways of stimulating and rewarding learning, changing the roles of managers to include coaching and facilitating and much more.
- *A one way transaction from more powerful to less powerful:* The full potential of improved performance through empowerment can never be realized as long as it is understood only as power being given up or shared. It is a process of creation of competence not a process of power distribution. This can be achieved through continuous competence enhancement and its applications at all levels in the organization. The power and influence of managers increase when their subordinates gain more competence and apply it towards better job performance.

Potential Pitfalls

- *Greater potential for chaos:* This could arise because of different employees performing at different levels which could leave the customers, internal and external, confused and unsure about the services provided. Departments may have their own interpretation of different company policies leading to further confusion and chaos.

- *Lack of clarity:* The speed and flexibility in decision making could lead to fuzzy job definitions where responsibilities and resultant accountabilities are not clear. Employees may feel too stretched out and frustrated where everyone is held responsible for almost everything that goes on the organization.
- *Breakdown of hierarchical control:* Empowerment brings along with itself, a breakdown of hierarchical levels as well loosening of cross functional demarcations. Control is shared both horizontally as well as vertically. Although cross-functional teams may work effectively towards problem solving, sharing of functional control is generally deeply resented by the concerned managers.
- *Demoralization:* The basic philosophy behind empowerment is based on the assumption that employees are desirous of more power and control over their work. This may just be a perception of those managers who like to take on additional responsibilities and hence may not be true for many employees, who become seriously demoralized when they are given higher responsibility and accountability.

❖ 5 Questions for Top Management to Ask

1. Are we ready for improvement?
2. Have we driven out fear?
3. Have we eliminated cross-functional barriers?
4. Are the managers acting as a facilitator?
5. Do we evaluate to obtain necessary feedback and follow up?

CHAPTER

11

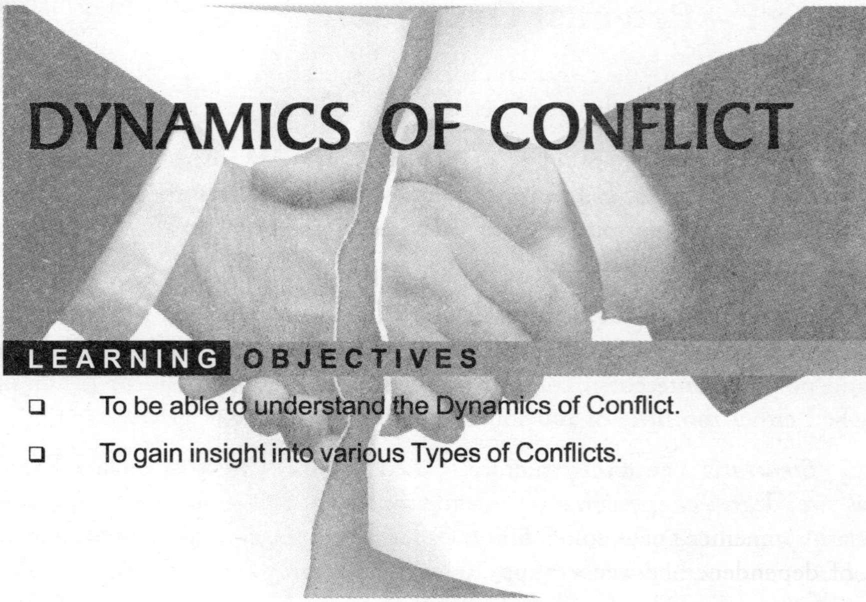

DYNAMICS OF CONFLICT

LEARNING OBJECTIVES

- To be able to understand the Dynamics of Conflict.
- To gain insight into various Types of Conflicts.

INTRODUCTION

Conflict is a part of life. Inside and outside the organization, people are being constantly subjected to conflict. Conflict surface due to limitation of resources, competition and differences in values, goals, attitudes, expectations, etc. Whatever may be the reason, if conflicts are not managed properly they may adversely affect the organization.

Effective management of conflict requires, the understanding of the concept of conflict. What is conflict? It is defined as "A process in which an effort is purposely made by 'A' to offset the effort of 'B' by some of blocking that will resulting in frustrating 'B' in attaining his or her goals or furthering his or her interest". Conflict also should be defined as the actual or the threatened use of force in any continuing relationship. Force is the attempt to override opposition by an act designed to produce injury to the other party.

STAGES OF CONFLICT

The various attempts to understand the conflict show that the conflict does not emerge all of a sudden. It is a process. It moves from one place to another and finally it takes the form of individual, group or class conflict. The stage of conflicts may be explained in the following manner.

Stage I – Potential Opposition

The first step in the conflict process is the absence of conditions that create opportunities for conflict to arise they did not lead directly to conflict, but one of these conditions is necessary if conflict is to arise.

Communication: It is one of the most important factors, which causes conflict. The communication source represents those opposing forces that arise from semantic difficulties,.misunderstandings and noise in the communication channels.

Researchers indicate that semantic difficulties, insufficient exchange of information and noise in the communication channel are barriers to communication and potential antecedent conditions to conflict. The potential for conflict increases, when either too little or too much communication takes place.

Structure: The term structure is used in this context to include variables such as size, degree of specialization in the task assigned to group members, jurisdictional clarity, member goal compatibility, leadership styles, rewards systems and the degree of dependence between groups. Research indicates that size and specialization act as forces to stimulate conflict. The larger the group and more specialized the activities, the greater the likelihood of conflict. Tenure and conflict have been found to be inversely related. The greater the ambiguity in precisely defining the responsibilities, the greater the potential for conflict to emerge. There is some evidence that a chosen style of leadership, tight and continuous observation with general control of the others behaviours increases conflict potential. Rewards systems too, are found to create conflict when members gain is at another's expense. Finally, if a group is dependent on the other group or if interdependence allows one group to gain at another's expense, opposing forces are stimulated.

Personal variables: Personal factors include the individual value systems that each person has and the personality characteristics and that account for individual differences. The evidence indicates that certain personality types – for example, individuals who are highly authoritarian and dogmatic and who demonstrate low esteem, lead to potential conflict.

Stage II – Cognition and Personalization

In the first stage, the conditions generate frustration and now it becomes actual conflict. The antecedent conditions can only lead to conflict when one or more of the parties are affected by, and cognitive of the conflict. It is necessary one or more of the parties must be aware of the existence of the antecedent conditions, when individuals become emotionally involved, that parties experience anxiety, tenseness frustration or hostility.

Stage III – Behaviour

When a member engages in an action that frustrates the attainment of another's goals or prevents the furthering of the other's interests. This action must be intended, that is, there must be a knowing effort to frustrate another. The conflict behaviour could be overt and covert.

Types of Conflict

Conflict can be classified into various types depending on their nature. Following are some of them:

(a) ***Perceived conflict:*** Perceived conflict is one in which people perceive that conflicting conditions exist in the work organizations. But there is potential ground for perceived conflict to turn into real conflict.

(b) ***Latent conflict:*** It is one which does not emerge in open. Although parties to conflict realize the fact of conflict for various reasons they do not show it openly.

(c) ***Manifest conflict:*** It is one in which not only there is recognition of conflict, but its explicit or open expression. This is a stage of open conflict

❖ Line and Staff Conflict

In an organization, there are people who represent line and others who represent staff positions. It is found from various studies that line managers consider themselves superior than the staff managers. Such conflicts are known as line and staff conflicts.

❖ Organised and Unorganised Conflict

As the name indicates there are times conflicts are expressed in organized or unorganized way. For example, if the parties to the conflict decide that they can successfully counter-effect the other party, they may use organized conflict. Union-management conflict in the form of a strike, or lockout all can be termed as organized. On the other hand, when parties view that organized conflict cannot bring solutions, they take on to unorganized conflict. For example, absenteeism, late coming, turnover are termed as unorganized conflict.

Levels of Conflict

Since our aim is to understand and manage conflict in organizations, we limit the levels of conflict to individual level, group level and organization level.

Interpersonal Conflicts

When individual joins the organization, they enter into not only economic contract but also, social and psychological contract. Individually have a number of needs and in order to satisfy these needs they join the organization. While satisfying the organizational needs, they try to satisfy their own individual needs. Not only the individuals bring their beliefs, values and customs etc. As a result of this, individuals join together knowingly or otherwise form groups and social systems.

People not liking one another or not agreeing with one another, expression of hostility towards one another, pointing out the weakness of other person and criticism, etc, characterize interpersonal conflicts. Some of the factors which are responsible for interpersonal conflict could be, competition, differing values, stereotype behaviour, exploitative nature of human beings etc.

Competitive environment can be a major source of interpersonal conflict. A competitive environment emerges in an organization where competence is rewarded and people who are able to show results are given more attention. Others experience a feeling of dissatisfaction because their self respect is challenged. In such a situation, the hostility may be directed either on to the person who has been rewarded or to the authority, which has rewarded him.

People working in the organization may have different preferences, values and beliefs, cultural back ground etc, this may also lead to interpersonal conflicts , like some managers may view trade unionism as made as a negative sign in the union management relations, other managers may not view that way. Hence, managers belonging to second category may not have tensed interpersonal relations with the union members.

Stereotyping and sharp judgment lead people to evaluate others first and form opinions of them through hurried judgments. These types of personal distortions, lead people to behave in biased ways towards each others resulting in conflicts. In a country like India, where workers belonging to different castes, religions, regional linguistic segments constitute the total workforce. In such a situation, managers belonging to one particular sect may interact with workers belonging to another sect in a manner which leads to conflict.

Interpersonal conflicts may arise in teamwork situations due to the exploitatory tendencies of some team members. It is common human nature that individuals have a tendency to take undue share in the outcome although their contribution to the achieving of goals may not be proportional. This type of situation leads to interpersonal conflict in the work teams.

❖ Strategies for Interpersonal Conflict Resolutions

(i) *Lose-Lose:* A lose-lose approach to conflict resolution is where both parties lose. It has been pointed out that this approach can take several forms. One of the most common approach is to compromise or take the middle ground in a dispute. A second approach is to pay off one of the parties in the conflict. These payments often take the form of bribes. A third approach is to use an outside party or arbitrary. A final type of lose-lose strategy appears when the parties in a conflict resort to bureaucratic rules or existing regulations to resolve the conflict. In all four of these approaches, both the parties in the conflict lose It is some time the only ways that conflicts can be resolved., but it is generally less desirable than the win-lose or specially, the win-win strategy.

(ii) *Win-Lose:* A win-lose strategy is a very common way of resolving conflict. In a competitive type of culture, one party in a conflict situation attempts to marshal its forces to win, and the other party loses. The following are the characteristics of the win-lose situation.

(a) There is a clear we-they distinction between the parties.

(b) Parties direct their energies towards each other in an atmosphere of victory and defeat.

(c) Parties see the issues from their own point of view.

(d) The emphasis/on solution rather than on the attainment of goals, values or objectives.

(e) Conflicts are personalized and judgmental.

(f) There is no differentiation of conflict-resolving activities from other group processes, nor is there a planned sequence of those activities.

Example of win-lose strategies can be found in superior-subordinate relationships, line-staff confrontations, union-management relations, and many other conflict situations found in today's organization. It is functional in the sense of creating a competitive drive to win and it can lead to cohesiveness among the individuals or groups in the conflict situation. On the dysfunctional side, a win-lose strategy ignores other solutions such as cooperative, mutually agreed upon outcome; there are pressures to confirm which may stifle a questioning, creative resolution for conflict resolution; and highly structured power relationships tend to emerge rapidly. Those who suffer the loss may learn something in the process, but loser always tend to be bitter and vindictive. A much heavier strategy is to have both parties of a conflict situation to win.

(iii) ***Win-win:*** A win-win strategy of conflict resolution is probably the most desirable from a human and organizational stand point. Energies and creativity are aimed at solving the problems rather than beating the other party. The needs of both the parties in a conflict situation are met and both parties receive rewarding outcomes. Although it is often difficult to accomplish a win-win outcome of an interpersonal conflict, this should be a major goal of the management of conflict.

Intergroup Conflicts

Groups in the organization could be classified into two types: formal groups and informal groups. Individuals are members of different groups for different purposes. Successful intergroup performance is a function of number of factors. The umbrella concept that overrides these factors is coordination. Each of the following factors can affect at coordination.

Interdependence: In any organization, groups or departments do not exist in isolation. The departments depend upon each other. There are three types of interdependence that could be identified when two groups/departments function with relative independence but when their combined output contributes to the organization's overall goals, pooled interdependence exists. Sequential interdependence is said to exist when one group depends on another for its input but the dependency is only one way. For example, one group says, parts assembly – depends on another say purchasing – for its input, but the dependency is only one way. In the above example, if purchasing fails to order an important component that goes into the assembly process, then the parts assembly department may have to slow down or temporarily close its assembly operations. The most complex form of interdependence is reciprocal. In these instances groups exchange inputs and outputs. For example, sales and product development groups in an organization are reciprocally interdependent. Sales then relay this back to product development so they can create new models or products. The long implications are that if product development does not come up with new products that potential customers find desirable, sales personnel are not going to get orders. So there is a high interdependence, product development needs sales for information on customer needs so it can create new products successfully and sales depend on the product development group to create products that it can successfully sell. This high degree of dependency translates into greater interaction and increased coordination demands.

Task certainty: The task certainty or uncertainty can also create intergroup conflict. The greater the uncertainty in a task, the more custom the response.

Conversely, low uncertainty encompasses routine task with standardized activities. Problems that group members face tend to contain few exceptions and are easy to analyze. Such group activities tend themselves to standardized operating procedures. For example, manufacturing task in a tyre factory are made up of highly routine task. These are activities that are unstructured, with many exceptions and problems that are hard to analyze. Of course, a lot of group tasks fall somewhere in the middle or combine both routine and non-routine tasks.

The key to tasks uncertainty is that non routine tasks require considerably more processing of information. Further, groups that do such tasks do not have to interact much with other groups. In contrast, groups that undertake tasks that are high in uncertainty face problems that require custom responses. This in turn leads to a need for more and better information.

Overload on some groups: It gives rise to conflicts. The overloaded groups may start feeling unhappy about the situation and may start demanding incentives and differential treatment may give rise to defensive and other reactions from the less worked-units. If the more loaded units are given any extra incentives, status and treatment differences filter into the organization—giving rise to a new kind of conflict.

Status differences: Some groups are ranked informally by managers in relation to their status. The groups, which are ranked low, resent such ranking and they start demonstrating their power by creating problematic situations to make their presence felt. For example, the line managers may treat personnel departments as support systems and there by of a lower status. In response, the personnel people may delay recruitments, insists on procedures to demonstrate that they cannot relegate to a lower status.

Role ambiguities: The lack of a proper definition of roles of different departments and the absence of mechanism to clear the ambiguities may also lead to conflicts. It is not sufficient to define the roles of various departments once for all. As any organization grows, new roles may get added and new departments may get created. Wherever such changes takes place and inadequate attention is paid to introduce such changes and clarify the roles continuously through a process of involvement of the people concerned, conflicts may increase.

Lack of understanding of each other's functions: One of the factor which lead to interdepartmental conflicts is lack of understanding of other department's role, may lead to indifference and lack of enthusiasm in collaborating with or appreciating the problems of the other departments. For example, line managers often do not realize functions and problems of the departments like personnel or finance. As a result, they make too many demands on them and when the response is not prompt, there are conflicts.

Differential reward systems: It is another potential source for intergroup conflicts. Some groups by the nature of the task they perform have less opportunities for promotion and a few others have relatively more opportunities. Some departments may give more opportunities for overtime work and some others may not.

❖ Managing Intergroup Relations and Conflicts

Rules and procedures: The simple and less costly method of managing intergroup conflict is to establish in advance, roles and procedures which will regulate the interdepartmental regulations. In complex organizations, without standard operating procedures, it will be difficult to manage complex interdepartmental relations. For example, any functional department requires additional manpower for some tasks to be completed, it should request the personnel department to arrange for it in advance.

Hierarchy: In case the rules and regulations are inadequate to regulate the intergroup relation, then the use of organization's hierarchy becomes the primary methods for managing intergroup relations. This means that the coordination is achieved by referring problems to a common superior in the organization. The major limitation to this method is that it increases demand on the common superior's time. If all differences were resolved by this means, the organization's chief executive would be overwhelmed with resolving intergroup problems, leaving little time for other matters.

Planning: Another factor which could bring the intergroup conflict down is appropriate planning. If each work group has specific goals for which it is responsible, then each knows what it is supposed to do. Intergroup tasks that create problems are resolved in terms of the goals and the contributions of each group. For example, in assembly line each area/departments should have a set of goals which define their area of responsibility and acts to reduce intergroup conflicts.

Integrating departments: When intergroup relations become too complex to be coordinated through plans, task forces, teams and the like, organizations may create integrating departments. These are permanent departments with members formally assigned to the task of integrating between two or more groups. While they are permanent and expensive to maintain, they tend to be used when an organization has a number of groups with conflicting goals, non-routine problems, and intergroups decisions that have a significant impact on the organization's total operations. They are also excellent devices to manage intergroup conflicts for organizations facing long term retrenchments.

There are other behavioural strategies developed by experts, which include avoidance, diffusion and confrontation.

Avoidance: Avoidance would indicate not facing the conflict. There are various ways people use to avoid conflict. They are ignoring the conflict situation or taking it easy by agreeing to the demands of one of the parties. All these methods of not wanting to face the conflict situation out of fear that the person may not be able to respond or resolve the conflict can be termed as avoidance strategies. Avoidance strategies do not help particularly if the leadership positions are involved. Leaders who avoid the conflicts are seen as lacking courage, and subordinates may increasingly create conflicting situations to weaken such leaders. Also, any issue once avoided may surface again in course of time. However, when intense emotions are involved, avoidance may serve as a good escape strategy. When the people involved are in more congenial or harmonious moods, the issues can be slowly taken up. This strategy however, tends to increase the self-confidence of the people involved in resolving the conflict.

Diffusion: This strategy involves postponement or delaying decisions to cool down the aroused tempers. It may involve focusing on unnecessary issues to avoid the main problem for some time. This strategy may help in temporarily avoiding the problem, but leaves anxiety about future and dissatisfaction of the parties.

Confrontation: This is facing the conflict. Confrontation may involve negotiation and use of authority. Power or authority may be used to sort out the conflict. The authority figure may decide in favour of one of the parties or the other, he may reprimand somebody or punish one of the parties, or take decision to rectify the situation. Negotiation is another mechanism of confrontation.

Class Conflicts

Conflict is inevitable in the industrial organization. Labour and management oppose each other in numerous ways in the course of daily work. Most industrial jobs are repetitive, monotonous, difficult, dirty and even accident prone. As a result of this, management uses strict supervision to get the work done. On the other hand, the normal sentiment of the worker is one of discontent. The interests of these two parties are in conflict with each other. For example, the main aim of the employers is to maximize profit. The management considers wages to workmen as one of its costs of production and in many industries, a major cost of production. Therefore, it is to the management's advantage to keep the costs of labour low, either through minimum wages, maximizing hours, reducing the number of employed working men, or making their labour more efficient through the use of machinery. On the other hand, workers expect more returns for their efforts in production or they expect wages to be commensurate with their work. Thus the interests of the workers and the management are diametrically opposed. The difference of opinion may be anything like, wages, bonus, working conditions, disciplinary matters etc. Workers and management may agree on such general goals as the maintenance of high levels of productivity and wages and the profitability of the enterprises.

Class conflict could be manifest or latent; organized or unorganised. Normally, strike is the most manifested or organised form of class conflict in industry. The strike may be used for a wide variety of purposes. Its aim may be to demonstrate worker resentment or to wage as sustained battle against the management. It may be the result of a calculated strategy, or a spontaneous outburst on the shop floor. Strikes are only one way in which industrial discontent is expressed. A doctrine in the number of strikes does not necessarily mean that discontent is less – it may merely mean that discontent is finding expression in other ways or is not finding expression at all. The decline of the strike as one form of conflict activity is not to be taken as a sign of the removal of conflict situation itself. Again, class conflict could be classified into two types. Basic conflict exists when a group feels that its share in rewards is unjust from a long-term point of view, procedural conflict arises from disagreements about short-term variations in rewards and conditions of work.

The second form of conflict is latent or unorganised conflict. The parties feel the differences of opinion but do not express so openly to be visible. The unorganised conflict even could be the result of a personal reaction to the frustrations of the industrial situations. The latent conflict is expressed through withdrawal of effort resulting in poor productivity, absenteeism and poor time keeping. It is important to remember that the strike is merely the most dramatic expressions of conflict. The proverbial tip of the iceberg.

CHAPTER

12

CONFLICT MANAGEMENT

LEARNING OBJECTIVES

- To understand the overall Conflict Resolution Mechanisms.
- To have insight into different methods of Conflict Resolution.

INTRODUCTION

A simple definition of conflict is that it is any tension that is experienced when one perceives that one's needs or desires are or are likely to be thwarted or frustrated. Such tensions could arise because the person experiences two incompatible desires within the self — that is, experiencing intrapersonal conflict — such as wanting to see a good movie tonight, but at the same time feeling the need to stay at home and study for exam that is to be held the next morning. Here, one goes through intrapersonal tensions or conflict in the process of deciding "to be or not to be". Tensions can also arise because of interpersonal conflict which can be defined as a state in which the concerns of two or more parties appear to be incompatible. The process starts when one party perceives that the other is frustrated or is about to frustrate some concern of the individual (Thomas, 1976). Chung and Megginson (1981) describe conflict as the struggle between incompatible or opposing needs, wishes, ideas, interests, or people. Conflict, they say, arises when individuals or groups encounter goals that both parties cannot obtain satisfactorily.

This suggests that conflict could arise due to incongruence in —

1. *Goals* (that is, the desired end state or preferred outcomes of two or more parties are incompatible).
2. *Values* (people having diametrically opposing value systems and experiencing problems in reconciling value differences),
3. *Cognition* (having conflicting ideas or thoughts);
4. *Affect* (incompatible feelings and emotions); and
5. *Behaviours* (acting in ways that are unacceptable to the other).

Traditional and Behavioural Views of Conflict

The traditional view of conflict has been that it is bad and should be avoided at all costs with the result that sometimes there is a tendency to suppress conflict and push it under the rug. By ignoring the presence of conflict, we somehow try to wish it away. The current behavioural view is that conflict is: a naturally occurring phenomenon; inevitable; inherent in any system; not always bad; and that, in fact, an optimum level of conflict energizes the system, clears the air, helps to solve problems, and acts as a catharsis. Thus, the current view of conflict is that it could be functional to individuals, groups, and to organizations *(Cosec,* 1956).

The Functionality of Conflict

Conflict is useful in as much as healthy tensions bring about many useful changes in the system. More often than not, conflict *clears the air* since people give vent to their emotions and get bad feelings off their chest. Having got rid of anger and other stifling emotions harboured for a long time within themselves by having now verbalised them, individuals can enter into healthy working relationships since they have worked through their feelings. Conflict is also useful in another sense. If there are no tensions at all in a system, then the system is likely to remain static and people are likely to feel bored with the status quo after a time. Imagine, for instance, a couple in a household, who over several years, have had absolutely no difference of opinion whatsoever on any matter, and the one tows the other's line all the time! It is possible that through the years, their marriage has become rather dull and eventless! In an organisational setting, if things go on very smoothly and people stick to their daily routines over extended periods of time through the years without any disagreements, work will probably get done, but there will be no innovation in the organization nor any incentive for the members to take a fresh look at how things ought to be changed in the interests of improving efficiency or effectiveness or both. In such organizations, work and the workers will tend to become mediocre since there will be no stimulation at the workplace. Thus, an optimum level of conflict seems essential for innovation since it stimulates people and keeps interpersonal interactions and the workplace moving in an exciting, healthy, and creative manner. We can illustrate this with an example.

Let us say that the sales and production departments are constantly fighting with each other. The vice-president might ask the heads of both departments to get together and discuss the problems so as to come up with a solution which will be mutually agreeable and beneficial to both parties. He might insist that this be done in the next three weeks. Thus, forcing the two departments to act jointly might result in their coming up with creative ideas that they might not have otherwise thought of. Thus, conflict could result in collaborative and creative problem solving if properly handled.

Intergroup conflicts (conflicts between two or more groups) foster intragroup cohesion as a common enemy is faced and dealt with by the group members. Thus, group cohesion can increase through conflict. At the organizational level, conflict can bring about changes in structure and processes since it acts as a stimulus for examining established systems which are no longer useful. New rules, regulations, procedures and norms, and changes in other dimensions of structure and processes are often brought about because of conflicting situations. For instance, it is possible that the cumbersome formal communication system in an organization might create tensions among members at different hierarchical levels. Because of the frequent tensions, management might examine the problem and arrive at an improved, functional communication system which would facilitate and speed up organisational work. Thus, structural and process changes are sometimes the result of conflict in organisations.

Conflict could also, serve as a power equaliser, that is, equalise power between two contending parties. This is manifest during union-management negotiations. When union and management go to the bargaining table, management does not feel as powerful as it normally does. In this conflicting situation, both the union members and management meet as two powerful groups with very little differential power advantages at the bargaining table. While management has the power over the purse strings, the union, due to sheer strength of numbers, has the power to even bring the organisation's operations to a halt!

Conflict contained within reasonable limits, thus serves several useful purposes and can be functional for individuals, groups, and to the institution. However, if conflict is allowed to develop beyond control, it could tend to become destructive, resulting in such aversive consequences as strikes, sabotage, and other dysfunctional behaviours. There, thus, seems to be an optimum level of conflict that is very useful for the development of creativity, healthy problem-solving behaviours, and productivity. This optimum level is depicted visually in Figure 12.1. Because too little conflict creates conditions of inertia and boredom in the system, and excessive conflict results in destructive and dysfunctional tendencies, conflict has to be "managed". Managers have to monitor the level of conflict in the system, and if there is too little or no conflict at all, managers may even have to induce some level of conflict to energise the system. As the level of conflict tends to go beyond the optimum level, the manager must act to resolve the conflict in a manner that will be beneficial to the organisation.

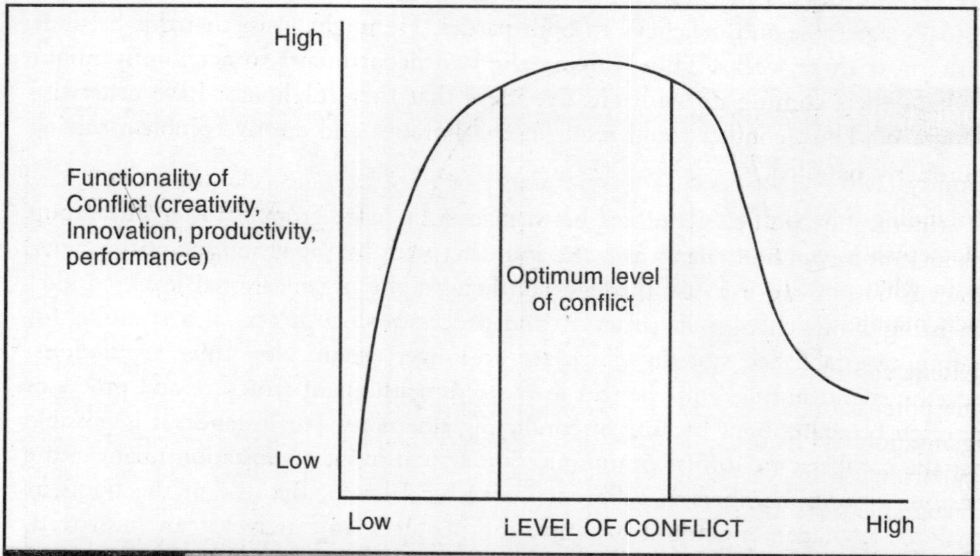

FIGURE 12.1 **Functionality of Conflict**

The Dynamics of Conflict

It is useful to understand the dynamics of conflict. Conflict gives rise to a series of behaviours and responses between or among parties. For instance, if a manager (M) perceives a subordinate (S) to be talking to another person instead of attending to some urgent work that he has been asked to do, then M experiences tensions since what he expects to happen (S working on the urgent assignment) and what he sees happening (S talking to another person) are at variance. M then calls S and in a severe tone of voice asks why S is wasting time instead of working on the urgent project. S gets annoyed with M for being so harsh and retaliates by saying if somebody comes and talks to him on official business, he cannot very well refuse to talk to him and what does M expect him to do? Tell the individual that his boss will not approve of his talking? M considers this response as insolent and becomes angrier. Thus, a chain reaction of behaviours and responses is set, as depicted in Figure 12.2.

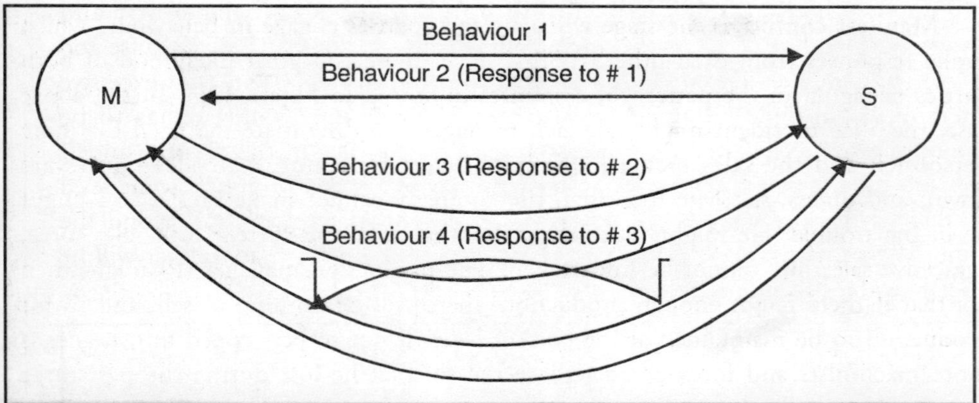

FIGURE 12.2 Chain Reactions or Behaviours and Responses in Conflicting Situations

Pondy (1967) developed a process model of conflict which is very useful in understanding how conflict starts and what stages it goes through. His model of the conflict episode is adapted and portrayed in Figure 12.3. Pondy delineates five stages in what he calls a "conflict episode": latent conflict, perceived conflict, felt conflict, manifests conflict and conflict aftermath.

Latent conflict is the stage in which factors exist in the situation which could become potential conflict inducing forces. For instance, if resources are limited in an organisation and there are demands for different kinds of resources (men, materials, money) from various departments in the system, then the situational factors are very favourable for conflicting situations to develop. This is the latent conflict stage.

Perceived conflict is the stage when one party perceives the other to be likely to thwart or frustrate his or her goals. For example, the production manager might hear the sales manager say that without more salespersons, he cannot achieve the targeted sales for the year. On hearing this, the production manager perceives the likelihood of a conflict developing between the sales manager and himself, since he is in need of more machinists and some foremen in his department as well. Since the resources in the organization are limited, if more salespersons are hired, less money will be available to hire more machinists and foremen for the production department. At this stage, the production manager is perceiving the possibility of a potential conflict developing between the two departments.

Felt conflict is the stage when the conflict is not only perceived but actually felt and recognised. In the above case, when the vice-president schedules a joint meeting of the department heads to discuss resource allocations, the production manager literally "feels" the impact of the impending confrontation in the ensuing meeting. Both parties anticipate some powerful exchange of words, probably rehearse their act, and experience anxiety.

Manifest conflict is the stage when the two parties engage in behaviours which evoke responses from each other. At this stage, there is a great likelihood of both parties engaging in the pattern of responses indicated in Figure 12.3. In the above case, the Vice President might ask each manager to substantiate the need for more personnel, and the sales manager (S) might start by saying that sales figures are down, and unless, sales are increased, the company cannot make profits and might be in big trouble. He might make the point that with the current lean sales force, aggressive sales just cannot be undertaken. The production manager (P) might then say that if there is not enough production, there will be nothing to sell, and so for production to be maintained at the current level (if not to be stepped up), he needs more machinists and foremen to replace the six that he lost during the past three months. He might also make a case for procuring better raw materials to produce better quality goods which will be more attractive to customers. S might then respond that making sophisticated goods in great quantities is not going lo increase sales unless there is adequate advertising for the products, and there are salespersons lo sell them. The arguments could thus go back and forth at the manifest conflict stage when the parties to the conflict air their opinions and feelings.

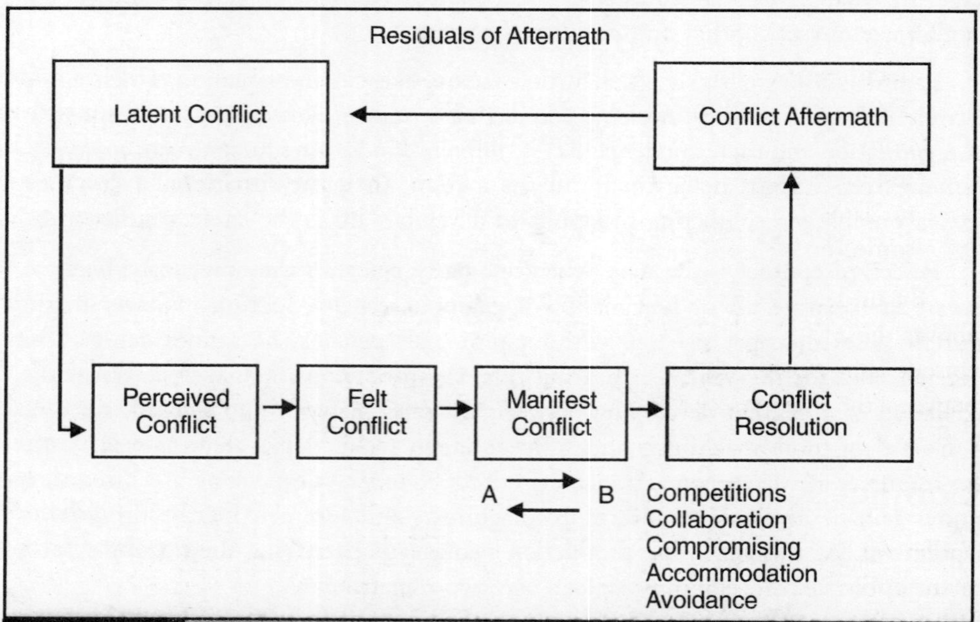

FIGURE 12.3 **Stages Conflict**

Conflict aftermath is the stage where, after the conflict is resolved in some way, there is still some residual tension left in the parties, which among other things, provides the basis for latent conflict for the next episode. For the sake of clarity, Conflict Resolution has been added as an additional box in Figure 12.3 to elucidate that conflict aftermath is a direct function of the results of the conflict resolution style adopted and exercised in any given situation.

Conflict Resolution

It can take place in a number of different ways, and there are at least five different modes in which conflict between parties tends to get resolved. Both parties could:

1. *Collaborate* with each other and find ways to resolve the problems taking a "win-win" approach to conflict resolution;
2. They could *compete* for the resources taking a "win-Iose" approach with the attitude "let the stronger party win";
3. One could *accommodate* to the needs of the other by surrendering his or her desires;
4. They could *compromise* and share the resources between them; or
5. One or both could *avoid* facing the conflict. These are discussed later in greater detail. Depending on how the conflict has been resolved, there will be an 'aftermath' or residue. If the conflict has been resolved to the satisfaction of both parties, all is well. If one or both parties feel aggrieved, there will be residual tensions left which will then become potent forces that set the stage for latent conflict for the next cycle of the episode which can be triggered by some incident.

By understanding the dynamics of conflict and their resolution as discussed above, the manager will be able to understand which stage any particular conflict episode is in and what would be the appropriate action to take to resolve the conflict between the parties so as to judiciously 'manage' conflict.

Conflict Resolution Models

Earlier we had stated that conflict has to be 'managed'. It has to be resolved as soon as the optimum level is crossed and before dysfunctional consequences start occurring. What are the different conflict resolution modes and how can the manager know which type of conflict resolution style should be adopted under what kinds of circumstances? Thomas (1976) has offered a contingency approach to resolving conflicts which we will now discuss.

If two groups or parties A and B experience conflict, each could be more concerned about their own self or they could experience more concern for the other. When concern for the self is very low, they could be very unassertive, and if concern for the self is high, they could be very assertive. If their concern for the other is low, they would tend to be uncooperative, and if it is high, they would be very cooperative. We could depict these on two axes as in Figure 12.4.

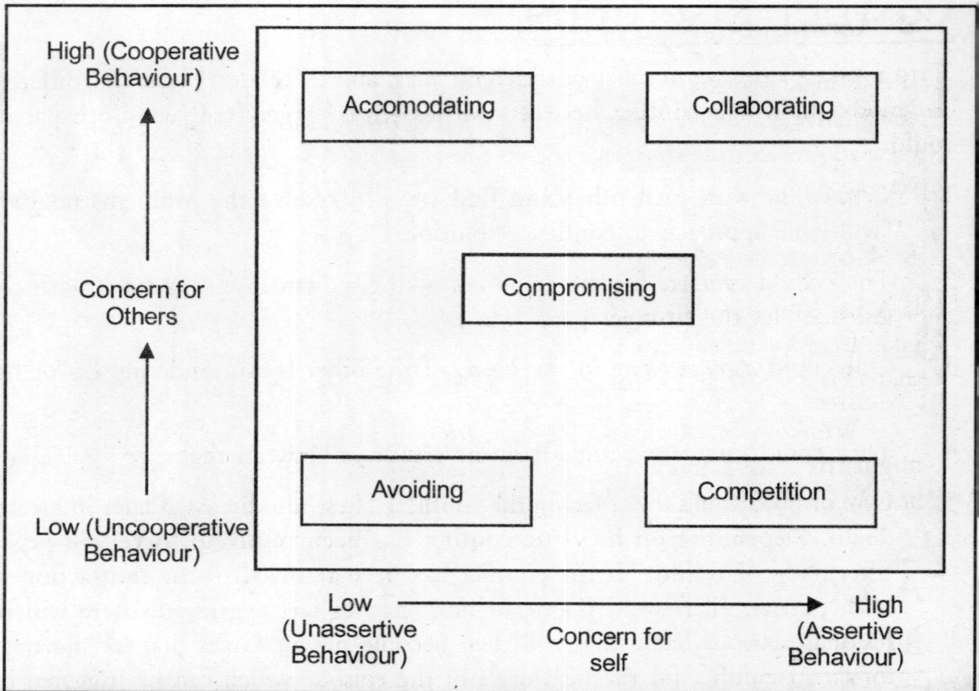

FIGURE 12.4 **Conflict Resolution Model**

❖ Avoidance

If in a conflicting situation, party A is concerned neither about himself nor the other. A is likely to avoid facing or handling the conflict. When the situation is thus ignored or neglected, then B might just get the better of A by taking advantage of A's avoidance behaviour.

❖ Competing

If on the other hand, A has very high concern for himself and very low concern for the other, then A will take a highly competitive stance and would approach the conflict situation from a "I win-you lose" stance. This, competitive mode of handling the conflict will then resolve who wins and who loses in the situation.

❖ Collaboration

If A has high concern both for the self and for the other, then A would approach the conflict situation in a collaborative mode with a desire to solve whatever problem exists in a way that would benefit both parties. A "win-win" stance will be taken in such a case and the resolution of the conflict will result in satisfying experiences for both parties.

❖ Accommodation

If A is highly concerned about the other and not so much about himself, that is, A is cooperative but very unassertive about satisfying his own concerns, then, he will be eager to give in to B and please B. To ensure that B's concerns are satisfied, A would be very accommodating and thus try to resolve conflicts through a policy of appeasement.

❖ Compromise

If A has a medium level of concern for both himself and the other, then, he would take a compromising stand with an attitude of "give and take" and be willing to share the resources, so that neither totally wins nor totally loses.

While all of us are capable of using all five conflicting handling modes, we might, by temperament or habit, be predisposed to use one or two modes more heavily or frequently than the others.

A Contingency Approach to Conflict Management

Is there "one best" mode for conflict resolution? Is collaboration always good, and competition or avoiding always bad? Perhaps not! All five modes come in handy in different situations and each has its own advantages and disadvantages. So long as we understand which mode works best in what kind of a situation, while also simultaneously recognizing their drawbacks, we can learn to be more flexible in the use of our conflict-handling styles to suit the different types of conflicting situations we find ourselves in. Recognizing the problems with each style also helps us to be aware of the dangers when our scores are either too high or too low on each of these modes.

When is each of these modes most useful? The following points (taken from Thomas and Kilmann, 1974) clarify the most appropriate situations under which each mode can be used profitably.

❖ Competing

Competing is a power oriented mode of resolving tensions and one uses what ever power one has or can muster: skills, knowledge, abilities, rank, being well-connected, etc., to win. Competing is useful when you know that resources are limited and the system has to be pruned. For instance, in times of budget cuts, the departments that do not contribute directly to the company's profits are usually eliminated on the basis of competitive power plays. Also, in times of emergencies, where quick, decisive action has to be taken and there is no time to seek collaborative, compromising, or accommodating solutions, the competing mode is useful. Here, one uses power and makes unilateral decisions taking the "win-lose" approach. Likewise, when one has to take unpopular decisions such as enforcing discipline, unpopular rules, cost cutting and so on, unilateral power-based strategies to put an end to conflicts are appropriate. Using power is also important to resolve conflicts on matters which are of vital importance to the company, and where one is aware of the right solutions.

There are some things that people should be concerned about when they score *high* on this mode. If individuals are highly power-oriented, they are likely to surround themselves with those who would always agree with them, that is, "yes-men" (because people know that it is politically unwise for them to disagree with such people). Thus, the only information that will be shared by the agreeable others with such power oriented individuals will be what the latter would like to hear. This shuts the high power people off from critical feedback which can be usefully applied for enhancing the effectiveness of the organisation. Also, since in a competitive environment, people feel compelled to come across to others as competent and knowledgeable, they never ask for information or guidance when they do not know how to handle issues, and hence, the organisation ultimately suffers as a result of lower quality performance.

When people score very *low* on the competing mode, they are likely to feel powerless in many situations, not realizing that they do have power but are just inept at or uncomfortable with using it. By trying to use the power one has, and becoming skilled at it, one could enhance one's influence, thereby enhancing one's effectiveness. Another drawback in scoring low on this mode is that such individuals find it difficult to take a firm stand on issues even when they know they are right. Concerns for others' feelings could force them to postpone making vital decisions and communicating them in a timely manner. This, in no way helps the organisation or its members.

Thus, while the competing mode is useful in certain situations, people have to be careful not to surround themselves with "yes-men" and not to foster ignorance and duplicity in the system. People low on this mode can learn to use their power more and enhance their own as well as their organization's effectiveness.

Collaborating

Collaborating involves an attempt to work with the other person to find solutions that would be satisfying to both parties. Here, the underlying concerns of both parties are explored in depth, the disagreements examined in detail, and resolutions arrived at by combining the insights of both the parties. A creative solution usually emerges because of the joint efforts of both the parties who are keen on both gaining from the situation without hurting the other.

Collaboration is a very useful mode when the two sets of concerns of the two parties are both too important to be compromised. Hence, finding integrated solutions becomes imperative. The example cited earlier where the marketing and production managers had their different concerns is a good case where the Vice President, could use a collaborative mode to resolve the conflict. Collaboration is also essential when the commitment of both parties is essential for important projects to succeed. This is achieved by addressing both people's concerns and arriving at a consensual decision. In addition, collaboration is also the best mode when the objectives of the party are:

1. To learn (testing one's own assumptions, trying to understand the other's point of view, etc.);
2. To merge insights that different people bring to a problem because of their backgrounds, training, disciplines, or orientations; or
3. To work through hard feelings which are interfering with a desired interpersonal relationship.

When people score *high* on collaborating, they have to be concerned about how they spend their time and use other organizational resources. Collaboration is time and energy consuming. Not all situations need collaborative solutions. The overuse of collaboration and consensual decision making may reflect risk aversion tendencies or an inclination to diffuse responsibility.

When people score *low* on collaborating, they may fail to capitalise on situations which would benefit immensely from joint problem solving. Also, by ignoring the concerns of employees, decisions and policies may be evolved which make the organisational members both unhappy and uncommitted to the system.

Compromising

Compromising is taking an intermediate position on both the assertive and cooperative dimensions. In compromising, the party tries to find some expedient, mutually acceptable solution which partially satisfies both parties, though neither is fully satisfied. A compromising stance addresses the issue without avoiding it, but does not explore the alternatives in a way that would be completely satisfying to both parties as in the case of collaboration. Compromising involves "splitting the difference", exchanging concessions, and seeking a quick middle ground solution.

Compromising is a useful mode when the goals pursued are important, but not so important that it is worth potential disruptions by taking very assertive or unyielding positions. For instance, the production and maintenance department might both want 50 hours of overtime to be sanctioned to each, but when only a total of 80 hours are made available to both, each might agree to use 40 hours. Each has compromised by giving up some, but not all. They have split the difference. Compromising is also a good conflict resolution mode when two parties with equal power are strongly committed to mutually exclusive goals such as in labour-management bargaining situations. Here, invariably, a final resolution of the conflict is reached by both parties making compromises on their original demands.

Compromise is an expedient mode to settle complex issues in the short run till a more thorough and permanent solution to the problem can be found. This is particularly true when solutions have to be arrived at under extreme time pressures. It can also be used as a backup mode when both collaboration and competition fail to work effectively in resolving conflicts.

When people score *high* on compromising, they should be wary of the fact that this mode of operation on a constant or consistent basis can create a climate of 'gamesmanship' in the work environment, which might then lead to distrust among members. That is, people might know that the resolution would involve "splitting the difference" and hence jack up the level of their original demands, as sometimes happens in the case of budget requests, where who ever plays the game 'right' is likely to gain additional advantages. Thus, people start playing games with each other which results in distrust among the members. It is also possible that when people concentrate heavily on the tactics of compromising, they may lose sight of values, principles, and long term objectives and company welfare. For instance, in the example where the maintenance and production departments split the overtime among them, it may have caused less frictions between the departments and their members, but without adequate maintenance, the machines might not be working as well as they should. This would result in further machine breakdowns. Because of the downtime and the time required for repairs, future demand for overtime for the production workers is bound to increase. It is also possible that because of constant machine breakdowns the quality of goods manufactured is sometimes affected Thus, compromise as a conflict resolution mode might offer an easy way out, but is also likely to produce adverse overall effects for the organization if that is the main or only approach to conflict resolution taken by managers in the organisation.

If people score *low* on compromising, it might indicate that they find it hard to make concessions and that they might be caught in power struggles and find it almost impossible to get out of awkward situations in a graceful manner. Compromise is a safety valve when collaboration or competition fails to yield results. A low score might also indicate the opposite — that the individual is too embarrassed or shy to bargain, and hence does not want to enter into such bargaining situations.

Avoiding

Avoiding is a mode used when the individual is both unassertive and uncooperative that is, the person has a very low concern for his own and his opponent's needs. While avoiding, the individual might diplomatically sidestep a conflicting issue, postpone addressing it till later, or totally withdraw physically and/or psychologically from a threatening situation.

Avoiding can be very functional when the issue involved in the conflict is trivial, or not of passing importance, or when more pressing issues are to be handled by the individual within a limited time frame. Avoiding can also be the only alternative when one's power is very low and there is no chance of satisfying one's own concerns. For instance, if the personality of the head of the department is such that whenever a clerk enters his cabin he just yells at and abuses the individual, the clerks will simply avoid going to the department head's cabin when he is inside since there is no way that the personality of the individual can be changed by the clerical staff who are low on the hierarchical ladder. Avoidance is also tactical when the potential damage of confronting the situation outweighs the benefits of resolution. A very capable clerk who was in line for promotion in the Reserve Bank several years ago, threw a paper weight at his supervisor who was both incorrect and argumentative in handling a situation. The clerk's anger was mitigated by taking out his frustration on his boss. But because of this impetuous act, the head of the department gave a ruling that the clerk should not be promoted for the next eight years despite his superior abilities and seniority. This is an instance where the clerk would have been well advised to avoid the conflict with his supervisor. The costs of the confrontation for him far outweighed whatever satisfaction he might have derived by handling the conflict in this manner.

Avoiding is also advisable in the following situations:

1. When you desire that people should cool down so that they regain their composure and perspective, after which the tensions can be handled more productively;
2. When more information is needed to make a good decision;
3. When someone else can resolve the conflict more effectively — in the above case of the clerk throwing the paperweight, the section manager could have more effectively resolved the tensions; and

4. When the issue which provokes the conflict is symptomatic of another more basic underlying matter, and attempting to resolve the surface issue will not help the situation. The example of the following case where a faculty member avoided her chairman well illustrates this point. The faculty member, who was very productive in research and had several papers to present in international conference was always harassed by the chairman who said that she made "too many demands" on the resources of the system whenever she asked for travel funds. It was known to all in the department that the chairman was miffed that his pay raises were not anywhere as close to hers because he did not do any research. People felt that this bothered him to such an extent that he was antagonistic towards her. To avoid the conflict with the chairman, the professor started to apply for travel funds from the dean's office and the dean then twisted the chairman's arms and she got paid without ever approaching the chairman.

When managers score *high* on avoidance, they have to be concerned that,

1. Decisions on important issues might constantly be made by default;
2. Coordination of efforts might suffer in the system because critical decisions and inputs are avoided; and
3. Inordinate amounts of time and energy can be expended by all when people get the message that the system is "too cautious" about making decisions and they also had better be so.

When individuals score *low* on avoiding (that is, they always want to confront every single issue), they might be hurting other people's feelings, and stirring up hostilities (which they do not intend to), because they make it a point to confront every insignificant situation. They might also be spending a lot of time on trivial issues.

Accommodating

Accommodating might take the form of selfless generosity, or obeying another's orders rather unwillingly, or giving in to another person's point of view. In all these cases, the individual neglects his or her own concern to satisfy the concerns of the other party. There is an element of self-sacrifice in this mode. Accommodating is useful in situations where the individual realizes that he or she is wrong. By yielding to the other's point of view, the individual indicates to the other that he/she is reasonable. Also, when an issue is much more important to the other person than to the individual, by being accommodating, the person maintains goodwill and a cooperative relationship, and also builds social credits so that the other person gives in when a later issue becomes important to this individual. Think of the situation where two employees want to leave the office early on a particular day — one because her child is sick, and the other because she wants to pay a casual visit to her cousin- but only one can go early. Would it surprise us when the latter quite willingly accommodates the former this time?

Accommodation is also expedient when continued competition would only damage one's cause because one is outmatched and is losing. As an example, when the department head has ears only for his favourite manager, there is not much point in trying to improve the working of the department in ways that would displease the favourite manager. Accommodation is also usually the choice mode of operation when preserving harmony and avoiding disruption are especially important, as frequently happens in many homes.

When people are *high* on accommodation, they might be deferring too much to the wishes of others and pay very little attention to their own ideas and concerns even though they may realise that they are not getting the attention they deserve. This might even lower one's self-esteem in addition to depriving one of influence, respect, and recognition from others since it negates the potential contributions that individuals are capable of making to the organisation.

When individuals score *low* on accommodating, they should start thinking about whether they lack the goodwill of others (since accommodating on some issues is important as a gesture of goodwill), and whether they are perceived by others as unreasonable, uncompromising, rigid, and demanding. Such people should also engage in introspection to find out if they know –

1. when to give up;
2. how to admit when they are in the wrong; and
3. can recognize legitimate exceptions to rules.

In sum, all five conflict handling modes are useful under different situations and there are advantages and disadvantages to having either too high or too low scores on each of these. It would be useful to build up a repertoire of conflict handling behaviours so that we can take a contingency approach to handling conflict situations.

Conflict in Organisations

In organisations, conflicts can be interpersonal, intragroup, intergroup or intra organisational in nature. Intra organisational conflict encompasses vertical, horizontal, line-staff, and role conflict. Let us briefly examine these.

Vertical conflict refers to conflicts that occur between individuals at different levels. Conflict between the superior and subordinate is an example of vertical conflict Such conflicts could happen because of perceived transgression of psychological contract, inadequate and (or ineffective communication, selective perceptions, misperceptions, incongruence in goals, values, cognition, affect, and behaviour, and any number of other reasons.

Horizontal conflict refers to tensions between employees or groups at the same hierarchical level. Horizontal conflict occurs because of interdependence among the parties concerned in the work situation and/or the common pooled resources shared. For instance, a common typists' pool requires several departments to share a central resource which is likely to produce tensions among the departments, each of which will be inclined to prioritize its own work. Incompatibility of goal and time orientations often results in horizontal conflicts. For example, the production department of a company might want to minimise costs and the marketing department might be keen on increasing custom made products. Here the goal of one is efficiency and the other is of customer satisfaction. In such cases where there is an incompatibility in the goals of two or more units, conflicts will arise. Differences in time orientations are also instrumental in inter-unit conflicts. For example, the operation of the sales department will have a shorter time frame as they make on-the-spot sales. If they want the research and development department who operate on a much longer time frame to come up with new ideas quickly, it is not going to work. Conflicts will take place between the units due to the misunderstandings and frustrations experienced by both parties. Horizontal conflict increases as:

1. Functional interdependence increases among people or groups at the same level (i.e., one has to depend on the other for the completion of its goals);
2. More units depend on common resources that have to be shared, for example, raw materials; and
3. The fewer the buffers or inventories for the resources shared.

Line-staff conflict refers to the conflicts that arise between those who assist or act in an advisory capacity (staff) and those who have direct authority to create the products, processes, and services of the organization (line). Staff managers and line managers usually have different personality predispositions, and goals, and come from different backgrounds. Staff managers have specialised skills and expertise acquired through training and education and have greater technical knowledge which is intended to help the line managers who are basically money makers for the organisation. Staff people serve as advisors for the line people in as much as they have the expertise to streamline methods and help in cost-cutting mechanisms. Line managers may however, feel that the staff people are a nuisance, coming in the way of their performance by always telling them how to do their job and thrusting their ideas and methods. It is not unusual for line people to resent the fact that they have to be "advised" by the staff people. The staff people often get frustrated that the line people do not consider all the ideas put forth by them and thereby fail to benefit.

Role conflict arises because different people in the organisation are expected to perform different tasks, and pressures build up when the expectations of the members clash in several ways.

This could be either because of:

1. *Intersender role conflict* — different role senders (bosses) expect the individual to perform different things and these expectations and their messages conflict with each other:
2. *Interrole conflict* — role requirements associated with membership in one group conflict with role requirements stemming from membership in another group;
3. *Intrasender role conflict* — when the same boss expects different incompatible behaviours from one person, and
4. *Person-role conflict* — where thereto requirements of an individual conflict with the individual's moral and ethical values. Examples of each of these would clarify the concepts.

An example of the intersender role is the president asking the manager to write up a report on the new project and submit it in the next four days, and the auditor asking the same manager to go with him to audit the branch offices today, tomorrow, and the day after! Here, the manager cannot possibly fulfill both role expectations. Inter-role conflict can be experienced by .a supervisor who just attended the managers' conference where he has been told that strict action should be taken against a group of strikers, and the same supervisor who is also a member of the union being told that "supervisors should protect the striking employees from harm". Here, the supervisor's membership to the two groups results in conflicting loyalties and role expectations. Intrasender role conflict will be experienced by a supervisor who is asked to get a lot of her section's work done, while also being asked to take charge of another section, because the supervisor of that section is on a week's casual leave without a replacement. Person-role conflict is likely to be experienced by an individual who is asked by the boss to bribe a government officer to get the job done for the department.

How can Managers 'manage' Conflict in organisations?

As we have already noted, managers should aim for optimum levels of conflict in organisations. Things should not be so dull that nobody cares what happens in the work setting, nor should they be so turbulent or traumatic that it is difficult for people to keep from getting at each other's throat!

Managers can reduce conflict in organisations through structural changes and other "organizational development" (O.D) strategies. Structural methods could involve decoupling or reducing interdependencies to the extent possible, buffering with inventory, and having better integrating or coordinating mechanisms for a comprehensive discussion of this. Other process oriented O.D. strategies could involve process consultation (where the dysfunctional ways in which people interact and deal with each other are examined and rectified), team building (which helps intra and intergroup members to work better with each other by understanding each other's position), and third party peace making (where a member external to the organisation helps people to sort out their differences). If the manager wants to resolve conflict by making the parties work in a collaborative mode, then superordinate goals which transcend the immediate goals of the two individual parties can be set. For instance, if the production and marketing departments are fighting for resources, the V.P. can say that if they jointly come up with a proposal that will increase the profits of the organisation by an additional 5 percent, each department can have 2 percent of the additional profits made. So, now, instead of worrying about their own departmental interests, the two will have to work in the interests of raising the organisation's profits of which they will each get a share!

Where things are quite and there is not much stimulation for innovation, managers can induce some cognitive tensions between groups, departments, or individuals. This can be done by disputing what is being said by one or both the parties, by playing the devil's advocate, and even creating goal conflict which will result in some competitive behaviours among the groups. This will spur them on to exchange ideas, generate new ideas and put vitality into the organisation.

❖ Summary

In this chapter, we examined conflict and its usefulness to organisations when it is properly managed. The importance of maintaining an optimum level of conflict was discussed. We looked at five different conflict handling modes and discussed the different kinds of conflict that organisations usually face and what managers can do to manage them.

Thus far, we have discussed several managerial processes in organisations. In the next two chapters, we will examine certain structural issues.

CASE STUDY

Managing Conflict

Treveni India Ltd. is an engineering company with its plant located near a big city in U.P. Shri Ramkrishnan, General Manager controls this plant. Shri P.K. Sharma, personnel manager assists and advises G.M. on personnel, industrial relations, and welfare matters. The plant employs about 800 workers. There is one workers union. All the office bearers are workers of the plant. There is one engineer forum as well.

Suresh, motor trolley operator attached to shop no.3 is required to carry material and parts from the shop to a point from where truck driver, Rahman ferries material to the assembly shop. Suresh is required to load the material, carry and unload the same near the truck. He has been doing this job for the last five years. His service records are generally satisfactory and he has 'average' ratings. He is aged 35 years. He was warned on three occasions in writing for his careless driving involving his trolley in accidents.

Vikramaditya Singh, aged 29 years appointed in this company three years ago joined shop no. 3 as foremen two months back. He reports to Shri T.V. Rao, Asstt. Production Manager.

On Tuesday morning, Suresh was loading some material on his trolley when foreman Singh was observing the work of operators, Ramlal was standing near his machine, while Suresh was preparing to start after loading the material. Singh turned towards him and said, "What is this Suresh? Why don't you do your work properly? Load some more items".

Suresh protested, "I have loaded enough. I have been doing this job for five years. I have never carried more than this load."

Singh did not permit Suresh to continue with his arguments. He advanced towards the material lying on the floor and put a few items on his trolley saying,

"Do you think you are here on a marriage party? I have set many scoundrels right. Now take it away and carry similar loads in future." Singh walked away.

Ramlal, who was listening to this altercation smiled and said, "*Ab mila hai sher ko sava sher*".

Suresh who was looking at the direction in which the foreman had gone, muttering some local abuses, now looked at Ramlal and shouted, "Is Singh your brother-in-law (sister's husband) that you are siding with him. "Shut up, else I will cut your tongue", shouted back Ramlal and there was a furor. Keshav Kohli, another operator working on the nearby machine rushed and intervened between Suresh and Ramlal requesting them to cool down. A few other workers also joined them. Vikramaditya Singh who heard the noise hurried back and told all workers to go back to their work.

Contd...

Singh who heard the noise hurried back and told all workers to go back to their work. Then he turned towards Suresh and told him sternly, "Now you scoundrel, if you don't move at once, I will suspend you." Suresh responded with angry eyes "*Dekh loonga*" then started and carried away his motor trolley. The foreman kept looking at him and said, "*Dekh to main loonga*".

Suresh carried the material near the truck and started unloading the same almost as if he was throwing it away in anger. Rahman the truck driver, smiled looking at Suresh and said. "Did you have a quarrel with your wife at home that you are acting like this? But, thank you. I am seeing you carrying a proper load for the first time. Keep it up, even if in anger. This will save time."

"All these asses are sold to foreman Singh", replied Suresh in anger.

" And you are also one of them," said Rahman jovially. In the meantime, his eyes fell on George, secretary of workers union who was going towards shop no. 3. He shouted, "*Hey George Sahab come here.*"

As George joined them, Suresh advanced towards him and narrated the entire incident asking him to intervene and restrain the foreman from acting as he did and advise him to behave properly with workers, and apologize for the incident. "Or else we will strike work", warned Suresh. George promised to look into the entire episode, advised Suresh to keep carrying on his work, saying that he will take whatever steps were necessary.

Soon after the incident, another motor trolley operator Khan, a great friend of Suresh, came to him. The two discussed the incident and decided to go together to George in the evening. They also discussed this incident with many other friends in the plant.

Vikramaditya Singh also kept track of the happening and met the secretary of engineers forum, Ram Singh, requesting him to take up the issue with the management to ensure discipline. Foreman Singh also reported the incident to Shri T. V. Rao Asstt. Production Manager and insisted an immediate issue of suspension orders for Suresh.

Shri Rao discussed the issue with personnel manager Shri P. K. Sharma who advised him that no action should be taken in a hurry. By the evening, secretaries of workers union and engineers forum met the Asstt. Production Manager and personnel manager separately and wanted them to take action so as not to allow the incident to develop into a bigger flare-up. Both the secretaries agreed with the personnel manager not to precipitate any action and allowed time to the management to resolve the conflict.

BASICS OF CONFLICT MANAGEMENT

Clarifying Confusion about Conflict

Conflict is when two or more values, perspectives and opinions are contradictory in nature and haven't been aligned or agreed about yet, including:

1. Within yourself when you're not living according to your values;
2. When your values and perspectives are threatened; or
3. Discomfort from fear of the unknown or from lack of fulfillment.

Conflict is inevitable and often good, for example, good teams always go through a "form, storm, norm and perform" period. Getting the most out of diversity means often-contradictory values, perspectives and opinions.

Conflict is often needed. It:

1. Helps to raise and address problems.
2. Energizes work to be on the most appropriate issues.
3. Helps people "be real", for example, it motivates them to participate.
4. Helps people learn how to recognize and benefit from their differences.

Conflict is not the same as discomfort. The conflict isn't the problem — it is when conflict is poorly managed that is the problem.

Conflict is a problem when it:

1. Hampers productivity.
2. Lowers morale.
3. Causes more and continued conflicts.
4. Causes inappropriate behaviours.

Types of Managerial Actions that cause Workplace Conflicts

1. Poor communications
   (a) Employees experience continuing surprises; they aren't informed of new decisions, programmes, etc.

(b) Employees don't understand reasons for decisions, and they aren't involved in decision making.

(c) As a result, employees trust the "rumour mill" more than management.

2. The alignment or the amount of resources is insufficient. There is:

(a) Disagreement about "who does what".

(b) Stress from working with inadequate resources.

3. "Personal chemistry", including conflicting values or actions among managers and employees, for example:

(a) Strong personal natures don't match.

(b) We often don't like in others what we don't like in ourselves.

4. Leadership problems, including inconsistent, missing, too-strong or uninformed leadership (at any level in the organization), evidenced by:

(a) Avoiding conflict, "passing the buck" with little follow-through on decisions.

(b) Employees see the same continued issues in the workplace.

(c) Supervisors don't understand the jobs of their subordinates.

Key Managerial Actions/Structures to minimize Conflicts

1. Regularly review job descriptions. Get your employee's input to them. Write down and date job descriptions. Ensure:

(a) Job roles don't conflict.

(b) No tasks "fall in a crack".

2. Intentionally build relationships with all subordinates.

(a) Meet at least once a month alone with them in office.

(b) Ask about accomplishments, challenges and issues.

3. Get regular, written status reports and include:

(a) Accomplishments.

(b) Currents issues and needs from management.

(c) Plans for the upcoming period.

4. Conduct basic training about:
   (a) Interpersonal communications.
   (b) Conflict management.
   (c) Delegation.
5. Develop procedures for routine tasks and include the employees' input.
   (a) Have employees write procedures when possible and appropriate.
   (b) Get employees' review of the procedures.
   (c) Distribute the procedures.
   (d) Train employees about the procedures.
6. Regularly hold management meetings, for example, every month, to communicate new initiatives and status of current programmes.
7. Consider an anonymous suggestion box in which employees can provide suggestions.

Ways People deal with Conflict

There is no one best way to deal with conflict. It depends on the current situation. Here are the major ways that people use to deal with conflict.

1. *Avoid it:* Pretend it is not there or ignore it.
   (a) Use it when it simply is not worth the effort to argue. Usually this approach tends to worsen the conflict over time.
2. *Accommodate it:* Give in to others, sometimes to the extent that you compromise yourself.
   (a) Use this approach very sparingly and infrequently, for example, in situations when you know that you will have another more useful approach in the very near future. Usually this approach tends to worsen the conflict over time, and causes conflicts within yourself.
3. *Competing*: Work to get your way, rather than clarifying and addressing the issue. Competitors love accommodators.
   (a) Use when you have a very strong conviction about your position.
4. *Compromising*: Mutual give and take.
   (a) Use when the goal is to get past the issue and move on.

5. *Collaborating*: Focus on working together.

   (a) Use when the goal is to meet as many current needs as possible by using mutual resources. This approach sometimes raises new mutual needs.

   (b) Use when the goal is to cultivate ownership and commitment.

❖ To manage a Conflict within Yourself — "Core Process"

It's often in the trying that we find solace, not in getting the best solution. The following steps will help you in this regard.

1. Name the conflict, or identify the issue, including what you want that you aren't getting. Consider:

   (a) Writing your thoughts down to come to a conclusion.

   (b) Talk to someone, including asking them to help you summarize the conflict in

   (c) Sentences or less.

2. Get perspective by discussing the issue with your friend or by putting it down in writing. Consider:

   (a) How important is this issue?

   (b) Does the issue seem worse because you're tired, angry at something else, etc.?

   (c) What's your role in this issue?

3. Pick at least one thing you can do about the conflict.

   (a) Identify at least three courses of action.

   (b) For each course, write at least three pros and cons.

   (c) Select an action — if there is no clear course of action, pick the alternative that will not hurt, or be least hurtful, to yourself and others.

   (d) Briefly discuss that course of action with a friend.

4. Then do something.

   (a) Wait at least a day before you do anything about the conflict. This gives you

   (b) Cooling off period.

   (c) Then take an action.

   (d) Have in your own mind, a date when you will act again if you see no clear improvement.

❖ To manage a Conflict with Another — "Core Process"

1. Know what you don't like about yourself, early on in your career. We often don't like in others what we don't want to see in ourselves.
   - (a) Write down 5 traits that really bug you when see them in others.
   - (b) Be aware that these traits are your "hot buttons".
2. Manage yourself. If you and/or the other person are getting heated up, then manage yourself to stay calm by
   - (a) Speaking to the person as if the other person is not heated up - this can be very effective!
   - (b) Avoid use of the word "you" — this avoids blaming.
   - (c) Nod your head to assure them you heard them.
   - (d) Maintain eye contact with them.
3. Move the discussion to a private area, if possible.
4. Give the other person time to vent.
   - (a) Don't interrupt them or judge what they are saying.
5. Verify that you're accurately hearing each other. When they are done speaking:
   - (a) Ask the other person to let you rephrase (uninterrupted) what you are hearing from them to ensure you are hearing them.
   - (b) To understand them more, ask open-ended questions. Avoid "why" questions - those questions often make people feel defensive.
6. Repeat the above step, this time for them to verify that they are hearing you when you present your position.
   - (a) Use "I", not "you".
   - (b) Talk in terms of the present as much as possible.
   - (c) Mention your feelings.
7. Acknowledge where you disagree and where you agree.
8. Work the issue, not the person. When they are convinced that you understand them:
   - (a) Ask "What can we do fix the problem?" They will likely begin to complain again. Then ask the same question. Focus on actions they can do, too.

9. If possible, identify at least one action that can be done by one or both of you.
   (a) Ask the other person if they will support the action.
   (b) If they will not, then ask for a "cooling off period".
10. Thank the person for working with you.
11. If the situation remains a conflict, then:
   (a) Conclude if the other person's behaviour conflicts with policies and procedures in the workplace and if so, present the issue to your supervisor.
   (b) Consider whether to agree or to disagree.
   (c) Consider seeking a third party to mediate.

Thoughts on Managing Conflict in the Organisation

Life is a never ending process of one conflict after another. Remember the time when you were a small child and had to choose between a tricycle and a cricket set or say a set of dolls and a new frock for a birthday present. That was probably your first exposure to a conflict situation. Of course, this is a simplistic example of a conflict, but has life been the same since? Probably not. Think back and recall how each succeeding conflict in your life over the years has been increasingly complex.

Conflict is a theme that has occupied the thinking of man more than any other with the exception of God and love. Conflict has always been widespread in society but it is only recently that it has generated a lot of interest and has been the focus of research and study. We are living in the age of conflict. Everyday the choices available to us regarding any decision are increasing in number. You may have wanted to become a manager, an entrepreneur or a computer scientist. On the other hand, your father might have wanted you to become a doctor, a lawyer or a chartered accountant. Thus, you faced a conflict not only at an intrapersonal level, in terms of the various choices confronting you, but also at an interpersonal level — your choice vs. your father's choice of a career for you.

Conflict is not confined at the individual level alone but is manifesting itself more and more in organisations. Employees have become more vociferous in their demands for a better deal. Various departments in an organisation face a situation full of conflicts due to a number of reasons like goal diversity, scarcity of resources or task interdependence, etc.

Management today is faced with the awesome responsibility of ensuring optimum levels of growth and productivity in an environment that is full of conflicting situations. A survey suggests that the modern manager spends over 20% of his time handling one form of conflict or the other. Top and middle level managers in the same survey have pointed out the importance of conflict management skills. We hope that the knowledge you will gain from this Unit will equip you better to manage conflict situations more deftly at your workplace.

TYPES OF CONFLICT

Conflict within an Individual

You can locate conflict at various levels. There could be conflict within oneself — the intrapersonal conflict. Basically, there are three types of such conflicts. You may have an excellent job offer in a city you are not willing to go to. In such a case, you are attracted to and repelled by the same object — an approach-avoidance conflict. Similarly, you may be attracted to two equally appealing alternatives like seeing a movie or going for a picnic — an approach conflict. You may also be repelled by two equally unpleasant alternatives like the threat of being dismissed if you fail to report against a friendly colleague who is guilty of breaking the organisation's rules — avoidance-avoidance conflict.

Conflict between Individuals

Conflict can also take an interpersonal form. Conflict between individuals takes place owing to several factors, but most common are personal dislikes or personality differences. When there are only differences of opinion between individuals about task related matters, it can be construed as technical conflict rather than interpersonal conflict. Of course, technical and interpersonal conflicts may influence each other due to role related pressures. The sale manager may put the blame for low sales volume on the production manager not meeting his production schedule and may start disliking the production manager as an incompetent person. It is often very difficult to establish whether a conflict between two parties is due to manifest rational factors, or it emanates from hidden personal factors.

Conflict between an Individual and a Group

These types of intragroup conflicts arise frequently due to an individual's inability to conform to the group norms. For example, most groups have an idea of a "fair day's work" and may pressurise an individual if he exceeds or falls short of the group's productivity norms. If the individual resents any such pressure or punishment he could come into conflict with other group members.

Usually, it is very difficult for an individual to remain a group-member and at the same time, substantially deviate from the group norm. So, in most cases, either he conforms to the group norm or quits (or is rejected by) the group. Of course, before taking any such extreme step, he or the other group members try to influence each other through several mechanisms leading to different episodes of conflict (much to the delight of the researchers in this field called Group Dynamics).

Conflict between Groups within an Organisation

Intergroup conflicts are one of the most important types of conflict to understand, as typically, an organisation is structured in the form of several interdependent task groups. Some of the usually chronic conflicts in most of the organisations are found at this level, e.g., Union vs. Management, one Union vs. another Union; one functional area like production vs. another functional area like maintenance; direct recruits vs. promotees, etc. The newly emerging field of Organisational Politics has started systematically investigating such types of conflict and in a later section on the effects of conflict we shall give examples of what happens to groups when their conflicts are not solved.

Conflict between Organisations

Conflict between organisations is considered desirable if limited to the economic context only. The *laissez - faire* economy is based on this concept. It is assumed that conflict between organisations leads to innovative and new products, technological advancement and better services at lower prices. However, in this Unit we shall refrain from probing into this macro level conflict.

Sources of Conflict

In the earlier sections, you have seen that it would be naive to think that conflicts in an organisation take place simply due to lack of understanding between people. A large number of potential sources of conflict exist in organisational life as antecedent conditions and realistic basis for some conflicts. In this section we shall quickly review some such sources.

Competition for Limited Resources

Any group exists for the purpose of attaining some goals with the help of available resources. These resources may be tangible like men, materials, and money or intangible like power, status or the manager's time. No organisation is capable of providing all the resources demanded by various units. Resources are limited and different groups have to compete for these scarce resources and many conflicts arise from this source.

Diversity of Goals

Groups in organisation have different functions to perform and as such they develop their own norms and goals. Theoretically, the achievement of these goals should achieve overall organisational goals but, often, in real life the reverse is true. Goals of one group are incompatible to the goals of another group. Take, for example, a company which manufactures electric fans that has a seasonal demand. Three departments-marketing, production and finance are involved. Since the demand for the product is seasonal, the marketing manager would like to have sufficient stock during the season. The production department has to gear up its capacity during the season but because of a tight labour market finds it difficult to hire labour temporarily and resorts to employ people on a permanent basis. This creates another problem. The finance manager says that as the storage costs are high, it is expensive to keep stock build up in the slack season, and maintaining the production line during slack season imposes an additional burden.

The example shows that each department develops its own goals, which may conflict with another department's goals and one department may try to achieve its goals at the expense of another. This happens quite often when the reward system is linked to group performance rather than to overall organisational performance.

Task Interdependence

Groups in an organisation do not function independent of one another. They have to interact with one another in order to accomplish their tasks. The sales department will have nothing to sell unless the financial department comes up with the money to buy raw materials. Thus, smooth interaction between various groups is essential for the efficient functioning of the organisation. Three types of interdependence can cause intergroup conflict – pooled, sequential and reciprocal.

❖ Pooled Interdependence

It exists when two work groups may not directly interact with each other but are affected by each other's actions. For example, when one independent product group performs poorly, all other groups may suffer financially. This can happen when rewards are contingent upon collective performance.

❖ Sequential Interdependence

It occurs when one group's performance depends on another group's prior performance. In a construction project, for example, the excavating team must prepare the foundation before the masons can work on the building structure. Since the masons depend on the excavators, conflict between the groups can occur when the excavators work is delayed.

❖ Reciprocal Interdependence

It occurs when two or more groups are mutually interdependent in accomplishing their tasks. For example, in developing and marketing a new product, three major departments (marketing, production and research) depend on each other to perform their tasks. Information possessed by one department is needed by another department. For example, the research department needs market information from the marketing department, and marketing needs research to provide customer services. When one group is unable to meet the expectations of another group, intergroup conflict usually results.

Differences in Values and Perception

A lot of conflict is generated within organisations because various groups within the organisation hold 'conflict' values and perceive situations in a narrow, individualistic manner. An example that comes readily to mind is that of the management labour conflict. Labour feels that management is exploiting it because in spite of making a profit, management does nothing for the economic welfare of labour. On the other hand, management feels that the profits should go to cash reserves so as to make the company an attractive proposition for investors. Another example is the conflict between engineering and manufacturing. Engineering lays stress on technological sophistication and precision and is accused by manufacturing of designing products that will last for 50 years but that the customers cannot afford. Similarly, engineering accuses manufacturing of making products of such limited durability that the company's reputation suffers.

Organisational Ambiguities

An implied conflict may emerge when two organisational units compete over new responsibility. Intergroup conflict stemming from disagreement about who has responsibility for ongoing tasks is an even more frequent problem. Newcomers to organisations are often struck by the ambiguity that exists about job responsibilities. Few organisations make extensive use of job descriptions or periodically update the job descriptions that do exist. Further, it is rare that the manager or employee consults his own job description. Managerial and staff jobs by their very nature are difficult to structure tightly around a job description.

❖ Introduction of Change

Change can breed intergroup conflict. Acquisitions and mergers, for example, encourage intergroup conflict, competition, and stress. When one organisation is merged into another, a power struggle often exists between the acquiring and acquired company. An attempt is usually made to minimise conflict by laying out plans for power sharing before the acquisition or merger is consummated. Frequently, the acquired company is given representation on the board of directors of the acquiring company. Nevertheless, power struggles are difficult to avoid.

❖ Nature of Communication

One of the major fallacies abounding about conflict is that poor communication is the cause of all conflicts. A typical statement is: "If we could just communicate with each other, we could eliminate our differences". Such a conclusion is not surprising considering the little time most of us have at our disposal communicating with one another. At the same time, evidence does suggest that problems in the communication channel such as noise, distortion, omission and overload to affect the process of collaboration and lead to misunderstanding. The potential for conflict increases when either too little or too much communication takes place. Apparently, an increase in communication is functional up to a point, where after it is possible to over communicate with a resultant increase in potential for conflict. Too much information as well as too little information can lay the foundation for a conflict.

❖ Aggressive Nature of People

Another factor that has a large potential for generating conflict within an organisation in personality characteristics that account for individual idiosyncracies and differences. Evidence suggests that certain personality types – for example, individuals who are highly authoritarian, arrogant, autocratic and dogmatic – lead to potential conflict. People have a natural need to find an outlet for their aggressive tendencies. Organisations are sometimes used as arenas for expressions of aggression – 'blowing of steam' – leading conflict.

This discussion on the sources of conflict is intended to emphasise that it is not possible to design an organisation which will remain conflict-free for all times to come. Conflict is inevitable in an organisation as some of these sources will always remain in any organisation. However, these sources are not to be confused with the causes of a conflict. A conflict, in ultimate analysis, is caused by perceptions and feelings people experience when an incompatibility exists between what they want and what someone else wants. When perception of incompatibility and feeling of frustration generate actions, conflict is manifested.

We can now move on to examine the modes through which conflict can be handled so as to result in optimal unit performance. You have already seen that when conflict level is too low, the unit performance is also likely to be low and there is a scope for a perceptive manager to stimulate conflict in order to enhance the performance of the group. Similarly, when the level of conflict is too high, conflict needs to be resolved so as to restore high performance and optimal level of conflict. So, in this section, we shall examine both the strategies of conflict management — stimulation as well as resolution.

STIMULATING PRODUCTIVE CONFLICT

Most of us since childhood have been taught to avoid conflict and even disagreement. How many times have you heard the statements "Don't Argue", "Stop fighting" or "It's better to turn the other cheek"? However, this tendency to avoid conflict is not always productive and there are times when there is a need to stimulate conflict. In an interesting experiment, series of groups were formed to tackle a problem. Some groups contained a planted member to challenge the majority opinion. Some groups did not have. Without fail, all groups that had a planted member came up with a more perceptive solution than the other groups. However, when the groups were asked to drop a member, all groups that had a planted member chose to drop the dissenting member despite clear evidence that the conflict was beneficial. Such resistance to conflict is what managers have to overcome in stimulating productive conflict.

Robbins (1978) suggested the following as signs where conflict stimulation is needed:

1. The organisation is filled with "yes men".
2. Employees are afraid of admit ignorance.
3. Compromise is stressed in decision making.
4. Managers put too much emphasis on harmony and peace.
5. People are afraid of hurting the feelings of others.
6. Popularity is given more importance than technical competence.
7. People show great resistance to change.
8. New ideas are not forthcoming.
9. There is an unusually low rate of employee turnover.

The presence of one or more of these signs is usually an indication of the need for conflict stimulation.

Once the need has been identified, you may adopt one or more of the following techniques:

(i) Manipulate communication channels.

(a) Deviate messages from traditional channels

(b) Repress information

(c) Transmit too much information

(d) Transmit ambiguous or threatening information.

(ii) After the organisation's structure (redefine jobs, alter tasks, reform units or activities).

(a) Increase a unit's size

(b) Increase specialization or standardisation

(c) Add, delete or transfer organisational members

(d) Increase interdependence between units.

(iii) Alter personal behaviour factors.

(a) Change personality characteristics of leader

(b) Create role conflict

(c) Develop role incongruence.

These are only a few of the suggestions possible. Depending upon your values and the organisation's value system, some of the suggestions may even sound unethical as you may feel that a desirable end-state does not always justify the questionable means (like transmitting threatening information). We leave it for you to decide. But if by stimulating your value-conflict, we become successful in helping you to understand the important option of conflict stimulation; we shall consider that such conflicts are functional.

Resolving Interparty Conflict: How and When

You have seen that stimulating conflict is a required mode of conflict management when groups are characterised by apathy, complacency, non-responsiveness to needed change, lack of enthusiasm for generating alternatives, etc. Though these symptoms are very much present in a number of work-units in Indian organisations (and hence calls for appropriate conflict stimulation interventions), the more commonplace are heightened manifest conflicts. So, for most practical purposes, you should not only possess the knowledge of different strategies of conflict-resolution but should also know when to use which strategy.

There is no dearth of literature in this area and different authors have given different taxonomies in reviewing possible conflict resolution strategies. Here we consider Feldman's (1985) strategies of intergroup conflict-resolution.

The primary dimension along which intergroup conflict-resolution strategies vary is how openly you as a manager should address the conflict. The chief characteristic of CONFLICT-AVOIDANCE strategies is that they attempt to keep the conflict from coming into the open. The goal of CONFLICT-DEFUSION strategies is to keep the conflict in abeyance and to 'cool' the emotions of the parties involved. CONFLICT-CONTAINMENT strategies allow some conflict to surface, but tightly control which issues are discussed and the manner in which they are discussed. CONFLICT-CONFRONTATION strategies are designed to uncover all the issues of the conflict and try to find a mutually satisfactory solution.

Conflict-avoidance Strategies

Ignoring the Conflict

This strategy is represented by the absence of action. You, as a manager, have often avoided dealing with dysfunctional aspects of conflict. Unfortunately, when you avoid searching for the causes of the conflict, the situation usually continues or becomes worse over time. Although ignoring the conflict generally is ineffective for resolving important policy issues, there are some circumstances in which it is at least a reasonable way of dealing with problems. One such circumstance in which ignoring the conflict is a reasonable strategy is when the issue seems to be symptomatic of other more basic conflicts. For example, two groups may experience conflict over the amount and quality of office space. Such conflicts often reflect more important issues about relative power and status. Resolving the office space problem would not address the key issues, and attention could be directed more fruitfully to the more basic concerns.

Imposing a Solution

This strategy consists of forcing the conflicting parties to accept a solution devised by a higher level manager. Imposing a solution does not allow much conflict to surface, nor does it leave room for the participants to air their grievances. So it also generally is an ineffective conflict-resolution strategy. Any peace that it does achieve is likely to be shortlived. Because the underlying issues are not addressed, the conflict reappears in other guises and in other situations.

Forcing a solution can, however, be appropriate when quick, decisive action is needed. For instance, when there is conflict over investment decisions, and delays can be very costly, forcing a solution may be the best strategy available to top management. Likewise, it may be necessary when unpopular decisions must be made and there is very little chance that the parties involved could ever reach agreement (Thomas. 1977). An example of this is when an organisation must cut back on the funding of programmes. It is unreasonable to expect that any department would agree to cut its staff and expenses for the greater good, yet some hard unpleasant decisions ultimately must be made.

CONFLICT-DEFUSION STRATEGIES

Smoothing

One way you can deal with conflict is to try to "smooth it over" by playing down its extent or importance. You may try to persuade the groups that they are not so far apart in their viewpoints as they think they are, point out the similarities in their positions, try to 'pat' group members whose feelings have been hurt, or play down the importance of the issue. By smoothing the conflict, you can hope to decrease its intensity and avoid escalation or open hostility. Like forcing a solution, smoothing generally is ineffective because it does not address the key points of conflict.

However, smoothing sometimes can serve as a stopgap measure to let people cool down and regain perspective. In the heat of the battle, people may make statements that are likely to escalate the conflict, and smoothing often can bring the disagreement back to a manageable level. Smoothing also may be appropriate when the conflict concerns non-work issues. For instance, intergroup conflict frequently occurs between older and younger employees because of their different political beliefs and moral values. Smoothing can help to defuse the tension so that the conflict does not spillover into central work issues.

Appealing to Superordinate Goals

You can defuse conflicts by focusing attention on that the groups share or the long-range aims that they have in common. This tends to make the current problem seem insignificant beside the more important mutual goals.

Finding superordinate goals that are important to both groups is not easy. Achieving these goals requires cooperation between the groups, so the rewards for achieving the goals must be significant. The most successful, and most frequently used, superordinate goal is organisational survival, i.e., if the sub-units do not cooperate sufficiently, the continued existence of the larger organisation itself will be severely jeopardised.

Conflict-containment Strategies

Using Representatives

One of the strategies you can use to contain conflict is the use of representatives. In order to decide an issue, you can meet with representatives of the opposing groups rather than deal with the groups in their entirely. The rational is that the representatives know the problems and can argue the groups' points of view accurately and forcefully.

Although this seems to be a logical way of proceeding, the research on the use of representatives as a means of solving intergroup conflict is fairly negative. Representatives are not entirely free to engage in compromise; rather, they must act out of loyalty, and are motivated to win (or at least avoid defeat) even though a solution to the intergroup problem may be sacrificed in the process. A representation who "gives in" is likely to face suspicion or rejection from group members, so if a representative cannot win, he or she will try to deadlock a solution or at least forestall defeat.

Although individual representatives have difficulty in negotiating an agreement because of their fear or rejection by their groups, two situational factors can increase the effectiveness of this strategy. First, the use of group representatives from each side can help to overcome individual anxiety about group rejection. The members of each team can provide mutual support when they need to make concessions in order to achieve agreement. Also, groups of negotiators may receive broader support and trust from their respective sides, since each representative may represent a different constituency or bring a different expertise to the negotiations. Most labour negotiations involve several representatives of both management and labour.

Resolving conflict through representatives is more effective before positions become fixed or are made public. After positions become fixed, representatives become even more intransigent, and "give in" is more likely to be attributed to the personal failure of the representatives than to situational factors.

Structuring the Interaction

Some managers assume that one way to decrease conflict is to increase the amount of contact between the groups (if the groups interacted more, they would like each other better and fight less). In reality, increased interaction can merely add fuel to the fire; the two groups spend their time looking for additional reasons to reinforce their negative stereotypes of each other.

However, structuring the interaction between the groups can be effective in resolving conflict. Providing a framework on how many issues are discussed and the manner in which they are discussed can facilitate conflict resolution.

There are many ways to structure the interaction between groups to deal with conflict; some of the most effective strategies include: (a) decreasing the amount of direct interaction between the groups in the early stages of conflict resolution; (b) decreasing the amount of time between problem solving meetings; (c) decreasing the formality of the presentation of issues; (d) limiting the recitation of historic events and precedents and focusing instead on current issues and goals and (e) using third-party mediators.

All these strategies allow some conflict to surface but prevent it from getting out of hand and reduce hardening of the groups' positions. Decreasing the amount of direct interaction between the groups early in the conflict helps to prevent the conflict from escalating. Decreasing the amount of time between problem solving, rather than a win-lose orientation to the conflict. Limiting how far back historically and how widely precedents can be cited helps to keep the focus on finding a solution to the current conflict. Finally, a mediator can act as a go-between, who transmits offers and messages, helps the groups to clarify their positions, presents each group's position more clearly to the other, and suggests some possible solutions that are not obvious to the opposing parties.

Structuring the interaction is especially useful in two situations: (a) when previous attempts to discuss conflict issues openly lead to conflict escalation rather than to problem solution; and (b) when a respected third party is available to provide and enforce some structure in the interactions between the groups.

Bargaining

Bargaining is the process of exchanging concessions until a compromise solution is reached. Bargaining can lead to the resolution of a conflict, but usually without much openness on the part of the groups involved and without much real problem solving. Typically, in bargaining each side begins by demanding more than it really expects to get. Both sides realise that concessions will be necessary in order to reach a solution, but neither side wants to make the first concession because it may be perceived as a sign of weakness. Thus, each party signals a willingness to be flexible in exchanging concessions without actually making an explicit offer: a tacit proposal can be denied later if it fails to elicit a positive response from the other party.

Bargaining continues until a mutually satisfactory agreement is reached, although such a solution can be reached without much open discussion of the conflict issues and without much effort to solve the underlying problems. Therefore, bargaining often results in a compromise agreement that fails to deal with the problem in a rational manner and is not in the long-term interests of either group.

For bargaining to be feasible at all as a conflict-resolution strategy, both parties must be of relatively equal power. Otherwise, one group simply will impose its will on the other, and the weaker group will have no means of obtaining concessions from the stronger one. Bargaining too, is more likely to work if there are several acceptable alternatives that both groups are willing to consider. Otherwise, bargaining is likely to end in a deadlock.

Conflict-confrontation Strategies

Problem solving

Problem solving is an attempt to find a solution that reconciles or integrates the needs of both parties who work together to define the problem and to identify mutually satisfactory solutions. In problem solving, there is open expression of feelings as well as exchange of task-related information. Alderfer (1977) summarises the most critical ingredients in successful problem solving:

1. Definition of the problem should be a joint effort based on shared fact finding rather than on the biased perceptions of the individual groups.
2. Problems should be stated in terms of specifics rather than as abstract principles.
3. Points of initial agreement in the goals and beliefs of both groups should be identified along with the differences.
4. Discussions between the groups should consist of specific, non-evaluative comments. Questions should be asked to elicit information, not to belittle the opposition.
5. The groups should work together in developing alternative solutions. If this is not feasible, each group should present a range of acceptable solutions rather than prompting the solution that is best for it while concealing other possibilities.
6. Solutions should be evaluated objectively in terms of quality and acceptability to the two groups. When a solution maximises joint benefits but favours one party, some way should be found to provide special benefits to the other party, to make the solution equitable.

7. All agreements about separate issues should be considered tentative until every issue is dealt with, because issues that are interrelated cannot be settled independently in an optimal manner.

There are two preconditions for successful, integrative problem solving. The first is a minimal level of trust between the groups. Without trust, each group will fear manipulation and may not reveal its true preferences. Secondly, integrative problem solving takes a lot of time and can succeed only in the absence of pressure for a quick settlement. However, when the organisation can benefit from merging the differing perspectives and insights of the two groups in making key decisions, integrative problem solving is especially needed.

Organisational Redesign

Redesigning or restructuring the organisation can be an effective, intergroup conflict-resolution strategy. This is especially true when the sources of conflict result from the coordination of work among different departments or divisions. Unlike the other strategies discussed so far, you may note, organisational redesign can be used either to resolve the conflict or to stimulate it.

One way of redesigning organisations is to reduce task interdependence between groups and to assign each group clear work responsibilities (i.e., create self-contained work-groups) to reduce conflict. This is most appropriate when the work can be divided easily into distinct projects. Each group is provided with clear project responsibilities and the resources needed to reach its goals. A potential cost of this strategy is duplication and waste of resources, particularly when one group can not fully utilise equipment or personnel.

Innovation and growth also may be restricted to existing project areas, with no group having the incentive or responsibility to create new ideas.

The other way to deal with conflict through organisational redesign is to develop overlapping or joint work responsibilities (e.g., integrator roles). This helps in maximising the use of the different perspectives and abilities of the different departments, but as you have already seen, it also tends to create conflict. On the other hand there may be tasks (e.g., developing new products) that do not fall clearly into anyone department's responsibilities but require the contributions, expertise, and coordination of several. Assigning new product development to one department could decrease potential conflict but at a high cost to the quality of the product. In this case, you might try to sustain task based conflict but develop better mechanisms for managing the conflict. For example, providing "integrating teams" can facilitate communication and coordination between the members of interdependent departments.

Organizational Conflict – The Good, The Bad and The Ugly

The issue that generates the most emotion, and frustrated comments, is conflict within the organization. We generally do not look at conflict as opportunity — we tend to think about conflict as unpleasant, counterproductive and time consuming. Conflict that occurs in organizations need not be destructive, provided the energy associated with conflict is harnessed and directed towards problem solving and organizational improvement. However, managing conflict effectively requires that all parties understand the nature of conflict in the workplace.

Two Views: The Good, The Bad

There are two ways of looking at organizational conflict. Each of these ways is linked to a different set of assumptions about the purpose and function of organizations.

❖ The Bad

The dysfunctional view of organizational conflict is imbedded in the notion that organizations are created to achieve goals by creating structures that perfectly define job responsibilities, authorities, and other job functions. Like a clockwork watch, each 'cog' knows where it fits, knows what it must do and knows how it relates to other parts. This traditional view of organizations values orderliness, stability and the repression of any conflict that occurs. Using the timepiece analogy we can see the sense in this. What would happen to time-telling if the gears in our traditional watches decided to become less traditional, and redefine their roles in the system?

To the 'traditional' organizational thinker, conflict implies that the organization is not designed or structured correctly or adequately. Common remedies would be to further elaborate job descriptions, authorities and responsibilities, increase the use of central power (discipline), separate conflicting members, etc.

This view of organizations and conflict causes problems. Unfortunately, most of us, consciously or unconsciously, value some of the characteristics of this 'orderly' environment. Problems arise when we do not realize that this way of looking at organizations and conflict only fits organizations that work in routine ways where innovation and change are virtually eliminated. Virtually all government organizations work within a very disorderly context — one characterized by constant change and a need for constant adaptation. Trying to "structure away" conflict and disagreement in a dynamic environment requires tremendous amounts of energy, and will also suppress any positive outcomes that may come from disagreement, such as improved decision making and innovation.

❖ The Good

The functional view of organizational conflict sees conflict as a productive force, one that can stimulate members of the organization to increase their knowledge and skills, and their contribution to organizational innovation and productivity. Unlike the position mentioned above, this more modern approach considers that the keys to organization success lie not in structure, clarity and orderliness, but in creativity, responsiveness and adaptability. The successful organization, then, NEEDS conflict so that diverging views can be put on the table, and new ways of doing things can be created.

The functional view of conflict also suggests that conflict provides people with feedback about how things are going. Even "personality conflicts" carry information to the manager about what is not working in an organization, affording the opportunity to improve.

If you subscribe to a flexible vision of effective organizations, and recognize that each conflict situation provides opportunity to improve, you then shift your view of conflict. Rather than trying to eliminate conflict, or suppress its symptoms, your task becomes managing conflict so that it enhances people and organizations, rather than destroying people and organizations.

So, the task is to manage conflict, and avoid what we call "the ugly"....where conflict is allowed to eat away at team cohesiveness and productivity.

The Ugly

We have the good (conflict is positive), the bad (conflict is to be avoided), and now we need to address the ugly. Ugly occurs where the manager (and perhaps employees) attempt to eliminate or suppress conflict in situations where it is impossible to do so. You know you have ugly in your organization when:

- many conflicts run for years.
- people have given up on resolving and addressing conflict problems.
- there is a good deal of private bitching and complaining but little attempt to fix the problem.
- staff show little interest in working to common goals, but spend more time and energy on protecting themselves.

When we get 'ugly' occurring in organizations, there is a tendency to look to the manager or formal leader as being responsible for the mess. In fact, that is how most employees would look at the situation. It is true that managers and supervisors play critical roles in determining how conflict is handled in the organization, but it is also true that the avoidance of ugliness must be a shared responsibility. Management and employees must work together in a cooperative way to reduce the ugliness, and increase the likelihood that conflict can be channeled into an effective force for change.

❖ Ugly Strategies

In future articles we will look at what you can do to proactively manage conflict to increase the probability that positive outcomes occur. Right now, let's look at some common strategies that result in the increase of ugly conflict.

Most of the ugly strategies used by managers, employees, and organizations as a whole are based on the repression of conflict in one way or another. We need to point that, in general, you want to avoid these approaches like the plague.

Ugly #1: Non action: The most common repressive management strategy is non action — doing nothing. Now, sometimes, doing nothing is a smart thing too, provided the decision to do nothing is well thought out and based on an analysis of the situation. Most of the time, people "do nothing" about conflict situations for other reasons, such as fear of bringing conflict into view, or discomfort with anger.

Unfortunately, doing nothing generally results in conflict escalating, and sets a tone for the organization..."we don't have conflict here". Everyone knows you have conflict, and if you seem oblivious, you also seem dense and out of touch.

Ugly #2: Administrative Orbiting: Administrative orbiting means keeping appeals for change or redress always "under consideration". While non action suggests obliviousness since it doesn't even acknowledge the problem, orbiting acknowledges the problem, but avoids dealing with it. The manager who uses orbiting will say things like "We are dealing with the problem", but the problem never gets addressed. Common stalls include: collecting more data, documenting performance, cancelling meetings, etc.

Ugly #3: Secrecy: A common means of avoiding conflict (or repressing it) is to be secretive. This can be done by employees and managers. The notion is that if nobody knows what you are doing, there can be little conflict. If you think about this for a moment, you will realize its absurdity. By being secretive, you may delay conflict and confrontation, but when it does surface it will have far more negative emotions attached to it than would have been the case if things were more open.

Ugly #4: Law and Order: The final "ugly strategy". Normally, this strategy is used by managers who mistakenly think that they can order people to eschew conflict. Using regulations, and power, the person using the approach "leans on" people to repress the outward manifestations of conflict.

Of course, this doesn't make conflict go away, it just sends it scuttling to the underground, where it will grow and increase its destructive power.

❖ Conclusion

The notion that conflict should be avoided is one of the major contributors to the growth of destructive conflict in the workplace. The 'bad' view of conflict is associated with a vision of organizational effectiveness that is no longer valid (and perhaps never was). Conflict can be directed and managed so that it causes both people and organizations to grow, innovate and improve. However, this requires that conflict not be repressed, since attempts to repress are more likely to generate very ugly situations. Common repression strategies to be avoided are: non-action, administrative orbiting, secrecy and law and order.

CHAPTER

13

CEO AND TOP MANAGEMENT: LEVERAGING THROUGH TEAMS

LEARNING OBJECTIVES

- To throw light on the role of CEO and Top Management in Teams in Organisational context.
- To draw a broad picture, on how to leverage through Teams.

How CEOs can make the Most of their Top Teams?

The most powerful CEOs often fail to create and manage the right environment in which top executive teams can be effective. This is the conclusion of research by Hay Group, the global professional services firm, published in the Hay Group Working Paper, "Top Teams — Why Some Work and Some Don't: Five Things the Best CEOs Do to Create Outstanding Executive Teams."

The research was based on a 4-year study of executive-level teams at leading global corporations in the telecommunications, airlines, beverages, computer software and manufacturing sectors. In each case, the team was led by a CEO or other executive decision maker and was made up of top business unit or geographic area leaders.

CEOs are under a new pressure to make Teams Deliver – Quickly

The study was commenced in 1998 and was coordinated by Hay Group Senior Vice President, Debra Nunes in conjunction with researchers from Harvard University and Dartmouth College. She said, "Average tenures of CEOs today are only about 18 months. As a result, they're under tremendous pressure to deliver results quickly. Assembling, managing and leading a top executive team is increasingly seen as critical to both the CEO's success, and the organization's. Given the increasingly important role of top teams, it's striking how many fall short of being truly effective."

"In our study, two-thirds of the teams failed to excel according to our criteria, and we discovered this was substantially tied to the team leader, usually the CEO, who often lacked an understanding of the dynamics of top teams," added Debra Nunes.

"Because executive teams are generally charged with issues central to the company's future, the cost of an underperforming team is great — both in terms of unrealized opportunity and in the loss of executives' commitment to the strategic agenda of the organization. On the other hand, truly effective teams can have a tremendously positive influence on the performance of the organization, and can be a critical driver of shareholder value," said Ms. Nunes.

Corporate Success is Dependent on Top Teams

The Hay Group study suggests that:

- effective top teams can help advance the CEO's strategy and agenda more quickly;
- make the organization more nimble and responsive to market changes; lead to higher perceived valuations from institutional investors.

According to Debra Nunes, "Institutional investors are increasingly aware of the importance of top teams in executing a company's 'big picture' strategy. In fact, a recent study of institutional portfolio managers suggests that 35% of an investment decision is driven by non-financial data, primarily 'execution of corporate strategy' and 'management credibility.' Since top teams exist primarily for these reasons, they are fast becoming a key component of a company's shareholder value proposition. And over time, we believe the role of top teams will only increase in importance."

She added, "In fact, Gillette's bond rating was recently upgraded by agencies which cited the top executive team created by the new CEO."

What constitutes a 'Real Team'?

It seems that many CEOs hold the (mistaken) belief that their 12-15 key "reports" are the top team. Probably this is not the case. These people exist in order to share information from each 'silo' of the business — they are not there to address the organization's biggest challenges and opportunities. And, significantly, they do not have a team dynamic.

Conversely, a real top team has "collective tasks and challenges that demand a high level of interdependency among its members." Also, they have clear and stable boundaries so that membership is not constantly changing. The most effective top teams were found to have only 6-8 members, handpicked by the CEO. Larger teams are likely to lack interdependence, have an unfocused agenda and unclear boundaries. And there is no need for a representative from every business unit so long as someone represents their interests.

The most effective teams tend to focus on the most consequential issues facing the business. They tend to stay away from operational matters and concentrate on big-picture mandates, including:

- mergers
- expansion into new markets
- sweeping reorganizations
- e-business strategy.

Debra Nunes argues that "Top executive teams have the potential to become entities that are smarter, more effective and more productive than the sum of their parts. In fact, resilient companies depend on top teams. But for those that are falling short, and risk becoming also-rans, there are steps that can maximize top team performance."

❖ CEOs need to be democratic but retain control

CEOs and other top executives have a variety of leadership styles, for example:

- coercion, expecting employees to comply with orders without question
- or pacesetting, demonstrating performance standards by personally modeling the way.

But the Hay Group research suggests that these styles are often ineffective, serving to alienate team members and retard the collaborative process.

"One of the most interesting anecdotal findings of our research is that the most charismatic CEOs make some of the worst team leaders. In a sense, their mythologies precede them, and their strong, forceful presences simply suck the air out of the room, creating an environment of worship rather than teamwork," said Ms. Nunes. "The challenge for these types of leaders, and others, is to turn off some of the skills and behaviours that have served them so well in their rise to the top, and turn on the listening and social skills that are not always reinforced in a hierarchical corporate culture."

Strong leaders were authoritative, gave strong direction, communicated the big picture and clearly articulated goals and behaviours expected of the team. But they were also democratic, allowing the team be a team and encouraging members to believe their voice would be heard, and that what they say matters.

Debra Nunes added, "The most successful team leaders have a spectrum of managerial styles that they deploy based on the situation. In general, they create the right conditions for teamwork and then step into the background to act as moderator and guide."

CEOs should provide more direction — even to the most insightful members of their team

There is an assumption that team members are powerful and committed and have the same core agenda. Not necessarily so. Team leaders need to be forceful and provide direction.

According to Debra Nunes, "One leader of an oil refining business gave his team a quick quiz asking each member to write down the team's number-one priority. When the 10 team members listed several different priorities related to safety, cost cutting, environmental compliance and new markets, the leader was shocked. 'Don't you guys realize that if we can't cut our refining costs by three cents a gallon, they're going to shut us down?' The team members were equally stunned by the simplicity of the mission. In fact, over the following year, the team took steps that reduced costs by five cents per gallon. The lesson here: You can never be too clear, or overstate the team's primary goal."

Top Teams need Members with Empathy and Integrity

The members of the most successful top teams are neither brighter, more driven nor more committed than people in less successful teams. But the members of the most successful teams excelled at working with others, bringing a high degree of emotional intelligence to the 'team dynamic'.

Emotionally intelligent team members:

- have self-control
- are adaptable

- exude self-confidence and self-awareness
- display high levels of empathy and integrity.

In fact, empathy and integrity are particularly significant. Hay Group research shows members of outstanding teams to be far more empathetic, having an understanding of the emotional makeup of others, than team members of less successful teams. In fact, on high performing teams, the research showed that 71% of participants said their team peers were sensitive to the unspoken emotions of their fellow members. On average performing teams, only 44% showed this characteristic.

According to Ms. Nunes, "Empathy is incredibly important to the successful team's dynamic. This is because members of a team will only 'buy in' to the team process if they feel they are being heard and understood. Resentment and withdrawal are the inevitable result if people feel their ideas and input are not being fairly evaluated."

The research also identified perception of integrity among and between team members as being essential for team success. A team member with 'integrity' was defined as one who "behaves consistently with the organization's or the team's values even when it is personally risky to do so." The researchers justified the importance of integrity through the trust it fosters among team members.

Just 3% of team members in average performing teams had taken the personal risk of challenging the team to live up to its values — compared to 44% of the members of high performing teams.

"No one wants to commit professional suicide by challenging his or her peers, especially the CEO. But if the team dynamic is healthy enough, members should feel comfortable about raising an opposing point of view," said Ms. Nunes. "In fact, productive conflict is desired as long as it's about ideas, not personalities. Top teams must be comprised of people who not only have the courage to identify, even create, conflict over ideas, but also the social skills to resolve friction constructively."

❖ Necessary Support and Development

The research identifies strong operational support as a necessity if a top team is to be successful. This support must include:

- sound data and forecasts
- teamwork training
- appropriate compensation tied to its ability to meet its goals.

Ms. Nunes concluded that, "Outstanding team leaders also periodically review the team's performance, providing helpful feedback, encouragement and continuous reinforcement and refinement of the team's goals. Some effective team leaders even provide individual coaching, taking aside a team member who's not contributing enough, or speaking privately with someone whose personality may be getting in the way. Again, the team leader must learn to wear several hats to make the team function as smoothly and effectively as possible."

TEAM-BASED TOP MANAGEMENT

(Questions Answered by Harold S. Resnick, A Leading Consultant for Team-building)

❖ What Exactly is the Term "Team-based Top Management"?

Chief executives around the world are realizing they have not tapped the great potential of their top management. More and more, firms' overall goals can only be achieved by using these highly skilled executives as a team.

A single person can make a big difference in an organization. But no single person has enough knowledge or experience to understand everything happening in a complex and sophisticated organization. Major gains in quality and productivity most often result from teams – groups of people pooling their skills, talents and knowledge. With proper chartering and leadership, teams can tackle complex and chronic problems and come up with effective, permanent solutions. Besides this pooling of skills and understanding, top management teams are better than solo performance at cross-functional, integrated performance.

An important knock-on effect of top management teams is that the core concepts of teamwork start to develop at all levels of the organization. Team members everywhere in the company start working together – without barriers or factions. All moving together in the same direction.

❖ When are Companies Most in need of Team-based Top Management?

An integrated top management team is essential when conditions prevail such as:

- The company is too complex for any one person to be able to know and handle all the variables.
- The interdependencies of team members mean good communications and connectivity are necessary for overall organizational success.
- Commitment to all goals by all members of top management is essential for the company to meet its many requirements.
- There are no obvious answers clearly known by one person. The team's collective knowledge and wisdom are needed to ensure success.

❖ Don't Most Senior Managements Already operate as a Team?

Much thought and attention has been paid to project teams, process improvement teams, functional organizational teams and self-directed work teams. But the executive team poses some unique requirements and challenges. First of all, a company's senior executives hold a collective set of responsibilities which is exclusively theirs. The success of the organization rests in their hands, and from their collective vision and direction, the organization's longer-term strategic direction and success will flow.

It is generally assumed that by the time a group of individuals reaches the senior executive level they have pretty well developed and honed their leadership skills, including those of serving on a wide variety of teams, and functioning as leaders of their own teams.

Unfortunately, the reverse is more often the case. In 35 years of consulting experience with hundreds of organizations across the globe, I seldom find an executive group functioning as a high-performance team. More often, the senior executive group consists of a number of fiercely independent individuals who enjoy competing with everyone, including each other. Power struggles are common, and separate fiefdoms dividing the organization along its functional structure is a common manifestation for what passes as a senior executive team. Of course, this is nonsense and a key reason why guidelines for team behaviour among top management are sorely needed.

❖ What was the Essence of the Traditional Model for Senior Management?

Traditionally, executives rose to the top of their organizations because of their high achievement focus and skills, honed over years of successful performance in competitive environments. Success has often been defined by the scope of an executive's power. For example, the size of the manager's organization, staff, budget and scope of decision making authority. Senior executives often see each other as rivals, both in terms of accumulating their share of the organization's power base, and their chances of getting the chief executive's job. And, sometimes this rivalry is used by CEOs as a valuable tool to stir the competitive pot and get the best results from each function.

In a stable marketplace with an organization seeking to maintain a consistent, predictable output, a functionally-driven organization where members of the top management team control their individual areas with little cross-functional involvement might be justified. Actually, just such a control-driven environment created the structures we've seen since the industrial revolution. But rapid shifts in the competitive marketplace have caused a major re-examination of the basic business models needed for the competitive environment we have now and will surely continue having in the decades ahead.

When the business environment is stable, executives function more as managers than leaders. They establish the core business strategy, agree on the organization's structure and the systems required to control the activities which will ensure achievement of the business plan. So, the system is essentially hierarchical. With such a system, the organization is divided up into its logical parts based on the functions performed. And, these functions are divided among top management with each responsible for a particular part.

Within this context, there is no compelling need for the members of top management to operate as an executive team. While they may need to share information and collectively review overall business results, course corrections are assigned to the functional members who own the source of the problem. So, the essence of the traditional model was designed to create and ensure stability and predictability. The assumption being that the whole is the sum of the parts, and if each part performs well, the whole will be achieved.

However, the core assumptions regarding business conditions and a stable economic environment no longer reflect the nature of the world. In today's changing marketplace, the economic environment is neither predictable nor stable. Economic growth is no longer assured, and competition abounds from all sides. For example, we now see many customized services replacing the previous assumptions which created the industrial revolution and mass production.

❖ What are the Requirements of this new Economic Environment?

The new reality is that in this changing environment a top-down, hierarchical, compartmentalized, control-oriented management culture simply will not work. It is too slow, too rigid, too far removed from the customer, too insensitive to feedback, and the layers of bureaucracy required by the hierarchy are too costly. The management system needed in this new era sees that the various elements of the system are interdependent and must function as an integrated whole. The entire system needs to be highly responsive to customer and marketplace feedback with the organization being very flexible.

Here, knowledge and the ability to solve problems no longer flow down from the top of the organization, far removed from the customer. The best sources of knowledge come from where the work gets down, not from the top. Knowledge and wisdom are not resident in the upper offices, and power is not derived by position or control.

"The new reality is that in this changing environment a top-down, hierarchical, compartmentalized, control-oriented management culture simply will not work."

The role of employees then shifts from one where individual differences need to be suppressed to one where individual differences – knowledge and skill – are the firm's most essential competitive advantage.

So, today's executives are responsible for guiding the work of a much more amorphous, flexible, distributed network of core competencies which must be brought together with speed and fluidity to meet the needs of rapidly changing markets, often using technologies with life cycles shorter than the products or services offered.

❖ Are Substantial Changes needed in the way Top Management operates?

A major consequence of these changes in the business world is that the role of top management must adapt and change as well. I see this new role as one where top managers guide an interdependent system, rather than control their own functional turf. And this presses the need for new skills and mindsets. Top management must now function primarily as leaders rather than managers. They must now guide the interdependent elements of a system, applying all the concepts of systematic thinking to their jobs, also seeing employees as their greatest resource instead of interchangeable parts.

For this to work, top management must also function as an interdependent system, essentially as a well-oiled executive team with the primary responsibility being the leadership of the firm more than the management of the firm.

❖ What are the Core Responsibilities of Leadership in an Organization?

Certainly the first role of a leadership team is establishing a vision. This defines the organization's core purpose, and sets the direction in which the firm will position itself, both for the external marketplace and for the workforce. The vision needs to be broad enough to encompass the hopes, dreams and desires for the future, but also specific enough for individuals to develop the definition and scope of their own work areas in the fulfillment of the vision.

To expect a vision to be accepted and embraced by the workforce, it must clearly embody the spirit and words of the executive team. It's essential for the message from the top management to be consistent and unanimous, since dissension at the senior level creates confusion and even competing behaviour at other levels of the organization.

The creation and acceptance of this vision must first be the team effort of top management. It's not going to work if individual executives submit their parts and wait for the CEO to pull it all together. It must be developed and embraced by all, so top management must function as an executive team throughout the process to both create the vision, and communicate their collective endorsement of the vision through words and actions.

❖ What comes after Top Management has established a Common Vision?

Alignment, which is the process by which the vision is translated into strategic direction, specific goals and business processes. And this also needs to be an integrated effort. The shift from a functional organization to a cross-functional process-driven organization requires a different way of thinking. Senior executives must be willing to let go of traditional power bases called functions or departments, and begin instead to take ownership of core cross-functional processes.

Goals must be based on the overarching strategic direction of the firm, rather than the individual functional goals traditionally used to set budgets and allocate resources. All the resources must be aligned to achieve the firm's goals and strategic direction, not to protect any individual power bases or special interests.

"Senior executives must be willing to let go of traditional power bases called functions or departments, and begin instead to take ownership of core cross-functional processes."

This process of aligning the entire firm along several core goals is potentially the most powerful role top management can play. When an organization is fully aligned, all the systems are working in concert with each other to reach common goals. Success is then defined by criteria such as customer satisfaction, market share, growth, profitability, and other factors pointing to the overall health and success of a business. So, any individual functional requirements are subordinated to the alignment created through these higher level goals.

In order for top management to align themselves and then the entire firm, they must first work together to determine strategic goals and direction. Those factors critical to the success of the firm's common goals can then be defined. From this point, core processes and their owners can be determined, and goals at other levels of the organization can be identified. This is work which can only be accomplished by a team working together, applying its best collective thinking to the process. Any efforts by individuals to protect their turf will endanger the whole. So, alignment requires a top-performing executive team whose primary focus is to set and then achieve the firm's overall goals.

❖ What are some Characteristics of an Effective Top Management Team?

The teams which function effectively usually show particular characteristics, and if any of these is missing, the team may become a group of disparate individuals who spend their time debating with each other and have a negative impact on each other's contribution – instead of an integrated team creating additional value through its work together. Some examples of these characteristics are:

- The atmosphere tends to be informal and relaxed. People are involved and interested without signs of boredom.
- There's a lot of discussion in which virtually everyone participates, and if the discussion gets off the subject, someone will bring it back quickly.
- The members listen to each other. People are not afraid of appearing foolish by putting forward a creative thought, even if it seems fairly extreme.
- There is constructive disagreement, and disagreements are not suppressed or overridden by premature team action.
- Most decisions are reached by consensus, and formal voting is at a minimum. The team does not accept a simple majority as a proper basis for action.
- Criticism is frequent, frank and relatively comfortable. There is little evidence of personal attack, either openly or in a hidden fashion.
- When action is taken, clear assignments are made and accepted.
- The team leader does not dominate, nor does the team defer unduly. The issue is not who controls, but how to get the job done.

❖ What about some of the reasons, why Top Management Teams Fail?

Teams can fail for many reasons, some to do with individuals and some with structure. Some of the most common problems are:

- Members do not have a vision of the additional power they can generate by working together as a team.
- It's not clear who makes what decisions, or what areas of decision making belong to this team as opposed to other divisions, board of directors, etc.
- Who's right becomes more important than what's right.
- There is a focus on individual vs. team success. This is a common condition among top management, especially around functional or departmental walls or barriers.
- Short-term gains become more important than long-term sustained growth and profitability.

CHAPTER

14

REWARDING TEAMS AND MEMBERS

LEARNING OBJECTIVES

- To understand basic concepts of Reward Management in an organisational set-ups.
- To know tools and types of Rewards for Teams and Members.

UNDERSTANDING THE CONCEPT AND TOOLS OF REWARD

Intrinsic Reward and Extrinsic Reward

Intrinsic reward is a psychological reward that is experienced directly by an individual. Examples are feelings of accomplishment, increased self-esteem, satisfaction of developing new skills, sense of fulfillment etc.

Extrinsic reward in contrast is a reward that is provided by an outside agent, such as a supervisor or work group. Examples are bonus, promotions, increase in salary, perks, appreciation or praise etc.

Dimensions of Reward Systems

Reward and incentives contribute to strategy implementation by shaping individual and group behaviour. Well-designed reward systems and incentive plans are consistent with an organization objectives and structure. They motivate employees to direct their performance toward the organization's, goals.

❖ What is a Reward?

- What reinforces or motivates an employee.
- What the employee perceives as reward, and not what the management considers as reward.
- Rewards may be extrinsic or intrinsic.
- Management can provide rewards but the individual employee determines their reward value.

Cost-reward Break-even Analysis

It is evident that many complex issues determine how employees will respond to economic rewards. There is no simple answer for the employer or the employee. The employee's solution to this complex problem in a rough type of cost-reward break-even analysis, in which the employee determines and compares personal costs and rewards to determine the point at which they are approximately equal; as shown in following figure. Employees consider all the costs of higher performance such as more effort. Then they compare these costs with probable rewards, which are always valued from the individual employee's point of view. Management can provide the rewards, but the individual employee determines their reward value.

The break-even point of costs and rewards is the point at which costs and rewards are equal for a certain level of performance, as shown by point B in the figure. Employee performance tends to be near the break-even point but below it, because typically the employee does not try to be so precise as to maximize the cost-reward relationship. Rather, the employee tries for a satisfactory relationship in which rewards are relatively favourable in relation to costs. Performance tends to be somewhere along the line A'B'.

In this figure, employee costs are shown rising more steeply near the highest level of performance to represent the additional difficulty that maximum effort and concentration require. Each employee's line will have a different shape, representing individual values. The reward line is shown as a straight line, such as that provided by a piece rate, but in most instances it rises only in steps after a certain amount of performance improvement occurs. If the reward line can be made to rise more steeply by means of larger rewards, then the break-even point will be at a higher level of performance.

Cost of performance in relation to reward for an employee. Employee's performance will tend to be in the area of A'B'.

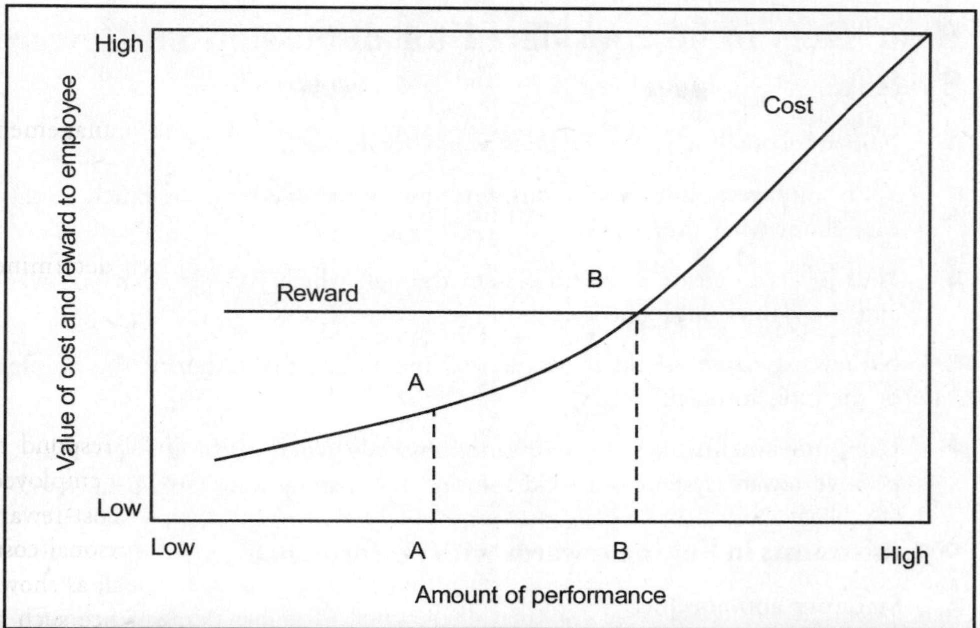

FIGURE 14.1 Cost of Performance to Reward

Key points to remember

- The things that get rewarded, get done.
- Proper linkage between rewards and performance is the single master key for improved performance.

❖ What is not a Reward?

- When it becomes a ritual or common facility/benefits.
- What the employees do not perceive as reward.
- When reward works as a disincentive.

❖ When Rewards do not have desired Impact?

- When one reward counters the other.
- When it is not given in proper way.
- When it is not for the right behaviour.
- When environmental factors are not conductive.
- When lack of faith on the bona fide of the giver.
- When employees do not perceive the value of reward.

Basic facts to be considered for discussion on Reward Systems

- Nobody works for you, everybody works for himself.
- Your employees don't care about what you want one-tenth as much as they care about what they want.
- Your job is to create a reward system through which you get what you want and the right things get done.
- No reward system works if people lack the ability, the authority, the training or the tools to do the job.
- Use punishments and negative sanctions only when nothing else works. A positive reward system is a solid solution for shaping long-term behaviour.

❖ Constraints in linking rewards with performance

- Statutory compulsions
- Industry wise wage boards
- Operative long-term settlements
- Labour unrest in the event of such a venture
- Lack of mutual trust
- Lack of visional and innovative Approaches on the part of management
- Lack of concerted efforts and commitments
- Lack of system based on fairness
- Fear on personal authority and whims.

The greatest single obstacle to the success of today's organisations is the giant mismatch between the behaviour we need and the behaviour we reward. For example:

- We need top managers to make sound, long range decisions, but we reward for short-term profits, and threaten their jobs when profits take a dive.
- We need managers to conserve costs and minimize red tape, but reward them with budget increases and new staff when they create more red tape.
- We need staff who will reduce needless paper work, but their job security is linked to amount of paper they have to shuffle.
- We need highly productive workers, but we don't pay them to produce.

Key point to remember

Each of us behave the way the reward system has taught us to behave.

Two lessons

1. You get more of the behaviour you reward. You don't get what you hope for, ask for, wish for or beg for. You get what you reward.
2. In trying to do right things, it's so easy to fall into the trap of rewarding the wrong activities and ignoring or punishing the right ones.

The result is that we hope for A, unwittingly reward B and wonder why we get B.

What is the linkage between the Rewards and Performance?

The linkage between performance, rewards and satisfaction may be established by the Figure 14.2.

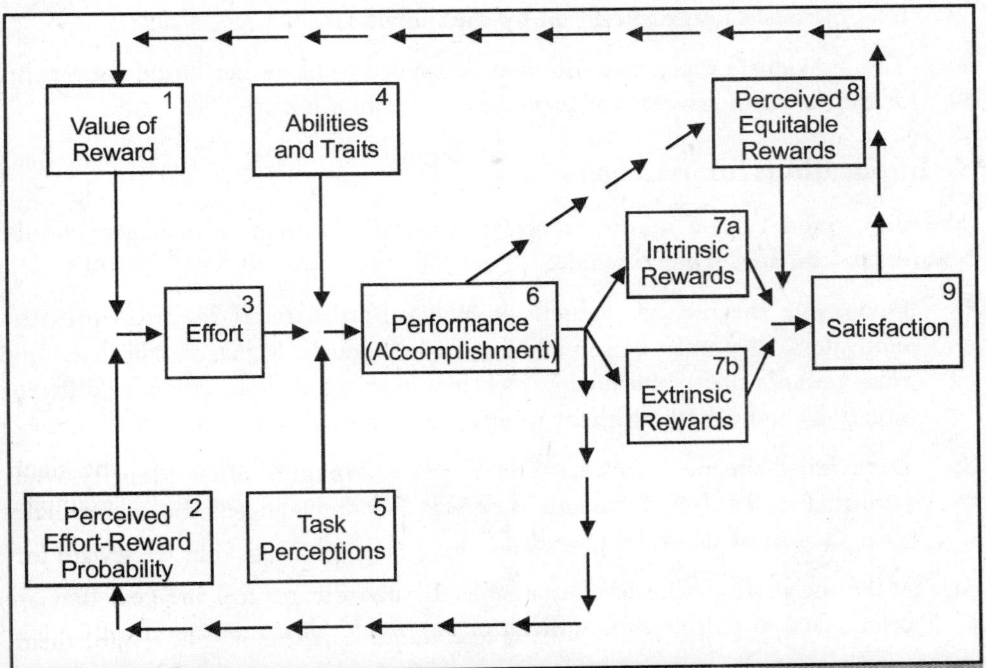

FIGURE 14.2 **Linkage between Performance Rewards and Satisfaction**

The value of the expected reward to the individual:

1. Combines with the individual's perception of the effort involved in attaining the reward and the probability of achieving it.

2. To produce a certain level of effort.
3. This effort combines with the individual's abilities and traits.
4. The way he or she sees the task.
5. To yield a specific performance level.
6. This resulting level of performance leads to intrinsic rewards (or negative consequences if the performance level is lower than expected) that are inherent in the task accomplishment.

7 a. And perhaps to extrinsic rewards.

7 b. (The wavy line in the model leading to the extrinsic rewards indicates that those rewards are not guaranteed, since they depend on how others assess the individual's performance and on the organization's willingness to reward that performance). The individual has his or her own idea about the appropriateness of the total set of rewards received.

8. Which, when measured against the rewards actually received. Results in the level of satisfaction experienced by the individual.
9. The individual's experience will then be applied to his or her future assessments of the values of rewards for further task accomplishment.

❖ Implications for Managers

The above model has a number of clear implications for how managers should reward subordinates. These include:

1. Determine the rewards valued by each subordinate. If rewards are to be motivators, they must be suitable for the individuals. Managers can determine what rewards their subordinates seek by observing their reactions in different situations and by asking them what rewards they desire.
2. Determine the performance you desire. Managers must identify what performance level or behaviour they want so they can tell the subordinates what they must do to be rewarded.
3. Make the performance level attainable. If subordinates feel the goal they are being asked to pursue is too difficult or impossible, their motivation will be low.
4. Link rewards to performance to maintain motivation. The appropriate reward must be clearly associated within a short period of time with successful performance.
5. Analyze what factors might counteract the effectiveness of the reward. Conflicts between the manager's reward system and other influences in the work situation

may require the manager to make some adjustments in the reward. For example, if the subordinate's work group favour low productivity, an above-average reward may be required to motivate a subordinate to high productivity.

❖ Implications for Organizations

The above model of rewards also has a number of implications for organizations. These include:

1. Organizations usually get what they reward for. The organization's reward system must be designed to motivate for desired behaviour and results.
2. The job itself can be made intrinsically rewarding. If jobs are designed to fulfill some of the higher needs of employees (such as independence or creativity). They can be motivating in themselves. This implication is obviously the basis of many job-enrichment programs. However, those individuals who do not desire enriched jobs should not be made to take them.
3. The immediate supervisor has an important role in the motivation process. . The supervisor is in the best position to define clear goals and to provide appropriate rewards for his or her various subordinates. The supervisor should therefore be trained in the motivation process and given enough authority to administer rewards.

What are the Common Fallacies in Reward Systems?

The great philosopher Yogi Berra once said. "You can observe a lot just by watching." Look around your workplace and you will certainly find examples of the right behaviour being ignored or punished and the wrong behaviour being rewarded. For example, does your organization:

- Need better results, but reward those who look busiest and work the longest hours?
- Ask for quality work, but set unreasonable deadlines?
- Want solid solutions to problems, but reward quick fixes?
- Talk about company loyalty, but offer no job security and pay the highest salaries to the most recently hired and those who threaten to leave?
- Need simplicity, but reward those who complicate matters and generate trivia?
- Ask for a harmonious work environment, but reward squeaking joints that complain the most?
- Need creative workers, but chastise those who dare to be different?

- Talk about frugality, but award the largest budget increases to those who exhaust all of their resources?
- Ask for teamwork, but reward one team member at the expense of another?
- Need innovation, but penalize unsuccessful risks and reward going by the book?

MONETARY AND NON-MONETARY REWARDS

Based on the practices of various organisations, a snapshot list of rewards is given below:

Monetary Rewards

- Salary increments
- Promotions
- Paid up insurance
- Loans
- Transport (car/two wheeler)
- Telephone
- Profit sharing
- Incentive cash
- Company accommodation
- Bonus
- Cash awards
- Furniture
- Company shares
- Other facilities

Non-monetary Rewards

❖ **Treats**

- Free lunch
- Picnics

- Dinner with boss
- Birthday treats
- Festival bashes
- Dinner for family

❖ Knick-knacks

- Desk accessories
- Company watches
- Tie pins
- Diaries
- Calenders
- Wallets
- T-shirts
- Bigger table
- Better chair
- Cabin

❖ Awards

- Trophies
- Plaques
- Citation
- Scroll
- Certificate
- Letter of appreciation

❖ Social acknowledgement

- Informal recognition
- Friendly greetings
- Smiles
- Solicitation of advice/suggestions
- Showing trust

- Membership of clubs
- Use of company facility for personal project
- Photograph on notice board/company journal
- Special praise by management
- Pat on back
- Opportunity for lecture

❖ Tokens

- Movie tickets
- Vacation trips
- Early off
- Coupons redeemable at stores
- Presents
- Special leave

❖ On the job

- More responsibility
- Job rotation
- Special assignment
- Training
- Security of tenure
- Representing company at public fora
- Trips on duty
- More authority
- Fair treatment
- Favourite work/job
- Facilities for self development
- Self goal setting
- Performance feedback
- Better designation

RECOGNITION PROGRAMME FOR TEAM MEMBERS: PRACTICES IN INDIAN COMPANIES

Components of employee recognition programs range from public appreciation to citations, team celebrations to sponsored family vacations, glittering trophies to colorful badges and cash awards to gift vouchers, all strung together to promote and reinforce the business objectives, values and belief systems of the organization. An in-depth look at the nitty gritties of employee reward and recognition programmes... the Indian way.

More and more organizations are tapping into the power of well designed employee recognition programs to motivate and inspire their human capital. The rewards range across a broad spectrum of monetary and non monetary offerings: from public appreciation to citations, team celebrations to sponsored family vacations, glittering trophies to colorful badges and cash awards to gift vouchers... all strung together to promote and reinforce the business objectives, values and belief systems of the organization. An in-depth look at the nitty gritties of employee reward and recognition programs... the Indian way.

COMPANY PRACTICE: SYMANTEC INDIA

A unique employee recognition initiative called Techwiz has been rolled out to recognize contributions to technical activities in Symantec beyond the boundaries of routine work. The basic idea is to award tech points to individuals for various technical activities, which can be redeemed later. These points accumulate over time and serve as a measure for the total extracurricular technical contribution of a person.

Two kinds of rewards are given to employees through this programme: material rewards like T-shirts, iPods, gift vouchers, etc. and status rewards like auto invites to high profile Symantec events — Inventor awards, breakfast with global leaders and trips to Cutting Edge. For active TechWiz performers, TechWiz PlatinumStar, TechWiz GoldStar and Tech Wiz SilverStar titles are conferred. An employee can accumulate these TechWiz points by engaging in two kinds of activities: standard activities (predecided under TechWiz programme and offering participation in programs like Cutting Edge, Road to Cutting Edge, Technology Forum activities, etc.) and non-standard activities (not pre-decided and those an employee thinks are worthy of recognition).

Tech Wiz is independent of the appraisal system and the managerial hierarchy. Most, if not all, the details of the programme are decided and administered by the people who have accumulated maximum TechWiz points i.e., those who are most active in Symantec Tech community.

Symantec also has Quarterly Awards that recognize managers for exemplifying superior people management skills and best practices in bringing order and consistency to management process while helping the organization to adapt to continuous change. One type of quarterly award honors an employee who has done outstanding work at his or her assigned job, helped others outside his or her normal area of responsibility, and expended extra effort or made personal sacrifices for the company. Quarterly awards also recognize employees who exemplify strong leadership in championing and supporting excellence.

Employees are rewarded for outstanding performance in reinforcing Symantec's values of customer-driven, trust, innovation, and action through contributions beyond normal assignments, achievements not specifically addressed by other plans or programs, and efforts in service to all current or potential, internal or external, Symantec customers.

Other than these, ongoing awards are granted for time-limited, focused achievements (for example, a project, special accomplishment) that are clearly beyond an employee's ongoing, normal work assignments and objectives. Service awards are a method of recognizing employees for their continued service to Symantec and expressing appreciation for employees' talent, passion and dedication in making Symantec successful.

The reward and recognition policy at NIS Sparta, or 'Reco', as they call it, recognizes exemplary performance and contribution of NISians. The focus is on recognition of multidimensional contribution at individual, departmental and organizational levels, in the form of both monetary and non monetary rewards. Objectives of 'Reco' are to acknowledge and promote achievement of individual and team objectives; to improve employee productivity and quality of work; and to improve customer service.

Individual recognition programmes include appreciation letters, citations, gift vouchers and paid vacations at resorts. Team achievement celebrations occur in the form of quarterly team celebrations (lunch/dinner/tea party and movie). Team pictures along with articles on the team's achievement are published in the company newsletter.

Excellence Club is awarded to five NISians who demonstrate adherence to the core values of learning and innovation, thus making outstanding contributions that impact profitability, customer satisfaction, leading to substantial financial impact in a year. As a token of appreciation for their outstanding achievements, the recipients of these awards attend a regional, Asian or international conference or a workshop. Winners of this award are portrayed as Brand Ambassadors of NIS Sparta.

Pathfinder Award is given to any business team member who demonstrates exemplary performance in getting value of orders. Employees can avail of a 3 days and 2 nights stay at a resort or premium hotel within the city or around with family. An appreciation letter is also given to the employee mentioning his specific achievement.

The Service Tenure Award recognizes an individual's long service and commitment and is given to employees who have completed two, five, ten, fifteen or twenty years of continuous service with NIS Sparta. The award comes in the form of gift vouchers for the value as per the category of tenure.

Company Practice: First Advantage

First Advantage's Allegiance Programme recognizes tenured employees through cash benefits, merchandise and certificates on completion of specific tenures in the organization ranging between 1 year to 7 years. Performance based variable pay over and above the fixed salary recognizes and rewards high performing individuals within the organization. Shift allowance for I working in staggered shifts benefits employees who work in unconventional timings. Zero Attrition incentive rewards supervisors who maintain zero attrition in their respective teams. The award recognizes and honours supervisors who have directly contributed to company's talent management objectives through their resource management skills. Absenteeism Incentives are given on a quarterly basis to individuals at the associate level for maintaining zero absenteeism. Scholarships are extended to employees for pursuing higher education, which will add value to the organization through professional skills development.

Pinnacle Awards Programme recognizes individuals for performance related achievements in seven categories. The individuals receive certificates of commendation and are also felicitated by the leadership team at the Pinnacle High Tea event. Accolades is a weekly recognition event for employees who have walked the extra mile to achieve organizational excellence or have received client appreciation. A letter from the MD is sent to family members thanking them for their support in the employee's success. Spot Awards are given to individuals on the operations floor. Peer appreciation is instantaneous and boosts self-confidence and morale. It promotes healthy competition amongst peer groups.

Company Practice: Haier Appliances

At Haier Appliances, a Best Branch Award is given to the branch which achieves maximum sales turnover with minimum sales return and outstanding. Best Sales Branch Manager Award (for achievement of maximum sales turnover), Best Collection Branch Manager Award (to boost collection from the market), Best Network Development Branch Manager (for the Branch Manger who has got maximum dealers or distributors and has retained old dealers), and Top 3 Sales Executive Awards (based on overall performance of executives for target achievement and collection) are also awarded. Haier also has reward and recognition schemes for customer service, commercial, HR and production functions.

We do recognition in various forms: recognition cards, team awards and senior leaders in any market have their individual, personalized awards for people making a positive difference. The most interesting aspect of Yum's recognition culture is that it does not necessarily flow top-down — team members and junior members of any team are as passionate about recognizing effort and achievement of their peers and superiors as the leadership is, of recognizing their teams. More often than not, recognition at *Yum* is not linked to monetary aspects. The focus is more on spotting and recognizing employees/partners doing the right thing.

Company Practice: GE JF Welch Technology Centre

Management awards recognize individuals or teams for significant achievements towards organizational business goals that have a high degree of challenge/difficulty in execution. The amount varies to reflect the magnitude of the achievement. The larger amounts are intended to recognize achievements that cut across organizational and technology lines in direct support of accelerating innovation and strengthening GE's competitive position.

The Golden Globe awards are specific to the consumer and industrial business and each award is given out to one employee each month, whose project is rated to be the best in a particular month. Employees are required to make a one/two page summary of the project and present the same to the panel of judges from within the employees on different project teams. The project is judged based on its relevance to the business and how it exemplifies the GE Growth Traits of external focus, inclusiveness, imagination and courage, expertise and clear thinker.

Gerald L. Philippe Awards represent GE's most prestigious employee volunteer recognition across the globe. All finalists receive recognition certificates. Each GE Business presents the top volunteers with special awards and $2,500.00 in cash grants to their favourite causes.

GE Global Research Awards like The Coolidge, Hull, Dushman and Whitney awards are the highest honours bestowed on individuals and teams for their technical contributions to the company. This is open to all GE Global Research employees across the four global research sites.

Thanks to You Awards reward and recognize unusual and significant accomplishments/contributions over and above the normal expectations of an employee's assignment. An award is not intended to be granted to employees for a level of performance for which they are already being compensated. It is also not meant to be a substitute for a salary adjustment, promotion, hiring bonus, suggestion award, retirement gift or other related personnel action.

Engineering Recognition Day is celebrated annually at JFWTC, in recognition of individual and team achievement, success and contribution to Aviation, Energy, Oil and Gas and Water and Process Technology businesses of GE Infrastructure. There are three categories of award for projects: product, technology and process excellence and four categories for individual excellence: Debutant, Playing Captain, Growth Leader and Enabler of the year. Awards are also given to the winners of the ERD theme contest and Cover page contest.

GE Transportation -- India Engineering Excellence Awards celebrate the achievements and milestones of the GE Transportation Engineering team in the year gone by. The awards are synonymous with the efforts of the team, the breadth and depth of technology that the team works on, and the impact they have had on GE's transportation business. These awards are based on four criteria: excellence in engineering, relevance to business objectives, enabling growth and performance.

Each Center of Excellence in the Infrastructure Engineering Team nominates the Project of the Month. A technical panel consisting of senior engineers decides which projects get awarded, based on certain criteria. The winning teams get a management award for their efforts. This programme helps give visibility to individual contributors and at the same time, senior engineers get exposure to the breadth and depth of technology, beyond their domain. These awards are announce every quarter in an all-employee meeting.

The GE India President Awards were instituted for the first time in 2009 and represent the highest recognition in India. The criteria for these awards are the growth traits, performance and leadership.

Patent and publication awards recognize top patent-holders and publication authors at the center by inviting them for an exclusive dinner with the leadership at the center in addition to the monetary award they receive.

JFWTC Annual Awards of Excellence represent the highest form of recognition for outstanding contribution by an employee at the centre. The JFWTC Awards are an epitome of innovation, excellence, creativity, leadership and more. There are five JFWTC Awards each being conferred to an individual based on a set of attributes defined. The awards have been named after renowned personalities who have earned their place of right in their sphere of work. A committee represented by employees across various teams at JFWTC have been formed that will be identifying the award winners. These awards are an endeavour to acknowledge and cherish the most distinguished among us and recognize breakthrough work done by them.

The committee has listed five categories of Awards covering various fields and aspects of an employee: CV Raman Innovation Award, Ramanujam Young Achiever Award, Radhakrishnan Mentor Award, JRD Tata Award for Building Reputation and Visvesvarayya Engineering Excellence Award.

The process of finalizing the awardees involves business leaders submitting nominations based on criteria specific to each award and then finalization by a core committee represented by senior engineers, scientists and members of leadership team from various JFWTC business groups. Winners are not only given cash awards and a memento but also gain an entry into the JFWTC Hall of Fame!

The GE Service Awards is an exclusive ceremony that recognizes the long-term commitment of employees to the Center. It an event that every employee looks forward to his/her career at the center as they dine with their families at the awards ceremony with some of the finest entertainment celebrities in country.

Company Practice: Freescale Semiconductor

Freescale's *BRAVO*! recognition programme provides timely, meaningful recognition to the employees. The programme provides both informal and formal ways to express appreciation and acknowledge hard work and results. *BRAVO*! informal recognition awards are non-monetary and must have a fair market value of less than $50. Informal recognition includes peer-to-peer, employee to manager, or manager to employee.

The formal recognition component recognizes more significant accomplishments or work that substantially exceeds the normal requirements of an employee's position. Using specific criteria, managers can award from $50 to $3,000 to an individual who has gone above and beyond. All *BRAVO*! awards are intended to be spontaneous and discretionary. Approximately 4,850 employees received *BRAVO*! globally last year.

In order to support cultural differences between organizations and regions, Freescale encourages its various business and corporate groups to put their own spin on recognition. Some incorporate elements of the *BRAVO*! programme while others have developed their own unique processes. Many groups publicly recognize teams and individuals during monthly! quarterly meetings, presenting *BRAVO*! certificates.

At the corporate level, monthly leadership teleconferences regularly seek and highlight outstanding examples of innovation, customer focus, exceptional teamwork and achievements of Indian employees.

COMPANY PRACTICE: SYSTIME

SYSTIME Quality Ace Award promotes the thought and understanding of quality across the organization and is given out every month to one individual. SYSTIME Annual Quality Award (conceptually based on Malcolm Baldrige Award) is an inter-unit team award given out annually to the best project or support team for a project ranked in terms of process adherence, quality and customer satisfaction among others. The award consists of a rotating trophy and certificates for winner and runner- up teams.

In addition to Distinction Awards, Special Achievement Awards, Excellence Awards, Leadership and Management Style Award, Distinction Award for specific levels and functions, SYSTIME has a Champion of the Year award, which is open for all categories. It emphasizes on exemplary and consistent performance both in employee's field of work and beyond assigned duties.

The Extra Mile Club has been constituted to promote a culture of innovation. Ideas from employees are assessed and implemented based on their feasibility and benefits. The selection of the most viable idea is done by the CEO on a monthly basis and the originator of the idea is inducted as a member of the prestigious Extra Mile Club. The selected SYSTIME gets a Welcome kit: a paper bag with a T-Shirt, Certificate and a badge that says "I have gone the extra mile!" He/she also gets a flag that is put up at his/her workstation with the same message. The special achievement is announced at the business meet and the above kit is handed over to the employee. The news is covered in the monthly employee newsletter, intranet and on all notice boards. A CEO communication announcing the winners is sent out. The originator of the idea is chosen to be a part of the team and implement the idea.

Peer to Peer Appreciation or Caring SYSTIME Programme is a channel used by SYSTIME to appreciate their colleagues' timely help and care. Any SYSTIME who wants to appreciate his team member or his colleague fills up a 'thank you' card designed especially for the programme and drops it in a box. All forms are removed at the end of the month from the drop box. They are screened and/top three appreciation forms are selected. The selected appreciation forms are announced during the business meet and the winners are invited for a lunch with the senior management.

Long Service Recognition or Wall of Fame is an attempt or a way to recognize the dedication and perseverance of the employees who have spent more than five years in the organization. To achieve this, framed pictures of the SYSTIME who have dedicated more than five years to SYSTIME are put up in the lobby area of the SYSTIME office building. For differentiation purposes, the entire lobby and reception area is painted "SYSTIME" green. The picture sizes vary, depending on the number of years spent and depict the name and date of joining and are demarcated using the metal plates indicating the number of years.

Company Practice: Small beginnings

While the value of a well designed and comprehensive recognition programme cannot be undermined, absence of a written policy is no reason to delay recognition in small doses. Go liberal with that unexpected pat on the back, the spontaneous words of praise and an occasional impromptu lunch out with the team. Monetary rewards and trophies are not the only way to raise those spirits. Perhaps he was stressing the immense power of public appreciation, when Abraham Lincoln, the 16th US President said, "That some achieve great success, is proof to all that others can achieve it as well." So, go on, take your pick from a wide variety of options to make your employees feel extra special. It will be worth it!

Payouts for the Team

Getting rank-and-file employees engaged in pursuit of organizational goals as individuals, as part of small work teams, or as broader organizational units, requires action and consistent follow-through by the management team. Unfortunately, management interventions that can spur such engagement – such as reward plans, communication devices, or training programs – are often created and implemented not as a coordinated system but independently. Even when part of a coordinated plan, they're often designed at cross-purposes. It's not at all unusual for companies to train people to work in high performing teams but then publicly celebrate or reward only the work of outstanding individuals.

Reward and recognition systems, communication and performance feedback devices, and training tools must be aligned. This begins with vision and mission statements but becomes real through work systems, communications, management coaching, personal and professional development, performance measurement and, of course, rewards systems. Improving where you're headed first requires understanding where you currently stand.

The Reinforcement Model

The reinforcement model is an easy way to look at your reward plan options. It begins with the organization's objectives and desired culture.

Business objectives tend to be straightforward. Profit, revenue growth, cycle time, EVA, financial return calculations, customer satisfaction, quality, new product development, and operating expense reduction are typical. Reward plans must aligned with these objectives to ensure management support. Objectives that would be nice accomplish are not as effective as ones that are key to success. Some objectives translate nicely into measures against which performance can be judged. Some require drilling down to find those activities, projects, and relevant contributory measures that, when addressed, will affect performance.

The best plans for losing weight or becoming physically, fit aren't those that helped some mythical other person in a book you read, but are those tailored to your unique needs and lifestyle. The same is true with reward plans. The best are those that the organization will embrace as important to meet its needs and so will follow through on. That means all levels of management accepting the plans as business strategies to engage employees in meeting the objectives. And that is a matter of culture.

Organizational culture (and how to influence it) has been the subject of many books and much academic research. The organization's vision, mission, history, operating norms, strategy, environment, and structure form culture. For the purpose of discussing reward plans, culture can be described as how the organization utilises its employees to get work done. It is more than work design. It is the way people are considered when there is a desire to improve performance.

One of the primary keys to success in improving the organizational performance is to ensure that reward plans reinforce the desired culture, or at least attempt to reduce the gap between the existing and desired culture.

What part of the continuum should you target? Simply put, the desired culture should be the one that best suits the needs of your business. If your desired culture differs from the existing one, it's important to structure any new reward or recognition system to reinforce the ideal culture, the one you're moving toward. For example, if your most influential reward plan is to recognize and celebrate outstanding performers and you want a culture of collaborative teamwork, you've got a disconnect. An organizational unit incentive plan that rewards results through teamwork would be more appropriate, or could be added to existing plans. Reward systems need to be aligned with the desired culture.

The reinforcement model looks at the continuum of rewards from fixed cost to employees (cost of doing business) to paying for results (investment in results). It has been observed that team rewards that focus on results provide the maximum return on the investments in people costs. Team rewards that tend to be more of a ritual (entitlement) without focusing on results do not provide leverage for organizational performance improvement.

Many organizations grope with the problem of adopting a suitable mechanism for rewarding team work, while the schemes will be organization and context specific, three distinct team rewards are illustrated below. One can classify rewarding teams into three main categories.

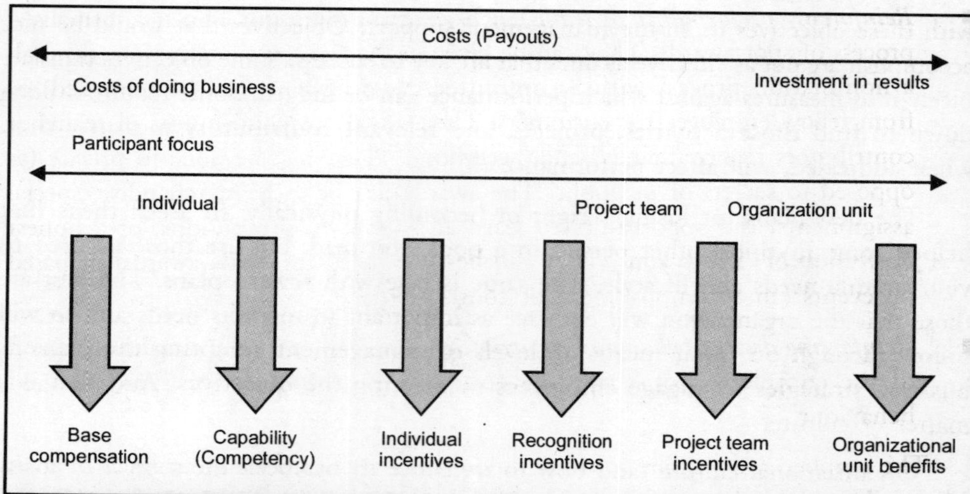

FIGURE 14.3 (A) The Reinforcement Model

RECOGNITION PLANS

Recognition plans are investments in human capital and often reflect the culture of the organization. These plans can apply to individuals, project teams, or permanent work groups (organizational units, by our definition). Recognition can take the form of a simple, "thank you", a cash spot bonus, or a trip to Bali.

The critical distinction between recognition and incentive plans is certainty. Recognition is after-the-fact, awarded after behaviour is exhibited or results accomplished; it is not" do this and get that" according to a preannounced schedule, but "we saw you do this – thanks". Recognition plans do not guarantee awards.

There are as many variations of recognition plans as there are creative minds. They are very powerful, and generally underutilised, tools for encouraging repeat positive performance and in building team morale. Getting the most out of a recognition plan requires ongoing attention and regular refreshing so that it stays meaningful to employees.

Most recognition plans fall into one of these categories:

- ***Celebrating organizational objectives:*** Picnics, pizza parties, special lunches, regular meetings to share accomplishments and challenges, and information—trading sessions are all examples of recognising both the objectives of the organization and the importance of people in meeting those objectives. They are inexpensive, fun, significant, and make a positive cultural statement. They must be frequent, open, honest, and involving. They are about focus and celebration, rather than manipulation and hype.

- ***Reinforcing performance of teams, or organizational units***: This is a formalised process of spot awards. They can be given at management's discretion, through a nomination process with a committee deciding who will be rewarded, or from fellow employees or customers. They single out contributors or teams of contributors to say "thanks" and "well-done". They can be done in private (as opposed to secret) or in public. The awards can be cash, merchandise, special assignments, the opportunity to learn and develop, promotions, or a honest expression of "thank you". They can be time-based (monthly awards) or based on events (an accomplishment or contribution).
- ***Reinforcing desired behaviours or activities***: These are generally social recognition of the completion of a training course, special project, or even changed behaviour.

The number and visibility of recognition plans says a lot about an organization's culture. The more dynamic and meaningful the plans, the more appreciated the employees feel.

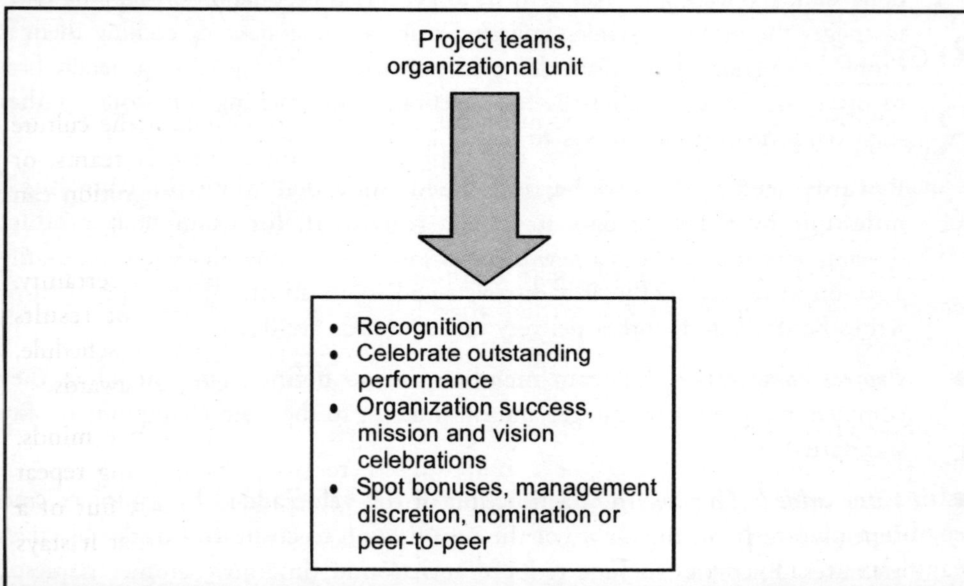

FIGURE 14.3 (B) Recognition Plans

Project Team Incentives

Project teams are usually, but not always, formed by management to tackle specific projects or challenges with a defined timeframe — reviewing processes for efficiency or cost-savings recommendations, launching a new software product, or implementing enterprise resource planning systems are just a few examples. In other cases teams self-form around specific issues or as part of continuous improvement initiatives such as team-based suggestions systems.

Project teams can have cross-functional membership or simply be a subset of an existing organizational unit. The person who sponsors the team — its "champion" — typically creates an incentive plan with specific objectives measures and an award schedule tied to achieving those measures. To qualify as an incentive, the plan must included preannounced goals, with a do this, get that guarantee for teams. The incentive usually varies with the value added by the project.

Project team incentive plans usually have some combination of these basic measures:

- ***Project milestones:*** Hit a milestone, on budget and on time, and all team members earn a defined amount. Although sound in theory, there are inherent problems in tying financial incentives to hitting milestones. Milestones often change for good reason (technology advances, market shifts, other developments) and you don't want the team and management to get into a negotiation on slipping dates to trigger the incentive. Unless milestones are set in stone and reaching them is simply a function of the team doing its normal, everyday job, it's generally best to use recognition as -after-the-fact celebration of reaching milestones, rather than tying financial incentives to it.

  Rewards need not always be time-based, such that when the team hits a milestone by a certain date it earns a reward. If, for example, a product development team debugs a new piece of software on time, that's not necessarily a reason to reward it. But if it discovers and solves an unsuspected problem or writes better code before a delivery date, rewards are due.

- ***Project completion***: All team members earn a defined amount when they complete the project on budget and on time (or to the team champion's quality standards).

- ***Value added***: This award is a function of the value added by a project, and depends largely on the ability of the organization to create and track objectives measures. Examples include reduced turnaround time on customer requests, improved cycle times for product development, cost savings due to new process efficiencies, or incremental profit or market share created by the product or service developed or implemented by the project team.

One warning about project incentive plans: they can be very effective in helping teams stay focused, accomplish goals, and feel like they are rewarded for their hard work, but they tend to be exclusionary. Not everyone can be on a project team. Some employees (team members) will have an opportunity to earn an incentive that others (non team members) do not. There is a lack of internal equity. One way to address this is to reward core team members with incentives for reaching team goals, and recognize peripheral players who supported the team, either by offering advice, resources, or a pair of hands, or by covering for project team members back at their regular job.

Some projects are of such strategic importance that you can live with these internal equity problems and non-team members' grousing about exclusionary incentives. The bottom line, though, is this tool should be used cautiously.

One type of project incentive plan can help sidestep perceived equity problems, however: incentives for self-formed teams. Under this plan employees are encouraged to form their own teams — usually between five and eight people — to take on a specific objectives and emerge with a way to make things better. Team-based suggestion systems are one manifestation of this plan, with cost reduction as a common target.

In well-designed plans, teams have the responsibility of not only for coming up with an idea or solution, but of writing up a business and implementation plan, getting managers affected by the change to sign off, developing the cost justification (savings, or degree of performance improvement), submitting it to management for approval, and then taking an active role in idea implementation.

Again, a preannounced reward schedule — do this, get that, usually based on cost reduction — is used for all such incentive plans. Special consideration is given to projects for which cost reduction is not an appropriate goal.

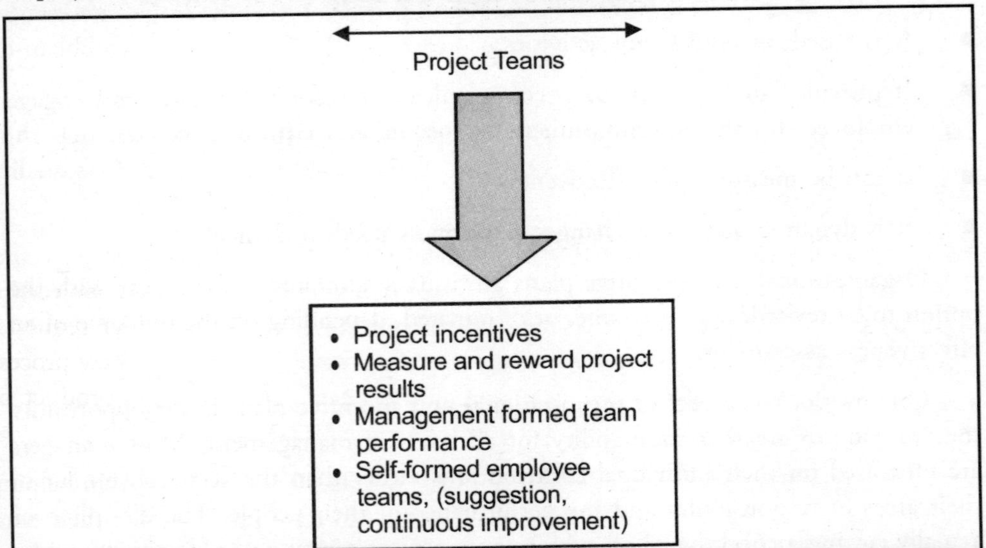

FIGURE 14.3 (C) **Project Team Incentives**

ORGANISATIONAL UNIT INCENTIVE

Organizational unit incentive plans cover a defined population, usually an organizational unit — an entire company, a division, a department, a work group. The unit appears on an organizational chart. Participation may be limited to certain levels of employees in that organizational unit (for example: everyone, all management employees, all workmen, or everyone but those on the management incentive plan). The performance award schedule is preannounced; participants know how much they can earn as a function of performance against the measures. It focuses on the primarily business objective and can use performance measures most appropriate for the participating organizational unit. Sometimes, levels of measurement are combined. For example, 25 percent of payout is based on how well the whole company does on return on assets, 25 percent on how well the division improves cycle time, and 50 percent split between two measures at the department level. All measures, however, should be aligned with the primary business objectives.

Organizational unit incentive can be the most powerful reward plan type to support a culture of teamwork. They can make a business strategy come alive. A good plan is a powerful way to leverage human capital to improve performance because of the following:

- It engages all or most of the employee base.
- It pays out only when the improvement occurs.
- It is based on results, not activities.
- It provides an opportunity to communicate, reinforce, educate, and engage employees for the accomplishment of specific and critical objectives.
- It can be measured for effectiveness.
- It is dynamic because it changes as business needs a change.

Organizational unit incentive plans are usually announced for a year with the option to be revised, kept the same, or terminated, depending on the outcome of an effectiveness assessment.

One overlooked aspect of organizational unit incentive plans is the opportunity they provide to create accountability for all levels of management. Most managers are measured on their individual contributions rather than the accomplishment of their areas of responsibility and the performance of their people. The discipline of actually cutting a check based on performance against measurable objectives provides the opportunity and discipline to follow through, recalibrate, and actually find out what you got for your money (something lacking in MBO and traditional measurements plans.)

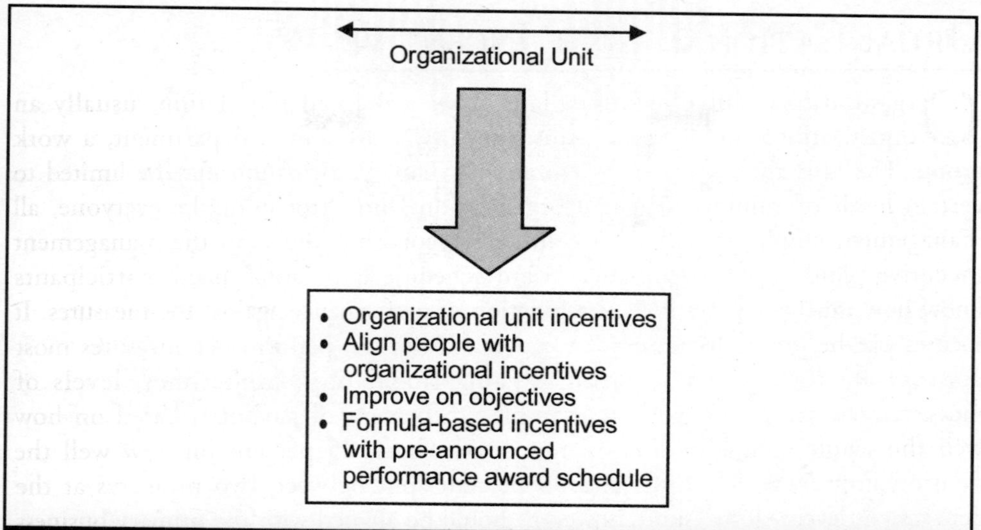

FIGURE 14.3 (D) **Organizational Unit Incentives**

Some organizational unit incentive plans are really awareness and communications plans in drag. It is rare that the plan designers realize they have designed a plan that is a methodology for the distribution of payouts based on a formula, rather than a plan that improves performance. These are long-line-of-sight plans. ("Line of sight" is the extent to which employees believe that they or their work group, department, or the like can actually contribute to affecting the measures.) Economic value added (EVA), earnings before taxes, return on capital assets, and customer satisfaction indexes are examples of measures often not understood by employees, making those measures have a long line of sight. Company-wide measures, covering diverse divisions and departments and sometimes international operations, also contribute to a long line of sight. The existence of the plan has little affect on the performance because the measures are too remote to the average employee.

These long-line-of-sight organizational unit incentive plans can be effective if management understands what "effective" means. These plans are for communication of critical objectives, the opportunity to educate employees about the measures, and to reinforce the vision and mission. The question then becomes: Is the value of a plan worth the expense? Usually the answer is yes, particularly when the company has purposely decided to pay people slightly below the competitive labour market and make up the difference, and more, through the organizational unit incentive plan. The measures used in a plan for this strategy need to be calibrated to ensure a payout of at least enough to span the gap between the market and the organizational's pay, but it is the upside opportunity that makes it attractive to the employee. The fact that the payout is variable with overall performance protects the company from payout unless the performance is there.

CHAPTER

15

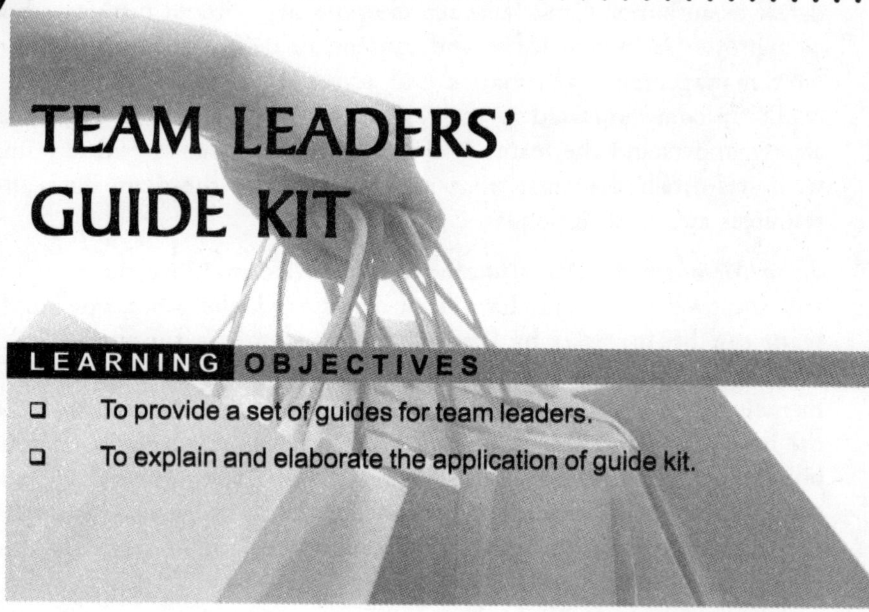

TEAM LEADERS' GUIDE KIT

LEARNING OBJECTIVES

- To provide a set of guides for team leaders.
- To explain and elaborate the application of guide kit.

WHY TEAMS DON'T PERFORM KNOWING AND UNDERSTANDING THE PERFORMANCE BARRIERS

Teams that aren't performing well or those being formed that won't ever perform well are the victims of a mismatch of people with the project, the process, and the product. In quantifying these factors, we often overlook the most complex and critical success element – the people who will do the work. While there are numerous reasons why teams fail, we have identified those that are most often the root cause. This section of the chapter discusses ten key reasons teams don't perform as well as they could.

1. ***The People Don't Understand the Team's Mission:*** The team needs a clearly understood and agreed upon objective, i.e., why it is being formed and what it is expected to accomplish. What is the team's active time frame? Is it event or calendar driven? Is this an ad hoc, single project team, a cross-functional/department work team, a continuing, open-ended assignment, or spell it out. How will the team and its members interface with the rest of the organization? What will be its reporting process? What are its constraints (functional,

political, etc.). Is this a research/study team, an idea or concept team, an implementation team, an advisory team? And, what will be its work product?

2. ***The Team Lacks Empowerment:*** Once the team's mission is set, thoroughly define its authority. Can it take action on its own without further authorization or approval? Is its role advise and consent, or define and do? The team must have management's affirmative and active support. Its authority must be explicitly communicated to the rest of the organization so that others may clearly understand the team's goal and role. This issue is critically important with self-directed teams; what real muscle does the team have and what resources are at its disposal?

3. ***Team Members Are Not Matched To The Mission:*** Once the team's mission and empowerment status have been determined, the process of building the team can begin. Start by identifying the requisite functional, technical, experiential, and other background skills that will be needed by the prospective members. Then, closely examine the team's intended work product to determine the best mix of thinkers, doers, analyzers, innovators, planners, implementors, builders, crafters, documenters, and researchers. These natural approaches to accomplishment are critically important for the team's success, and often make the difference between "mission accomplished," or holding a postmortem critique to determine what went wrong.

4. ***There is a Poor Fit of Each Member to His/Her Role:*** Poor judgement in the formation of a team precludes the team's full creative capacity from ever being realized, i.e., the team has a short oar before it ever begins the race. Evaluate each member in terms of two performance perspectives; the individual's actual performance and expertise prior to the team assignment, and *their team performance potential*. The team requires certain skill-sets, behavioural and personality traits, and individual approaches to team work. To perform effectively, a team needs to operate as a unified group, and within a larger environment with a possibly different culture than that which develops inside the team. Each member has a role which must not be materially different than that demonstrated outside of the team. The team environment may alter an individual's conduct by degree, but it is unreasonable to expect a completely different kind of performance in a team role than has otherwise been demonstrated.

5. ***People Don't Understand Each Other's Natural Approaches:*** Inscribed on the temple of Apollo at Delphi is the sage advice to, "Know thyself." The corollary to this advice is "know thyself and then know thy fellow teammate." Every team member is unique in some way that allows each to contribute a special knack or gift to the team. Each member knows what he/she will or won't do, or resists doing. Knowing the other person's approach to team work is a powerful

tool in building the needed synergy. Assumptions about another person's conduct are quite often erroneous, leading to misunderstandings, miscommunications, and mistakes and to a missed mission. Know each other, then the expectations of and for the team will be realistically based.

6. ***No Development of the Individuals' Innate Talents:*** Since each member brings their own skill and behaviour set to the team, the team leader must allow that strength to flourish. Otherwise, each person will not produce to her/his full capability, and neither will the team reach its combined potential. Team membership should provide the opportunity for continued individual development and contribution, not stunt it or set it aside for the time being.

7. ***Team Roles Don't Match Individuals' Personal Fulfillment Goals:*** Every individual has their own set of professional aspirations. Each person hopes to realize at least some of his/her goals or to make significant progress toward them in every assignment. Most of us not only need to be recognized for our noteworthy achievements, but most importantly for those achievements that are on our own path to success; affirmation that we are indeed on the right path. An individual's team role is really a subset of her/his overall mission within the company, and therefore must be compatible with the reason why that person joined the company. The team role must effectively answer a subtle phrasing of the question, "What's in it for me?" which really addresses more than just the need for continued employment or the chance to demonstrate one's "team spirit." We all need to feel good about our accomplishments, and that's a very personal thing. Do you know the personal goals of each team member?

8. ***Performance isn't Linked to Organizational Goals:*** In addition to aligning an individual's team role with his/her personal goals is the need to firmly link a team member's performance to the goals of the organization. The answer to "Why are we doing this?" must emphasize the organization's need for *team* mission accomplishment which can be realized only through *individual* performance. As individuals, the need to be a part of . . . not apart from . . . the "big picture" can be achieved through an understanding of how one's team performance contributes to the company's goals. The team's mission must be to help the organization achieve its mission. If the team fails, the organization will suffer. If the team succeeds, individual recognition and reward will come from both the team and the organization.

9. ***There's no Linkage of Personal Performance and Team Responsibility:*** Teams have both a responsibility and an obligation for performance. One does not abrogate his/her individual responsibility for performance by becoming part of a team. A team must not be a hiding place for someone thinking to shirk the "burden" of individual performance. If anything, team members are "under the microscope" to an even greater degree. Outstanding performance on a

team quite often leads to more rapid and significant advancement toward one's goals than might otherwise be the case. Similarly, the weak team member must bear an appropriate portion of the responsibility for a team's failure.

10. ***Inability to Transform Team Member Conflict into Synergy:*** 'Synergy' does not imply "one big happy family." What it means for a team is the blending of often diverse and unique individual skills and sometimes conflicting behaviours into a mutually supportive effort focused on an objective to which all members commit themselves. "The total being greater than the sum of its parts," will be realized only if management and the team itself – meaning the individual members can direct and channel their individual strengths into a cohesive gel that allows each to work to her/his fullest and best capability. Team members must also rely on each other to offset any individual weaknesses, shortcomings, or resistance. Team members must barter their skills, behaviours, and approaches in a manner which does indeed "accentuate the positive" and which turns controversy, diversity, and differences of opinion into the "stuff " from which innovation and new ideas and processes are spawned. If the team is forced to operate at the level of its common denominator, there will be no synergy and the team will fail. Management and the team leader(s) must absolutely know how to structure the team (its infrastructure) in a manner that makes this synergy possible. It all starts with knowing and understanding the team members as individuals who each bring their own skills, motivations, behaviours, energies and foibles to the task.

Use Your Team for Recruitment: A Retention Strategy

Selecting and retaining top notch staff is key for business success. Talented people who continue to develop skills and increase their value to your organization and to your customers are your most important resource. How do you select and retain talented people? How do you create an environment in which talented people continue to grow and contribute?

The primary elements of any plan to improve the quality of the staff you employ include improving the quality of new hires, identifying and retaining superior employees, and developing employees (especially those with high potential for growth). A performance development approach to providing job expectations and feedback will assist with this process.

At the same time, you need to take a hard look at underperforming staff members. Ask whether each individual is in the wrong job. Determine whether you have provided specific and clear requirements so the individual knows what you expect from him. Make sure you have provided feedback against measurable goals and objectives so the person knows he is not meeting expectations. Decide if a performance improvement plan will help the individual contribute within your organization. If you have done your part to create an environment in which an individual can succeed — and the person is not succeeding — let the person go. Your organization will be better off for his absence and the individual will have the opportunity to locate a job in which he can perform.

Part 1: Two Roles for Team Members

How would you like to increase your pool of candidates for selection, add value to your interview process, heighten employee loyalty, build supportive peer relationships, and improve retention rates simultaneously? By implementing a team recruitment strategy, you will achieve all this and more. There are four steps in the team recruitment process: defining manpower needs, finding and enticing quality candidates to respond to those needs, interviewing and selecting the best applicants, and orienting newly selected employees into the business. The most effective team-recruitment approach will include employees at all four stages of the process.

While there are myriad methods of involving employees in the recruitment process, this article highlights the three most commonly used inclusion strategies: employee as agent, employee as contributing evaluator, and employee as sponsor or peer mentor.

❖ Employee as Agent

Establishing a modest recruitment incentive programme will encourage positive public relations and improve employees' perceptions of their relationship with the company. An existing employee adds value to a recruitment campaign for several reasons.

Because employees have an operational understanding of the various roles and responsibilities of the business, they will be more likely to introduce candidates who match position requirements.

- Increasing candidate selection will reduce reliance on external agency services and save time and money.
- Employees will feel valued when a personally recommended candidate is considered.
- Positive public relations will manifest naturally when employees know that they can benefit from attracting others to the business.
- Participation will foster a spirit of contribution to the big picture.

Normally, an employee is offered a modest monetary incentive in comparison to external agency fees. Half of the amount is paid after the contract is signed, and the balance is provided upon successful completion of a probationary period (encouraging peer support even after the initial offer is made.)

❖ Employee as Contributing Evaluator

Inviting employees to participate in the interview process as contributing evaluators augments employee perceptions of value and offers frontline insights regarding candidate suitability and fit within an existing team structure. While employees may or may not participate actively during the interview session, their post-interview comments to the human resources staff and managers can be very helpful in evaluating first round interviewees. This method of inclusion has a wide range of benefits.

- Gives a voice to the departmental members who will ultimately work with the new employee.
- Increases employees' perception of value through inclusion.
- Fosters positive working relationships between managers and reporting staff.
- Serves as a practical training exercise for interviewing skills.
- Supports a spirit of cooperation across organizational levels.
- Provides key, frontline, operational insights regarding a candidate's ability to respond to position requirements.
- Supports ownership and empowerment of departmental activity.

Part 2: The Third Role

❖ Employee as Sponsor or Peer Mentor

There is nothing more unsettling for a new employee than to show up on her first day of work with little knowledge about what she is supposed to do, how she will fit in, or who the key people in her team are. The lack of information and support is a major cause of stress for new employees at every level. While a good orientation process might help to lessen that stress, employee sponsorship (sometimes referred to as a "buddy system") will prevent it from occurring. Employee sponsorship is normally associated with very large organizations. The US Air Force uses a sponsorship programme to help new recruits adapt to both their new position and community. The same approach can, and should be used for small and medium sized private companies and organizations. A sponsorship programme benefits both sponsor and new employee in many ways.

- Initial perceptions of new employees are improved — taken care of from prior to day one.
- Sponsor feels valued as a contributing member of the organization.
- Sponsor is periodically reminded of company policies, goals, mission and vision.
- Peer relationships based on team support are fostered.
- Communication skills of employees are exercised and improved.
- A sense of community is created and nurtured.
- New employees understand the big picture and how they fit in prior to their first day.

A basic sponsorship programme includes a letter and information packet sent from the sponsor to the new employee's home address *prior* to the first work day. The package might include information relating to the history of the company; key biographies and roles and organizational chart; position descriptions and how they support business goals; welcome letters from relevant managers (including the president); administrative comments and policies; social opportunities described; benefits summary; and area information (maps, Internet sites, restaurants, clubs, attractions, etc.) The sponsor personalizes the package with a cover letter providing contact information, key dates and times for personnel processing and induction, and general comments.

Sponsors are usually selected from the new employee's peer group. For example, a new graphic artist would be assigned a fellow graphic artist as a sponsor. A different sponsor should be selected for each new recruit, until everyone in the department has had a chance to sponsor. This should be done at every level of the organization. While most of the information in the sponsorship package is canned, it should be personalized to the greatest extent possible for each new employee.

The introduction of the "buddy," prior to the new employee starting work, will help the new employee feel welcome. The sponsor provides a focal point for the new employee to get help and information. The sponsor provides an early notification system for potential problems and lost opportunities to integrate the new employee effectively.

❖ Summary

By incorporating these three team-approach recruitment methods, retention efforts will be simultaneously strengthened through improved perceptions of new recruits and active participation of existing employees. Fostering a sense of community by inclusion will make recruiting and retention efforts more effective.

IMPROVING YOUR STAFF'S SELF-CONFIDENCE

One of a manager's most important responsibilities is increasing subordinates' self-confidence; employees then have a more optimistic but realistic view of their skills and talents.

Increasing self-confidence offers more than psychic rewards. If employees feel good about themselves, chances are you will notice that productivity and morale both improve. Why? First, self-confident people are decisive rather than tentative. They can focus on their work responsibilities instead of worrying about the reactions of others, and they are optimistic about reaching their objectives.

Second, self-confident people are risk-takers, and taking risks is crucial in technical organizations. These people are expressive; they forge ahead instead of waiting for someone else to show the way. People who lack self-confidence, on the other hard, tend to play "catch up", rather than focus on progress.

Third, people who feel good about themselves are likely to increase the self-confidence of those around them. Self-confident people are respected by colleagues and management, and they return that respect.

One note of caution here: I'm not talking about over-confidence. People must accurately perceive their abilities so they will accept tasks that are appropriate to their skills. Managers play an important role in working with researchers, to assign tasks so individuals can determine for themselves which challenges they can handle.

Once we decide that improving self-confidence among the staff is a vital responsibility for a manager, how do we go about it? By accepting, praising, appreciating, encouraging, and reassuring. Let's examine these actions.

Accepting

Accept your employees for who they are, not just for what they do. People who feel valued, rather than feeling constantly scrutinized, will be more secure. And since secure people are less threatened by mistakes, security fosters innovation. (By 'mistakes,' I'm excluding life or corporate-threatening errors, which clearly require drastic measures.) Secure employees develop a realistic form of self-confidence, since they are more likely to recognize their deficiencies and admit them to others.

How do we translate this accepting attitude into action? When you see something you don't like, you may need to stifle the urge to say, "Do it my way." Instead, both parties may benefit if you let the person continue and learn. Don't rule out the possibility that you may also learn something—many chiefs' ideas have been proven wrong by curious, intelligent, and secure subordinates.

It's difficult to maintain an accepting attitude in the midst of others' mistakes, but it will make you a better manager.

Praising

Good managers take the time to listen to their employees, and are concerned about employees' self-esteem. Although we all know how good it feels to be praised, many managers are too insensitive, too busy, or too concerned with their own egos to praise subordinates.

Here are some guidelines:

- Praise must be deserved, otherwise it will be counterproductive (or scorned).
- A spontaneous comment is the most genuine form of praise.
- Never suppress the urge to praise.
- Comments should be specific, so the recipient knows exactly what is being praised.
- Expand a specific comment into general praise: "That memo was especially persuasive; you definitely have a way with words."

You can praise people by recognizing them as individuals or members of a group. There are many options here. For example, sponsor dinners, give out plaques, allow trips to represent the company, or send a formal letter detailing what the employee has done so well.

Usually, the problem is not an inability to find the proper reward vehicle, but rather the manager's reluctance to praise.

Appreciating

Appreciation is akin to praise, but while praise acknowledges that the employee has excelled at some skill or task, appreciation explains what the employee's effort has done for an individual, team or company.

To appreciate, show your staff how their accomplishments have benefited you (as well as the company), and make it clear that you appreciate their efforts. (If you really have trouble appreciating your subordinates, ask yourself whether you can meet your career objectives without them).

While the value of praise is determined by whether the recipient feels it's deserved, the value of appreciation is largely determined by the giver. Managers should show appreciation when it's due. This is the right way to treat people; otherwise, managing becomes manipulating.

Show appreciation through personal comments and notes, but make it sincere: "I just found out that I've been promoted. It was partly due to your great work. Thanks!" You will also find that appreciation will be reciprocated, resulting in a far more pleasant and productive work environment. Among the most rewarding events for a manager is receiving a note of thanks from a subordinate.

Encouraging

When does an employee most need encouraging? After a mistake. This is when you can help the employee admit errors and learn from them: One word of encouragement during a failure is worth a whole book of praise after a success.

It's important to appreciate that the greatest threat to self-confidence is criticism even a single remark. Although some believe 'constructive' criticism improves performance and fosters personal growth, criticism is almost always destructive. Regression, not growth, is the most likely consequence of criticism.

Self-criticism, the only kind you should encourage among subordinates and yourself, is the exception in most work environments.

Secure and self-confident group members, who see each other as friends, are more likely to self-criticize. Almost paradoxically, external criticism tends to stifle self-criticism by threatening morale and status.

If the manager frequently finds fault, then group members will become defensive and lose self-esteem. What is needed is less managerial criticism coupled with increased managerial praise and encouragement.

Reassuring

Reassuring is defined as "restoring to assurance or confidence." (Reassuring is directed to someone who generally feels inadequate, while encouraging is a response to something specific, like a mistake.)

Studies have shown that more than two-thirds of business executives have feelings of personal inadequacy and doubt. I'm sure it's not only top management, but also researchers, who need reassurance.

People like to be praised for what they do well, but they need reassurance in areas where they are less confident. Let them know they're making progress in overcoming a deficiency, that their problem is trivial, or that no one is perfect.

James Newton, in *Uncommon Friends,* gives a perfect example of the place and power of reassurance: "When Thomas Edison was improving his first light bulb, he handed a finished bulb to a young helper, who nervously carried it upstairs, step by step. At the last moment, the boy dropped it. The whole team had to work another 24 hours to make another bulb. Edison looked around, then handed it to the same boy. The gesture probably changed the boy's life. Edison knew that more than the bulb was at stake."

The more important a person is to us, the more we need signals from him or her that our relationship is healthy and productive. Therefore, managers must frequently reassure, particularly in R&D, where the disappointments commonly outnumber the successes.

There is a danger: if you overdo reassurance, the beneficiary might feel patronized. Reassurance is best done empathetically when you try to see things from the other's point of view and identify with those feelings: "I know things look pretty dismal now. That's the way I felt just before I finally solved that sticky production problem."

On the most productive teams, leaders and subordinates have a realistic self-confidence. Researchers' self-confidence can easily be increased or decreased, and it's up to you as a manager to sustain it. The entire team will find their jobs more enjoyable and you'll be ready to tackle the toughest problems.

Tips for Interview-based Evaluation

Put the interviewee at ease

- Ensure privacy and congenial atmosphere
- Opening comments should be friendly
- Avoid irrelevant small talk on weather and news—it tends to be artificial.

Explain how the interviewee and the organization can benefit from an open interview

- Mention that the interview is a two-way decision. The applicant must decide if the job is to his liking as much as the interviewer must assess the suitability of the applicant. This can achieved only through openness and trust which is mutually beneficial.

Explain areas that will be covered in during the job interview

- Tell the applicant the areas that you will cover during the interview, job history, education current life etc.
- Explain that he will be allowed to ask questions during or at the end of the interview, as the case may be.
- Put applicant at ease by indicating what to expect.

Ask questions that elicit answers to the job constructs in each area

- Refer to the questions on constructs you have structured.
- Apply construct questions.
- Avoid asking questions routinely.
- Display interest in the answers

Describe the job and the organization

- Describe the job description.
- Discuss company history.
- Discuss development opportunities
- Discuss methods of performance appraisal.
- Discuss salary and benefits.

Ask the interviewee if there are any questions

- Answer openly and truthfully any questions.

Close interview

- Summarize conversation.
- Inform applicant of next stage, i.e. phone call or letter.
- Thank applicant for coming.

Job Interview Questioning Techniques

The way you approach and open the interview is important to its overall success. The types of questions you ask and the way you ask them are of prime importance. There are two types of questions.

- Directive
- Non-directive

Both can be used effectively in the interview to gain the information you require from the job applicant.

Directive Questions

A directive question leads the applicant onto making a specific response by limiting him to a choice of a yes or no answer.

- "Do you prefer early morning or late afternoon schedules?"
- "Did you hear about us through an employment agency?"

Directive questions can often be effective in gaining precise answers or exact information, but, because they limit the applicant to a choice or yes or no answer, they often discourage free response and result in very little information. Questions that provide for little information are generally those that can be answered in one or two words. A definite answer will be offered, but the applicant probably will volunteer any additional information.

Also, the applicant may give the answer he thinks you are looking for, Poorly phrased questions may actually give away the answer. Giveaway questions are those which tell the applicant the answer the interviewer thinks he should give.

Non-directive Questions

Non directional questions allow the applicant to respond freely without being forced to make a choice or respond with a yes or no answer.

- "What type of work schedule do you prefer?"
- "How did you happen to hear about our company?"

They may be used to direct the conversation to an area of the interviewer's interest, but do not control the applicants response. The applicant is free to express his thoughts without being forced to make a choice, or respond with a yes or no. Non-directive questions are prefixed by the following:

- how
- why
- what
- when
- where

The Employee Evaluation Interview Situation

Do

- Have as much privacy as possible
- Call applicant by name when calling him into the office
- Ensure the applicant knows your name

- Greet applicant courteously and sincerely
- Make the applicant feel that you are pleased with his interest in the position
- Establish an informal but business like atmosphere
- Make the applicant feel important
- Talk to the applicant as though you were the only contact he would ever have with the company
- Compliment a good employment record
- Interrupt the conversation to keep interview on track
- Use active listening
- Relax and the applicant will relax
- Keep information given, confidential
- Remember the applicant's time is valuable
- Investigate applicant's work record/performance thoroughly
- Watch for gaps in work record
- Check job records and references
- Use application blanks and other data in planning the interview
- Make an outline in advance, of the main items of information you want to obtain during the interview
- Plan the time required for the interview.

Don't

- Interview when worried, upset, ill or under stress
- Hold an interview in a noisy place
- Keep applicants waiting unnecessarily
- Give the impression of being abrupt or harsh
- Allow outside interruptions
- Seek information you already have
- Antagonize the applicant
- Show emotion at any physical handicap
- Hurt the applicant's feelings or destroy his faith in himself

- Forget applicant is sensitive to every word the interviewer speaks
- Appear to lose interest in the interview
- Dominate the interview
- Pry into personal lives
- Break or delay an appointment
- Fall into a set pattern of interviewing
- Waste time on a long interview if the applicant is clearly not suitable
- Conduct the interview in a haphazard manner.

Opening the Evaluation Process

Do

- Open the interview with handshake and clear introduction
- Smile and be pleasant
- Open the interview with some topic of common interest
- Create an atmosphere in which the applicant feels confident and at ease.

Don't

- Flounder for a cue when opening the conversation
- Appear ill at ease
- Give an impression of being harried or brusque.

Obtaining information and assisting the employee/ applicant

Do

- Give the interviewee time to think
- Give the interviewee time to answer one question before asking another
- Stimulate interviewee to do most of the talking
- Encourage interviewee to talk about his work experiences
- Try to bring out attitudes, experience capacities and opinions
- Elicit facts about abilities, interests, health and motivation
- Use simple why, what, where and how questions.

Don't

- Make the interviewee speak up to you
- Use trick questions
- Cross-examine
- Crowd interviewee for answers
- Ask 'yes' or 'no' questions unless necessary
- Phrase questions to indicate desired answers
- Let interview wander.

Giving the Interviewee Information

Do

- Know and give information on job requirements
- Talk about your division, products and services
- Answer all questions
- Talk in lay terms
- Provide sufficient information in order for the applicant to give a considered decision
- Explain opportunities for advancement.

Don't

- Oversell the job
- Talk too much
- Sell the job to the applicant
- Use jargon
- Knowingly misrepresent the facts
- Offer unsolicited advice
- Tell the applicant your troubles or your successes
- Commit yourself as to religion, politics or other beliefs
- Encourage unsuitable applicants to fit into the organization.

Observing the Interviewee

Do

- Carefully note appearance, attitude, impressions, ability, knowledge
- Watch every action, word and pause with respect to the position
- Watch voice inflection, facial expression, posture, gestures, eyes and general behaviour to supplement the spoken word
- Appraise temperament and qualifications in terms of success on the job
- Be thorough in your explanation of the duties of the job, then ask the applicant if he is interested and capable. Watch the reaction.

Don't

- Hire applicants for jobs where their limitations would not suit
- Make the applicant self conscious by being too intent in observation
- Be ostentatious in recording observations or information obtained.

Evaluating the Interviewee

Do

- Keep the job in mind during the interview
- Keep the applicants future potential in mind
- Be objective
- Remember, it is better to make a mistake and not hire a good applicant than to be in doubt and hire a bad one
- Have a reliable grading system and grade the applicant
- Look at yourself — are you a credit to your company?

Don't

- Hire merely because there is not a suitable applicant
- Buy a hard luck story
- Be influenced to overlook an applicants shortcomings
- Make decision until you have grounds
- Hire applicants whose past work history lacks creditability

- Commit yourself to employ the applicant until you have covered every phase in the applicant's background
- Accept previous experience as an absolute guarantee of ability.

Closing the Interview

Do

- Close the interview in a friendly constructive manner
- Ask the applicant if he has any further questions

Don't

- Fail to tell the applicant if you plan to hire someone else
- Offer excuses or put blame for not hiring upon another department or individual.

CHAPTER

16

TEAM BUILDING TOOL KIT

LEARNING OBJECTIVES

- To make available ready to use Team Building Tools.
- To provide tips on application of Team Building Tools.

TRUST ME, I AM A TEAM WORKER

Team-building through trust building is a major agenda for organisations today. Much of our intellectual and scientific research as well as the ethical norms of our human behaviour are governed by trust, though it does not come naturally. One must want and work for it.

As trust grows, the barriers that prevent candour and openness relax. People become more expressive, impulsive, frank and spontaneous. They even begin to risk conflict and confrontation for deeper communication, involvement and commitment. Decision making becomes easier. These principles hold as true for work teams as for other interpersonal relationships.

To gauge your trust orientation profile take the following quiz. Each pair of statements in the quiz represents one particular characteristic of trust, which is listed in the scoring key with regard to the characteristic of Trust/Mistrust. Interpret your scores and set your positive or negative trust profile, accordingly.

Scoring Procedure

For each statement of the quiz given below, distribute five points between the two alternatives (A and B). Base your answers on how you actually behave or feel or how you actually perceive the situation, not on how you think you should respond. Although some sets of alternatives might seem to be equally true, assign more points to the alternative that is more representative of your personal experience.

1. If A is completely characteristic of you or your views and B is completely uncharacteristic, then write 5 under A and 0 under B.
2. If A is considerably characteristic of you and B is somewhat characteristic, write 4 under A and 1 under B.
3. If A is only slightly more characteristic of you than B, write 3 under A and 2 under B.
4. Each of the above three combinations may be reserved. If you feel that B is slightly more characteristic of you than A, write 2 under A and 3 under B, and so on for A=1 and B=4; or A=0 and B=5.
5. Be sure the numbers you assign to each pair add up to 5.

The Quiz

1. (a) My co-workers have all the knowledge and experience they need to do their jobs effectively.

   (b) My co-workers seem to lack the knowledge and/or experience they need to do their jobs effectively.
2. (a) I cannot predict how my co-workers will respond in a given situation.

   (b) I can predict how my co-workers will respond in a given situation.
3. (a) I share my honest thoughts and feelings with my co-workers.

   (b) I keep honest thoughts and feelings with my co-workers.
4. (a) I trust my co-workers; I believe they won't let me down.

   (b) I "play it safe" and trust only myself; this way no one else can let me down.
5. (a) I encourage my co-workers to comment on their thoughts and feelings.

   (b) I would prefer not to hear my co-workers expressions of their thoughts and feelings.

6. (a) When I am in a bind, I know I can depend on my co-workers to bail me out.

   (b) When I am in a bind, I have to rely exclusively on myself.

7. (a) My abilities are superior to those of my co-workers.

   (b) My co-workers and I are all at the same level of competence.

8. (a) My co-workers and I cooperate with one another.

   (b) My co-workers and I compete with one another.

9. (a) My co-workers behave as if they think they are better than I am.

   (b) My co-workers treat me as an equal.

10. (a) I can count on my co-workers to meet the deadlines and performance standards defined for their work

    (b) I cannot count on my co-workers to meet the deadlines and performance standards defined for their work.

11. (a) When faced with a problem, I figure out the best solution and present the idea to my co-workers.

    (b) When faced with a problem, I collaborate with my co-workers to define the problem, explore alternatives and arrive at a solution.

12. (a) My team is warm, accepting and free of hostility.

    (b) There is hostility in my team.

13. (a) I wonder if my co-workers appreciate my work; I sometimes think they question the value of my contributions.

    (b) I know that my co-workers are concerned about my well being; they "play fairly" and respect my unique contributions.

14. (a) I prefer my own solutions to problems.

    (b) I am willing to accept solutions proposed by my co-workers.

15. (a) No matter what I share with my team members, they are not judgmental.

    (b) I am careful about what I share with my team members because they may judge me harshly.

16. (a) The term 'commitment' doesn't seem to mean much to my co-workers.

    (b) I can depend on my co-workers to follow through on their commitments.

TABLE 16.1 Take a breath and get set to analyse yourself

Key to scoring of statements with regard to characteristics of Trust/ Mistrust			
No.	**Characteristic**	**Trust**	**Mistrust**
1.	Expert vs. Inept	A	B
2.	Dependable vs. Capricious	B	A
3.	Open vs. Closed	A	B
4.	Willingness to take risk vs. Unwillingness to take risk	A	B
5.	Cooperative vs. Competitive	A	B
6.	Mutual vs. Superior	B	A
7.	Accountable vs. Unaccountable	B	A
8.	Open-minded about problems vs. Fixated on predetermined solutions	A	A
9.	Respectful vs. Disrespectful	B	A
10.	Genuine vs. Hypocritical	B	A

Interpretation

Transfer your scores from the scoring table to the lines that follow in order to compute your trust-orientation score.

Total trust score = +

Total mistrust score = –

Trust orientation =

Plot your trust orientation score on the continuum that follows:

– 40<	–	+ 10	–
– 30	–	+ 20	–
– 20	–	+ 30	–
– 10	–	+ 40>	–
0	–		
Mistrust		Trust	

The various dimensions described in the scoring table regarding trust/mistrust-building attitudes hold true in relationships between two people and among members in a group.

In case you get a negative profile and are in a need to foster more trust building attitudes, you have to take certain remedial steps. Remember that trust has to be nurtured and maintained if you wish to enjoy your interpersonal relationships and attain your objectives. Trust building takes hard work, time and energy; it also involves risk. For trust to grow deeper each person needs to be a person worthy of trust and must continue to earn the right to be trusted. Team work has to be fostered.

Solutions increasingly will come as a result of collaborative action of groups of individual who have multiple motives but can focus on a single objective.

Team unity through trust building should thus became a major agenda for organisations all over if they want to foster growth round the clock.

TEAM EFFECTIVENESS CHECKLIST

How Efficient are your Workplace Teams?

Use the below evaluation to determine the effectiveness of your team. Score from 1 (hardly at all) to 5 (greatly).

1. Teams need to be organized around horizontal processes that include different disciplines, functions, or skills.
(a) To what extent is there one key process that provides the focus for our team?
(b) To what extend does our team represent all of the functions or disciplines that contribute to this process?
(c) To what extent is our team composed of the skills needed to maintain and improve this process?
(d) To what extent does our team have the ability to add or delete competencies?

2. Teams need to have a shared view of what is to be accomplished, a goal toward which all team members contribute.
(b) To what extent is there a specific goal (or goals) that our team needs to accomplish?
(c) To what extent do our goals align with and contribute to the overall business goals and objectives?
(d) To what extent are our team goals clear and defined in simple terms, so that all team members understand what the team is trying to do?
(e) To what extent are our team goals shared among all users of the team's output?

3. Teams need to have agreed-upon ways of working that cut across boundaries.
(a) To what extent has our team defined how it will solve problems, make decisions, and handle conflict in the team?

Contd...

(b)	To what extent does our team have a process for dealing with poor performance or discipline issues within the team?
(c)	To what extent does our team dedicate time to assessing team members' abilities to work as a team?
(d)	To what extent is our team clear about roles, about who does what to accomplish team goals?
(e)	To what extent do all members of our team feel empowered to voice their opinions so that the team makes better and more informed decisions than individuals acting alone?

4.	**Teams need shared measures of success and ways of rewarding achievement.**
(a)	To what extent are our team's goals measurable and operational?
(b)	To what extent do all members of our team feel personal responsibility for team results?
(c)	To what extent do team members share in the rewards earned by our team?

❖ Scoring

> 65

Your team is most likely a true team and is functioning reasonably well. You might want to focus on the few key scores that were lowest or the category that received the lowest scores, and do some fine tuning.

45-65

There are probably some significant weaknesses in the way your team is functioning. Look to see if the weaknesses are across the board or if there are targeted categories that need immediate attention.

< 45

Your score was fairly low; you should examine whether your team is really a team and whether team members understand what it means to be a team.

EMPLOYEE SURVEY QUESTIONNAIRE SAMPLE

Why an Employee Survey?

By being proactive, asking your employees' opinions and hearing what they have to say, you will improve your potential for bottom-line success through expanded knowledge of your employees' attitudes that can drive how you execute your strategic initiatives. Whether initiated by line management or human resources, the information gleaned from an Employee Survey can help you set a course for improved profitability and success.

_______ current activities reflect a strong focus on the customer.

_______ does a good job communicating about changes or decisions that affect employees.

_______ is a good company to work for.

_______ is committed to providing competitive products and services.

_______' image is that of a high quality company.

_______'s standards for business ethics are high.

At _______, my suggestions are given serious consideration.

Being committed to excellence through continuous improvement in all activities to increase value for our customers.

Being the catalyst of change and innovation at the forefront of the industry.

Benefits available are appropriate for my needs and those of my family.

Career paths exist for someone like me in this company.

Conditions in my work area allow me to be highly productive.

Considering everything, I am satisfied at _______ .

From my point of view the five most important issues raised in this survey are:

Having a clear corporate 'culture' (a clear set of values, a clear style of management, etc.)

Having a minimum of "corporate politics" (favouritism in handling conflict, advancement based on "looking good," etc.)

How long have you worked for _______?

How long have you worked for the company?

I am able to balance work priorities with my personal life.

I am able to contact senior management as needed.

I am adequately recognized for my good work.

I am aware of available training and development activities.

I am committed to producing the highest quality work for our customers/ members.

I am compensated fairly for the work I do.

I am expected to find new and better ways to get the job done.

I am given a real opportunity to improve my skills in this company.

I am given the training I need to do my job effectively.

I am happy to encourage friends and colleagues to work at _______ .

I am involved in decisions that affect my work.

I am made to feel that I am an important part of _______.

I am proud to work for _______.

I am provided with opportunities to improve my skills.

I am recognized by my manager for my contributions.

I am satisfied with the increases in compensation.

I am satisfied with the information I receive from management on what's going on in the company.

I am treated fairly by my supervisor.

I believe _______ will use this survey's feedback to make improvements.

I believe real changes can be made in my Department/Function as a result of this survey.

I believe that the HR department heeds my opinion with regard to Work and Family benefit needs.

I believe that the IT department asks my opinion with regard to technology needs.

I can clearly explain the business goals of my local business unit to others.

I can get the information I need to do my job.

I can see the link between my work and _______ objectives.

I feel encouraged to come up with new and better ways of doing things.

I feel favoritism is not a problem in my department.

I feel I have job security.

I feel the company values honest answers.

I feel the company's benefits meet my needs.

I find my work challenging.

I get the training I need to do a first-class job.

I have a clear understanding of _______ pay policy.

I have all the information I need to do my job well.

I have clear measures for each of my objectives.

I have enough information to do my job well.

I have participated in a Performance Management Process.

I have seen improvements as a result of the ____ action plans that were created.

I have the flexibility to arrange my work schedule to meet my personal/family responsibilities.

I have the freedom I need to meet customer needs.

I have the materials and equipment I need to do my work right.

I have the materials and equipment to do my job right.

I have the necessary resources to perform my job.

I have the training and support to do my job right.

I know how my job impacts the mission of _______.

I know what is expected of me in my job.

I participate in training and development opportunities that are available to me.

I plan to be working for _______ a year from now.

I support the _______ values in my day-to-day actions.

I understand the criteria used to decide my compensation.

I understand the issues facing our customers/members.

I would share the costs of an improved benefits plan.

In general, career moves are handled fairly at _______.

In my department/function, decisions get made without unreasonable delay In my department/function, projects are managed well (from initiation and planning to execution and close-out).

In my job, I focus on problem solving instead of fault finding.

In my work group, we ask our internal customers what they require from us.

In my work group, we participate in deciding how the work gets done.

In the last 12 months, my manager has talked to me about my progress Job promotions are fair and equitable.

Managers communicate a clear sense of direction for my organisation.

My co-workers and I work well together to accomplish our organization's goals.

My department works well together to accomplish our organization's goals.

My fellow employees are committed to doing quality work.

My group works well together to accomplish our organization's goals.

My job is enjoyable and challenging.

My job makes good use of my skills and abilities.

My manager assists me to identify my training and development needs.

My manager delegates work effectively.

My manager encourages my professional development.

My manager gets input and buy-in from me when making key decisions that impact my section.

My manager has enough authority to get the work done.

My manager has set performance goals for my job.

My manager holds me accountable for the work that I do.

My manager is available to me when I have questions or need help.

My manager is effective in involving his/her employees in solving the problems we face as a unit.

My manager is fair and even handed in the treatment of all employees.

My manager keeps me in the loop so that I know what is happening in the organization that impacts my work.

My manager role models effective leadership (i.e., behaviour that is ethical, moral, consistent, positive, just).

My manager role models high standards for quality work.

My manager sets a good example.

My skills and abilities are utilized effectively by the company.

My supervisor provides me with adequate feedback.

My training meets my needs for my current job.

My work gives me a feeling of personal accomplishment.

My work group focuses on fixing the problem rather than finding someone to blame.

My workgroup looks for ways to change processes to improve productivity.

Our department staff meetings are filled with open and honest participation.

Our organization has clearly identified the customers/members who receive our work.

Our senior leaders establish a clear direction for the company.

Our team's current activities reflect a strong focus on the customer.

Overall, I feel the organization is successful.

Overall, my workload is reasonable.

People get ahead as fast here as they do in other places.

Please comment on any other issue you would like to raise.

Rate your overall satisfaction with your job at _______.

Senior management gives staff a clear picture of the direction in which _______ is headed.

Technology available is appropriate for my needs and those of my customer.

The amount of pay you receive for your job compared to others doing similar work in our industry.

The extent to which you are kept informed about matters that affect you.

The extent to which you receive recognition when you do a good job.

The freedom you have to use your own judgment in getting the job done.

The information from this year's survey will be used constructively by management.

The internal practices of _______ support my ability to deliver a high standard of quality to my customers.

The last time I asked someone from a different function for help, I got it.

The organization values diversity.

The people I work with cooperate to get the work done.

The senior administration cares about my ideas.

The tools and equipment I need to do my job right are readily available.

There are opportunities for promotion in my role.

There is cooperation among team members.

There is someone at work who encourages my development.

Timely follow up on questions for benefits, employee relations issues.

We have a plan to implement the organization's work.

We have a set of values and beliefs that guide our decisions about work.

We have prioritized our major goals.

We know who is responsible for what, who needs to be informed, and who, if anyone, has veto power.

We resolve conflict honestly, effectively and quickly.

What is lacking in your work environment that might help you perform better?

What is your level in the organization?

What would make our organization more effective?

Understand your own Conflict Management Style

Instructions

Imagine that you are in situations where you do not agree with another person and try to respond to the following with that orientation.

Below, you will find several pairs of statements describing possible behavioural responses to situations. For each pair, circle the 'a' or the 'b' statement which is most characteristic of your own behaviour. In some cases, neither the 'a' nor the 'b' statement would be representative of you behaviour, even so, try to select that which comes closest to what you may be likely to do.

The responses which you circle will offer you a good understanding of your conflict handling style.

1.	A	I frequently decide that I should not bother about the differences in our view points.
	B	I try to get my way.
2.	A B	I try not to hurt the others feeling so that our relationship can be maintained I do all that is necessary to avoid tensions.

Contd...

3.	A B	I get all the issues out in the open and discuss them I try to postpone issues till I have the time to think
4.	A B	I try to seek a solution which is neither totally what I want nor what the other person wants I try to assert my viewpoint
5.	A B	Many times i let the other person take on the responsibility of solving problem situation Instead of trying to negotiate the things on which i might disagree with another, I usually emphasis the aspects on which we both agree
6	A B	I am very goal oriented and pursue my own goals I try to patch up so that our friendship is not spoilt
7.	A B	I establish a middle ground I do not think that I should worry about the differences
8.	A B	I take a middle ground I insist on my points being heard
9.	A B	I firmly pursue my goals I try to avoid friction
10	A B	I usually try to find solution which is more compromising in nature I usually try to handle all of the other party's as well as My own concerns
11	A B	I try not to handle controversial issues If it makes him happy, I let him have his way
12	A B	I try not to create unpleasantness for myself I try to win my own position
13	A B	I try to be logical and show him the advantages of my position I try to be sensitive to his wishes
14	A B	To make the other person happy, I let him have his say I will give in some, if he will give in some
15	A B	I start working through the differences immediately I try to see what is fair for both
16	A B	I try to deal with both persons, wishes I let him solve the problem
17	A B	I usually search for compromise solution I usually let go of my own wishes so that the other persons, needs are taken care of
18	A B	I try to establish a middle ground I try to satisfy both our wishes
19	A B	I firmly stick to my point of view I work out a solution with the other person
20	A B	If the matter is that important to him, I let him have his way I insist on a compromise

Contd...

21	A B	I usually get every ones concerns out in the open I usually try to give in and preserve our friendship
22.	A B	While negotiating, I consider other's feelings I deal with the issue directly, placing all the cards on the table
23	A B	I feel strongly about pursuing my goals I feel compromise solutions work best
24	A B	I take time to think over the issue before starting to discuss it I give in some to gain some
25	A B	I would rather not hurt the other's feelings I jointly work out the problem with the other person
26	A B	I try not to hurt the other's feelings I convince the other of the logic of my statement
27	A B	I express my ideas and ask for his I try to convince him of the benefits of my ideas
28	A B	I firmly pursue my goals I try to get all the issues out on the table.
29	A B	I generally avoid controversial situations I pursue a policy of give and take
30	A B	I invariably work with the other person's help to come up with a solution I try my best to do whatever is necessary to avoid tensions

Score Sheet

S. No.	Competing	Collaborating	Compromising	Avoiding	Accommodating
1	B			A	
2				B	A
3		A		B	
4	B		A		
5				A	B
6	A				B
7			A	B	
8	B		A		
9	A			B	
10		B	A		
11				A	B
12	A			B	

Contd...

	Competing	Collaborating	Compromising	Avoiding	Accommodating
13	A				B
14			B		A
15		A	B		
16		A		B	
17			A		B
18		B	A		
19	A	B			
20			B		A
21		A			B
22		B			A
23	A		B		
24			B	A	
25		B			A
26	B				A
27	B	A			
28	A	B			
29			B	A	
30		A		B	
Total					
	Competing	**Collaborating**	**Compromising**	**Avoiding**	**Accommodating**

FOCUSED TEAM BUILDING ACTIVITIES

Team Activity No. 1

❖ Searching for Common Causes and Effects of poor Time Utilization

Here is a checklist of common causes of waste in organizations based around time wasters. These are prime targets when seeking to improve productivity. The old adage, "time is money" is no more true than in business. Apply your team members job knowledge, together with this checklist to identify areas for improvement.

TIP: Measure the before and aftereffects wherever possible. That is, you should attempt to quantify each cause of waste time you attack, in terms of money, time and material. This way you can objectively assess the difference you have made.

❖ Waste of Time

- Lack of proper planning, keeping workers waiting between jobs or waiting for material
- Failure on the supervisor's part to thoroughly understand orders and instructions received
- Lack of knowledge of what constitutes a full day's work
- Failure to make orders and instructions clear to workers
- Failure to insist that tools supplies, and portable equipment be kept in proper places
- Ordering overtime work that could be avoided
- Not seeing that workers are supplied with proper tools and equipment for every job
- Allowing workers intentionally to do less work than they can
- Failure to inform human resources department when more labour is required
- Keeping too many workers
- Failure to write records and requisitions intelligibly
- Failure to question and correct workers who lay off
- Allowing workers to get habit of talking, visiting, killing time
- Failure to get workers to start on time, slack supervision
- Delay in making decisions
- Unnecessary absenteeism or tardiness on the supervisor's part
- Being late with reports
- Not investigating immediately when repairs are needed
- Unnecessary visiting and conversation on the job
- Failure on the supervisors's part to organize his/her time and work
- Lack of proper planning, keeping workers waiting between jobs or waiting for material

Team Building Activity No. 2

❖ Not being Alert to or Ignoring new Ideas

The list below are symptomatic of lost productivity through ignoring new ideas and thinking. Have your team members apply their job knowledge, and experience together with this checklist to determine if this has happened in the past. How can new ideas in the future be fully evaluated?

Build this checklist into your team, building activities to make an improvement to productivity, and therefore job security, in your organization. Stress that it is everyone's interest to be alert to new thinking and where appropriate, install such thinking into processes and methods. Be alert to questions along the lines of 'What's in it for us?' Would fair and equitable financial reward be in order?

TIP: Measure the before and aftereffects wherever possible. That is, you should attempt to quantify each cause of waste you attack, in terms of money, time and material. This way you can objectively assess the difference you have made.

❖ Waste of Potentially Good Ideas

- Failure to listen and comment when workers offer suggestions.
- Failure to encourage workers to offer suggestions.
- Not asking workers advice on problems.
- Failure to read and study about the work and about business methods.
- Failure to get from new employees helpful ideas which they may bring from previous employment.
- Not consulting enough with other departments, such as engineering, etc.
- Failure to consider or refer to the proper person all usable suggestions no matter where they come from.
- Failure to take proper interest in meetings.
- Failure to benchmark performance of organization with other similar organizations and the sector as a whole.

Team Activity No. 3

❖ Searching for Improvements in Process Methods and Material Supplies Wastage

The checklist below lists some common causes of waste in organizations relating to the business process methods and materials used therein. Apply your team members job knowledge and experience, together with this checklist to improve problems highlighted during team meetings. Build this checklist into your team building activities to make an improvement to productivity, and therefore job security, in your organization.

TIP: Measure the before and after effect wherever possible. That is, you should attempt to quantify each cause of waste you attack, in terms of money, time and material. This way you can objectively assess the difference you have made.

❖ Waste of Methods and Supplies

- Failure to explain money value of materials and supplies to employees
- Inadequate supervision resulting in spoilage of material
- New employees not instructed properly
- Employees not instructed on new work
- Procedures, blueprints, sketches, diagrams, etc. torn or illegible
- Machines out of order or not adjusted or out of date
- Failure to follow each job through
- Failure to give clear instructions and orders
- Permitting improper or rough handling of material and supplies.
- Not paying attention to workers' eyesight and health as possible cause of spoiled work
- Lack of discipline among workers, thereby encouraging carelessness and sub standard work
- Allowing employees to use supplies unsuited to work; too good or not good enough
- Inability to trace defective work to the person who did it so that it can be corrected
- Taking employees ability for granted; not making sure employees are qualified for the work they are doing, especially new ones
- Not knowing the right kind of supplies to order
- Ordering more materials and supplies than necessary and not returning excess stock
- Failure to see materials are stored appropriately
- Failure to investigate all bare wires, leaky valves, pipes, fittings on steam, water, gas, electric, and compressed air lines, etc.
- Allowing workers to use oil, compressed air, small tools, chemicals, etc. for personal use

- Letting defective material go through as standard
- Lack of system to control outgoing supplies to prevent loss/theft
- Scrapping material that could be salvaged
- Permitting the waste or abuse of such supplies as brooms, stationary, oilers, light bulbs, shovels, rubber hose etc.

Team Activity No. 4

❖ Searching for Improvements in Equipment/Machinery Utilization and Efficiency

Here is a checklist of common causes of waste in organizations based around common causes of excessive cost relating to methods and supplies. Apply your job knowledge, together with this checklist to make a difference over time. Build this checklist into your team building activities to make an improvement to productivity, and therefore job security, in your organization.

TIP: Measure the before and aftereffects wherever possible. That is, you should attempt to quantify each cause of waste you attack, in terms of money, time and material. This way you can objectively assess the difference you have made.

❖ Causes of Poor Equipment/Machinery Utilization and or Efficiency

- Failure to plan work so that effective and efficient utilization is made of all available machinery
- Failure to inspect machinery to keep it in good condition and to prevent breakdown
- Foreman's lack of knowledge on possible use and capacity of machines
- Failure to make regular examination of wire ropes, belts, chain drives, gear drives, conveyors, lubrication systems, valves etc.
- Using unnecessary large and powerful machine for small work
- Lack of cooperation with maintenance department; upkeep, repairs, painting etc.
- Not protecting idle machinery from weather, dust, dirt, rust, fumes etc.
- Allowing machinery to stay dirty through lack of periodic cleaning
- Failure to inspect for proper lubrication of all moving parts
- Failure to make needed repairs promptly

- Lack of instruction to employees on the proper operation of machinery
- Lack of proper discipline to prevent abuse of machinery and equipment
- Allowing employees to make 'shoestring' repairs
- Failure by the foreman to keep informed on the latest technology
- Failure to pay attention to workers opinions on value and condition of machinery.
- Abusing small machines on large work
- Repairing machinery that should be scrapped; may cost more than replacing.

Team Activity No. 5

❖ Searching for Improvements in Manpower Utilization and Efficiency Failure to get the best efforts of which Employees are Capable

- Failure to commend exceptional performance
- Failure to explain as much about the work so as to make it interesting
- Lack of interest in employees progress and affairs
- Failure to admit mistakes
- Lack of attention to employees ability and temperament in assigning work
- Failure to view employees as individuals in order to motivate them
- Countenancing the formation of cliques
- Rating employees on any grounds but competence; racial, religious, fraternal, etc.
- Keeping an employee in a job for which he is not mentally of physically suitable
- Permitting employees to work when they are sick
- Not giving employees the support and help they need
- Failure to promote an employee when it is possible and appropriate
- Lack of due consideration of problems affecting wages and working conditions
- Failure to train an understudy.

❖ Failure to control the Turnover of Capable Employees

- Not appreciating the direct and indirect costs of labour turnover

- Too much 'bossing' and not enough intelligent direction
- Too strict or too lax enforcement of discipline
- Not keeping promises which could have been fulfilled
- Making promises which cannot be fulfilled with regard to wages, promotion, etc.
- Discharging employees without sufficient cause; improper use of the discharge procedure as a penalty
- Keeping an employee on a job for which he may have a strong dislike
- Favouritism; treating one person better than another
- Taking sides in employee's arguments
- Criticizing a worker in front of the group
- Failure to conduct an exit interview
- Failure to correctly interpret managements real aims and policies to workers
- Failure of the foreman to do all he can to fairly adjust wage and work conditions
- Failure to get full production as quickly as possible from new workers
- Not inducting new employees appropriately; policies, procedures, pay, terms and conditions of employment, facilities, etc.
- Incomplete job instruction for new employees
- Failure to impress on new employees what is expected in terms of quality and quantity of work
- Failure to select suitably qualified and experienced employees
- Impatience with new employees who learn slowly
- Failure to get other workers to show a friendly, helpful attitude to new employees
- Failure to establish sound relationship and regular contact with new employees
- Failure to instruct new employees in all aspects of safety.

Team Activity No. 6

❖ Searching for Health and Safety at Work Issues

Poor health and safety observance and adherence to regulations can and will lead to accidents. Accidents cost the organizations every day.

Apply the job knowledge and experiences of team members, together with the checklist below to reveal potential or known problem areas for improvement. Build this checklist into your team building activities to make an improvement to safety and productivity, in your organization.

TIP: Measure the before and aftereffects wherever possible. That is, you should attempt to quantify each cause of waste you attack, in terms of money, time and material. This way you can objectively assess the difference you have made in the area of accident prevention.

❖ Common Causes of Accidents

- Failure to recognize accident prevention as part of the business process
- Failure to give all employees thorough instruction in safe practice
- Failure to install and maintain safeguards
- Allowing employees to work with guards out of place
- Failure to display safety signs and keep them legible
- Failure to thoroughly understand accident costs
- Poor housekeeping
- Lack of understanding of what constitutes an accident hazard
- Failure to keep accident records, to analyze them, and to use the information
- Not setting a good example in safe practice
- Lack of regular and conscientious safety inspections
- Failure to enforce consistently all safety rules and regulations
- Allowing employees to work without the necessary safety apparel
- Failure to recognize personal responsibilities for accidents
- Failure to stimulate and maintain interest of employees in accident prevention
- Lack of cooperation with statutory regulations.

Team Activity No. 7

❖ Searching for Causes of Poor Interpersonal Relationships/non-cooperation

Here is a checklist of common causes of poor interpersonal relationships and a lack of cooperation at work. Apply your job knowledge, together with this checklist to make a difference over time. Build this checklist into your team building activities to make an improvement to productivity, and therefore job security, in your organization.

TIP: Measure the before and aftereffects wherever possible. That is, you should attempt to quantify each cause of waste you attack, in terms of money, time and material. This way you can objectively assess the difference you have made.

❖ Failure to cooperate

- With other others at the same level in other departments
- With clerical, engineering, sales, personnel departments, etc.
- Lack of a thorough understanding of company policies and failure to explain them to employees
- Failure to deal with gossip and rumors
- Passing the buck; up, across or down the organization
- Not adequately representing the employees
- Permitting disgruntled employees to agitate and unsettle other employees
- Failure to give support to unpopular company policies
- Failure to promote friendliness and cooperation among employees
- Thoughtless criticism by the supervisor himself/herself of any company policy or of any individual in the organization
- Not cooperating whole- heartedly with management in its educational activities such as apprentice training, bulletin boards, customer relationship management initiatives, employees magazines, suggestions schemes, safety meetings.

Team Activity No. 8

❖ Searching for Causes of Poor Space Utilization

Some common causes of excessive cost relating to poor utilization and planning of space at work are given below. Each cause is fertile ground for improving productivity. Apply the job knowledge and experiences of your team members, together with this checklist to reveal problem areas and work up a ideas for each highlighted problem. Build this checklist into your team building activities to make an improvement to productivity, and therefore job security, in your organization.

TIP: Measure the before and aftereffects wherever possible. That is, you should attempt to quantify each cause of waste you attack, in terms of money, time and material. This way you can objectively assess the difference you have made.

❖ Causes of Poor Space Utilization

- Improper stacking and storage of materials
- Not enough attention to routing of materials through processes
- Wrong placement of machines and other permanent equipment
- Allowing employees to leave portable tools, ladders, etc., in the way of other employees
- Failure to keep passage ways clear
- Keeping materials which should be scrapped
- Lockers, oil tanks, stock supplies, etc., in inconvenient places
- Letting unused machinery and equipment take up valuable space
- Leaving needed space unused for want of needed repairs to roof floor, etc.
- Allowing dark spots in plant and office; ineffective lighting
- Failure to maintain order and good housekeeping
- Keeping unnecessary materials at the workplace.

❖ Additional Resources

These resources are available to promote focused team building. The focus has to be in terms orientating efforts towards improving productivity.

A meeting place for like-minded management practitioners who desire to contribute in a positive way to the success of their organizations (or their clients) and the development of human resources within those organizations.

Here you will find organizational development resources that can and will make a difference to your organization/business if applied and pursued with diligence and tenacity. This resource includes programmes, techniques, tips, procedures, extracts/summaries from appropriate research and instruments.

All of which have been developed to improve your skills and knowledge base and thereby constantly improve business productivity

Intended benefits to you

This resource is intended to provide a self development resource, that will inter alia:

- Develop management skills
- Develop the ability to influence the hearts and minds of others (leadership)

- Enable you to set high (attainable) standards for yourself, your organization and its people in terms of standards of work performance and ethic
- Develop and improve self-motivation to produce tangible results, whatever the hierarchical level in the organization
- Improve personal marketability, in that if you apply these resources in your work place successfully and can demonstrate the 'before and after' effect you will be one of those rare business breeds i.e. an added value employee (as opposed to an added cost employee)
- Provide a better understanding of the 'Ying and Yang' of it all, i.e. the cyclical nature of business, society, human nature etc. Most, if not all of the factors, affecting our business systems are not new, neither is what drives it, like human behaviour, the desire to trade, and accumulate wealth. The advent of the printing press, the steam engine, the discovery of sea routes to the East and later the 'New' world to the West (so what is new about the global economy?), for instance, brought about changes, challenges, opportunities similar to those we face today in our work places and communities.

This understanding is an important component in team—building and in your efforts to improve your organizations productivity through coordinating the behaviour and efforts of others.

Intended benefits to your organization

- ***Quite simply, improve productivity:*** Not doing so will ensure that change is forced on you and your organization, ultimately leading to the loss of jobs, impoverishment of the organization's host community and possibly the demise of the organization itself.

INDEX